# FAITH AND RATIONALITY

# Faith and Rationality:

## Reason and Belief in God

ALVIN PLANTINGA AND
NICHOLAS WOLTERSTORFF, EDITORS

UNIVERSITY OF NOTRE DAME PRESS
NOTRE DAME LONDON

**Library of Congress Cataloging in Publication Data**

Main entry under title:

Faith and rationality.

1. Faith and reason—Addresses, essays, lectures.
2. Religion—Philosophy—Addresses, essays, lectures.
I. Plantinga, Alvin. II. Wolterstorff, Nicholas.
BT50.F34 1983 200'.1 83-14843
ISBN 0-268-00964-3
ISBN 0-268-00965-1 (pbk.)

Manufactured in the United States of America

# Contents

# Introduction

## Nicholas Wolterstorff

This book is a series of essays on the topic of faith and reason. But there are many such essays, and many such books. What, if anything, makes this one significantly different? From near the beginning of Christianity there have been reflections on this topic. It could hardly have been otherwise, given that the culture with which Christianity first interacted, once it had emerged from Judaism, was the heavily philosophical culture of Hellenism. What, after all these years of discussion, merits anybody's attention in these *additional* essays on this ancient topic?

I judge that what is significant and unique about these essays is the weaving in and out of four fundamental themes. They are essays around these four themes.

(1) Perhaps the most basic theme is that of the collapse of *classical foundationalism.* Those words, for most readers, will require a bit of explanation.

The last decade or so has seen radically new developments in the field of philosophical epistemology. Among the most significant of these developments is the rise of metaepistemology. Rather than just plunging ahead and developing epistemological theories, philosophers have stood back and reflected seriously on the structural options available to them in their construction of such theories. This has had a most illuminating effect. We have come to see the structure of various epistemological debates more clearly than ever before. We have come to see more clearly than before the assumptions behind various positions staked out in these debates. We have been able to formulate with more clarity traditional positions on various issues.

After immersing themselves in metaepistemology, thereby acquiring a clearer picture of the structure of epistemological options, philosophers have naturally looked about to find out which of these various options have actually been developed in the West. What caught their attention is the extraordinarily long dominance of *one* structural option—that option which has come to be known as classical foundationalism. Before

I explain what that option is, let me first say that classical foundationalism, along with the other positions which are structural options to it, may be (and has been) formulated as a theory of three different things. It may be formulated as a theory of *rationality,* it may be formulated as a theory of *knowledge,* and it may be formulated as a theory of *authentic science* (scientia, Wissenschaft). For the purposes of these introductory comments let me, without more ado, explain it as a theory of rationality—that is, as a theory of what is rational for a given person to accept, to believe.

Any foundationalist whatsoever, whether a classical foundationalist or one of some other stripe, will begin by making a distinction between those of our beliefs which we hold on the basis of others of our beliefs and those which we do not hold on the basis of other beliefs of ours—those which we hold *immediately,* as the tradition said. From here the foundationalist will go on to insist that not only can this distinction be drawn abstractly but that in fact it can be made out within any person's set of beliefs. Most people, on first hearing of this claim, seem not to boggle at the suggestion that some of our beliefs are held on the basis of other beliefs of ours. But many do boggle at the suggestion that some of our beliefs are held immediately. So that is where the foundationalist concentrates his endeavors at persuasion. This is the way things *must be,* he argues. Maybe I believe *p* on the basis of my belief that *q,* and *q* on the basis of my belief that *r,* and so on. But somewhere this chain has to have a beginning. Somewhere, somehow, I have to have some beliefs induced in me *on which* I can then begin to base others, but which are themselves not based on others. The foundationalist proceeds then to give examples of such immediately held beliefs. Almost all of us who accept the proposition that $1 + 1 = 2$ do not do so on the basis of yet other beliefs of ours; we just "see" that it is true. And when a person is of the conviction that he feels dizzy, he does not base his conviction on yet other beliefs of his. He just immediately knows that he feels dizzy.

Having drawn this quasi-psychological distinction between those of our beliefs which are mediated by other beliefs and those which are produced immediately, the foundationalist goes on to argue that beliefs of both kinds can be rational. Often, indeed, he will argue that if some of a person's mediate beliefs are rational, then there *must* also be some of his immediate beliefs which are rational. Here we need not trace out this necessity-argument of his. Suffice it to say that on his view, beliefs of both sorts can be held rationally.

All foundationalists agree on yet one or two more things. They hold that for at least some of the beliefs which we hold on the basis of other beliefs, what makes it rational to hold the former is that those latter *support* them. The latter provide adequate evidence for the former—strictly, the propositions believed in the latter provide adequate evidence for the propositions believed in the former. Now suppose one starts from a belief B*p* which it is rational for the person to hold because he holds it on the basis of another belief B*q* such that *q* adequately supports *p*. And suppose he holds B*q* on the basis of yet another belief B*r* such that *r* adequately supports *q*. And so on. All foundationalists insist that if one follows out such chains of "believing on the basis of what provides adequate evidential support for," beginning from a rationally held mediate belief, one will always end exclusively with *immediately* held beliefs which it is *rational* for the person to hold. Those stopping points may then be thought of as the foundation of the person's structure of rational beliefs. On so much, foundationalists of all species would agree.

It is easy to surmise where they differ. They differ on how one proposition must be related to another for the one to provide adequate evidential support to the other. Thus one finds different theories of evidence among foundationalists. And, perhaps more importantly, they differ on which beliefs may properly be held immediately. Thus they differ on what is to be found in the foundation of a structure of rationally held beliefs. They all agree that every person's structure of rationally held beliefs will have this foundation/superstructure character. But they disagree on just what is to be found in the foundation—and on how the superstructure is supported by the foundation.

I can now pick out that particular species of foundationalism which has been called *classical* foundationalism. The classical foundationalist is the foundationalist who holds that just two sorts of propositions can be candidates for propositions which it is rational to hold immediately. The foundation of a rational belief-structure will, on his view, contain just two sorts of propositions. It will contain propositions which are *self-evident* to the person in question—propositions which he just sees to be true. $1 + 1 = 2$ would be an example of something self-evident to most of us. Second, it will contain propositions about one's states of consciousness which one cannot mistakenly believe to be true (or mistakenly believe to be false). That I am dizzy would be an example. These have been called *incorrigible* propositions in the philosophical tradition. Propositions which are self-evident for the person in question and propositions which are incorrigible for him—such propositions may properly be accepted immediately. They may properly be found in the foundations of a person's belief-structure. They are candidates for being properly basic. So contends the classical foundationalist. (Plantinga in his essay gives a slightly different explanation of "classical foundationalism." The difference, for my purposes here, makes no difference. What I here call "classical foundationalism" he there calls "modern foundationalism.")

I was observing that philosophers in the past decade have become much more aware than ever before of the structural options available to the epistemologist. One of those structural options is classical foundationalism, and most, if not all, philosophers would agree that this option, along with close relatives of it, has constituted the dominant epistemological tradition in the West. What must now be added is that most philosophers who have seen clearly the structure of this particular option have rejected it. On close scrutiny they have found classical foundationalism untenable. And it makes no difference now whether it is construed as a theory of rational acceptance, or of knowledge, or of scientia. It has seemed unacceptable as any of these. (Some of the reasons for this judgment are traversed in Plantinga's essay. It should be added that several writers in this volume have contributed to producing this general consensus that classical foundationalism is untenable.) Thus in a most fundamental way traditional epistemology has come "unstuck" in recent years—with the result that the field of epistemology is now filled with fascinating turmoil and chaos, and with new probes in many directions.

The following essays—especially those by the philosophers Alston, Mavrodes, Plantinga, and Wolterstorff—are written in the context of these new developments in epistemology. Up to this time there has been almost no exploration of the significance of these new developments for our understanding and assessment of religious—and more specifically, Christian—belief. Such exploration is at the very heart of these essays. Looking back from the position of these new developments in epistemology, one can see that almost all discussions on faith and reason for many centuries have taken for granted either the truth of classical foundationalism or some close relative of it, or they have departed from that position without any clear awareness of what they were departing from. These essays, by contrast, are written from the position of a clear realization of what constitutes classical foundationalism and a vivid awareness of its collapse. Actually, at several points they go beyond an exploration of the bearing of these recent developments in epistemology on our understanding of religious belief. They make a contribution to general epistemology. They make a contribution to the general, postfoundationalist dialogue on epistemology that is now taking place.

One thing more must be said here. Some philosophers have concluded from the collapse of the classical foundationalist theory of knowledge that the concept of knowledge itself must be discarded. (Cf. Richard Rorty.) And some have concluded from the collapse of the classical foundationalist theory of rationality that the distinction between rational and nonrational beliefs must be discarded. They have affirmed that "anything goes." (Cf. Paul K. Feyeraband.) Most emphatically these essays do not draw those conclusions. They are neither agnostic nor antinomian. So important, indeed, is this theme of opposition to agnosticism and antinomianism in these essays that I might well have singled it out for separate attention as one of the major themes around which these essays are organized.

(2) A second theme which weaves in and out of these essays is that of the evidentialist challenge to religious belief, a challenge first issued decisively in the European Enlightenment. Though these essays stand in that long line of reflections on faith and reason which begin with the church fathers, the context in which our discussion occurs is very different from the context in which their discussion occurred, with the result that, for all its affinities with those earlier discussions, ours is significantly different. One facet of our context is the one already discussed: we live in the situation where the main epistemological tradition of the West has collapsed among those knowledgeable concerning recent thinking in epistemology. Another facet of our context is that the fundamental contentions of the Enlightenment still prove persuasive to many.

The Enlightenment was not only an intellectual phenomenon but also a broadly cultural phenomenon. Eighteenth-century European man lived in the midst of the collapse of tradition and authority. Traditional ways of relating to the earth and of organizing society were rapidly being rejected in favor of ways that were "better"—ways that more effectively secured desired ends. And the authoritative hold of the Christian church on the European populace had been destroyed by the Reformation and the wars of religion. For many in Europe these developments yielded an exhilarating sense of liberation. The shackles of tradition and authority had been thrown off, and man was now free. That theme is sounded powerfully, for example, in Kant's famous essay "What Is Enlightenment?" But obviously liberation from tradition and authority poses this crucial decision: If we are not to guide our decisions by those, by what then? Will not any alternative merely place us under different shackles? And if guidance by a shared tradition and authority is no longer available, what then can unify society and secure a commonwealth?

The answer that the Enlightenment gave to these anxious questions was Reason. We are to be guided by Reason. Reason is something that each of us possesses intrinsically. It is not something extrinsic to us. Thus, to follow the voice of Reason is not to submit to some new external authority. It is to follow *one's own* voice. It is to submit to what is of the very essence of oneself. And that, of course, is not really to submit to anything. It is to be free. Furthermore, Reason belongs to all of us in common. It belongs to the very essence of what it is to be human. To follow the voice of Reason is to follow a voice that all of us hear. Reason offers the genuine possibility of being the foundation for a commonwealth. "Sapere aude!" says Kant. "Have the courage to use your own intelligence! is . . . the motto of the enlightenment."

Now the form assumed by the vision of the Enlightenment when it came to matters of religion was what may be called the *evidentialist challenge* to religious belief. The challenge can be seen as consisting of two contentions. It was insisted, in the first place, that it would be *wrong* for a person to accept Christianity, or any other form of theism, unless it was *rational* for him to do so. And it was insisted, secondly, that it is not rational for a person to do so unless he holds his religious convictions on the basis of other beliefs of his which give to those convictions adequate evidential support. No religion is acceptable unless rational, and no religion is rational unless supported by evidence. That is the evidentialist challenge.

I suggest, in my essay, that this challenge was clearly issued by John Locke—and that perhaps he was the first to issue it clearly and forcefully. The basis for the challenge, in Locke, was his adherence to classical foundationalism with respect to rationality. Though Descartes was certainly a classical foundationalist, it is doubtful that he was that for anything other than scientia. He seems not to have held that for anyone to have any knowledge at all, that person must satisfy the demands of classical foundationalism. And certainly he did not hold that for anyone to believe anything rationally, he must satisfy those demands. In effect, what Locke did was take the classical foundationalist demands that Descartes had laid down for scientific belief and lay them down for rational belief in general. If anyone was to believe anything rationally, he had to satisfy the demands of classical foundationalism. Locke noticed that the central claims of Christianity, and of theism generally, are neither self-evident to us nor incorrigible reports of our states of consciousness. And so he insisted that to be rational in holding them we needed evidence for them. If we are to be rational in holding them, they must occur in the superstructure of our system of belief. And concerning the contention that one ought never to believe what it is not rational to believe, Locke, as a good precursor of the Enlightenment, seems to have had no doubt whatsoever.

I think I do not exaggerate when I say that almost everybody in the West has regarded the evidentialist challenge as tenable. We in the West still live very much in the shadow of the Enlightenment. Some have thought that the challenge could not be met; no adequate evidence is available for Christianity, nor for theism, they have insisted. For such people the evidentialist challenge constitutes the ground of an objection to Christianity. Others, including Locke, have thought that the challenge could be met, or was already being met. They then have gone about assembling what they regarded as the adequate evidence, or showing that the adequate evidence is already in hand.

It is in this context that the final two essays in this volume should be read. They are background essays. Marsden's project is to discover how American evangelical academics in the nineteenth century understood the relation between faith and reason. What he discovers is that they pervasively saw themselves as meeting the evidentialist challenge both with respect to theism and with respect to Christianity. He also shows, however, that the rise of evolutionary theory profoundly disturbed that confidence, with the result that evangelicals in academia became a bewildered and intimidated lot for almost a century. David Holwerda in his essay discusses an important contemporary theologian, Wolfhart Pannenberg, who has enthusiastically embraced the evidentialist challenge and the Enlightenment spirit behind it, and has gone on to try to provide the evidence for Christianity that the challenge requires from those who are Christians.

Lest a mistaken impression be conveyed here, it must be said that though most Christians have accepted the validity of the evidentialist challenge, there have been some who, instead of trying to meet it or show that it has been met, have rejected it. Karl Barth is certainly one of the premier twentieth-century examples of this. With a swipe of the hand Barth made clear that he would have nothing to do with this challenge. To accept it, he said, would be to prefer Reason to Christ and thus to fall prey to an idol. What Barth does not do, however, is show just where the challenge is mistaken. That one or the other of the two theses making up the challenge is in his judgment false—on that Barth is clear. And that accepting it amounts in his judgment to replacing Christ with the idol of Reason—on that too he is clear. But wherein the challenger sees the structure of rationality mistakenly—on that Barth is far indeed from clear.

It is characteristic of the following essays that they too reject the evidentialist challenge. Where they go well beyond Barth and others, however, is that they show just where the challenger sees things wrongly—just where his perspective on rationality is askew. If I may be pardoned a bit of overly dramatic rhetoric: in these essays the evidentialist challenge of the Enlightenment is challenged and overcome.

(3) It is met and overcome in such a way that the resultant positions bear a close affinity to positions long held on the relation of faith to reason by the Continental Reformed (Calvinist) tradition. Thus a third theme which weaves in and out of these essays is what might be called, admittedly not very felicitously, "Calvinist epistemology," or "Reformed epistemology."

Characteristic of the Continental Calvinist tradition has been a revulsion against arguments in favor of theism or Christianity. Of course, at its beginnings this tradition was not appraising the giving of such arguments in the context of the Enlightenment insistence on the importance of Reason. It was instead appraising it in the context of the long medieval tradition of natural theology. But whatever the context, that this tradition has characteristically viewed in a dim light the project of offering evidence for theism and for Christianity is clear. Sometimes the bold position was staked out that such offering of arguments is pernicious. Barth has his antecedents! Sometimes the less bold position was affirmed, that little or nothing of worth is to be gotten from constructing such arguments. But most often the position taken was that such arguments are unnecessary for putting a person in the position where he is within his rights in being a Christian. Thus well before the evidentialist challenge was issued clearly and forcefully by Locke and his ilk, it was characteristic of those in the Reformed tradition to have taken up a position in opposition to the challenge. In short, the Continental Reformed tradition has characteristically been antievidentialist. The third theme that weaves in and out of these essays, then, is that of the antievidentialist impulses of the Reformed tradition. Of course, by taking up an antievidentialist position in their response to the Enlightenment, these essays *perforce* ally themselves with that impulse in the Reformed tradition. The point is that this is by no means an unwitting alliance. Particularly in Plantinga's essay there is a detailed tracing out of the connections among the demise of classical foundationalism, the evidentialist challenge, and the antievidentialist impulse characteristic of the Reformed tradition.

(4) Though less prominent in these essays than the others, there is a fourth theme which is perhaps worth singling out for attention. Marsden shows in his essay that it was the conviction of American evangelical academics in the nineteenth century that science, if competently pursued, would always prove compatible with Christianity. They were confident that if it did prove incompatible on some issue, that would be due to the scientist's having failed, somewhere along the line, to practice his science with full competence. It has been characteristic of the Continental Reformed tradition to contest this assumption. Science competently pursued, it has long said, may well be in conflict with Christian conviction. It went on to add, more strikingly, that in at least some cases the Christian theorist would be fully within his rights, maybe even obliged, to reject the science and hold on to his Christian convictions in such a situation of conflict. For science, it said, is not the result of neutrally assembling facts and then in Baconian fashion arriving at inductive generalizations. We all, in the practice of science, are guided by fundamental visions of life and reality. Theoretical reason is not autonomous. Thus two people who are guided by different visions may both practice science competently but wind up with differing results which science, by itself, is incapable of adjudicating.

The dominant tradition in the West has seen consensus as the appropriate goal and expectation of scientific inquiry. This alternative tradition has seen the pluralism of the academy as the well-nigh inevitable outcome even of fully competent theorizing. This theme of the inevitable pluralism of the academy is a fourth of the fundamental themes around which these essays are organized.

* * * * *

These essays arose out of a yearlong project of the Calvin (College) Center for Christian Studies on the topic of "Toward a Reformed View of Faith and Reason." Senior fellows of the Center for that year (1979–80) were David Holwerda (theology), George Marsden (history), Robert Manweiler (physics), Alvin Plantinga (philosophy), and Nicholas Wolterstorff (philosophy), all from Calvin College, and George Mavrodes from the Philosophy Department of the University of Michigan. Student fellows were Ronald Feenstra, Mike Hakkenberg, and Pieter Pereboom. Adjunct fellows were William P. Alston, of the Philosophy Department of Syracuse University, and Henk Hart, from the Institute for Christian Studies in Toronto. The work of six of these has found its way into the volume.

Though, of course, most of the interaction among the fellows took place in conversation, some of it took place by way of brief papers which the fellows addressed to each other. Among these were some delightful stories which George Mavrodes wrote at various points in the yearlong dialogue. Looking back at these, we judge that they remain interesting and illuminating. Accordingly the volume contains two of these, "The Stranger" and "Turning." The essays by the philosophers Plantinga, Alston, Wolterstorff, and Mavrodes address the issue of the rationality of Christian belief, and those by Marsden and Holwerda, already mentioned, explicate some features of the historical setting within which our contemporary discussion of these issues takes place.

In these introductory comments I have made clear that this book is more than a mere assortment of essays on the topic of faith and reason. The essays are bound together by virtue of being essays around those four themes which I singled out. But though the essays are united in fundamental ways in their treatment of various issues, there has been no attempt to "cover the field." Nothing is said, for example, about the role of Scripture in Christian belief and the rationality of accepting something on the say-so of Scripture—though certainly this is an important topic which falls within the area of our concern. It seemed to us more important to explore certain issues in depth, and to suggest new ways of approaching these matters, than to try to "cover the field." Furthermore, the emphases in the volume as a whole are no doubt different from those that one would find in an idealized treatment which discussed topics at a length directly proportional to their importance. Some of us, at the beginning of the project, fully expected that equal emphasis would be given to those two main divisions of traditional discussions on faith and reason: the rationality of Christian belief and the bearing of faith on theorizing. That proved not to be the case; the former topic drew the main focus of our attention, and that is reflected in this book. About this, all that can be said is that a project of this sort acquires a life and a mind of its own, and it seemed to us better to give our explorations their lead than to rein them in and turn to something else just for the sake of achieving a balance of attention which justly reflects our estimate of the relative importance of various topics.

* * * * *

In the essays by Plantinga and Wolterstorff there are extensive discussions on the nature of rationality. Nowhere in the essays, however, is there any explicit discussion on the nature of faith. A certain understanding of faith is presumed throughout. But as it turns out, nowhere is that understanding explicitly articulated. To prevent certain misunderstandings it may be well then to close this introduction with a brief examination of what we take to be the nature of the faith of which we are speaking. Of course, this is not the place for a full disquisition on the nature and manifestations of faith. I shall concentrate my attention on getting clear as to what constitutes the *core* of faith and, then, on the relation of faith to the believing of propositions.

Since it is Christian faith that we especially have in mind, it seems appropriate to proceed by looking at how the sacred documents of Christianity —the writings of the New and Old Testament—understand faith rather than by exploring the ordinary use of the word "faith" and then defining the derivative phrase "Christian faith."

Various writers of the New Testament record Jesus as having urged his hearers to take up the stance of *faith.* Likewise, those and other New Testament writers urge their own readers to take up this same stance of faith. Indeed, they urge their readers to take up this stance toward Jesus himself. It is clear that when the writers urged this stance on their readers, and when Jesus urged it on his hearers, they and he saw themselves as doing so on behalf of God. God himself calls us to the stance of faith. Let us then look at what the New Testament writers called their readers to, and what Jesus called his hearers to, when they and he, speaking on behalf of God, called them to faith.

Sometimes when the New Testament writers represent God as requiring faith of us, they are thinking of faith as one among other things that God requires of us. Faith is then one among other "virtues." Paul, in 1 Corinthians 13, urges faith along with hope and love on his hearers. At other times, however, they use the word "faith" to cover the core of that total stance toward God to which, on behalf of God, they call us. Faith in things not seen, hope, and love are then three of the requisite manifestations of faith. It is faith in this sense, as the core of that comprehensive stance toward God to which God calls us, that I shall be considering. I shall to a considerable extent follow R. Bultmann's excellent, though indeed highly tendentious, discussion on *pistis* in Kittel's *Theological Word Book of the New Testament.*

"In primitive Christianity," says Bultmann, "*pistis* became the leading term for the relation of man to God." (205) The term thus chosen to refer to what it is that God requires of man in man's relationship to him is a term whose root meaning, in its various grammatical forms in both classical and Hellenistic Greek, is *trust* (reliance, belief in, confidence). The objects of *pisteuein* are characteristically such things as contracts and oaths, laws, armaments, and persons. Likewise the words of a person can be the object of trust, in which case the sense of *pisteuein* shades toward our "believe." And sometimes, not surprisingly, *pisteuein* has the nuance of "to obey."

In New Testament usage, too, the root meaning of the term is *trust.* The fact that faith, at its core, is trust in God comes to the fore especially in the great chapter on the heroes of faith, Hebrews 11. Sarah, in verse 11, trusts the promises of God; Abraham, in verses 17ff., both trusts the promises of God and trusts God's miraculous power; and Noah, in verse 7, trusts God's warnings and sets about building the ark. The same note of trust in God's power and promises comes explicitly to the fore in Paul's reference to Abraham's faith in Romans 4:16ff.

But, of course, trust is characteristically, indeed inevitably, manifested in a variety of different actions and states of being. If one trusts someone, then naturally one believes what he says, does what he asks, addresses him in various ways, expectantly hopes for what he promises, experiences union with him, and so on. Perhaps even more important than this observation of fact, however, is that trust *requires* such things of one, in the sense that the absence of such acts and states indicates a deficiency in one's trust. It will prove useful to call those actions and states which are required of some person, if some trust of his is not to be deficient, the *authentic manifestation* of that trust. The New Testament writers do not speak only of faith. They speak as well of what belongs to the authentic manifestation of faith. They speak of what is required of us if our faith in God is not to be deficient.

One thing that over and over comes to the fore, when faith in God is spoken of, is the *obedience* required by faith. Apart from the actions of obedience there is no well-formed faith in God—this in addition to the fact that the stance of faith itself marks an obedient response to God. "By faith Abraham obeyed the call." (Heb. 11:8) In other passages what comes to the fore is that an expectant *hope* in God's promises and actions is required for well-formed faith. "Faith gives substance to our hopes." (Heb. 11:1) Frequently also there is emphasis on the *faithfulness* (fidelity, endurance) required of the one who fully trusts in God. And often what is in view when faith in God is spoken of is the *belief* required by well-formed faith—in particular, the acceptance of the words of God and of those who speak on his behalf. (Cf. John 2:22: "And they believed the Scripture and the word which Jesus had spoken.") Then, too, faith in God finds its manifestation in worship of God, in praise of him, in address (prayer) to him, and so on.

All this has its antecedents in the Old Testament; there too the required manifestations of trust in God include obedience, hope, fidelity, believing, and such.[1] Unique to the New Testament are two additional, qualifying, phenomena. First, Jesus himself, not only God, is often said to be the appropriate object of our faith, this frequently being expressed with the locution "believe in." "We have believed in Jesus Christ," says Paul in Galatians 2:16, "in order to be justified by faith in Christ." Second, to be a person of faith one must believe the apostolic proclamation, the *kerygma,* the Good News of God's saving actions culminating in the resurrection and the attendant Lordship of Jesus and the call to our appropriate acknowledgement of these events. "This," says Paul, is "the word of faith which we proclaim. If on your lips is the confession, 'Jesus is Lord,' and in your heart the faith that God raised him from the dead, then you will find salvation. For the faith that leads to righteousness is in the heart, and the confession that leads to salvation is upon the lips." (Romans 10: 8ff.) Here it is clear that what Paul dominantly has in mind, as he speaks of faith, is the acceptance in the heart and the confession on the lips of the message that Jesus is the Lord, risen from the dead.[2]

About this last dimension of New Testament faith, the confessing acceptance of the apostolic *kerygma,* Bultmann says this: "it is apparent that acknowledgment of Jesus as Lord is intrinsic to Christian faith along with acknowledgment of the miracle of His resurrection, i.e., acceptance of this miracle as true. The two statements constitute an inner unity. The resurrection is not just a remarkable event. It is the soteriological fact in virtue of which Jesus became the *kyrios*. . . . Naturally, in view of the inner unity, either one of the statements can be made alone, or the event of salvation can be described differently or more explicitly. The totality is always in view." (209)

Finally, it comes as no surprise to learn that sometimes, in New Testament usage, the message itself, not just the confessing *acceptance* of the message, is spoken of as *pistis*. Thus Paul speaks in Galatians 1:23 of "proclaiming the faith."

I have observed that Christian faith incorporates belief (i.e., acceptance) of the apostolic *kerygma* concerning God's saving acts and our appropriate response. It is clear, though, that the belief-component of a person's Christian faith includes more than that. It includes as well the *applications* of the *kerygma* to one's own life—it includes, for example, not only the belief that Jesus Christ came into the world to save sinners but also the belief that he came into the world to save *me*. Second, it typically includes various convictions to the effect that God acts in one's own experience. Paul's conviction that God was calling him to go from Asia Minor to Macedonia is an example. As Jonathan Edwards was fond of emphasizing, the person who trusts in God now "reads," and is required to "read," vast stretches of his own experience in new ways.

It is sometimes asked nowadays whether faith understood in the New Testament sense has a "propositional content." No doubt different people understand different things by "proposition." But suppose we mean by a proposition simply whatever can be believed to be true. Then the answer to the question is surely Yes. Genuine, full-fledged faith always requires belief; and belief always has a "what's believed," a *quae creditur*, a propositional content. As we have just seen, this propositional content of the belief-component of well-formed faith includes, though also goes beyond, the apostolic *kerygma*.

Of course the New Testament writers do not believe that the *quae creditur* of the belief-component of a person's faith is to be entertained in some coolly tentative fashion. The news of God's action, says Paul, is confessed and held in our hearts. If the phrase "propositional content of Christian faith" suggests to some an attitude of cautious tentativeness, that suggestion must be firmly repudiated. Neither do the New Testament writers hold that the *kerygma* which is believed is something devised by theologians. It is delivered to us by God himself. So if the phrase "propositional content of Christian faith" suggests the labored deliverances of theologians, that suggestion too must be firmly repudiated. And perhaps what bears repetition is that faith as a whole is not identical with belief. Indeed, belief is not even the organizing center of faith. Trust is that. Belief enters, first of all, by virtue of the fact that the one who trusts in God and Jesus Christ believes what they say. Faith requires believing the words of the one trusted. But also it requires believing the relevant specifications of that message for one's own life. And beyond this it requires, or at least typically results in, various beliefs about the working of God in one's own experience. In these various ways belief is one of the requisite and typical manifestations of faith. The one who fully trusts in God will display obedience, hope, and endurance. But also he will believe. In calling us to faith, God calls us to belief.

It may be added that some of the belief required for genuine, well-formed faith is not only required by such faith but is required if there is to be faith in God at all, even *malformed* and underdeveloped faith. One *cannot,* for example, trust God if one does not even believe that God exists. No doubt it was this point that the writer of Hebrews had in mind when he said, almost by the way, that "whoever would draw near to God must believe that he exists and that he rewards those who seek him."

It is worth noting, in conclusion, that the believed and confessed *kerygma* is often spoken of by the New Testament writers as *known.* We in our age are inclined to offer religious convictions as paradigm examples of what is "merely believed," not known. Not so the New Testament writers. The person who trusts (in) God also believes, that is, accepts, what he says; and this acceptance may well be a case of knowledge. Thus Paul says that "if we have died with Christ, we believe that we shall also live with him. For we know that Christ being raised from the dead will never die again." (Romans 6:8–9) And again, "we too believe, and so we speak, knowing that he who raised the Lord Jesus will raise us also with Jesus and bring us with you into his presence." (2 Cor. 4:13–14) The *kerygma* of the Christian faith is believed, as the trusted word of the One that one trusts; but it is believed (accepted) in such a manner as to be not *merely* believed but known.[3] The same pattern is to be seen in John. For example, in John 6:69 we read these words of Peter, addressed to Jesus: "and we have believed, and have come to know, that you are the Holy One of God." (Among other such passages see John 17:8 and 1 John 4:16.) Noticing that John often speaks of "knowing and believing" or "believing and knowing," one might wonder whether, in his thought, there is a natural sequence in the relation of belief and knowledge. Does belief find its fulfilment in knowledge, as Augustine so consistently taught, or does knowledge somehow find its fulfilment in confessing belief? Bultmann's comments on this seem correct: The two are indissolubly bound up together. "In antithesis to Gnosticism it is apparent that knowledge can never take us beyond faith or leave faith behind. As all knowledge begins with faith, so it abides in faith. Similarly, all faith is to become knowledge. If all knowledge can only be a knowledge of faith, faith comes to itself in knowledge. Knowledge is thus a constitutive element in genuine faith." (227)

And just as the believing which belongs to faith is often spoken of as being knowledge, so, similarly, there is little if any difference between trusting God—having faith in him—and *acknowledging* him (as God). Where "know" has the sense of *acknowledge,* as it frequently does in the

Bible, trusting God is knowing God. To have faith in God is to know him; to know God is to have faith in him.

## NOTES

1. Bultmann gives a fine summary of the Old Testament understanding of faith: "In the O.T. to believe in God is to acknowledge Him as such. This includes trust and hope, fear and obedience. But these are a unity, since trust is taken radically and thus includes the overcoming of both anxiety and self-confidence. Faith is a daring decision for God in man's turning aside both from the menacing world and also from his own strength. As is sometimes stressed, it is thus faith in spite of appearances. As a confident decision for God it contains within itself suppressed temptation. This faith in God is not just general trust. It is grounded in what God has done in the past. Hence it has its own firm relation to the future. It is the assurance that God will do what He has promised. Its opposite is murmuring and doubt, whereby God is tempted. It is expectant hope and stillness. Again, it has a firm relation to the present as obedience to God's commands, in the fulfilment of which the covenant faithfulness of the people must be demonstrated." (198)

2. About believing *in* Christ, Bultmann observes the following: "If this decisive act and attitude of faith are orientated to Christ, it might seem as though Christian faith were pushing the relation to God into the background. Nevertheless, the faith which is orientated to Christ believes precisely in God's act in Christ. . . . God and Christ are not set before the believer as two different objects of faith which are either co-ordinated or subordinated. On the contrary, God Himself meets us in Christ." (217)

3. Paul also uses the word "knowledge" when expressing his convictions concerning the working of God in his own experience and destiny.

# Reason and Belief in God

Alvin Plantinga

Belief in God is the heart and center of the Christian religion—as it is of Judaism and Islam. Of course Christians may disagree, at least in emphasis, as to how to think of God; for example, some may emphasize his hatred of sin; others, his love of his creatures. Furthermore, one may find, even among professedly Christian theologians, supersophisticates who proclaim the liberation of Christianity from belief in God, seeking to replace it by trust in "Being itself" or the "Ground of Being" or some such thing. It remains true, however, that belief in God is the foundation of Christianity.

In this essay I want to discuss a connected constellation of questions: Does the believer-in-God accept the existence of God by *faith*? Is belief in God contrary to reason, unreasonable, irrational? Must one have *evidence* to be rational or reasonable in believing in God? Suppose belief in God is *not* rational; does that matter? And what about proofs of God's existence? Many Reformed or Calvinist thinkers and theologians have taken a jaundiced view of natural theology, thought of as the attempt to give proofs or arguments for the existence of God; are they right? What underlies this hostility to an undertaking that, on the surface, at least, looks perfectly harmless and possibly useful? These are some of the questions I propose to discuss. They fall under the general rubric *faith and reason,* if a general rubric is required. I believe Reformed or Calvinist thinkers have had important things to say on these topics and that their fundamental insights here are correct. What they say, however, has been for the most part unclear, ill-focused, and unduly inexplicit. I shall try to remedy these ills; I shall try to state and clearly develop their insight; and I shall try to connect these insights with more general epistemological considerations.

Like the Missouri River, what I have to say is best seen as the confluence of three streams—streams of clear and limpid thought, I hasten to add, rather than turbid, muddy water. These three streams of thought are first, reflection on the evidentialist objection to theistic belief, according to which belief in God is unreasonable or irrational because there is insufficient evidence for it; second, reflection on the Thomistic conception of faith and reason; and third, reflection on the Reformed rejection to natural theology. In Part I I shall explore the evidentialist objection, trying to see more clearly just what it involves and what it presupposes. Part II will begin with a brief look at Thomas Aquinas' views on faith and knowledge; I shall argue that the evidentialist objection and the Thomistic conception of faith and knowledge can be traced back to a common root in *classical foundationalism*—a pervasive and widely accepted picture or total way of looking at faith, knowledge, belief, rationality, and allied topics. I shall try to characterize this picture in a revealing way and then go on to argue that classical foundationalism is both false and self-referentially incoherent; it should therefore be summarily rejected. In Part III I shall explore the Reformed rejection of natural theology; I will argue that it is best understood as an implicit rejection of classical foundationalism in favor of the view that belief in God is properly basic. What the Reformers meant to hold is that it is entirely right, rational, reasonable, and proper to believe in God without any evidence or argument at all; in this respect belief in God resembles belief in the past, in the existence of other persons, and in the existence of material objects. I shall try to state and clearly articulate this claim and in Part IV to defend it against objections.

The attentive reader may note two styles of print: large and small. The main lines of the argument are to be found in the large print, where technicalities and side issues will be kept to a minimum. The sections in small print will amplify, qualify, and add detail. I hope what I have to say will be of use to the philosophical and theological neophyte as well as to those with more training and experience. Readers interested just in the main line of argument are invited to skip the sections in small print; readers who find the large print too cursory and simplistic are invited to consult the small.

## PART I: THE EVIDENTIALIST OBJECTION TO BELIEF IN GOD

My first topic, then, is the evidentialist objection to theistic belief. Many philosophers—W. K. Clifford,[1] Brand Blanshard,[2] Bertrand Russell,[3] Michael Scriven,[4] and Anthony Flew,[5] to name a few—have argued that belief in God is irrational or unreasonable or not rationally acceptable or intellectually irresponsible or somehow noetically below par because, as they say, there is *insufficient evidence* for it. Bertrand Russell was once asked what he would say if, after dying, he were brought into the presence of God and asked why he had not been a believer. Russell's reply: "I'd say 'Not enough evidence God! Not enough evidence!'"[6] We may have our doubts as to just how that sort of response would be received; but Russell, like many others, held that theistic belief is unreasonable because there is insufficient evidence for it.

### *A. How Shall We Construe "Theistic Belief"?*

But how shall we construe "theistic belief" here? I have been speaking of "belief in God"; but this is not entirely accurate. For the subject under discussion is not really the rational acceptability of belief *in* God, but the rationality of belief that God exists—that there *is* such a person as God. And belief in God is not at all the same thing as belief that there is such a person as God. To believe that God exists is simply to accept as true a certain proposition: perhaps the proposition that there is a personal being who has created the world, who has no beginning, and who is perfect in wisdom, justice, knowledge, and power. According to the book of James, the devils do that, and they tremble. The devils do not believe *in* God, however; for belief in God is quite another matter. One who repeats the words of the Apostles' Creed "I believe in God the Father Almighty, . . ." and means what he says is not simply announcing the fact that he accepts a certain proposition as true; much more is involved than that. Belief in God means *trusting* God, accepting God, accepting his purposes, committing one's life to him and living in his presence. To the believer the entire world speaks of God. Great mountains, surging ocean, verdant forests, blue sky and bright sunshine, friends and family, love in its many forms and various manifestations—the believer sees these things and many more as gifts from God. The universe thus takes on a personal cast for him; the fundamental truth about reality is truth about a *person.* So believing in God is indeed more than accepting the proposition that God exists. But if it is more than that, it is also at least that. One cannot sensibly believe in God and thank him for the mountains without believing that there *is* such a person to be thanked and that he is in some way responsible for the mountains. Nor can one trust in God and commit oneself to him without believing that he exists; as the author of Hebrews says, "He who would come to God must believe that he is and that he is a rewarder of those who seek him." (Heb. 11:6)

So belief in God must be distinguished from the belief that God exists. Having made this distinction, however, I shall ignore it for the most part, using "belief in God" as a synonym for "belief that there is such a person as God." The question I want to address, therefore, is the question whether belief in God—belief in the existence of God—is rationally acceptable. But what is it to believe or assert that God exists? Just which belief is it into the rational acceptability of which I propose to inquire? Which God do I mean to speak of? The answer, in brief, is: the God of Abraham, Isaac, and Jacob; the God of Jewish and Christian revelation: the God of the Bible.

To believe that God exists, therefore, is first of all to hold a *belief* of a certain sort—an existential belief. To assert that God exists is to make an *assertion* of a certain sort—an existential assertion. It is to answer at the most basic level the ontological question "What is there?" This may seem excessively obvious. I would not so much as mention it, were it not for the fact that some philosophers and theologians seem to disagree. Oddly enough, they seem to use the phrase "belief in God" and even "belief that God exists" in such a way that to believe in God is not to hold any such existential beliefs at all. Much of what Rudolph Bultmann says, for example, seems to suggest that to believe in God is not at all to believe that there exists a being of a certain sort. Instead, it is to adopt a certain attitude or policy, or to make a kind of resolve: the resolve, perhaps, to accept and embrace one's finitude, giving up the futile attempt to build hedges and walls against guilt, failure, and death. And according to the philosopher Richard Braithwaite, a religious assertion is "the assertion of an intention to carry out a certain behavioral policy, subsumable under a sufficiently general principle to be a moral one, together with the implicit statement, but not necessarily the assertion, of certain stories."[7] But then it looks as if according to Braithwaite when the Christian asserts "I believe in God the Father Almighty" he is not, contrary to appearances, asserting that he believes that there exists a *being* of a certain kind; instead he is asserting that he intends to carry out a certain behavioral policy. As *I* use the phrase "belief in God," however, that phrase denotes a *belief,* not a resolve or the adoption of a policy. And the assertion that God exists is an *existential* assertion, not the assertion of an intention to carry out a certain policy, behavioral or otherwise. To believe or assert that God exists is to believe or assert that there exists a being of a certain very special sort.

*What* sort? Some contemporary theologians, under the baneful influence of Kant, apparently hold that the name "God," as used by Christians and others, denotes an *idea,* or a *concept,* or a *mental construct* of some kind. The American theologian Gordon Kaufman, for example, claims that the word 'God' "raises special problems of meaning because it is a noun which by definition refers to a reality transcendent of and thus not locatable within experience."[8] In a striking echo of one of Kant's famous distinctions, Kaufman distinguishes what he calls the "real referent" of the term "God" from what he calls "the available referent":

> The real referent for "God" is never accessible to us or in any way open to our observation or experience. It must remain always an unknown X, a mere limiting idea with no content.[9]
>
> For all practical purposes, it is the *available referent* — a particular imaginative construct — that bears significantly on human life and thought. It is the "available God" whom we have in mind when we worship or pray; . . . it is the available God in terms of which we speak and think whenever we use the word "God." In this sense "God" denotes for all practical purposes what is essentially a mental or imaginative construct.[10]

Professor John Hick makes a similar suggestion; in his inaugural address at the Claremont School of Theology he suggested that when Christians speak to God, they are speaking of a certain *image,* or *mental construction,* or *imaginative creation* of some sort.

Now these are puzzling suggestions. If it is Kaufman's "available referent" "in terms of which we speak whenever we use the word 'God'," and if the available referent is a mental or imaginative construct, then presumably when we say "there is a God" or "God exists" we are affirming the existence of a certain kind of mental or imaginative construct. But surely we are not. And when Christians say that God has created the world, for example, are they really claiming that an image or imaginative construct, whatever precisely that may be, has created the world? That seems at best preposterous. In any event, the belief I mean to identify and discuss is not the belief that there exists some sort of imaginative construct or mental construction or anything of the sort. It is instead the belief, first, that there exists a *person* of a certain sort — a being who acts, holds beliefs, and has aims and purposes. This person, secondly, is immaterial, exists *a se,* is perfect in goodness, knowledge, and power, and is such that the world depends on him for its existence.

### *B. Objections to Theistic Belief*

Now many objections have been put forward to belief in God. First, there is the claim that as a matter of fact there is no such thing as belief in God, because the sentence "God exists" is, strictly speaking, nonsense.[11] This is the positivists' contention that such sentences as "God exists" are unverifiable and hence "cognitively meaningless" (to use their charming phrase), in which case they altogether fail to express propositions. On this view those who claim to believe in God are in the pitiable position of claiming to believe a proposition that as a matter of fact does not so much as exist. This objection, fortunately, has retreated into the obscurity it so richly deserves, and I shall say no more about it.[12]

Second, there is the claim that belief in God is *internally inconsistent* in that it is impossible, in the broadly logical sense, that there be any such person as theists say God is. For example, theists say that God is a person who has no body but nonetheless acts in the world; some philosophers have retorted that the idea of a bodiless person is impossible, and the idea of a bodiless person *acting* is *obviously* impossible. Some versions of some of these objections are of great interest, but I do not propose to discuss them here. Let me just record my opinion that none of them is at all compelling; so far as I can see, the concept of God is perfectly coherent. Third, some critics have urged that the existence of God is incompatible with other beliefs that are plainly true and typically accepted by theists. The most widely urged objection to theistic belief, the deductive argument from evil, falls into this category. According to this objection the existence of an omnipotent, omniscient, and wholly good God is *logically incompatible* with the presence of evil in the world—a presence conceded and indeed insisted upon by theists.[13] For their part, theists have argued that there is no inconsistency here;[14] and I think the present consensus, even among those who urge some form of the argument from evil, is that the deductive form of the argument from evil is unsuccessful.

More recently, philosophers have claimed that the existence of God, while perhaps not inconsistent with the existence of the amount and kinds of evil we actually find, is at any rate *unlikely* or *improbable* with respect to it; that is, the probability of God's existence with respect to evil is less than that of its denial with respect to evil. Hence the existence of God is improbable with respect to what we know. But if theistic belief *is* improbable with respect to what we know, then, so goes the claim, it is irrational or intellectually improper to accept it. Although this objection—the probabilistic argument from evil—is not of central concern here, it bears an interesting relation to one of my main topics—the question whether belief in God is properly basic. So suppose we briefly examine it. The objector claims that

(1) God is the omnipotent, omniscient, wholly good creator of the world

is improbable or unlikely with respect to the amounts and varieties of evil we find in the world. Perhaps *some* of the evil is necessary to achieve certain good states of affairs, but there is so *much* evil, much of which seems, on the face of things, utterly gratuitous. The objector claims, therefore, that (1) is improbable or unlikely, given

(2) There are $10^{13}$ turps of evil

where the turp is the basic unit of evil—equal, as you may have guessed, to $1/10^{13}$ (the evil in the actual world).

The burden of the free-will defense is that it is *possible* that it was not within God's power to create a world containing as much good as the actual world contains but fewer than $10^{13}$ turps of evil—and this even if God is omniscient and omnipotent. That is, it *could* be that

(3) God is the omnipotent, omniscient, wholly good creator of the world, and it was not within his power to create a world containing more good than the actual world contains but fewer than $10^{13}$ turps of evil.

Let us suppose, for the moment, that (3) is indeed possible. It is a familiar theorem of the probability calculus that

(4) If *A* entails *B* and *B* is improbable on *C*, then *A* is improbable on *C*.

Hence if (1) is improbable or unlikely on (2), then (3) is improbable on (2). The objector is therefore committed to supposing that (3) is unlikely or improbable on (2).

Now I have argued elsewhere [15] that it is quite implausible to suppose (3) unlikely or improbable given the truth of (2), and hence implausible to suppose that (1) is improbable on (2). Call this response to the objector "the low-road reply." Here I want to pursue instead the *high-road* reply.

Suppose we stipulate for purposes of argument that (1) is in fact improbable on (2). Let us agree that it is unlikely, given the existence of $10^{13}$ turps of evil, that the world has been created by a God who is perfect in power, knowledge, and goodness. What is supposed to follow from that? How is this to be construed as an objection to theistic belief? How does the argument go from there? It does not follow, of course, that theism is false. Nor does it follow that one who accepts both (1) and (2) (and, let us add, recognizes that (1) is improbable with respect to (2)) has an irrational system of beliefs or is in any way guilty of noetic impropriety. For it *could* be, obviously enough, that (1) is improbable with respect to (2) but probable with respect to something else we know. I might know, for example, both that

(5) Feike is a Frisian, and 9 out of 10 Frisians cannot swim,

and

(6) Feike is a Frisian lifeguard, and 99 out of 100 Frisian lifeguards can swim;

it is plausible to hold that

(7) Feike can swim

is probable with respect to (6) but improbable with respect to (5). If, furthermore, (5) and (6) are all we know about Feike's swimming ability, then the view that he can swim is epistemically more acceptable for us than the view that he cannot—even though we know something with respect to which the former is improbable.

Indeed, we might very well *know* both (5) and (7); we might very well know a pair of propositions $A$ and $B$ such that $A$ is improbable on $B$. So even if it were a fact that (2) is evidence against (1) or that (1) is improbable on (2), that fact would not be of much consequence. But then how can this objection be developed? How can the objector proceed?

Presumably what he means to hold is that (1) is improbable, not just on (2) but on some appropriate body of *total evidence*—perhaps all the evidence the theist has, or perhaps the body of evidence he is rationally obliged to have. The objector must be supposing that there is a relevant body of total evidence here, a body of evidence that includes (2); and his claim is that (1) is improbable with respect to this relevant body of total evidence.

Suppose we step back a moment and reconsider the overall structure of the probabilistic argument. The objector's claim is that the theist is irrational in accepting belief in God because it is improbable with respect to (2), the proposition that there are $10^{13}$ turps of evil—a proposition whose truth the theist acknowledges. As we have seen, however, even if the existence of God is improbable with respect to (2), that fact is utterly insufficient for demonstrating irrationality in the theist's structure of beliefs; there may be many propositions $A$ and $B$ such that even though $A$ is improbable on $B$, we can nonetheless accept both in perfect propriety. What the objector must be supposing, then, is something like this. For any theist $T$ you pick, there is a set of propositions $T_s$ that constitute his *total evidence*; and now for any proposition $A$ the theist accepts, he is rational in accepting $A$ only if $A$ is not improbable with respect to $T_s$. And the objector's claim is that the existence of God *is* improbable with respect to $T_s$ for any (or nearly any) theist.

Suppose we say that $T_s$ is the theist's *evidential set.* This is the set of propositions to which, as we might put it, his beliefs are responsible. A belief is rationally acceptable for him only if it is not improbable with respect to $T_s$. Now so far we have not been told what sorts of propositions are to be found in $T_s$. Perhaps these are the propositions the theist *knows* to be true, or perhaps the largest subset of his beliefs that he can rationally accept without evidence from other propositions, or perhaps the set of propositions he knows *immediately*—knows, but does not know on the basis of other propositions. However exactly we characterize this set $T_s$, the presently pressing question is this: Why cannot belief in God be itself a member of $T_s$? Perhaps for the theist—for some theists, at any rate—belief in God is a member of $T_s$, in which case it obviously will not be improbable with respect to $T_s$. Perhaps the theist is entirely within his epistemic rights in *starting from* belief in God, taking that proposition to be one of the ones probability with respect to which determines the rational propriety of *other* beliefs he holds. If so, the fact, if it is a fact, that theistic belief is improbable with respect to the existence of evil does not even begin to show that the theist is irrational in accepting it. The high-road reply to the probabilistic argument from evil, therefore, leads directly to one of the questions I am fundamentally concerned with: What sorts of beliefs, if any, is it rational or reasonable to *start from*? Which beliefs are such that one may properly accept them without evidence, that is, without the evidential support of other beliefs? One who offers the probabilistic argument from evil simply *assumes* that belief in God does not have that status; but perhaps he is mistaken.

### *C. The Evidentialist Objection Stated*

Now suppose we turn explicit attention to the evidentialist objection. Many philosophers have endorsed the idea that the strength of one's belief ought always to be proportional to the strength of the evidence for that belief. Thus, according to John Locke a mark of the rational person is "the not entertaining any proposition with greater assurance than the proofs it is built upon will warrant." According to David Hume "A wise man . . . proportions his belief to the evidence." In the nineteenth century we have W. K. Clifford, that "delicious *enfant terrible*" as William James calls him, insisting that it is wicked, immoral, monstrous, and maybe even impolite to accept a belief for which you do not have sufficient evidence:

> Whoso would deserve well of his fellows in this matter will guard the purity of his belief with a very fanaticism of jealous care, lest at any time it should rest on an unworthy object, and catch a stain which can never be wiped away.[16]

He adds that if a

> belief has been accepted on insufficient evidence, the pleasure is a stolen one. Not only does it deceive ourselves by giving us a sense of power which we do not really possess, but it is sinful, because it is stolen in defiance of our duty to mankind. That duty is to guard ourselves from such beliefs as from a pestilence, which may shortly master our body and spread to the rest of the town. (184)

And finally:

> To sum up: it is wrong always, everywhere, and for anyone to believe anything upon insufficient evidence. (186)

(It is not hard to detect, in these quotations, the "tone of robustious pathos" with which James credits him.) Clifford, of course, held that one who accepts belief in God *does* accept that belief on insufficient evidence and has therefore defied his duty to mankind. More recently, Bertrand Russell has endorsed the same idea: "Give to any hypothesis which is worth your while to consider," he says, "just that degree of credence which the evidence warrants"; and in his view the evidence warrants no credence in the existence of God.

### *1. A. Flew: The Presumption of Atheism*

Still more recently Anthony Flew has commended what he calls Clifford's "luminous and compulsive essay" (perhaps "compulsive" here is to be understood as "compelling"); and Flew goes on to claim that there is, in his words, a "presumption of atheism." What is a presumption of atheism, and why should we think there is one? Flew puts it as follows:

> What I want to examine is the contention that the debate about the existence of God should properly begin from the presumption of atheism, that the onus of proof must lie upon the theist.
>
> The word 'atheism,' however, has in this contention to be construed unusually. Whereas nowadays the usual meaning of 'atheist' in English is 'someone who asserts there is no such being as God,' I want the word to be understood not positively but negatively. I want the original Greek preface 'a' to be read in the same way in 'atheist' as it is customarily read in such other Greco-English words as 'amoral,' 'atypical,' and 'asymmetrical.' In this interpretation an atheist becomes: not someone who positively asserts the non-existence of God; but someone who is simply not a theist.[17]
>
> What the protagonist of my presumption of atheism wants to show is that the debate about the existence of God ought to be conducted in a particular way, and that the issue should be seen in a certain perspective. His thesis about the onus of proof involves that it is up to the theist: first to introduce and to defend his proposed concept of God; and second, to provide sufficient reason for believing that this concept of his does in fact have an application. (14–15)

How shall we understand this? What does it mean, for example, to say that the debate "should properly begin from the presumption of atheism?" What sorts of things do debates begin from, and what is it for one to begin from such a thing? Perhaps Flew means something like this: to speak of where a debate should begin is to speak of the sorts of premises to which the affirmative and negative sides can properly appeal in arguing their cases. Suppose you and I are debating the question whether, say, the United States has a right to seize Mideast oil fields if the OPEC countries refuse to sell us oil at what we think is a fair price. I take the affirmative and produce for my conclusion an argument one of whose premises is the proposition that the United States has indeed a right to seize these oil fields under those conditions. Doubtless that maneuver would earn me few points. Similarly, a debate about the existence of God cannot sensibly start from the assumption that God does indeed exist. That is to say, the affirmative cannot properly appeal, in its arguments, to such premises as that there is such a person as God; if she could, she would have much too easy a time of it. So in this sense of "start" Flew is quite right: the debate cannot start from the assumption that God exists.

Of course, it is also true that the debate cannot start from the assumption that God does *not* exist; using "atheism" in its ordinary sense, there is equally a presumption of aatheism. So it looks as if there is in Flew's sense a presumption of atheism, alright, but in that same sense an equal presumption of aatheism. If this is what Flew means, then what he says is entirely correct, if something of a truism.

In other passages, however, Flew seems to understand the presumption of atheism in quite a different fashion:

> It is by reference to this inescapable demand for grounds that the presumption of atheism is justified. If it is to be established that there is a God, then we have to have good grounds for believing that this is indeed so. Until or unless some such grounds are produced we have literally no reason at all for believing; and in that situation the only reasonable posture must be that of either the negative atheist or the agnostic. (22)

Here we have a claim much more contentious than the mere suggestion that a debate about the existence of God ought not to start from the assumption that indeed there is such a person as God; here Flew is claiming that it is irrational or unreasonable to accept theistic belief in the absence of arguments or evidence for the existence of God. That is, Flew claims that if we know of no propositions that serve as evidence for God's existence, then we cannot rationally believe in God. And of course Flew, along with Russell, Clifford, and many others, holds that in fact there are not sufficient grounds or evidence for belief in God. Flew, therefore, seems to endorse the following two principles:

(8) It is irrational or unreasonable to accept theistic belief in the absence of sufficient evidence or reasons

and

(9) We have no evidence or at any rate not sufficient evidence for the proposition that God exists.

*2. M. Scriven: Atheism Is Obligatory in the Absence of Evidence.*

According to Michael Scriven, if the arguments for God's existence fail, then the only rational posture is not merely not believing in God; it is atheism, the belief that there is no God. Speaking of the theistic proofs, he says, "It will now be shown that if they fail, there is no alternative to atheism."[18] He goes on to say: "we need not have a proof that God does not exist in order to justify atheism. Atheism is obligatory in the absence of any evidence for God's existence. . . . The proper alternative, where there is no evidence, is not mere suspension of belief, e.g., about Santa Claus; it is *disbelief*". (103) But Scriven's claim seems totally arbitrary. He holds that if the arguments *for* God's existence fail and the arguments *against* God's existence *also* fail, then atheism is rationally obligatory. If you have no evidence *for* the existence of God, then you are rationally obliged to believe there is no God – whether or not you have any evidence *against* the existence of God. The first thing to note, then, is that Scriven is not treating

(10) God exists

and

(11) God does not exist

in the same way. He claims that if there is no evidence for (10), then the only rational course is to believe its denial, namely (11). But of course he does not propose the same treatment for (11); he does not suggest that if there is no evidence for (11), then we are rationally obliged to believe *its* denial, namely (10). (If he *did* propose that (11) should be treated like (10), then he would be committed to supposing that if we had no evidence either way, the rational thing to do would be to believe the denial of (10), namely (11), and *also* the denial of (11), namely (10).) Why then does he propose this lack of parity between (10) and (11)? What is the justification for treating these propositions so differently? Could not the theist just as sensibly say, "If the arguments for *atheism* fail and there is no evidence for (11), then theism is rationally obligatory"? Scriven's claim, initially at any rate, looks like a piece of merely arbitrary intellectual imperialism.

Scriven speaks of *obligations, duties,* with respect to belief: in the absence of evidence, he says, atheism is *obligatory.* What sorts of principles of epistemic obligation underlie this claim? Obviously we cannot sensibly hold that for *any* proposition $A$, if $S$ has no evidence for $A$, then $S$ is rationally obliged to believe $\sim A$; for then if $S$ has no evidence for $A$ and also none for $\sim A$, $S$ will be obliged to believe both $A$ and $\sim A$. Some of what Scriven says suggests that it is just *existential* propositions with respect to which $S$ is obliged to toe this very demanding line:

> Recalling that to get even a little evidential support for the existence of a Being with supernatural powers will require that that little be of very high quality ('little' does not mean 'dubious'), we see that the failure of all the arguments, i.e., of all the evidence, will make even agnosticism in the wide sense an indefensible exaggeration of the evidential support. (105)

He then adds, via a footnote:

> Technical note: attempts to formulate the general principle of evidence involved here have usually run into difficulties related to those made familiar in the paradoxes of confirmation. For example, negative existential hypotheses in natural language can be supported by the failure of proofs of their contradictories; but positive existential hypotheses are not made plausible by the failure of disproofs of their denials. (105)

Perhaps the last sentence is the key: Scriven believes that positive existential hypotheses have a very different standing from negative existential hypotheses. In the absence of evidence, he seems to think, one is obliged to believe the denial of a positive existential hypothesis, whereas of course the same does not hold for negative existential hypotheses. It is hard to see any reason for thus discriminating against positive existential hypotheses—why should they be thought of as less credible, *ab initio,* than negative existential hypotheses? Indeed, according to Carnap and many of his followers, universal propositions have an a priori probability of zero; since the negative existential $\sim(\exists x)Fx$ is equivalent to a universal proposition $((x) \sim Fx)$, it too would have an a priori probability of zero, so that its positive existential denial would have an a priori probability of 1.[19] Now it is no doubt a bit excessive to claim that the a priori credibility of positive existential propositions is 1, but is there any reason to suppose that in the absence of evidence either way, negative existentials have a stronger claim on us than positive existentials? It is at the least very hard to see what such reason might be.

In any event Scriven's suggestion is entirely unsuccessful. Consider

(12) There is at least one human being that was not created by God.

It is a necessary truth that

(13) If God exists, then God has created all the human beings there are.

(If you think (13) *is not* necessary, then replace "God" in (12) and (13) by "the being who is identical with God and has created all the human beings there are.") (12) is a positive existential proposition; hence on Scriven's suggestion we ought to believe its denial unless we have evidence for it. Hence if the arguments for (12) fail, we should accept its denial. But any argument for (12), given the necessity of (13), can be transformed into an argument for the nonexistence of God—an argument which is successful if the original argument for (11) is. So if the arguments for the nonexistence of God fail, then so do the arguments for (12). But, by Scriven's principle, if the arguments for (12) fail, we are rationally obliged to believe its denial, that is,

(14) Every human being has been created by God.

On this principle, therefore, if the arguments *against* the existence of God fail, we are rationally obliged to believe that every human being has been created by God; and if both the arguments for and the arguments against the existence of God fail, then we are obliged to believe both that God does not exist and that we have all been created by him. No doubt Scriven would view this as an unsatisfactory result.

Scriven's extravagant claim, then, does not look at all promising. Let us therefore return to the more moderate evidentialist position encapsulated by

(8) It is irrational or unreasonable to accept theistic belief in the absence of sufficient evidence or reasons

and

(9) There is no evidence or at any rate not sufficient evidence for the proposition that God exists.

### *3. The Evidentialist Objection and Intellectual Obligation*

Now (9) is a strong claim. What about the various arguments that have been proposed for the existence of God—the traditional cosmological and teleological arguments for example? What about the versions of the *moral* argument as developed, for example, by A. E. Taylor and more recently by Robert Adams? What about the broadly inductive or probabilistic arguments developed by F. R. Tennant, C. S. Lewis, E. L. Mascall, Basil Mitchell, Richard Swinburne, and others? What about the ontological argument in its contemporary versions?[20] Do none of these provide evidence? Notice: the question is not whether these arguments, taken singly or in combinations, constitute *proofs* of God's existence; no doubt they do not. The question is only whether someone might be rationally justified in believing in the existence of God on the basis of the alleged evidence offered by them; and that is a radically different question.

At present, however, I am interested in the objector's other premise —the claim that it is irrational or unreasonable to accept theistic belief in the absence of evidence or reasons. Why suppose *that* is true? Why should we think a theist must have evidence, or reason to think there *is* evidence, if he is not to be irrational? Why not suppose, instead, that he is entirely within his epistemic rights in believing in God's existence even if he has no argument or evidence at all? This is what I want to investigate. Suppose we begin by asking what the objector means by describing a belief as *irrational.* What is the force of his claim that theistic belief is irrational, and how is it to be understood? The first thing to see is that this objection is rooted in a *normative* view. It lays down conditions that must be met by anyone whose system of beliefs is *rational,* and here "rational" is to be taken as a normative or evaluative term. According to the objector there is a right way and a wrong way with respect to belief. People have responsibilities, duties, and obligations with respect to their believings just as with respect to their actions, or if we think believings are a kind of action, their *other* actions. Professor Brand Blanshard puts this clearly:

> everywhere and always belief has an ethical aspect. There is such a thing as a general ethics of the intellect. The main principle of that ethic I hold to be the same inside and outside religion. This principle is simple and sweeping: Equate your assent to the evidence.[21]

and according to Michael Scriven

> Now even belief in something for which there is no evidence, i.e., a belief which goes beyond the evidence, although a lesser sin than belief in something which is contrary to well-established laws, is plainly irrational in that it simply amounts to attaching belief where it is not justified. So the proper alternative, when there is no evidence, is not mere suspension of belief, e.g., about Santa Claus; it is disbelief. It most certainly is not faith.[22]

Perhaps this sort of obligation is really just a special case of a more general moral obligation; perhaps, on the other hand, it is unique and *sui generis.* In any event, says the objector, there are such obligations: to conform to them is to be rational and to go against them is to be irrational.

Now here what the objector says seems plausible; there do seem to be duties and obligations with respect to belief, or at any rate in the general *neighborhood* of belief. One's own welfare and that of others sometimes depends on what one believes. If we are descending the Grand Teton and I am setting the anchor for the 120-foot rappel into the Upper Saddle, I have an obligation to form such beliefs as *this anchor point is solid* only after careful scrutiny and testing. One commissioned to gather intelligence —the spies Joshua sent into Canaan, for example—has an obligation to get it right. I have an obligation with respect to the belief that Justin Martyr was a Greek apologist—an obligation arising from the fact that I teach medieval philosophy, must make a declaration on this issue, and am obliged not to mislead my students here. The precise nature of these obligations may be hard to specify: What exactly *is* my obligation here? Am I obliged to believe that Justin Martyr was a Greek apologist if and only if Justin Martyr *was* a Greek apologist? Or to form a belief on this topic only after the appropriate amount of checking and investigating? Or maybe just to tell the students the truth about it, whatever I myself believe in the privacy of my own study? Or to tell them what is generally thought by those who should know? In the rappel case, do I have a duty to believe that the anchor point is solid if and only if it is? Or only only if it is? Or just to check carefully before forming the belief? Or perhaps there is no obligation to *believe* at all, but instead an obligation to *act on* a certain belief only after appropriate investigation. In any event, it seems plausible to hold that there are obligations and norms with respect to belief, and I do not intend to contest this assumption.

These duties or obligations with respect to belief—call them "intellectual duties"—may assume a wide variety of forms. There may be duties with respect to *acquiring* belief; perhaps there are ways of acquiring belief such that one is rationally obliged to try not to acquire belief in those ways. There may be duties pertaining to the *sustaining* of a belief; perhaps there are conditions under which one is obliged to try to maintain a belief, other circumstances in which one ought to be willing to consider giving it up, and still others in which one's epistemic duty is to try to divest oneself of it. There may be other sorts of epistemic duties: duties having to do with the strength of belief, with one's openness to the influence of one's elders and betters, and the like.

Furthermore, these duties can be understood in several ways. First, we could construe them teleologically; we could adopt an intellectual utilitarianism. Here the rough idea is that our intellectual obligations arise out of a connection between our beliefs and what is intrinsically good and intrinsically bad; and our intellectual obligations are just special cases of the general obligation so to act as to maximize good and minimize evil. Perhaps this is how W. K. Clifford thinks of the matter. If people accepted such propositions as *this DC10 is airworthy* when the evidence is insufficient, the consequences could be disastrous; so perhaps some of us, at any rate, have an obligation to believe that proposition only in the presence of adequate evidence. The intellectual utilitarian could be an *ideal* utilitarian; he could hold that certain epistemic states are intrinsically valuable—knowledge, perhaps, or believing the truth, or a skeptical and judicial temper that is not blown about by every wind of doctrine. Among our duties, then, is a duty to try to bring about these valuable states of affairs. Perhaps this is how Professor Chisholm is to be understood when he says:

> Let us consider the concept of what might be called an "intellectual requirement." We may assume that every person is subject to a purely intellectual requirement: that of trying his best to bring it about that, for every proposition that he considers, he accepts it if and only if it is true.[23]

Of course a person could fulfill this obligation just by trying to bring it about that he considered only a few utterly obvious propositions; he might ask his friends, perhaps never to mention to him any but the most obvious truths—truths of elementary arithmetic, for example. Presumably something must be said about a willingness to consider many propositions and many different kinds of propositions. But that there is something like the obligation Chisholm mentions is surely plausible.

Second, we could construe intellectual obligations *aretaically*; the objector could adopt what Professor Frankena calls a "mixed ethics of virtue" with respect to the intellect. There are valuable noetic or intellectual states (whether intrinsically or extrinsically valuable); there are also the corresponding intellectual virtues, the habits of acting so as to produce or promote or enhance those valuable states. One's intellectual obligations, then, are to try to produce and enhance these intellectual virtues in oneself and others.

Third, we could construe intellectual obligations *deontologically*; we could adopt a pure ethics of obligation with respect to the intellect. Perhaps there are intellectual obligations that do not arise from any connection with good or evil but attach to us just by virtue of our being the sorts of creatures we are and having the sorts of noetic powers we do in fact display. The above quotation from Chisholm could also be understood along these lines. Intellectual obligations, therefore, can be construed *variously*, and of course there will be intellectual *permissions* corresponding appropriately to the obligations.

Now perhaps the evidentialist objector thinks there are intellectual obligations of the following sorts. With respect to certain kinds of propositions perhaps I have a duty not to believe them unless I have evidence for them. Perhaps I have a duty not to accept the denial of an apparently self-evident proposition unless I can see that it conflicts with other propositions that seem self-evident. Perhaps I have a duty to accept such a proposition as *I see a tree* under certain conditions that are hard to spell out in detail but include at least my entertaining that proposition and my having a certain characteristic sort of visual experience along with no reason to think my perceptual apparatus is malfunctioning.

Of course these obligations would be *prima facie* obligations; in special sorts of circumstances they could be overridden by other obligations. I have an obligation not to take bread from the grocery store without permission and another to tell the truth. Both sorts of obligation can be overridden, in specific circumstances, by other obligations—in the first case, perhaps, an obligation to feed my starving children and in the second (when the Nazis are pounding on the door) an obligation to protect a human life. So we must distinguish *prima facie* duties or obligations from *all-things-considered* or *on-balance* (*ultima facie*?) obligations. I have a *prima facie* obligation to tell the truth; in a given situation, however, that obligation may be overridden by others, so that my duty, all things considered, is to tell a lie. This is the grain of truth contained in situation ethics and the ill-named "new morality."

And *prima facie* intellectual obligations, like obligations of other sorts, can conflict. Perhaps I have a *prima facie* obligation to believe what seems to me self-evident, and what seems to me to follow self-evidently from what seems to me self-evident. But what if, as in the Russell paradoxes, something that seems self-evidently false apparently follows, self-evidently, from what seems self-evidently true? Here *prima facie* intellectual obligations conflict, and no matter what I do, I will violate a *prima facie* obligation. Another example: in reporting the Grand Teton rappel I neglected to mention the violent electrical storm coming in from the southwest; to escape it we must get off in a hurry, so that I have a *prima facie* obligation to inspect the anchor point carefully, but another to set up the rappel rapidly, which means I cannot spend a lot of time inspecting the anchor point.

Thus lightly armed, suppose we return to the evidentialist objector. Does he mean to hold that the theist without evidence is violating some intellectual obligation? If so, which one? Does he claim, for example, that the theist is violating his all-things-considered intellectual obligation in thus believing? Perhaps he thinks anyone who believes in God without evidence is violating his all-things-considered intellectual duty. This, however, seems unduly harsh. What about the 14-year-old theist brought up to believe in God in a community where everyone believes? This 14-year-old theist, we may suppose, does not believe in God on the basis of evidence. He has never heard of the cosmological, teleological, or ontological arguments; in fact no one has ever presented him with any evidence at all. And although he has often been told about God, he does not take that testimony as evidence; he does not reason thus: everyone around here says God loves us and cares for us; most of what everyone around here says is true; so probably *that is* true. Instead, he simply believes what he is taught. Is he violating an all-things-considered intellectual duty? Surely not. And what about the mature theist—Thomas Aquinas, let us say—who thinks he *does* have adequate evidence? Let us suppose he is wrong; let us suppose all of his arguments are failures. Nevertheless he has reflected long, hard, and conscientiously on the matter and thinks he *does* have adequate evidence. Shall we suppose he is violating an all-things-considered intellectual duty here? I should think not. So construed, the objector's contention is totally implausible.

Perhaps, then, the objector is to be understood as claiming that there is a *prima facie* intellectual duty not to believe in God without evidence. This duty can be overridden by circumstances, of course, but there is a *prima facie* obligation to believe propositions of this sort only on the basis of evidence. The theist without evidence, he adds, is flouting this obligation and is therefore not living up to his intellectual obligations. But here too there are problems. The suggestion is that I now have the *prima facie* duty to comply with the following command: either have evidence or do not believe. But this may be a command I cannot obey. I may not know of any way to acquire evidence for this proposition; and of course if the objector is right, there is no adequate evidence for it. But it is also not within my power to refrain from believing this proposition. My beliefs are not for the most part directly within my control. If you order me now, for example, to cease believing that the earth is very old, there is no way I can comply with your order. But in the same way it is not now within my power to cease believing in God now. So this alleged *prima facie* duty is one such that it is not within my power to comply with it. But how can I have a duty, *prima facie* or otherwise, to do what it is not within my power to do?

### *4. Can I Have Intellectual Obligations If My Beliefs Are Not within My Control?*

This is a difficult and vexing question. The suggestion here is that I cannot now have a *prima facie* obligation to comply with a command which it is not now within my power to obey. Since what I believe is not normally within my power, I cannot have an obligation to believe a certain proposition or to refrain from believing it; but then, *contra* the objector, I do not have an obligation to refrain from believing in God if I have no evidence. This response to the objector is, I think, inadequate. In the first place the response is unbecoming from the theist, since many of those who believe in God follow St. Paul (for example, Romans 1) in holding that under certain circumstances failure to believe in God is culpable. And there are cases where most of us—theist and nontheist alike—do in fact believe that a person is culpable or condemnable for holding a given belief, as well as cases where we hold a person responsible for *not* accepting certain beliefs. Consider the following. Suppose someone comes to believe that Jews are inferior, in some important way, to Gentiles. Suppose he goes on to conclude that Jews should not be permitted to share public facilities such as restaurants and hotels with the rest of us. Further reflection leads him to the view that they should not be provided with the protection of law and that the rest of us have a right to expropriate their property if that is convenient. Finally, he concludes that they ought to be eliminated in order to preserve the purity of the alleged Aryan race. After soul-searching inquiry he apparently believes in all honesty that it is his duty to do what he can to see that this view is put into practice. A convincing sort, he gets the rest of us to see things his way: we join him in his pogroms, and his policy succeeds.

Now many of us will agree that such a person is culpable and guilty. But wherein does his guilt consist? Not, presumably, in doing what he believes he ought to do, in trying to carry out his duty as he sees it. Suppose, to vary the example, he tries to encourage and institute these abhorrent policies at considerable cost to himself: he loses his job; his friends turn their backs on him; he is finally arrested and thrown into prison. Nonetheless he valiantly persists. Does he not deserve moral *credit* for doing what he sees as his duty? His guilt, surely, does not consist solely in his taking the *actions* he takes; at least part of the guilt lies in accepting those abhorrent views. If he *had not* acted on his beliefs—out of fear of the consequences, perhaps—would he not have been guilty nonetheless? He would not have caused as much trouble, but would he not have been guilty? I should think so. We do in fact sometimes think that a person is guilty—has violated norms or obligations—by virtue of the beliefs he holds.

We might suppose, following Alan Donagan, [24] that a person is blameworthy for his beliefs only if he has arrived at them *carelessly* or *dishonestly*. But the fact is, I think, that if someone held the sort of heinous views I mentioned above, we would consider him blameworthy and guilty even if appearances supported his claim that he arrived at these views only after careful, conscientious, and soul-searching inquiry.

Further, suppose we did hold that a person could not be guilty by virtue of accepting beliefs he is led to by conscientious and honest inquiry. What is the importance of the qualifying clause? Well, we think that the person who arrives at his noxious views by such inquiry has at any rate done his best; and even if he arrives at the wrong views, we can ask no more of him than that he do his best. On the other hand, the person who arrives at similar views *carelessly* or *thoughtlessly* is in the wrong for not having exercised sufficient care. But what if a person holds the view that honest and careful inquiry nearly always leads one astray? What if he believes that those views are nearest the truth that have been arrived at, not by inquiry, honest or otherwise, but on impulse? Or suppose he holds that *how* one arrives at beliefs is of no consequence; what counts is only the depth and passion and persistence with which one holds them. Suppose he then holds his offensive beliefs with depth and passion and persistence; can he be guilty by virtue of holding beliefs he has acquired and holds in just the way he thinks beliefs ought to be acquired and held? Is he not then doing his best, and can we expect more of him? If *doing one's best* excuses holding heinous beliefs arrived at through honest inquiry, then does it not equally excuse *S*'s holding heinous beliefs arrived at in whatever way *S* thinks beliefs ought to be arrived at—no matter *what way* *S* thinks beliefs ought to be arrived at? But could a person really escape guilt for offensive racial views, for example, by pleading that while he had arrived at these views impulsively and without thought, that is how he thought such views *ought* to be arrived at? And what about the person who accepts the view that there really are no moral distinctions—that the whole institution of morality is a confused and superstitious remnant of the infancy of our race? Could a person escape accountability for his actions by virtue of his failure to believe in accountability? These are difficult questions, but I think the answer in each case is No. A person who carelessly arrives at morally repugnant beliefs is guilty even if he holds that beliefs should be arrived at carelessly. A person who does not accept morality at all can nonetheless be guilty.

Or so, at any rate, we ordinarily think. Part of the explanation of our so thinking, I believe, lies in our views as to what sorts of beliefs a person of good will *can* virtuously acquire. We do not think any normal human being could honestly arrive at the view that it does not matter how one treats his fellows, that if inflicting severe pain on someone else affords a certain mild pleasure, then there can be no real objection to so doing. We do not believe anyone of good will could honestly come to the conclusion that, say, an entire racial group could rightly be eliminated to avoid the possibility of racial contamination. It is not, of course, that we think it logically impossible that someone should honestly arrive at this view; it is rather that we think it simply would not or could not happen, given what is in fact the makeup of human beings. If we are theists, we will perhaps believe that God has created us in such a way that we can simply see that heinous actions are indeed heinous; and if a normal person comes to believe that such actions are perfectly right and proper, it must be because of some fault in him. Perhaps at some time in the past he *decided* to accept these views, and the pressure of that commitment has brought it about that now in fact he does believe them. A part of what is involved in our blaming people for holding corrupt beliefs, I think, is our supposing that the normal human condition is to reject them, just as the normal human condition is to accept *modus ponens,* say, as valid. We think a normal human being will find injustice—the sort depicted, for example, in the story the prophet Nathan told King David—despicable and odious. In the face of this natural tendency or prompting, to accept the view that such behavior is perfectly proper requires something like a special act of will—a special act of *ill* will. Such a person, we think, *knows better,* chooses what in some sense he knows to be wrong. And if we think a person really *lacks* this inclination to see some actions as morally wrong, then we do not hold him responsible; we think instead that he is in some way defective. According to the McNaughton Rule, one who does not know the difference between right and wrong is in fact *insane* and accordingly cannot be brought to trial. One who cannot see the difference between right and wrong is like someone who was born blind, or is unable to do elementary arithmetical calculations, or cannot see that *modus ponens* is valid.

So we do find some opinions and views morally objectionable. We also object, from a moral point of view, to some kinds of conscientious action; we hold that a person may be doing what is wrong or wicked in acting a certain way, even if he thinks that way of acting is morally permissible—even, indeed, if he thinks that way of acting is his duty. Our objection here is that we believe he *ought not* to think that way of acting is permissible or obligatory; the fact that he *does* think so shows that if he is a normal, well-formed human being, then at some point he has made a morally wrong decision. We think those whom we hold responsible for their views *really know better.* They have rejected what is plain to anyone of good will. They have ignored or suppressed the promptings and leadings of nature—the natural tendency to find unjust behavior reprehensible, for example—and have instead chosen a different route—perhaps one that legitimizes a desire for self-aggrandizement, one that gives free rein to that perverse and aboriginal sin, *pride.* Even if our beliefs are not directly within our control, therefore, most of us recognize that a person can be guilty or culpable by virtue of the beliefs he holds.

The theist, accordingly, should not reply to the evidentialist objector by claiming that since our beliefs are not within our control, we cannot have a *prima facie* duty to refrain from believing certain propositions. But there is a second reason why this response to the evidentialist is inadequate. I have been using the terms "accept" and "believe" interchangeably, but in fact there is an important distinction they can nicely be used to mark. This distinction is extremely hard to make clear but nonetheless, I think, important. Perhaps we can make an initial stab at it as follows. Consider a Christian beset by doubts. He has a hard time believing certain crucial Christian claims—perhaps the teaching that God was in Christ, reconciling the world to himself. Upon calling that belief to mind, he finds it cold, lifeless, without warmth or attractiveness. Nonetheless he is committed to this belief; it is his position; if you ask him what he thinks about it, he will unhesitatingly endorse it. He has, so to speak, thrown in his lot with it. Let us say that he *accepts* this proposition, even though when he is assailed by doubt, he may fail to *believe* it—at any rate explicitly—to any appreciable degree. His commitment to this proposition may be much stronger than his explicit and occurrent belief in it; so these two—that is, acceptance and belief—must be distinguished.

Take another example. A person may accept the proposition that alleged moral distinctions are unreal, and our tendency to make them is a confused and superstitious remnant of the infancy of our race—while nonetheless sometimes finding himself compelled to believe, for example, that gross injustice is wicked. Such a person adopts as his position the proposition that moral distinctions are unreal, and he accepts that proposition; but (at certain times and in certain conditions) he cannot help believing, *malgré lui,* that such distinctions are not unreal. In the same way, someone with solipsistic inclination—acquired, perhaps, by an incautious reading of Hume—could *accept* the proposition that, say, there really is no external world—no houses, horses, trucks, or trees—but find himself, under certain conditions, regularly believing that there are such things.

Now I am quite aware that I have not been able to make this distinction between acceptance and belief wholly clear. I think there is such a distinction in the neighborhood, however, and I believe it is important. It is furthermore one the objector may be able to make use of; for while it is plausible to hold that what I believe is not within my direct control, it is also plausible to suppose that what I *accept* is or can be at least in part a matter of deliberate decision, a matter of voluntarily taking up a certain position. But then the objector can perhaps restate his objection in terms of *acceptance.* Perhaps (because of an unfortunate upbringing, let us say) I cannot refrain from believing in God. Nevertheless it is within my power, says the evidentialist objector, to refuse to *accept* that proposition. And now his claim that there are duties with respect to our beliefs may be reconstrued as the claim that we have *prima facie* duties with respect to our acceptances, one of these duties being not to accept such a proposition as *there is such a person as God* in the absence of evidence.

Finally, while we may perhaps agree that what I believe is not *directly* within my control, some of my beliefs are indirectly within my control, at least in part. First, what I accept has a long-term influence upon what I believe. If I refuse to accept belief in God, and if I try to ignore or suppress my tendency to believe, then perhaps eventually I will no longer believe. And as Pascal pointed out, there are other ways to influence one's beliefs. Presumably, then, the evidentialist objector could hold that it is my *prima facie* duty not to accept belief in God without evidence, and to do what I can to bring it about that I no longer believe. Although it is not within my power now to cease believing now, there may be a series of actions, such that I can now take the first and, after taking the first, will be able to take the second, and so on; and after taking the whole series of actions I will no longer believe in God. Perhaps the objector thinks it is my *prima facie* duty to undertake whatever sort of regimen will at some time in the future result in my not believing without evidence. Perhaps I should attend a Universalist-Unitarian church, for example, and consort with members of the Rationalist Society of America. Perhaps I should read a lot of Voltaire and Bertrand Russell and Thomas Paine, eschewing St. Augustine and C. S. Lewis and, of course, the Bible. Even if I cannot now stop believing without evidence, perhaps there are other actions I can take, such that if I were to take them, then at some time in the future I will not be in this deplorable condition.

So far, then, we have been construing the evidentialist objector as holding that the theist without sufficient evidence—evidence in the sense of other propositions that prove or make probable or support the existence of God—is violating a *prima facie* intellectual obligation of some sort. As we have seen, the fact that belief is not within direct control may give him pause; he is not, however, without plausible replies. But the fact is there is a quite different way of construing the evidentialist objection; the objector need not hold that the theist without evidence is violating or has violated some duty, *prima facie, ultima facie,* or otherwise. Consider someone who believes that Venus is smaller than Mercury, not because he has evidence, but because he read it in a comic book and always believes everything he reads—or consider someone who holds this belief on the basis of an outrageously bad argument. Perhaps there is no obligation he has failed to meet; nevertheless his intellectual condition is defective in some way; or perhaps alternatively there is a commonly achieved excellence he fails to display. Perhaps he is like someone who is easily gulled, or has a serious astigmatism, or is unduly clumsy. And perhaps the evidentialist objection is to be understood, not as the claim that the theist without evidence has failed to meet some obligation, but that he suffers from a certain sort of intellectual deficiency. If this is the objector's view, then his proper attitude toward the theist would be one of sympathy rather than censure.

But of course the crucial question here is this: Why does the objector think these things? Why does he think there *is* a *prima facie* obligation to try not to believe in God without evidence? Or why does he think that to do so is to be in a deplorable condition? Why is it not permissible and quite satisfactory to believe in God without any evidence—proof or argument—at all? Presumably the objector does not mean to suggest that *no* propositions can be believed or accepted without evidence, for if you have evidence for *every* proposition you believe, then (granted certain plausible assumptions about the formal properties of the evidence relation) you will believe infinitely many propositions; and no one has time, these busy days, for that. So presumably *some* propositions can properly be believed and accepted without evidence. Well, why not belief in God? Why is it not entirely acceptable, desirable, right, proper, and rational to accept belief in God without any argument or evidence whatever?

## PART II: AQUINAS AND FOUNDATIONALISM

In this section I shall give what I take to be the evidentialist objector's answer to these questions; I shall argue that his answer is not in the least compelling and that the prospects for his project are not bright. But it is not only evidentialist objectors that have thought theists need evidence if their belief is to be rational; many Christians have thought so too. In particular, many Christian thinkers in the tradition of natural theology have thought so. Thomas Aquinas, of course, is the natural theologian *par excellence*. Thomist thought is also, as it seems to me, the natural starting point for philosophical reflection on these topics, Protestant as well as Catholic. No doubt there are mountains between Rome and Geneva; nevertheless Protestants should in these matters be what Ralph McInerny calls "peeping Thomists"—at any rate they should *begin* as peeping Thomists. We must therefore look at some of Aquinas' views on these matters.

## *A. Aquinas and Evidentialism*

### *1. Aquinas on Knowledge*

According to Aquinas it is possible for us to have scientific knowledge —*scientia*—of the existence and immateriality, unity, simplicity, and perfection of God. As Aquinas sees it, *scientia* is knowledge that is inferred from what is *seen* to be true:

> Any science is possessed by virtue of principles known immediately and therefore seen. Whatever, then, is an object of science is in some sense seen.[25]

Aristotle suggests that the principles of a science must be *self-evident*; and Aquinas sometimes seems to follow him in holding that *scientia*, properly speaking, consists in a body of propositions deduced syllogistically from self-evident first principles—or perhaps *scientia* consists not just in those syllogistic conclusions but in the syllogisms themselves as well. Logic and mathematics seem to be the best examples of science so thought of. Consider, for example, propositional logic: here one can start from self-evident axioms and proceed to deduce theorems by argument forms—*modus ponens*, for example—that are themselves self-evidently valid in an obvious sense.[26] Other good examples of science, so thought of, would be first order logic and arithmetic.[27] And here it would be the *theorems*, not the axioms, of these systems that would constitute science. *Scientia* is *mediate* knowledge, so that one does not have *scientia* of what is self-evident. Strictly speaking, then, only those arithmetical truths that are not self-evident would constitute science. The proposition $3 + 1 = 4$ is unlikely to appear as an axiom in a formulation of arithmetic; since it is self-evident, however, it does not constitute *scientia*, even if it appears as a theorem in some axiomatization of arithmetic.

Of course the "first principles" of a science—the axioms as opposed to the theorems, so to say—are also *known*. They are known *immediately* rather than mediately, and are known by "understanding."

> Now a truth can come into the mind in two ways, namely, as known in itself, and as known through another. What is known in itself is like a principle, and is perceived immediately by the mind. And so the habit which perfects the intellect in considering such a truth is called 'understanding'; it is a firm and easy quality of mind which sees into principles. A truth, however, which is known through another is understood by the intellect, not immediately, but through an inquiry of reason of which it is the terminus.[28]

Like many of Aquinas' distinctions, this one comes from Aristotle:

> Now of the thinking states by which we grasp truth, some are unfailingly true; others admit of error—opinion, for example, and calculation, whereas scientific knowledge and intuition are always true; further, no other kind of thought except intuition is more accurate than scientific knowledge, whereas primary premises are more knowable than demonstrations, and all scientific knowledge is discursive. From these considerations it follows that there will be no scientific knowledge of the primary premises, and since, except intuition, nothing can be truer than scientific knowledge, it will be intuition that apprehends the primary premises. (*Posterior Analytics,* II,19)

Following Aristotle, then, Aquinas distinguishes what is self-evident, or known through itself (*per se nota*), from what is known through another (*per aliud nota*); the former are "principles" and are apprehended by understanding, while the latter constitute science. Aquinas' central point here is that self-evident propositions are known *immediately.* Consider a proposition like

(1) $2 + 1 = 3$

and contrast it with one like

(2) $281 \times 29 = 8{,}149.$

We know the first but not the second *immediately*: we know it, and we do not know it by way of inference from other propositions or on the basis of our knowledge of other propositions. Instead, we can simply see that it is true. Elsewhere Aquinas says that a proposition that is self-evident to us (*per se notam quod nos*) is such that we cannot grasp or apprehend it without believing, indeed, knowing it. (2), on the other hand, does not have this status for us; few of us can simply see that it is true. Instead we must resort to calculation; we go through a chain of inferences, the ultimate premises of which are self-evident.

Of course self-evident propositions are *known,* even though they do not constitute *scientia* in the strict sense. Indeed, their epistemic status, according to Aquinas, is higher than that of propositions known by demonstration. More exactly, *our* epistemic condition, in grasping a truth of this sort, is superior to the condition we are in with respect to a proposition of which we have knowledge by demonstration. The emerging picture of scientific knowledge, then, is the one to be found in Aristotle's *Posterior Analytics*: we know what is self-evident and what follows from what is self-evident by self-evident argument forms. Knowledge consists of *scientia* and *intellectus,* or understanding. By understanding we grasp first principles, self-evident truths; from these we infer or deduce further truths. What we know consists in what we find self-evident together with what we can infer from it by logical means. And if we take this picture seriously, it looks as if knowledge is restricted to what is necessarily true in the broadly logical sense.[29] Presumably a proposition is *per se nota* only if it is necessarily true, and any proposition that follows from necessary truths by self-evident argument forms will itself be necessarily true. As Aristotle puts it, "Since the object of pure scientific knowledge cannot be other than it is, the truth obtained by demonstrative knowledge [Aquinas' *scientia*] will be necessary." (*Posterior Analytics,* I, 3)

As a picture of Aquinas' view of science, however, this is at best incomplete; for Aquinas obviously believes we have knowledge, scientific knowledge, of much that is not logically necessary. He thinks there is such a thing as natural science (*scientia naturalis*), whose subject matter is changeable material objects:

> On the other hand there is the fact that demonstrative knowledge (*scientia*) is found in the intellect. Had the intellect no knowledge of material things, it could not have demonstrative knowledge (*scientia*) of them. Thus there would be no natural science (*scientia naturalis*) dealing with changeable material beings. (ST, Ia, 84, 1)

Aquinas means to say, furthermore, not merely that in natural science we know some necessary truths about contingent and changeable objects (as we do in knowing, for example, that whatever is moved is moved by another); he means that among the truths we know are such contingent propositions as that there is a tree outside the window and that its branches are moving in the wind.

Thus he objects to Plato's view that what we know are the forms or ideas rather than the sensible objects around us: "This may be shown to be false for two reasons. Because first, since the ideas are immaterial and unchanging, demonstrative knowledge of change and matter (such as is characteristic of natural science) would be ruled out, as would any demonstration in terms of material or changeable explanatory principle." (ST, Ia, 84, 1)

According to Aquinas, therefore, we have *scientia* of what changes, and presumably some of this *scientia* involves contingent propositions. Indeed Aquinas elsewhere holds that the kind of knowledge most characteristic of human beings and most proper to them is knowledge of material objects:

> Cognitive faculties are proportioned to their objects. For instance, an angel's intellect, which is totally separate from corporeal reality, has as its proper object intelligible substances separate from corporeal reality, and it is by means of these intelligible objects that it knows material realities. The proper object of the human intellect, on the other hand, since it is joined to a body, is a nature or whatness (quidditas) found in corporeal matter—the intellect, in fact, rises to the limited knowledge it has of invisible things by way of the nature of visible things. (ST, Ia, 84, 8 Resp.)

> We know incorporeal realities . . . by analogy with sensible bodies, which do have images, just as we understand truth in the abstract by a consideration of things in which we see truth. (ST, Ia, 84, 8, ad 3)

There are two sorts of propositions whose truth we simply *see*. First, there are those that are self-evident, or *per se nota*; these are the object of *intellectus* or understanding, and we see their truth in the way in which we see that 2 + 1 = 3. Second, there are propositions "evident to the senses," as he puts it: "That some things move is evident to the senses" (ST, Ia, 2, 3), as is the proposition that the sun moves.[30] His examples of propositions evident to the senses are for the most part propositions whose truth we determine by *sight*. Although of course Aquinas did not think of vision as the only sense yielding knowledge, he did give it pride of place; because it is immaterial, he says, it is "more of a knower" than the other senses. It is not easy to see just what Aquinas means by "evident to the senses," but perhaps the following is fairly close: a proposition is evident to the senses if we human beings have the power to determine its truth by looking at, listening to, tasting, touching, or smelling some physical object. Thus

(3) There is a tree outside my window,

(4) The cat on the mat is fuscous,

and

(5) This wall is yellow

are propositions evident to the senses.

In the first place, then, there are those propositions we simply see to be true; in the second place there are those propositions we see to follow from those in the first group. These propositions can be deduced from those in the first group by arguments we see to be valid.[31] So the basic picture of knowledge is this: we know what we see to be true together with what we can infer from what we see to be true by arguments we can see to be valid.

### 2. *Aquinas on Knowledge of God*

Now Aquinas believes that human beings (even in our earthly condition here below) can have knowledge, *scientific* knowledge, of God's existence, as well as knowledge that he has such attributes as simplicity, eternity, immateriality, immutability and the like. In *Summa Theologiae* Aquinas sets out his famous "Five Ways," or five proofs of God's existence: in *Summa Contra Gentiles* he sets out the proof from motion in much greater detail; and in each case he follows these alleged demonstrations with alleged demonstrations that God possesses the attributes just mentioned. So natural knowledge of God is possible. But the vast majority of those who believe in God, he thinks, do not have knowledge of God's existence but must instead take it on faith. Only a few of us have the time, inclination, and ability to follow the theistic proofs; the rest of us take this truth on faith. And even though God's existence is demonstrable—even though we are capable of *knowing* it—nevertheless it is appropriately proposed to human beings as an object of faith. The reason, in brief, is that our welfare demands that we believe the proposition in question, but *knowledge* of it is exceedingly hard to come by:

> For the rational truth about God would have appeared to only a few, and even so after a long time and mixed with many errors; whereas on knowing this depends our whole welfare, which is in God. (ST, Ia, I,1)

> From all this it is clear that, if it were necessary to use a strict demonstration as the only way to reach a knowledge of the things we must know about God, very few could ever construct such a demonstration and even these could do it only after a long time. From this it is evident that the provision of the way of faith, which gives all easy access to salvation at any time, is beneficial to man.[32]

So most of those who believe in God do so on faith. Fundamentally, for Aquinas, to accept a proposition on faith is to accept it on God's authority; faith is a matter of "believing God" (ST, IIa, IIae, ii, 2): "for that which is above reason we believe only because God has revealed it" (SCG, I, 9). Now what about those who believe in God on faith even though they do not know that God exists? How can that be a rational procedure? So far as I know, Aquinas does not explicitly address this question. He does discuss a closely related question, however: the question whether those who believe (take on faith) what is "above reason" are irrational or foolish, or in his terms, "believe with undue levity":

> [1] Those who place their faith in this truth, however, "for which the human reason offers no experimental evidence," do not believe foolishly, as though "following artificial fables" (II Peter 1:16). For these "secrets of divine Wisdom" (Job 11:6) the divine Wisdom itself, which knows all things to the full, has deigned to reveal to men. It reveals its own presence, as well as the truth of its teaching and inspiration, by fitting arguments; and in order to confirm those truths that exceed natural knowledge, it gives visible manifestation to works that surpass the ability of all nature. Thus, there are the wonderful cures of illnesses, there is the raising of the dead, and the wonderful immutation in the heavenly bodies; and what is more wonderful, there is the inspiration given to human minds, so that simple and untutored persons, filled with the gift of the Holy Spirit, come to possess instantaneously the highest wisdom and the readiest eloquence. When these arguments were examined, through the efficacy of the above-mentioned proof, and not the violent assault of arms or the promise of pleasures, and (what is most wonderful of all) in the midst of the tyranny of the persecutors, an innumerable throng of people, both simple and most learned, flocked to the Christian faith. In this faith there are truths preached that surpass every human intellect; the pleasures of the flesh are curbed; it is taught that the things of the world should be spurned. Now, for the minds of mortal men to assent to these things is the greatest of miracles, just as it is a manifest work of divine inspiration that, spurning visible things, men should seek only what is invisible. Now, that this has happened neither without preparation nor by chance, but as a result of the disposition of God, is clear from the fact that through many pronouncements of the ancient prophets God had foretold that He would do this. The books of these prophets are held in veneration among us Christians, since they give witness to our faith. (SCG, I, 6)

Here the point, I think, is the following. It is of course totally proper and entirely sensible to take a belief on God's say-so, to accept it on his authority. Clearly I am not foolish or irrational in believing something on the authority of my favorite mathematician, even if I cannot work it out for myself. I may thus come to believe, for example, that the four-color problem has been solved. But then a fortiori I would not be foolish or irrational in accepting a belief on the basis of *God's* authority. If I know that God proposes *p* to me for belief, then, clearly enough, it is eminently sensible to believe *p*. The question is not whether it is foolish to believe something on God's authority, but whether it is foolish to believe that God has in fact proposed a given item for my belief. Obviously, if he *has,* then I should believe it; but what is my reason or motive for supposing that in fact it is *God* who has proposed for our belief, for example, the teaching of the Trinity?

This is the question Aquinas addresses in the above passage; he means to argue that it is not foolish or irrational to take it that God has proposed for our belief just those items Christians suppose that he has—the articles of faith. What he means to say, I think, is that to believe in the mysteries of the faith is not to be foolish or to believe with undue levity, because we have *evidence for* the conclusion that God has proposed them for our belief. This evidence consists in the fulfillment of prophecy and in the signs and wonders accompanying the proclamation of these mysteries. Aquinas refers here to "works that surpass the ability of all nature," such as "wonderful cures of illness," "the raising of the dead," and the like. The greatest miracle of all, he says, is the marvelous rapidity with which the Christian faith has spread, despite the best efforts of tyrants and despite the fact that "In this faith there are truths preached that surpass every human intellect; the pleasures of the flesh are curbed; it is taught that the things of the world should be spurned."

I think he means to suggest, furthermore, that if we did *not* have this evidence, or some other evidence, we would be foolish or irrational in accepting the mysteries of the faith. It is just because we have evidence for these things that we are not irrational in accepting them. Here by way of contrast he cites the followers of Mohammed, who, he says, do not have evidence: "It is thus clear that those who place any faith in his words believe foolishly." (SCG, I, 6)

What is important to see here is the following. Aquinas clearly believes that there are some propositions we are rationally justified in accepting, even though we do not have evidence for them, or reason to them from other propositions, or accept them on the basis of other propositions. Let us say that a proposition is *basic* for me if I believe it and do not believe it on the basis of other propositions. This relationship is familiar but hard to characterize in a revealing and nontrivial fashion. I believe that the word "umbrageous" is spelled u-m-b-r-a-g-e-o-u-s: this belief is based on another belief of mine, the belief that that is how the dictionary says it is spelled. I believe that $72 \times 71 = 5112$. This belief is based upon several other beliefs I hold: that $1 \times 72 = 72$; $7 \times 2 = 14$; $7 \times 7 = 49$; $49 + 1 = 50$; and others. Some of my beliefs, however, I accept but do not accept on the basis of any other beliefs. Call these beliefs *basic.* I believe that $2 + 1 = 3$, for example, and do not believe it on the basis of other propositions. I also believe that I am seated at my desk, and that there is a mild pain in my right knee. These too are basic for me; I do not believe them on the basis of others. Now the propositions we are rationally justified in accepting as basic, thinks Aquinas, are the ones we see to be true: those that are self-evident or evident to the senses. As for the rest of the propositions we believe, we are rational in accepting them only if they stand in a certain relationship to those that are properly basic. Among the nonbasic propositions we rationally accept, some we see to follow from those that *are* basic; these are the propositions we know. Others are not known to us, do not follow from basic propositions, but are nonetheless rationally acceptable because they are *probable* or likely with respect to them. I believe Aquinas means to hold, more generally, that a proposition is rationally acceptable for us only if it is at least probable with respect to beliefs that are properly basic for us—that is, with respect to beliefs that are self-evident or evident to the senses. And hence on his view, as on the evidentialist objector's, belief in God is rational for us only if we have evidence for it.

Here I should point out that there are suggestions of another line of thought in Aquinas: he sometimes suggests that there is a sort of *intuitive* or *immediate* grasp of God's existence:

> It remains to investigate the kind of knowledge in which the ultimate felicity of an intellectual substance consists. For there is a common and confused knowledge of God which is found in practically all men; this is due either to the fact that it is self-evident that God exists, just as other principles of demonstration are—a view held by some people, as we said in Book One —or, what seems indeed to be true, that man can immediately reach some sort of knowledge of God by natural reason. For when men see that things in nature run according to a definite order, and that ordering does not occur without an orderer, they perceive in most cases that there is some orderer of the things that we see. But who or what kind of being, or whether there is but one orderer of nature, is not yet grasped immediately in this general consideration. (SCG, III, 38)

Aquinas would also hold, presumably, that someone who has such immediate and intuitive apprehension of God's existence is not irrational in believing that there is a God. It is not entirely easy to see how to fit this suggestion into his generally Aristotelian way of looking at the matter; perhaps here we must see Aquinas as an early Calvinist. See below, Part III, sections A and C.

### *B. Foundationalism*

Aquinas and the evidentialist objector concur, then, in holding that belief in God is rationally acceptable only if there is evidence for it—only if, that is, it is probable with respect to some body of propositions that constitutes the evidence. And here we can get a better understanding of Aquinas and the evidentialist objector if we see them as accepting some version of *classical foundationalism.* This is a *picture* or total way of looking at faith, knowledge, justified belief, rationality, and allied topics. This picture has been enormously popular in Western thought; and despite a substantial opposing groundswell, I think it remains the dominant way of thinking about these topics. According to the foundationalist some propositions are properly basic and some are not; those that are not are rationally accepted only on the basis of *evidence,* where the evidence must trace back, ultimately, to what *is* properly basic. The existence of God, furthermore, is not among the propositions that are properly basic; hence a person is rational in accepting theistic belief only if he has evidence for it. The vast majority of those in the western world who have thought about our topic have accepted some form of classical foundationalism. The evidentialist objection to belief in God, furthermore, is obviously rooted in this way of looking at things. So suppose we try to achieve a deeper understanding of it.

Earlier I said the first thing to see about the evidentialist objection is that it is a *normative* contention or claim. The same thing must be said about foundationalism: this thesis is a normative thesis, a thesis about how a system of beliefs *ought* to be structured, a thesis about the properties of a correct, or acceptable, or rightly structured system of beliefs. According to the foundationalist there are norms, or duties, or obligations with respect to belief just as there are with respect to actions. To conform to these duties and obligations is to be rational; to fail to measure up to them is to be irrational. To be rational, then, is to exercise one's epistemic powers *properly*—to exercise them in such a way as to go contrary to none of the norms for such exercise.

Although for ease of exposition I am taking the relevant foundationalist claim as one about *duties,* or *norms,* or *obligations,* it could also be construed as a claim about *excellence.* So taken, the foundationalist claims that to achieve a certain characteristic excellence, a system of beliefs ought to be structured in a certain way. The claim could also be construed as about *defects,* as the claim that a system of beliefs not structured in that way is defective.

I think we can understand foundationalism more fully if we introduce the idea of a *noetic structure.* A person's noetic structure is the set of propositions he believes, together with certain epistemic relations that hold among him and these propositions. As we have seen, some of my beliefs may be based upon others; it may be that there are a pair of propositions

*A* and *B* such that I believe *B*, and believe *A on the basis of B.* An account of a person's noetic structure, then, would specify which of his beliefs are basic and which nonbasic. Of course it is abstractly possible that *none* of his beliefs is basic; perhaps he holds just three beliefs, *A, B,* and *C*, and believes each of them on the basis of the other two. We might think this improper or irrational, but that is not to say it could not be done. And it is also possible that *all* of his beliefs are basic; perhaps he believes a lot of propositions but does not believe any of them on the basis of any others. In the typical case, however, a noetic structure will include both basic and nonbasic beliefs. It may be useful to give some examples of beliefs that are often basic for a person. Suppose I seem to see a tree; I have that characteristic sort of experience that goes with perceiving a tree. I may then believe the proposition that I see a tree. It is *possible* that I believe that proposition *on the basis of* the proposition that I seem to see a tree; in the typical case, however, I will not believe the former on the basis of the latter because in the typical case I will not believe the latter at all. I will not be paying any attention to my experience but will be concentrating on the tree. Of course I *can* turn my attention to my experience, notice how things look to me, and acquire the belief that I seem to see something that looks like *that*; and if you challenge my claim that I see a tree, perhaps I *will* thus turn my attention to my experience. But in the typical case I will not believe that I see a tree on the basis of a proposition about my experience; for I believe *A* on the basis of *B* only if I believe *B*, and in the typical case where I perceive a tree I do not believe (or entertain) any propositions about my experience. Typically I take such a proposition as basic. Similarly, I believe I had breakfast this morning; this too is basic for me. I do not believe this proposition on the basis of some proposition about my experience—for example, that I seem to remember having had breakfast. In the typical case I will not have even considered *that* question—the question whether I *seem* to remember having had breakfast; instead I simply believe that I had breakfast; I take it as basic.

Second, an account of a noetic structure will include what we might call an index of *degree* of belief. I hold some of my beliefs much more firmly than others. I believe both that 2 + 1 = 3 and that London, England, is north of Saskatoon, Saskatchewan; but I believe the former more resolutely than the latter. Some beliefs I hold with maximum firmness; others I do in fact accept, but in a much more tentative way.

Here we might make use of the personalist interpretation of probability theory; think of an index of degree of belief as a function $B_S(A)$ from the set of propositions a person *S* believes or disbelieves into the real numbers between 0 and 1. $B_s(A) = n$, then, records something like the degree to which $S$ believes $A$, or the strength of his belief that $A$. $B_s(A) = 1$ proclaims $S$'s utter and abandoned commitment to $A$; $B_s(A) = 0$ records a similar commitment to not-$A$; $B_s(A) = .5$ means that $S$, like Buridan's ass, is suspended in equilibrium between $A$ and not-$A$. We could then go on to consider whether the personalist is right in holding that a rational noetic structure conforms to the calculus of probability. I have argued elsewhere that he is *not* right.[33]

Third, a somewhat vaguer notion: an account of $S$'s noetic structure would include something like an index of *depth of ingression.* Some of my beliefs are, we might say, on the periphery of my noetic structure. I accept them, and may even accept them firmly, but I could give them up without much change elsewhere in my noetic structure. I believe there are some large boulders on the top of the Grand Teton. If I come to give up this belief (say by climbing it and not finding any), that change need not have extensive reverberations throughout the rest of my noetic structure; it could be accommodated with minimal alteration elsewhere. So its depth of ingression into my noetic structure is not great. On the other hand, if I were come to believe that there simply is no such thing as the Grand Teton, or no mountains at all, or no such thing as the state of Wyoming, that would have much greater reverberations. And suppose I were to come to think there had not been much of a past (that the world was created just five minutes ago, complete with all its apparent memories and traces of the past) or that there were not any other persons: these changes would have even greater reverberations; these beliefs of mine have great depth of ingression into my noetic structure.

We must note that basicality, degree of belief, and depth of ingression are not related in any simple way. Some propositions I take as basic I believe with maximum firmness— that $2 + 1 = 3$, for example, or that I seem to see a blue pen in my hand. Others I accept much less firmly. I believe I visited a certain university in northern England five years ago. I do not believe this proposition on the basis of others (for example, propositions about what my journal says or what my wife remembers or thinks she remembers), so this proposition is basic for me. But I do not believe it nearly as firmly as that $2 + 1 = 3$. Thus there are substantial differences in the degree to which I believe propositions I take as basic. Furthermore, there are some propositions I believe on the basis of others, that I believe more firmly than some I take as basic. The belief that I visited that university in northern England is basic for me, but I do not believe it as firmly as that $21^2 = 441$ or that "umbrageous" is spelled u-m-b-r-a-g-e-o-u-s, neither of which is basic for me. In the same way basicality and depth of ingression can vary inversely, as can the latter and degree of belief.

Furthermore, a belief can easily change status from nonbasic to basic and vice versa. *Now* the proposition that $21 \times 21 = 441$ is not basic for me; I accept it on the basis of the belief that I have just calculated it, and that is how it came out. Later, however, I may remember that 21 × 21 = 441 and forget that I calculated it. In that case I will simply remember it and no longer believe it on the basis of other beliefs; it will be basic for me. The same may happen for "umbrageous." Having just looked it up, I believe that it is spelled that way on the basis of my belief that that is how the dictionary says it is spelled; later I may remember that it is spelled that way but no longer remember having looked it up.

Finally, it might be thought that we can determine what a person takes as basic by asking a Chisholm-like[34] question: perhaps something like "What is your reason for believing *p*?" or "Why do you believe *p*?"[35] But this, I think, is incorrect. Suppose I seem to see a tree and believe that I do see a tree; you ask me what my reasons are for thinking that I see a tree. The first thing to note is that the question can be taken variously. I may take it as a request for my reason for thinking it is a *tree* that I see rather than, say, a large cactus. I might then respond by saying that it looks to me like a tree (and not like a cactus). I might also interpret your query as a request for my reasons for believing I *see* a tree (as opposed, for example, to hearing or smelling one); again I might respond by citing some proposition about my experience. Or I might take your query as a request to give *you* a reason for believing there is a tree there. You cannot see the tree—you have broken your glasses or you have the hiccups and have adopted the folk remedy of putting a brown paper bag over your head; I know that you believe that when I am appeared to treely, then 99 chances out of 100 there is a tree lurking in the neighborhood. So I might take your question variously, and many ways of taking it are such that if I do take it that way, then I will respond by citing a proposition about my experience.

But does it follow that I believe the proposition *I see a tree* (call it "T") on the basis of that experiential proposition? I should think not. Surely it does not follow that at *t*, the time of the query, I believed T on the basis of the experiential proposition. At *t* perhaps I did not even *believe* the experiential proposition; I may have been concentrating on the tree rather than on my own experience; and surely it is not possible that at a time *t* I accept a belief *B* on the basis of a belief *A* if at *t* I do not even believe *A*. Of course at *t**, the time of my response, I do presumably accept the experiential proposition; does it follow that at *t** I believe T on the basis of that experiential proposition? No. As I said, I might be trying to give you a reason to believe that there is a tree there, or I might be explaining why I believe I *see* as opposed to hear or smell a tree, or explaining why I think I see a *tree* as opposed to a large cactus. In these cases I might respond by citing an experiential proposition, but why suppose that I am believing that I see a tree *on the basis of* the experiential proposition, or indeed, on the basis of any other proposition? Again, suppose you ask me what my reasons are for believing that *2 + 1 = 3* or that *modus ponens* is a valid form of argument. I may very well reply, "Well, it just seems self-evident." Must we conclude that my belief that *2 + 1 = 3* is based upon a proposition about my experience? I should think not. Does the fact that I cite an experiential proposition when queried in this way show that I do not take *modus ponens* as basic? Surely not. So we cannot in this fashion determine what propositions are basic for a person, and it is not altogether easy to say just when a proposition *is* basic for a person. But we can say at least this much. A *necessary* condition for *S*'s believing *A* on the basis of *B* is *S*'s believing both *A* and *B*, and a sufficient condition is *S*'s believing *A*, believing *B*, believing that *B* is good evidence for *A*, and believing that he believes *A* on the basis of *B*.

Now foundationalism is best construed, I think, as a thesis about *rational* noetic structures. A noetic structure is rational if it could be the noetic structure of a person who was completely rational. To be completely rational, as I am here using the term, is not to believe only what is true, or to believe all the logical consequences of what one believes, or to believe all necessary truths with equal firmness, or to be uninfluenced by emotion in forming belief; it is, instead, to do the right thing with respect to one's believings. It is to violate no epistemic duties. From this point of view, a rational person is one whose believings meet the appropriate standards; to criticize a person as irrational is to criticize her for failing to fulfill these duties or responsibilities, for failing to conform to the relevant norms or standards. To draw the ethical analogy, the irrational is the impermissible; the rational is the permissible.

Here I am taking "rationality" in terms of *duty,* but as we have seen, we could in addition or alternatively take it as the possession of an epistemic excellence or the avoidance of an epistemic defect.

A rational noetic structure, then, is one that could be the noetic structure of a wholly rational person; and foundationalism, as I say, is a thesis about such noetic structures. We may think of the foundationalist as beginning with the observation that some of our beliefs are based upon others. According to the foundationalist a rational noetic structure will *have a foundation*—a set of beliefs not accepted on the basis of others; in a rational noetic structure some beliefs will be basic. Nonbasic beliefs, of course, will be accepted on the basis of other beliefs, which may be accepted on the basis of still other beliefs, and so on until the foundations are reached. In a rational noetic structure, therefore, every nonbasic belief is ultimately accepted on the basis of basic beliefs.

Perhaps we can put the matter as follows. According to the foundationalist the basis relation is, first, a one-many relation; a belief *A* will often be based upon *several* beliefs $B_1 \ldots B_n$. Second, in a rational noetic structure this relationship is *irreflexive*. It may be doubted whether anyone is so benighted as to believe *A* on the basis of *A*, but even if it could be done, it should not be. For in a rational noetic structure, if *A* is believed on the basis of *B*, then *B* is in an important sense *prior* to *A*; and no proposition is prior to itself. From this point of view the term "self-evident" is something of a misnomer. A self-evident proposition—$2 + 1 = 3$, for example—is not one for which we have good evidence, but for which the evidence is *itself*; it is, instead, a proposition that is evident, or known, in itself, *without* evidence. That means that one does not believe it on the basis of other propositions. *2* + *1* = *3* is self-evident; this is not to say that it is its own evidence, but that no evidence is needed for it.

Third, according to the foundationalist the basis relation is *asymmetric* in a rational noetic structure; if my belief that *A* is based upon my belief that *B*, then my belief that *B* must not be based on my belief that *A*. More exactly, suppose *N* is a rational noetic structure. Then if the belief that *A*, in *N*, is based upon $B_1 \ldots B_n$, none of the $B_i$ will be based upon *A*. So for example, if I am rational and my belief that the Bible is authoritative is based upon my belief that God is its author and whatever God says is true, then my belief that God is the author of the Bible will not be based upon the beliefs that the Bible is authoritative and says that God is its author.

So the first main thesis of foundationalism is that the basis relation in a rational noetic structure is irreflexive and asymmetric. The second main thesis is one we have already met. In a rational noetic structure some beliefs will not be based on any other beliefs; some beliefs will be *basic*. These beliefs are the foundation of that noetic structure.

Perhaps we can see a bit more of the articulation of a rational noetic structure as follows. Let us say that a belief *B* is an *immediate basis* of a belief *A* in a noetic structure *N* if *A* is based on *B* in *N* and there is no belief *C* such that *C* is based on *B* in *N* and *A* is based on *C* in *N*. Then in a rational noetic structure

(6) Every nonbasic belief has an immediate basis.

Let us say further that a belief is *$0^{th}$ level in N* if it is basic in *N*, *$1^{st}$ level in N* if it is immediately based on some belief that is $0^{th}$ level in *N*, and, in general, *$n + 1^{st}$ level in N* if it is immediately based upon at least one belief that is $n^{th}$ level in *N*. In a rational noetic structure *N*

(7) Every belief *B* in *N* will belong to a highest level in *N*;

that is, there will be some level such that *B* belongs to that level and to no higher level. (7) guarantees that no belief is immediately based upon itself. For suppose B were immediately based on *B*. By (7) *B* belongs to a highest level l. But since *B* is immediately based upon *B*, it also belongs to a higher level l + 1, which is impossible. Similarly, (7) guarantees that the immediate-basis-of relation is asymmetric. One more piece of terminology: say that *the* level of a belief *B* in a noetic structure *N* is the highest level of *B* in *N*. Then in a rational noetic structure *N*

(8) If *A* is based on *B* in *N*, then the level of *A* is higher than the level of *B*.

We might put this by saying that if *A* is based on *B* in *N*, then *B* is *prior* to *A* in *N*; this is the respect I mentioned in which the basing proposition is prior to the based proposition. From (8) it follows that the basis relation is asymmetric and irreflexive.

In a rational noetic structure every nonbasic belief will be immediately based on some beliefs $A_1 \ldots A_n$, each of these will be immediately based on some other beliefs $B_1 \ldots B_n$, and so on until the foundations are reached. So from any nonbasic belief $B$ there is a path downward through the noetic structure to the foundations—typically several different paths, terminating in several different basic beliefs. Perhaps we can put this more precisely as follows. A *path from A to B in N* is a set of propositions $A, B_n, \ldots B_1, B$ such that, in $N$, $A$ is immediately based upon $B_n$, $B_n$ is immediately based upon $B_n - 1 \ldots$, $B_2$ is immediately based on $B_1$, and $B_1$ is immediately based on $B$. A *path from A in N* is any path in $N$ from $A$ to any other proposition. A path from $A$ to $B$ *can be extended to a path from A to C* if there is a path from $B$ to $C$. And a path from A *terminates at C* if it can be extended to a path from $A$ to $C$ and there are no paths from $C$. Then in a rational noetic structure $N$

(9) If $A$ is believed on the basis of $B$ in $N$, then there is a path from $A$ to $B$ in $N$.

In such a noetic structure, furthermore,

(10) If $A$ is nonbasic in $N$, then there is a path from $A$ to some belief $B$ that is basic in $N$;

(11) If there is a path from $A$ to $B$ in $N$, and $B$ is nonbasic in $N$, then the path from $A$ to $B$ can be extended to a path from $A$ to $C$, where $C$ is basic in $N$;

and

(12) Every path from a nonbasic belief $A$ terminates in the foundations.

According to the foundationalist, therefore, every rational noetic structure has a foundation, and all nonbasic beliefs are ultimately accepted on the basis of beliefs in the foundations. But a belief cannot properly be accepted on the basis of just *any* other belief; in a rational noetic structure, $A$ will be accepted on the basis of $B$ only if *B supports A* or is a member of a set of beliefs that together support $A$. It is not clear just what this relation—call it the "supports" relation—is; and different foundationalists propose different candidates. Presumably, however, it lies in the neighborhood of *evidence*; if $A$ supports $B$, then $A$ is evidence for $B$, or makes $B$ evident; or perhaps $B$ is likely or probable with respect to $B$. This relation admits of degrees. My belief that Feike can swim is supported by my knowledge that nine out of ten Frisians can swim and Feike is a Frisian; it is supported more strongly by my knowledge that the evening paper contains a picture of Feike triumphantly finishing first in the fifteen-hundred meter freestyle in the 1980 summer Olympics. And the foundationalist holds, sensibly enough, that in a rational noetic structure the strength of a nonbasic belief will depend upon the degree of support from foundational beliefs.

There is a great deal more to be said about this supports relationship, but no space to say it here. Things would be neatest for the foundationalist if the supports relation could be seen as like the probability relation, as a function from pairs of beliefs into the real numbers between 0 and 1. Then perhaps he could explain Locke's *dictum* that strength of belief ought to be proportional to strength of evidence as follows: If *S*'s noetic structure is rational, then for any nonbasic belief $A$, $P(A/F) \geq B_S(A)$; that is, the support afforded to $A$ by the foundations of *S*'s noetic structure is at least as strong as *S*'s belief that $A$. Problems arise for knowledge (as opposed to rational belief), however. Suppose we agree that if the support from the foundations for each of a pair of propositions *A* and *B* is sufficient for knowledge, then the support for their conjunction, *A and B*, is also sufficient for knowledge. Then the lottery paradox shows that if the supports relation conforms to the probability calculus, there will be no degree of support (less than 1) such that a proposition's being supported to that degree is sufficient (so far as support goes) for knowledge. There are further perplexities here, but the foundationalist will certainly hold that there *is* such a supports relationship, and that in a rational noetic structure, strength of nonbasic belief is a function of support from the foundations.

By way of summary, then, let us say that according to foundationalism: (1) in a rational noetic structure the believed-on-the-basis-of relation is asymmetric and irreflexive, (2) a rational noetic structure has a foundation, and (3) in a rational noetic structure nonbasic belief is proportional in strength to support from the foundations.

### *C. Conditions on Proper Basicality*

Next we note a further and fundamental feature of classic varieties of foundationalism: they all lay down certain conditions of proper basicality. From the foundationalist point of view not just any kind of belief can be found in the foundations of a rational noetic structure; a belief to be properly basic (that is, basic in a rational noetic structure) must meet certain conditions. It must be capable of functioning foundationally, capable of bearing its share of the weight of the whole noetic structure. Thus Thomas Aquinas, as we have seen, holds that a proposition is properly basic for a person only if it is self-evident to him or "evident to the senses."

Suppose we take a brief look at self-evidence. Under what conditions does a proposition have it? What kinds of propositions are self-evident? Examples would include very simple arithmetical truths such as

(13) $2 + 1 = 3$;

simple truths of logic such as

(14) No man is both married and unmarried;

perhaps the generalizations of simple truths of logic, such as

(15) For any proposition $p$ the conjunction of $p$ with its denial is false;

and certain propositions expressing identity and diversity; for example,

(16) Redness is distinct from greenness,
(17) The property of being prime is distinct from the property of being composite,

and

(18) The proposition *all men are mortal* is distinct from the proposition *all mortals are men.*

There are others; Aquinas gives as examples:

(19) The whole is greater than the part,

where, presumably, he means by "part" what we mean by "proper part," and, more dubiously,

(20) Man is an animal.

Still other candidates—candidates which may be less than entirely uncontroversial—come from many other areas; for example,

(21) If $p$ is necessarily true and $p$ entails $q$, then $q$ is necessarily true,
(22) If $e^1$ occurs before $e^2$ and $e^2$occurs before $e^3$, then $e^1$ occurs before $e^3$,

and

(23) It is wrong to cause unnecessary (and unwanted) pain just for the fun of it.

What is it that characterizes these propositions? According to the tradition the outstanding characteristic of a self-evident proposition is that one simply sees it to be true upon grasping or understanding it. Understanding a self-evident proposition is sufficient for apprehending its truth. Of course this notion must be relativized to *persons*; what is self-evident to you might not be to me. Very simple arithmetical truths will be self-evident to nearly all of us, but a truth like $17 + 18 = 35$ may be self-evident only to some. And of course a proposition is self-evident to a person only if he does in fact grasp it, so a proposition will not be self-evident to those who do not apprehend the concepts it involves. As Aquinas says, some propositions are self-evident only to the learned; his example is the truth that immaterial substances do not occupy space. Among those propositions whose concepts not everyone grasps, some are such that anyone who *did* grasp them would see their truth; for example,

(24) A model of a first-order theory T assigns truth to the axioms of T.

Others—*17 + 13 = 30,* for example—may be such that some but not all of those who apprehend them also see that they are true.

But how shall we understand this "seeing that they are true"? Those who speak of self-evidence explicitly turn to this visual metaphor and expressly explain self-evidence by reference to vision. There are two important aspects to the metaphor and two corresponding components to the idea of self-evidence. First, there is the *epistemic* component: a proposition $p$ is self-evident to a person $S$ only if $S$ has *immediate* knowledge of $p$—that is, knows $p$, and does not know $p$ on the basis of his knowledge of other propositions. Consider a simple arithmetic truth such as $2 + 1 = 3$ and compare it with one like $24 \times 24 = 576$. I know each of these propositions, and I know the second but not the first on the basis of computation, which is a kind of inference. So I have immediate knowledge of the first but not the second.

But there is also a phenomenological component. Consider again our two propositions; the first but not the second has about it a kind of luminous aura or glow when you bring it to mind or consider it. Locke speaks, in this connection, of an "evident luster"; a self-evident proposition, he says, displays a kind of "clarity and brightness to the attentive mind." Descartes speaks instead of "clarity and distinctness"; each, I think, is referring to the same phenomenological feature. And this feature is connected with another: upon understanding a proposition of this sort one feels a strong inclination to accept it; this luminous obviousness seems to compel or at least impel assent. Aquinas and Locke, indeed, held that a person, or at any rate a normal, well-formed human being, finds it impossible to withhold assent when considering a self-evident proposition. The phenomenological component of the idea of self-evidence, then, seems to have a double aspect: there is the luminous aura that $2 + 1 = 3$ displays, and there is also an experienced tendency to accept or believe it. Perhaps, indeed, the luminous aura *just is* the experienced impulsion toward acceptance; perhaps these are the very same thing. In that case the phenomenological component would not have the double aspect I suggested it did have; in either case, however, we must recognize this phenomenological aspect of self-evidence.

Aquinas therefore holds that self-evident propositions are properly basic. I think he means to add that propositions "evident to the senses" are also properly basic. By this latter term I think he means to refer to *perceptual* propositions—propositions whose truth or falsehood we can determine by looking or employing some other sense. He has in mind, I think, such propositions as

(25) There is a tree before me,

(26) I am wearing shoes,

and

(27) That tree's leaves are yellow.

So Aquinas holds that a proposition is properly basic if and only if it is either self-evident or evident to the senses. Other foundationalists have insisted that propositions basic in a rational noetic structure must be *certain* in some important sense. Thus it is plausible to see Descartes as holding that the foundations of a rational noetic structure include, not such propositions as (25)–(27), but more cautious claims—claims about one's own mental life; for example,

(28) It seems to me that I see a tree,

(29) I seem to see something green,

or, as Professor Chisholm puts it,

(30) I am appeared greenly to.

Propositions of this latter sort seem to enjoy a kind of immunity from error not enjoyed by those of the former. I could be mistaken in thinking I see a pink rat; perhaps I am hallucinating or the victim of an illusion. But it is at the least very much harder to see that I could be mistaken in believing that I *seem* to see a pink rat, in believing that I am appeared pinkly (or pink ratly) to. Suppose we say that a proposition with respect to which I enjoy this sort of immunity from error is incorrigible for me; then perhaps Descartes means to hold that a proposition is properly basic for *S* only if it is either self-evident or incorrigible for *S*.

By way of explicit definition:

(31) *p* is incorrigible for *S* if and only if (a) it is not possible that *S* believe *p* and *p* be false, and (b) it is not possible that *S* believe ~*p* and *p* be true.

The second clause serves to exclude necessary truths; given just the first clause, either Goldbach's conjecture or its denial would be incorrigible, even though no one knows whether it is true.

Here we have a further characteristic of foundationalism: the claim that not just any proposition is properly basic. Ancient and medieval foundationalists tended to hold that a proposition is properly basic for a person only if it is either self-evident or evident to the senses: modern foundationalists—Descartes, Locke, Leibniz, and the like—tended to hold that a proposition is properly basic for *S* only if either self-evident or incorrigible for *S*. Of course this is a historical generalization and is thus perilous; but perhaps it is worth the risk. And now let us say that a *classical foundationalist* is any one who is either an ancient and medieval or a modern foundationalist.

### *D. The Collapse of Foundationalism*

Now suppose we return to the main question: Why should not belief in God be among the foundations of my noetic structure? The answer, on the part of the classical foundationalist, was that even if this belief is *true*, it does not have the characteristics a proposition must have to deserve a place in the foundations. There is no room in the foundations for a proposition that can be rationally accepted only on the basis of other propositions. The only properly basic propositions are those that are self-evident or incorrigible or evident to the senses. Since the proposition that God exists is none of the above, it is not properly basic for anyone; that is, no well-formed, rational noetic structure contains this proposition in its foundations. But now we must take a closer look at this fundamental principle of classical foundationalism:

> (32) A proposition *p* is properly basic for a person *S* if and only if *p* is either self-evident to *S* or incorrigible for *S* or evident to the senses for *S*.

(32) contains two claims: first, a proposition is properly basic *if* it is self-evident, incorrigible, or evident to the senses, and, second, a proposition is properly basic *only if* it meets this condition. The first seems true enough; suppose we concede it. But what is to be said for the second? Is there any reason to accept it? Why does the foundationalist accept it? Why does he think the theist ought to?

We should note first that if this thesis, and the correlative foundationalist thesis that a proposition is rationally acceptable only if it follows from or is probable with respect to what is properly basic—if these claims are true, then enormous quantities of what we all in fact believe are irrational. One crucial lesson to be learned from the development of modern philosophy—Descartes through Hume, roughly—is just this: relative to propositions that are self-evident and incorrigible, most of the beliefs that form the stock in trade of ordinary everyday life are not probable—at any rate there is no reason to think they are probable. Consider all those propositions that entail, say, that there are enduring physical objects, or that there are persons distinct from myself, or that the world has existed for more than five minutes: none of these propositions, I think, is more probable than not with respect to what is self-evident or incorrigible for me; at any rate no one has given good reason to think any of them is. And now suppose we add to the foundations propositions that are evident to the senses, thereby moving from modern to ancient and medieval foundationalism. Then propositions entailing the existence of material objects will of course be probable with respect to the foundations, because included therein. But the same cannot be said either for propositions about the past or for propositions entailing the existence of persons distinct from myself; as before, these will not be probable with respect to what is properly basic.

And does not this show that the thesis in question is false? The contention is that

> (33) *A* is properly basic for me only if *A* is self-evident or incorrigible or evident to the senses for me.

But many propositions that do not meet these conditions *are* properly basic for me. I believe, for example, that I had lunch this noon. I do not believe this proposition on the basis of other propositions; I take it as basic; it is in the foundations of my noetic structure. Furthermore, I am entirely rational in so taking it, even though this proposition is neither self-evident nor evident to the senses nor incorrigible for me. Of course this may not convince the foundationalist; he may think that in fact I do *not* take that proposition as basic, or perhaps he will bite the bullet and maintain that if I really *do* take it as basic, then the fact is I *am*, so far forth, irrational.

Perhaps the following will be more convincing. According to the classical foundationalist (call him *F*) a person *S* is rational in accepting (33) only if either (33) is properly basic (self-evident or incorrigible or evident to the senses) for him, or he believes (33) on the basis of propositions that are properly basic for him and support (33). Now presumably if *F* knows of some support for (33) from propositions that are self-evident or evident to the senses or incorrigible, he will be able to provide a good argument—deductive, inductive, probabilistic or whatever—whose premises are self-evident or evident to the senses or incorrigible and whose conclusion is (33). So far as I know, no foundationalist has provided such an argument. It therefore appears that the foundationalist does not know of any support for (33) from propositions that are (on his account) properly basic. So if he is to be rational in accepting (33), he must (on his own account) accept it as basic. But according to (33) itself, (33) is properly basic for *F* only if (33) is self-evident or incorrigible or evident to the senses for him. Clearly (33) meets none of these conditions. Hence it is not properly basic for *F*. But then *F* is self-referentially inconsistent in accepting (33); he accepts (33) as basic, despite the fact that (33) does not meet the condition for proper basicality that (33) itself lays down.

Furthermore, (33) is either false or such that in accepting it the foundationalist is violating his epistemic responsibilities. For *F* does not know of any argument or evidence for (33). Hence if it is true, he will be violating his epistemic responsibilities in accepting it. So (33) is either false or such that *F* cannot rationally accept it. Still further, if the theist were to accept (33) at the foundationalist's urging but without argument, he would be adding to his noetic structure a proposition that is either false or such that in accepting it he violates his noetic responsibilities. But if there is such a thing as the ethics of belief, surely it will proscribe believing a proposition one knows to be either false or such that one ought not to believe it. Accordingly, I ought not to accept (33) in the absence of argument from premises that meet the condition it lays down. The same goes for the foundationalist: if he cannot find such an argument for (33), he ought to give it up. Furthermore, he ought not to urge and I ought not to accept any objection to theistic belief that crucially depends upon a proposition that is true only if I ought not believe it.

This argument can be made more rigorous. The classical foundationalist accepts

> (34) *p* is rationally acceptable for *S* only if either (1) *p* is self-evident or evident to the senses or incorrigible for *S*, or (2) there are paths in *S*'s noetic structure from *p* to propositions $q_1 \ldots q_n$ that (a) are basic for *S*, (b) are self-evident, evident to the senses, or incorrigible for *S*, and (c) support *p*.

Now (34) itself is obviously not evident to the senses. Furthermore it is not incorrigible for *F*. If (34) is contingent, then it will be possible that *F* believe it even though it is false, in which case it is not incorrigible. If it is noncontingent, then it is either necessarily true or necessarily false. If the former, it will be possible that *F* believe it false when it is true; if the latter, then it will be possible that *F* believe it true when it is false; so in neither case is it incorrigible. Still further, (34) is not plausibly thought self-evident; surely it is not such that one cannot understand it without believing it. So (34) is not self-evident, evident to the senses, or incorrigible for *F*. If (34) is true, therefore, then if *F* is to be rational in accepting (34), he must believe it on the basis of propositions that are self-evident, incorrigible, or evident to the senses, and support it. But no foundationalist has ever produced a successful argument for (34) from propositions that meet that condition. It is therefore unlikely that *F*'s acceptance of (34) conforms to the necessary condition of rationality (34) lays down.

Of course it *could* be that there are propositions $P_1 \ldots P_n$ such that (1) there is a path in *S*'s noetic structure from (34) to the $P_i$, (2) the $P_i$ do in fact support (34), and (3) the $P_i$ meet the condition for proper basicality laid down in (33) even if *F* cannot say what they are and even if the rest of us cannot think of any viable candidates. (Just as it could be that every theist accepts belief in God on the basis of propositions that both support that belief and are properly basic according to [33].) This seems unlikely, however, and in the absence of some reason to think there *are* propositions of that sort, the better part of valor is to reject (34).

We might try amending (34) in various ways. Nearly everyone accepts as basic some propositions entailing the existence of other persons and some propositions about the past; not nearly everyone accepts the existence of God as basic. Struck by this fact, we might propose:

(35) *p* is properly basic for *S* if and only if *p* is self-evident or incorrigible or evident to the senses for *S*, or is accepted as basic by nearly everyone.

There are problems with (35). It is meant to legitimize my taking as basic such deliverances of memory as that I had lunch this noon; but not nearly everyone takes that proposition as basic. Most of you, I daresay, have not so much as given it a thought; you are much too busy thinking about your own lunch to think about mine. So (35) will not do the job as it stands. That is of no real consequence, however; for even if we had an appropriate statement of (35), it would suffer from the same sort of malady as does (34). Not nearly everyone takes (35) as basic; I do not, for example. Nor is it self-evident, incorrigible, or evident to the senses. So unless we can find an argument for it from propositions that meet the conditions it lays down, we shall, if we believe it, be believing a proposition that is probably either false or such that we ought not believe it. Therefore we ought not believe it, at least until someone produces such an argument for it.

Now we could continue to canvass other revisions of (33), and in Part III I shall look into the proper procedure for discovering and justifying such criteria for proper basicality. It is evident, however, that classical foundationalism is bankrupt, and insofar as the evidentialist objection is rooted in classical foundationalism, it is poorly rooted indeed.

Of course the evidentialist objection *need* not presuppose classical foundationalism; someone who accepted quite a different version of foundationalism could no doubt urge this objection. But in order to evaluate it, we should have to see what criterion of proper basicality was being invoked. In the absence of such specification the objection remains at best a promissory note. So far as the present discussion goes, then, the next move is up to the evidentialist objector. He must specify a criterion for proper basicality that is free from self-referential difficulties, rules out belief in God as properly basic, and is such that there is some reason to think it is true.

An evidentialist objector need not be a classical foundationalist; indeed, he need not be a foundationalist *at all.* He could accept a coherence theory of rationality. This is a large and complicated topic; I cannot enter it here. The central issues, however, are two. In the first place, what is coherence? And is there any reason to think the theist's noetic structure does not display it? Second, suppose it does not; how do we determine in what direction it should be modified? Suppose, for example, that a given theist's noetic structure exhibits lack of coherence because it contains both belief in God and also, say, rejection of the idea that there is such a thing as agent causation. Perhaps his noetic structure is irrational, or at any rate defective, by virtue of this incoherence. But how can this be construed as an objection to theistic belief? Some change is called for, but why suppose that what he must do is give up theistic belief? Obviously there is another alternative; perhaps what he should do instead is accept agent causation.

## PART III: THE REFORMED OBJECTION TO NATURAL THEOLOGY

Suppose we think of natural theology as the attempt to prove or demonstrate the existence of God. This enterprise has a long and impressive history—a history stretching back to the dawn of Christendom and boasting among its adherents many of the truly great thinkers of the Western world. One thinks, for example, of Anselm, Aquinas, Scotus, and Ockham, of Descartes, Spinoza, and Leibniz. Recently—since the time of Kant, perhaps—the tradition of natural theology has not been as overwhelming as it once was; yet it continues to have able defenders both within and without officially Catholic philosophy.

Many Christians, however, have been less than totally impressed. In particular Reformed or Calvinist theologians have for the most part taken a dim view of this enterprise. A few Reformed thinkers—B. B. Warfield, for example—endorse the theistic proofs, but for the most part the Reformed attitude has ranged from tepid endorsement, through indifference, to suspicion, hostility, and outright accusations of blasphemy. And this stance is initially puzzling. It looks a little like the attitude some Christians adopt toward faith healing: it can't be done, but even if it could it shouldn't be. What exactly, or even approximately, do these sons and daughters of the Reformation have against proving the existence of God? What *could* they have against it? What could be less objectionable to any but the most obdurate atheist?

### *A. The Objection Initially Stated*

By way of answering this question, I want to consider three representative Reformed thinkers. Let us begin with the nineteenth-century Dutch theologian Herman Bavinck:

> A distinct natural theology, obtained apart from any revelation, merely through observation and study of the universe in which man lives, does not exist. . . .
>
> Scripture urges us to behold heaven and earth, birds and ants, flowers and lilies, in order that we may see and recognize God in them. "Lift up your eyes on high, and see who hath created these." Is. 40:26. Scripture does not reason in the abstract. It does not make God the conclusion of a syllogism, leaving it to us whether we think the argument holds or not. But it speaks with authority. Both theologically and religiously it proceeds from God as the starting point.
>
> We receive the impression that belief in the existence of God is based entirely upon these proofs. But indeed that would be "a wretched faith, which, before it invokes God, must first prove his existence." The contrary, however, is the truth. There is not a single object the existence of which we hesitate to accept until definite proofs are furnished. Of the existence of self, of the world round about us, of logical and moral laws, etc., we are so deeply convinced because of the indelible impressions which all these things make upon our consciousness that we need no arguments or demonstration. Spontaneously, altogether involuntarily: without any constraint or coercion, we accept that existence. Now the same is true in regard to the existence of God. The so-called proofs are by no means the final grounds of our most certain conviction that God exists. This certainty is established only by faith; that is, by the spontaneous testimony which forces itself upon us from every side.[36]

According to Bavinck, then, belief in the existence of God is not based upon proofs or arguments. By "argument" here I think he means arguments in the style of natural theology—the sort given by Aquinas and Scotus and later by Descartes, Leibniz, Clarke, and others. And what he means to say, I think, is that Christians do not *need* such arguments. Do not need them for what?

Here I think Bavinck means to hold two things. First, arguments or proofs are not, in general, the source of the believer's confidence in God. Typically the believer does not believe in God on the basis of arguments; nor does he believe such truths as that God has created the world on the basis of arguments. Second, argument is not needed for *rational justification*; the believer is entirely within his epistemic right in believing, for example, that God has created the world, even if he has no argument at all for that conclusion. The believer does not need natural theology in order to achieve rationality or epistemic propriety in believing; his belief in God can be perfectly rational even if he knows of no cogent argument, deductive or inductive, for the existence of God—indeed, even if there is no such argument.

Bavinck has three further points. First he means to add, I think, that we cannot come to knowledge of God on the basis of argument; the arguments of natural theology just do not work. (And he follows this passage with a more or less traditional attempt to refute the theistic proofs, including an endorsement of some of Kant's fashionable confusions about the ontological argument.) Second, Scripture "proceeds from God as the starting point," and so should the believer. There is nothing by way of proofs or arguments for God's existence in the Bible; that is simply presupposed. The same should be true of the Christian believer then; he should *start* from belief in God rather than from the premises of some argument whose conclusion is that God exists. What is it that makes those premises a better starting point anyway? And third, Bavinck points out that belief in God relevantly resembles belief in the existence of the self and of the external world—and, we might add, belief in other minds and the past. In none of these areas do we typically *have* proof or arguments, or *need* proofs or arguments.

Suppose we turn next to John Calvin, who is as good a Calvinist as any. According to Calvin God has implanted in us all an innate tendency, or nisus, or disposition to believe in him:

> 'There is within the human mind, and indeed by natural instinct, an awareness of divinity.' This we take to be beyond controversy. To prevent anyone from taking refuge in the pretense of ignorance, God himself has implanted in all men a certain understanding of his divine majesty. Ever renewing its memory, he repeatedly sheds fresh drops. Since, therefore, men one and all perceive that there is a God and that he is their Maker, they are condemned by their own testimony because they have failed to honor him and to consecrate their lives to his will. If ignorance of God is to be looked for anywhere, surely one is most likely to find an example of it among the more backward folk and those more remote from civilization. Yet there is, as the eminent pagan says, no nation so barbarous, no people so savage, that they have not a deep-seated conviction that there is a God. So deeply does the common conception occupy the

> minds of all, so tenaciously does it inhere in the hearts of all! Therefore, since from the beginning of the world there has been no region, no city, in short, no household, that could do without religion, there lies in this a tacit confession of a sense of deity inscribed in the hearts of all.
>
> Indeed, the perversity of the impious, who though they struggle furiously are unable to extricate themselves from the fear of God, is abundant testimony that this conviction, namely, that *there is some God,* is naturally inborn in all, and is fixed deep within, as it were in the very marrow. . . . From this we conclude *that it is not a doctrine that must first be learned in school,* but one of which each of us is master from his mother's womb and which nature itself permits no one to forget.[37]

Calvin's claim, then, is that God has created us in such a way that we have a strong tendency or inclination toward belief in him. This tendency has been in part overlaid or suppressed by sin. Were it not for the existence of sin in the world, human beings would believe in God to the same degree and with the same natural spontaneity that we believe in the existence of other persons, an external world, or the past. This is the natural human condition; it is because of our presently unnatural sinful condition that many of us find belief in God difficult or absurd. The fact is, Calvin thinks, one who does not believe in God is in an epistemically substandard position—rather like a man who does not believe that his wife exists, or thinks she is like a cleverly constructed robot and has no thoughts, feelings, or consciousness.

Although this disposition to believe in God is partially suppressed, it is nonetheless universally present. And it is triggered or actuated by a widely realized condition:

> Lest anyone, then, be excluded from access to happiness, he not only sowed in men's minds that seed of religion of which we have spoken, but revealed himself and daily discloses himself in the whole workmanship of the universe. As a consequence, men cannot open their eyes without being compelled to see him. (51)

Like Kant, Calvin is especially impressed in this connection, by the marvelous compages of the starry heavens above:

> Even the common folk and the most untutored, who have been taught only by the aid of the eyes, cannot be unaware of the excellence of divine art, for it reveals itself in this innumerable and yet distinct and well-ordered variety of the heavenly host. (50)

And Calvin's claim is that one who accedes to this tendency and in these circumstances accepts the belief that God has created the world—perhaps upon beholding the starry heavens, or the splendid majesty of the mountains, or the intricate, articulate beauty of a tiny flower—is entirely within his epistemic rights in so doing. It is not that such a person is justified or rational in so believing by virtue of having an implicit argument—some version of the teleological argument, say. No; he does not need any argument for justification or rationality. His belief need not be based on any other propositions at all; under these conditions he is perfectly rational in accepting belief in God in the utter absence of any argument, deductive or inductive. Indeed, a person in these conditions, says Calvin, *knows* that God exists.

Elsewhere Calvin speaks of "arguments from reason" or rational arguments:

> The prophets and apostles do not boast either of their keenness or of anything that obtains credit for them as they speak; nor do they dwell upon rational proofs. Rather, they bring forward God's holy name, that by it the whole world may be brought into obedience to him. Now we ought to see how apparent it is not only by plausible opinion but by clear truth that they do not call upon God's name heedlessly or falsely. If we desire to provide in the best way for our consciences—that they may not be perpetually beset by the instability of doubt or vacillation, and that they may not also boggle at the smallest quibbles—we ought to seek our conviction in a higher place than human reasons, judgments, or conjectures, that is, in the secret testimony of the Spirit. (book 1, chapter 7, p. 78)

Here the subject for discussion is not belief in the existence of God, but belief that God is the author of the Scriptures; I think it is clear, however, that Calvin would say the same thing about belief in God's existence. The Christian does not *need* natural theology, either as the source of his confidence or to justify his belief. Furthermore, the Christian *ought* not to believe on the basis of argument; if he does, his faith is likely to be "unstable and wavering," the "subject of perpetual doubt." If my belief in God is based on argument, then if I am to be properly rational, epistemically responsible, I shall have to keep checking the philosophical journals to see whether, say, Anthony Flew has finally come up with a good objection to my favorite argument. This could be bothersome and time-consuming; and what do I do if someone does find a flaw in my argument? Stop going to church? From Calvin's point of view believing in the existence of God on the basis of rational argument is like believing in the existence of your spouse on the basis of the analogical argument for other minds—whimsical at best and unlikely to delight the person concerned.

### *B. The Barthian Dilemma*

The twentieth-century theologian Karl Barth is particularly scathing in his disapproval of natural theology. *That* he disapproves is overwhelmingly clear. His *reasons* for thus disapproving, however, are much less clear; his utterances on this topic, as on others, are fascinating but Delphic in everything but length. Sometimes, indeed, he is outrageous, as when he suggests that the mere act of believing or accepting the Christian message is a manifestation of human pride, self-will, contumacy, and sin. Elsewhere, however, he is both more moderate and thoroughly intriguing:

> Now suppose the partner in the conversation [that is, natural theology] discovers that faith is trying to use the well-known artifice of dialectic in relation to him. We are not taking him seriously because we withhold from him what we really want to say and represent. It is only in appearance that we devote ourselves to him, and therefore what we say to him is only an apparent and unreal statement. What will happen then? Well, not without justice—although misconstruing the friendly intention which perhaps motivates us—he will see himself despised and deceived. He will shut himself up and harden himself against the faith which does not speak out frankly, which deserts its own standpoint for the standpoint of unbelief. What use to unbelief is a faith which obviously knows different? And how shocking for unbelief is a faith which only pretends to take up with unbelief a common position. . . . This dilemma betrays the inner contradiction in every form of a "Christian" natural theology. It must really represent and affirm the standpoint of faith. Its true objective to which it really wants to lead unbelief is the knowability of the real God through Himself in his revelation. But as a "natural" theology, its initial aim is to disguise this and therefore to pretend to share in the life-endeavour of natural man. It therefore thinks that it should appear to engage in the dialectic of unbelief in the expectation that here at least a preliminary decision in regard to faith can and must be reached. Therefore, as a natural theology it speaks and acts improperly. . . . We cannot experiment with unbelief, even if we think we know and possess all sorts of interesting and very promising possibilities and recipes for it. We must treat unbelief seriously. Only one thing can be treated more seriously than unbelief; and that is faith itself—or rather, the real God in whom faith believes. But faith itself—or rather, the real God in whom faith believes—must be taken

> so seriously that there is no place at all for even an apparent transposition to the standpoint of unbelief, for the pedagogic and playful self-lowering into the sphere of its possibilities.[38]

We must try to penetrate a bit deeper into these objections to natural theology, and suppose we start with Barth. Precisely what is the objection to which he is pointing? That somehow it is improper or un-Christian or dishonest or impious to try to prove God's existence; but *how* exactly? Barth speaks here of a *dilemma* that confronts the natural theologian. Dilemmas have horns; what are the horns of this one? The following, I think. In presenting a piece of natural theology, either the believer must adopt what Barth calls "the standpoint of unbelief" or he must pretend to his unbelieving interlocutor to do so. If he does the former, he deserts his Christian standpoint; but if he does the latter, he is dishonest, in bad faith, professing to believe what in fact he does not believe. But what *is* the standpoint of unbelief and what is it to adopt it? And how could one fall into this standpoint just by working at natural theology, just by making a serious attempt to prove the existence of God?

Perhaps Barth is thinking along the following lines. In *arguing* about the existence of God, in attempting to prove it, one implicitly adopts a certain stance. In adopting this stance one presupposes that it is not yet known whether there is a God; that remains to be seen; that is what is up for discussion. In adopting this stance, furthermore, the natural theologian implicitly concedes that what one ought to believe here depends on the result of the inquiry; if there are good arguments *for* the existence of God, then we—that is, we believers and unbelievers who together are engaged in this inquiry—ought to accept God's existence; if there are good arguments *against* the existence of God, we ought to accept its denial; and if the arguments on both sides are equally strong (and equally weak) then perhaps the right thing to do is to remain agnostic.

In adopting this stance one concedes that the rightness or propriety of belief and unbelief depends upon the outcome of a certain inquiry. Belief in God is right and proper only if there is on balance better reason to believe than not to believe—only if, that is, the arguments for the existence of God are stronger than those against it. But of course an inquiry has a starting point, and arguments have premises. In supposing the issue thus dependent upon the outcome of argument, one supposes the appropriate premises are available. What about these premises? In adopting this stance the natural theologian implicitly commits himself to the view that there is a certain set of propositions from which the premises of theistic and antitheistic arguments are to be drawn—a set of propositions such that belief in God is rational or proper only if it stands in the right relation to that set. He concurs with his unbelieving interlocutor that there is a set of propositions both can appeal to, a set of propositions accepted by all or nearly all rational persons; and the propriety or rightness of belief in God depends on its relation to these propositions.

What are these propositions and where do they come from? We shall have to enter that question more deeply later; for the moment let us call them "the deliverances of reason." Then to *prove* or *demonstrate* that God exists is to exhibit a deductive argument whose conclusion is that God exists, whose premises are drawn from the deliverances of reason, and each of whose steps is by way of an argument whose corresponding conditional is among the deliverances of reason. Aquinas' first three ways would be attempts to demonstrate the existence of God in just this sense. A demonstration that God does not exist, of course, would be structurally isomorphic; it would meet the second and third condition just mentioned but have as conclusion the proposition that there is no such person as God. An alleged example would be the deductive argument from evil—the claim that the existence of evil is among the deliverances of reason and is inconsistent with the existence of God.

Of course it might be that the existence of God does not thus follow from the deliverances of reason but is nonetheless *probable* or *likely* with respect to them. One could then give a probabilistic or inductive argument for the existence of God, thus showing that theistic belief is rational, or epistemically proper, in that it is more likely than not with respect to the deliverances of reason. Perhaps Aquinas' Fifth Way and Paley's argument from design can be seen as falling into this category, and perhaps the probabilistic argument from evil—the claim that it is unlikely that God exists, given all the evil there is—can then be seen as a structurally similar argument for the conclusion that unbelief is the proper attitude.

According to Barth, then, the natural theologian implicitly concedes that the propriety of belief in God is to be tested by its relationship to the deliverances of reason. Belief is right, or rational, or rationally acceptable only if it stands in the proper relationship to the deliverances of reason—only if, for example, it is more likely than not or at any rate not unlikely with respect to them.

Now to adopt the standpoint of unbelief is not, as Barth sees it, to reject belief in God. One who enthusiastically accepts and believes in the existence of God can nonetheless be in the standpoint of unbelief. To be in that standpoint it is sufficient to hold that belief in God is rationally permissible for a person *only if he or she has a good argument for it.* To be in the standpoint of unbelief is to hold that belief in God is rationally acceptable *only if it is more likely than not with respect to the deliverances of reason.* One who holds this belief, says Barth, is in the standpoint of unbelief; his ultimate commitment is to the deliverances of reason rather than to God. Such a person "makes reason a judge over Christ," or at any rate over the Christian faith. And to do so, says Barth, is utterly improper for a Christian.

The horns of the Barthian dilemma, then, are bad faith or dishonesty on the one hand and the standpoint of unbelief on the other. Either the natural theologian accepts the standpoint of unbelief or he does not. In the latter case he misleads and deceives his unbelieving interlocutor and thus falls into bad faith. In the former case he makes his ultimate commitment to the deliverances of reason, a posture that is for a Christian totally inappropriate, a manifestation of sinful human pride.

> And this attempt to prove the existence of God certainly cannot end in any other way than with the affirmation that even apart from God's grace, already preceding God's grace, already anticipating it, he is ready for God, so that God is knowable to him otherwise than from and through himself. Not only does it end with this. In principle, it begins with it. For in what does it consist but in the arrogation, preservation and affirmation of the self-sufficiency of man and therefore his likeness with God? (135)

### C. *Rejecting Classical Foundationalism*

Now I think the natural theologian has a sound response to Barth's dilemma: she can execute the maneuver known to dialectician and matador alike as "escaping between the horns." As a natural theologian she offers or endorses theistic arguments, but why suppose that her own belief in God must be based upon such argument? And if it is not, why suppose she must pretend that it is? Perhaps her aim is to point out to the unbeliever that belief in God follows from other things he already believes, so that he can continue in unbelief (and continue to accept these other beliefs) only on pain of inconsistency. We may hope this knowledge will lead him to give up his unbelief, but in any event she can tell him quite frankly that her belief in God is not based on its relation to the deliverances of reason. Indeed, she can follow Calvin in claiming that belief in God *ought* not to be based on arguments from the deliverances of reason or anywhere else. So even if "the standpoint of unbelief" is as reprehensible as Barth says it is, his dilemma seems to evaporate.

What is most interesting here is not Barth's claim that the natural theologian faces this dilemma; here he is probably wrong, or at any rate not clearly right. More interesting is his view that belief in God need not be based on argument. Barth joins Calvin and Bavinck in holding that the believer in God is entirely within his rights in believing as he does even if he does not know of any good theistic argument (deductive or inductive), even if he does not believe there is any such argument, and even if in fact no such argument exists. Like Calvin, Kuyper, and Bavinck, Barth holds that belief in God is *properly basic*—that is, such that it is rational to accept it without accepting it on the basis of any other propositions or beliefs at all. In fact, they think the Christian ought not to accept belief in God on the basis of argument; to do so is to run the risk of a faith that is unstable and wavering, subject to all the wayward whim and fancy of the latest academic fashion. What the Reformers held was that a believer is entirely rational, entirely within his epistemic rights, in *starting with* belief in God, in accepting it as basic, and in taking it as premise for argument to other conclusions.

In rejecting natural theology, therefore, these Reformed thinkers mean to say first of all that the propriety or rightness of belief in God in no way depends upon the success or availability of the sort of theistic arguments that form the natural theologian's stock in trade. I think this is their central claim here, and their central insight. As these Reformed thinkers see things, one who takes belief in God as basic is not thereby violating any epistemic duties or revealing a defect in his noetic structure; quite the reverse. The correct or proper way to believe in God, they thought, was not on the basis of arguments from natural theology or anywhere else; the correct way is to take belief in God as basic.

I spoke earlier of classical foundationalism, a view that incorporates the following three theses:

(1) In every rational noetic structure there is a set of beliefs taken as basic—that is, not accepted on the basis of any other beliefs,
(2) In a rational noetic structure nonbasic belief is proportional to support from the foundations,

and

(3) In a rational noetic structure basic beliefs will be self-evident or incorrigible or evident to the senses.

Now I think these three Reformed thinkers should be understood as rejecting classical foundationalism. They may have been inclined to accept (1); they show no objection to (2); but they were utterly at odds with the idea that the foundations of a rational noetic structure can at most include propositions that are self-evident or evident to the senses or incorrigible. In particular, they were prepared to insist that a rational noetic structure can include belief in God as basic. As Bavinck put it, "Scripture . . . does not make God the conclusion of a syllogism, leaving it to us whether we think the argument holds or not. But it speaks with authority. Both theologically and religiously it proceeds from God as the starting point" (above,

p. 64). And of course Bavinck means to say that we must emulate Scripture here.

In the passages I quoted earlier, Calvin claims the believer does not need argument—does not need it, among other things, for epistemic respectability. We may understand him as holding, I think, that a rational noetic structure may very well contain belief in God among its foundations. Indeed, he means to go further, and in two separate directions. In the first place he thinks a Christian *ought* not believe in God on the basis of other propositions; a proper and well-formed Christian noetic structure will *in fact* have belief in God among its foundations. And in the second place Calvin claims that one who takes belief in God as basic can *know* that God exists. Calvin holds that one can *rationally accept* belief in God as basic; he also claims that one can *know* that God exists even if he has no argument, even if he does not believe on the basis of other propositions. A foundationalist is likely to hold that some properly basic beliefs are such that anyone who accepts them *knows* them. More exactly, he is likely to hold that among the beliefs properly basic for a person *S*, some are such that if *S* accepts them, *S* knows them. He could go on to say that *other* properly basic beliefs cannot be known if taken as basic, but only rationally believed; and he might think of the existence of God as a case in point. Calvin will have none of this; as he sees it, one needs no arguments to know that God exists.

One who holds this view need not suppose that natural theology is of no use. In the first place, if there *were* good arguments for the existence of God, that would be a fact worth knowing in itself—just as it would be worth knowing (if true) that the analogical argument for other minds is successful, or that there are good arguments from self-evident and incorrigible propositions to the existence of other minds. Second, natural theology could be useful in helping someone move from unbelief to belief. The arguments are not successful from the point of view of classical foundationalism; probably, that is, they do not start from premises that are self-evident, incorrigible, or evident to the senses and then proceed by argument forms that are self-evidently valid to the conclusion that God exists. Nonetheless there may be (in fact there are) people who accept propositions and argument forms out of which a theistic argument can be constructed; for these people theistic arguments can be useful as a means of moving toward what Calvin sees as the best way to believe in God: as basic.

## PART IV: *IS* BELIEF IN GOD PROPERLY BASIC?

According to the Reformed thinkers discussed in the last section the answer is "Yes indeed." I enthusiastically concur in this contention, and in this section I shall try to clarify and develop this view and defend it against some objections. I shall argue first that one who holds that belief in God is properly basic is not thereby committed to the view that just about *anything* is; I shall argue secondly that even if belief in God is accepted as basic, it is not *groundless*; I shall argue thirdly that one who accepts belief in God as basic may nonetheless be open to arguments *against* that belief; and finally I shall argue that the view I am defending is not plausibly thought of as a species of *fideism*.

### *A. The Great Pumpkin Objection*

It is tempting to raise the following sort of question. If belief in God is properly basic, why cannot *just any* belief be properly basic? Could we not say the same for any bizarre aberration we can think of? What about voodoo or astrology? What about the belief that the Great Pumpkin returns every Halloween? Could I properly take *that* as basic? Suppose I believe that if I flap my arms with sufficient vigor, I can take off and fly about the room; could I defend myself against the charge of irrationality by claiming this belief is basic? If we say that belief in God is properly basic, will we not be committed to holding that just anything, or nearly anything, can properly be taken as basic, thus throwing wide the gates to irrationalism and superstition?

Certainly not. According to the Reformed epistemologist certain beliefs are properly basic in certain circumstances; those same beliefs may *not* be properly basic in other circumstances. Consider the belief that I see a tree: this belief is properly basic in circumstances that are hard to describe in detail, but include my being appeared to in a certain characteristic way; that same belief is not properly basic in circumstances including, say, my knowledge that I am sitting in the living room listening to music with my eyes closed. What the Reformed epistemologist holds is that there are widely realized circumstances in which belief in God is properly basic; but why should that be thought to commit him to the idea that just about *any* belief is properly basic in any circumstances, or even to the vastly weaker claim that for any belief there are circumstances in which it is properly basic? Is it just that he rejects the criteria for proper basicality purveyed by classical foundationalism? But why should *that* be thought to commit him to such tolerance of irrationality? Consider an analogy. In the palmy days of positivism the positivists went about confidently wielding their verifiability criterion and declaring meaningless much that was clearly meaningful. Now suppose someone rejected a formulation of that criterion—the one to be found in the second edition of A. J. Ayer's *Language, Truth and Logic,* for example. Would that mean she was committed to holding that

(1) T' was brillig; and the slithy toves did gyre and gymble in the wabe,

contrary to appearances, makes good sense? Of course not. But then the same goes for the Reformed epistemologist: the fact that he rejects the criterion of proper basicality purveyed by classical foundationalism does not mean that he is committed to supposing just anything is properly basic.

But what then is the problem? Is it that the Reformed epistemologist not only rejects those criteria for proper basicality but seems in no hurry to produce what he takes to be a better substitute? If he has no such criterion, how can he fairly reject belief in the Great Pumpkin as properly basic?

This objection betrays an important misconception. How *do* we rightly arrive at or develop criteria for meaningfulness, or justified belief, or proper basicality? Where do they come from? Must one have such a criterion before one can sensibly make any judgments—positive or negative—about proper basicality? Surely not. Suppose I do not know of a satisfactory substitute for the criteria proposed by classical foundationalism; I am nevertheless entirely within my epistemic rights in holding that certain propositions in certain conditions are not properly basic.

Some propositions seem self-evident when in fact they are not; that is the lesson of some of the Russell paradoxes. Nevertheless it would be irrational to take as basic the denial of a proposition that seems self-evident to you. Similarly, suppose it seems to you that you see a tree; you would then be irrational in taking as basic the proposition that you do not see a tree or that there are no trees. In the same way, even if I do not know of some illuminating criterion of meaning, I can quite properly declare (1) (above) meaningless.

And this raises an important question—one Roderick Chisholm has taught us to ask.[39] What is the status of criteria for knowledge, or proper basicality, or justified belief? Typically these are universal statements. The modern foundationalist's criterion for proper basicality, for example, is doubly universal:

(2) For any proposition $A$ and person $S$, $A$ is properly basic for $S$ if and only if $A$ is incorrigible for $S$ or self-evident to $S$.

But how could one know a thing like that? What are its credentials? Clearly enough, (2) is not self-evident or just obviously true. But if it is not, how does one arrive at it? What sorts of arguments would be appropriate? Of course a foundationalist might find (2) so appealing he simply takes it to be true, neither offering argument for it nor accepting it on the basis of other things he believes. If he does so, however, his noetic structure will be self-referentially incoherent. (2) itself is neither self-evident nor incorrigible; hence if he accepts (2) as basic, the modern foundationalist violates in accepting it the condition of proper basicality he himself lays down. On the other hand, perhaps the foundationalist will try to produce some argument for it from premises that are self-evident or incorrigible: it is exceeding hard to see, however, what such an argument might be like. And until he has produced such arguments, what shall the rest of us do—we who do not find (2) at all obvious or compelling? How could he use (2) to show us that belief in God, for example, is not properly basic? Why should we believe (2) or pay it any attention?

The fact is, I think, that neither (2) nor any other revealing necessary and sufficient condition for proper basicality follows from clearly self-evident premises by clearly acceptable arguments. And hence the proper way to arrive at such a criterion is, broadly speaking, *inductive*. We must assemble examples of beliefs and conditions such that the former are obviously properly basic in the latter, and examples of beliefs and conditions such that the former are obviously *not* properly basic in the latter. We must then frame hypotheses as to the necessary and sufficient conditions of proper basicality and test these hypotheses by reference to those examples. Under the right conditions, for example, it is clearly rational to believe that you see a human person before you: a being who has thoughts and feelings, who knows and believes things, who makes decisions and acts. It is clear, furthermore, that you are under no obligation to reason to this belief from others you hold; under those conditions that belief is properly basic for you. But then (2) must be mistaken; the belief in question, under those circumstances, is properly basic, though neither self-evident nor incorrigible for you. Similarly, you may seem to remember that you had breakfast this morning, and perhaps you know of no reason to suppose your memory is playing you tricks. If so, you are entirely justified in taking that belief as basic. Of course it is not properly basic on the criteria offered by classical foundationalists, but that fact counts not against you but against those criteria.

I say we must assemble examples of beliefs and conditions such that the former are *obviously* properly basic in the latter, but that is not exactly right. The sample set, by reference to which hypotheses as to the necessary and sufficient conditions of proper basicality must be tested, should contain belief-condition pairs <B,C> of that sort but also pairs where it is not clear whether B is justified in C, and pairs where it seems fairly clear but not obvious that B is justified in C. (Of course our sample set should display the same variety with respect to pairs <BC> where B is *not* justified in C.)

The sample set, furthermore, should be revisable in the light of theory and under the pressure of argument. Thus we may come to see that a pair <BC>, originally taken to be an example of a belief and circumstances such that the former is justified in the latter, is really not of that sort. Further, it may be that we cannot find any revealing criterion; we may have to be content with some necessary conditions and some sufficient conditions. Perhaps my being appeared to redly, for example, is both necessary and sufficient for my being justified in taking it as basic that I am appeared to redly. For other sorts of beliefs, however, it may be extremely difficult to find a condition that is both necessary and sufficient. Consider memory beliefs for example; my seeming to remember that *p* may be necessary for my justifiably taking it as basic that I do remember that *p,* but it clearly is not sufficient. If, for example, I know that my memory is faulty on the subject matter of *p*, then presumably I am not justified in taking it as basic that I remember that *p* when it seems to me that I do; and it may be very hard to find a condition that when conjoined with *it seems to me that I remember that p* yields a condition that is both necessary and sufficient for my being justified in taking it as basic that I remember that *p*.

Furthermore, it may be that the best we can do here is to give some sufficient conditions of *prima facie* justification. When I am being appeared to in a certain way, I am *prima facie* justified in believing that I perceive a tree. But this justification is defeasible; if I am told by an authority that there are a lot of fake trees around, visually indistinguishable at medium range from real trees, then I am no longer justified in taking it as basic that I see a tree. So the circumstance of being appeared to in a certain way confers *prima facie,* not *ultima facie,* justification upon my belief that I see a tree.

Accordingly, criteria for proper basicality must be reached from below rather than above; they should not be presented *ex cathedra* but argued to and tested by a relevant set of examples. But there is no reason to assume, in advance, that everyone will agree on the examples. The Christian will of course suppose that belief in God is entirely proper and rational; if he does not accept this belief on the basis of other propositions, he will conclude that it is basic for him and quite properly so. Followers of Bertrand Russell and Madelyn Murray O'Hare may disagree; but how is that relevant? Must my criteria, or those of the Christian community, conform to their examples? Surely not. The Christian community is responsible to *its* set of examples, not to theirs.

And hence criteria for proper basicality arrived at in this particularistic way may not be polemically useful. If you and I start from different examples—if my set of examples includes a pair <B,C> (where B is, say, belief in God and C is some condition) and your set of examples does not include <BC>—then we may very well arrive at different criteria for proper basicality. Furthermore I cannot sensibly use my criterion to try to convince you that B is in fact properly basic in C, for you will point out, quite properly, that my criterion is based upon a set of examples that, as you see it, *erroneously* includes <BC> as an example of a belief and condition such that the former is properly basic in the latter. You will thus be quite within your rights in claiming that my criterion is mistaken, although of course you may concede that, given my set of examples, I followed correct procedure in arriving at it. But of course by the same token you cannot sensibly use your criterion to try to convince me that B is *not,* in fact, properly basic in C. If criteria for proper basicality are arrived at in this particularistic way, they will not be or at any rate need not be polemically useful. Following this sort of procedure, we may not be able to resolve our disagreement as to the status of <B,C>; you will continue to hold that B is *not* properly basic in C, and I will continue to hold that it *is.*

Of course it does not follow that there is no truth of the matter; if our criteria conflict, then at least one of them is mistaken, even if we cannot by further discussion agree as to which it is. Similarly, either I am mistaken in holding that B is properly basic in C, or you are mistaken in holding that it is not. Still further, if I *am* mistaken in this matter, then if I take B as basic in C—that is, if I am in C and believe B without the evidential support of other beliefs—then I am irrational in so doing. Particularism does not imply *subjectivism.*

So, the Reformed epistemologist can properly hold that belief in the Great Pumpkin is not properly basic, even though he holds that belief in God is properly basic and even if he has no full-fledged criterion of proper basicality. Of course he is committed to supposing that there is a relevant *difference* between belief in God and belief in the Great Pumpkin if he holds that the former but not the latter is properly basic. But this should prove no great embarrassment; there are plenty of candidates. These candidates are to be found in the neighborhood of the conditions that justify and ground belief in God—conditions I shall discuss in the next section. Thus, for example, the Reformed epistemologist may concur with Calvin in holding that God has implanted in us a natural tendency to see his hand in the world around us; the same cannot be said for the Great Pumpkin, there being no Great Pumpkin and no natural tendency to accept beliefs about the Great Pumpkin.[40]

### *B. The* **Ground** *of Belief in God*

My claim is that belief in God is properly basic; is does not follow, however, that it is *groundless.* Let me explain. Suppose we consider perceptual beliefs, memory beliefs, and beliefs ascribing mental states to other persons, such beliefs as:

(3) I see a tree,

(4) I had breakfast this morning,

and

(5) That person is in pain.

Although beliefs of this sort are typically taken as basic, it would be a mistake to describe them as *groundless*. Upon having experience of a certain sort, I believe that I am perceiving a tree. In the typical case I do not hold this belief on the basis of other beliefs; it is nonetheless not groundless. My having that characteristic sort of experience—to use Professor Chisholm's language, my being appeared treely to—plays a crucial role in the formation of that belief. It also plays a crucial role in its *justification*. Let us say that a belief is *justified* for a person at a time if (a) he is violating no epistemic duties and is within his epistemic rights in accepting it then and (b) his noetic structure is not defective by virtue of his then accepting it.[41] Then my being appeared to in this characteristic way (together with other circumstances) is what confers on me the right to hold the belief in question; this is what justifies me in accepting it. We could say, if we wish, that this experience is what justifies me in holding it; this is the *ground* of my justification, and, by extension, the ground of the belief itself.

If I see someone displaying typical pain behavior, I take it that he or she is in pain. Again, I do not take the displayed behavior as *evidence* for that belief; I do not infer that belief from others I hold; I do not accept it on the basis of other beliefs. Still, my perceiving the pain behavior plays a unique role in the formation and justification of that belief; as in the previous case it forms the ground of my justification for the belief in question. The same holds for memory beliefs. I seem to remember having breakfast this morning; that is, I have an inclination to believe the proposition that I had breakfast, along with a certain past-tinged experience that is familiar to all but hard to describe. Perhaps we should say that I am appeared to pastly; but perhaps that insufficiently distinguishes the experience in question from that accompanying beliefs about the past not grounded in my own memory. The phenomenology of memory is a rich and unexplored realm; here I have no time to explore it. In this case as in the others, however, there is a justifying circumstance present, a condition that forms the ground of my justification for accepting the memory belief in question.

In each of these cases a belief is taken as basic, and in each case *properly* taken as basic. In each case there is some circumstance or condition that confers justification; there is a circumstance that serves as the *ground* of justification. So in each case there will be some true proposition of the sort

(6) In condition *C*, *S* is justified in taking *p* as basic.

Of course *C* will vary with *p*. For a perceptual judgment such as

(7) I see a rose-colored wall before me

*C* will include my being appeared to in a certain fashion. No doubt *C* will include more. If I am appeared to in the familiar fashion but know that I am wearing rose-colored glasses, or that I am suffering from a disease that causes me to be thus appeared to, no matter what the color of the nearby objects, then I am not justified in taking (7) as basic. Similarly for memory. Suppose I know that my memory is unreliable; it often plays me tricks. In particular, when I seem to remember having breakfast, then, more often than not, I have not had breakfast. Under these conditions I am not justified in taking it as basic that I had breakfast, even though I seem to remember that I did.

So being appropriately appeared to, in the perceptual case, is not sufficient for justification; some further condition—a condition hard to state in detail—is clearly necessary. The central point here, however, is that a belief is properly basic only in certain conditions; these conditions are, we might say, the ground of its justification and, by extension, the ground of the belief itself. In this sense basic beliefs are not, or are not necessarily, *groundless* beliefs.

Now similar things may be said about belief in God. When the Reformers claim that this belief is properly basic, they do not mean to say, of course, that there are no justifying circumstances for it, or that it is in that sense groundless or gratuitous. Quite the contrary. Calvin holds that God "reveals and daily discloses himself in the whole workmanship of the universe," and the divine art "reveals itself in the innumerable and yet distinct and well ordered variety of the heavenly host." God has so created us that we have a tendency or disposition to see his hand in the world about us. More precisely, there is in us a disposition to believe propositions of the sort *this flower was created by God* or *this vast and intricate universe was created by God* when we contemplate the flower or behold the starry heavens or think about the vast reaches of the universe.

Calvin recognizes, at least implicitly, that other sorts of conditions may trigger this disposition. Upon reading the Bible, one may be impressed with a deep sense that God is speaking to him. Upon having done what I know is cheap, or wrong, or wicked, I may feel guilty in God's sight and form the belief *God disapproves of what I have done.* Upon confession and repentance I may feel forgiven, forming the belief *God forgives me for what I have done.* A person in grave danger may turn to God, asking for his protection and help; and of course he or she then has the belief that God is indeed able to hear and help if he sees fit. When life is sweet and satisfying, a spontaneous sense of gratitude may well up within the soul; someone in this condition may thank and praise the Lord for his goodness, and will of course have the accompanying belief that indeed the Lord is to be thanked and praised.

There are therefore many conditions and circumstances that call forth belief in God: guilt, gratitude, danger, a sense of God's presence, a sense that he speaks, perception of various parts of the universe. A complete job would explore the phenomenology of all these conditions and of more besides. This is a large and important topic, but here I can only point to the existence of these conditions.

Of course none of the beliefs I mentioned a moment ago is the simple belief that God exists. What we have instead are such beliefs as:

(8) God is speaking to me,

(9) God has created all this,

(10) God disapproves of what I have done,

(11) God forgives me,

and

(12) God is to be thanked and praised.

These propositions are properly basic in the right circumstances. But it is quite consistent with this to suppose that the proposition *there is such a person as God* is neither properly basic nor taken as basic by those who believe in God. Perhaps what they take as basic are such propositions as (8)–(12), believing in the existence of God on the basis of propositions such as those. From this point of view it is not wholly accurate to say that it is belief in God that is properly basic; more exactly, what are properly basic are such propositions as (8)–(12), each of which self-evidently entails that God exists. It is not the relatively high-level and general proposition *God exists* that is properly basic, but instead propositions detailing some of his attributes or actions.

Suppose we return to the analogy between belief in God and belief in the existence of perceptual objects, other persons, and the past. Here too it is relatively specific and concrete propositions rather than their more general and abstract colleagues that are properly basic. Perhaps such items as:

(13) There are trees,

(14) There are other persons,

and

(15) The world has existed for more than five minutes

are not in fact properly basic; it is instead such propositions as:

(16) I see a tree,

(17) That person is pleased,

and

(18) I had breakfast more than an hour ago

that deserve that accolade. Of course propositions of the latter sort immediately and self-evidently entail propositions of the former sort, and perhaps there is thus no harm in speaking of the former as properly basic, even though so to speak is to speak a bit loosely.

The same must be said about belief in God. We may say, speaking loosely, that belief in God is properly basic; strictly speaking, however, it is probably not that proposition but such propositions as (8)–(12) that enjoy that status. But the main point, here, is this: belief in God, or (8)–(12), are properly basic; to say so, however, is not to deny that there are justifying conditions for these beliefs, or conditions that confer justification on one who accepts them as basic. They are therefore not groundless or gratuitous.

### *C. Is Argument Irrelevant to Basic Belief in God?*

Suppose someone accepts belief in God as basic. Does it not follow that he will hold this belief in such a way that no argument could move him or cause him to give it up? Will he not hold it come what may, in the teeth of any evidence or argument with which he could be presented? Does he not thereby adopt a posture in which argument and other rational methods of settling disagreement are implicitly declared irrelevant? Surely not. Suppose someone accepts

(19) There is such a person as God

as basic. It does not for a moment follow that he will regard argument irrelevant to this belief of his; nor is he committed in advance to rejecting every argument against it. It could be, for example, that he accepts (19) as basic but also accepts as basic some propositions from which, by arguments whose corresponding conditionals he accepts as basic, it follows that (19) is false. What happens if he is apprised of this fact, perhaps by being presented with an argument from those propositions to the denial of (19)? Presumably some change is called for. If he accepts these propositions more strongly than (19), presumably he will give the latter up.

Similarly, suppose someone believes there is no God but also believes some propositions from which belief in God follows by argument forms he accepts. Presented with an argument from these propositions to the proposition that God exists, such a person may give up his atheism and accept belief in God. On the other hand, his atheistic belief may be stronger than his belief in some of the propositions in question, or his belief in their conjunction. It is possible, indeed, that he *knows* these propositions, but believes some of them less firmly than he believes that there is no God; in that case, if you present him with a valid argument from these propositions to the proposition that God exists, you may cause him to give up a proposition he knows to be true. It is thus possible to reduce the extent of someone's knowledge by giving him a sound argument from premises he knows to be true.

So even if I accept (19) as basic, it may still be the case that I will give up that belief if you offer me an argument from propositions I accept, by argument forms I accept, to the denial of (19). But I do have other options. All your argument really shows is that there is trouble somewhere in my noetic structure. A change must be made somewhere, but the argument does not show *where*. Perhaps I will give up one of the premises instead, or perhaps I will give up their conjunction. Perhaps I will give up one of the argument forms involved in the inference of the denial of (19) from those premises; this would be in the spirit of Hilary Putnam's suggestion that we give up the logical law of distribution because it is incompatible with quantum mechanics. Still another possibility: I may find all of (19), these premises, and the above-mentioned argument forms more worthy of belief than the contention that those argument forms lead from those premises to the denial of (19); if so, then perhaps I should give up *that* belief.

So a person can accept belief in God as basic without accepting it dogmatically—that is, in such a way that he will ignore any contrary evidence or argument. And now a second question: Suppose the fact is belief in God *is* properly basic. Does it follow that one who accepts it dogmatically is within his epistemic rights? Does it follow that someone who is within his rights in accepting it as basic *remains* justified in this belief, no matter what counterargument or counterevidence arises?

Again, surely not. The justification-conferring conditions mentioned above must be seen as conferring *prima facie* rather than *ultima facie*, or all-things-considered, justification. This justification can be overridden. My being appeared to treely gives me a *prima facie* right to take as basic the proposition *I see a tree*. But of course this right can be overridden; I might know, for example, that I suffer from the dreaded dendrological disorder, whose victims are appeared to treely only when there are no trees present. If I do know that, then I am not within my rights in taking as basic the proposition *I see a tree* when I am appeared to treely. The same goes for the conditions that confer justification on belief in

God. Like the fourteen-year-old theist (above, p. 33), perhaps I have been brought up to believe in God and am initially within my rights in so doing. But conditions can arise in which perhaps I am no longer justified in this belief. Perhaps you propose to me an argument for conclusion that it is impossible that there be such a person as God. If this argument is convincing for me—if it starts from premises that seem self-evident to me and proceeds by argument forms that seem self-evidently valid—then perhaps I am no longer justified in accepting theistic belief. Following John Pollock, we may say that a condition that overrides my *prima facie* justification for *p* is *defeating condition* or *defeater* for *p* (for me). Defeaters, of course, are themselves *prima facie* defeaters, for the defeater can be defeated. Perhaps I spot a fallacy in the initially convincing argument; perhaps I discover a convincing argument for the denial of one of its premises; perhaps I learn on reliable authority that someone else has done one of those things. Then the defeater is defeated, and I am once again within my rights in accepting *p*. Of course a similar remark must be made about defeater-defeaters: they are subject to defeat by defeater-defeater-defeaters and so on.

Many believers in God have been brought up to believe, but then encountered potential defeaters. They have read books by skeptics, been apprised of the atheological argument from evil, heard it said that theistic belief is just a matter of wish fulfillment or only a means whereby one socioeconomic class keeps another in bondage. These circumstances constitute potential defeaters for justification in theistic belief. If the believer is to remain justified, something further is called for—something that *prima facie* defeats the defeaters. Various forms of theistic apologetics serve this function (among others). Thus the *free-will defense* is a defeater for the atheological argument from evil, which is a potential defeater for theistic belief. Suppose I am within my epistemic rights in accepting belief in God as basic; and suppose I am presented with a plausible argument—by Democritus, let us say—for the conclusion that the existence of God is logically incompatible with the existence of evil. (Let us add that I am strongly convinced that there *is* evil.) This is a potential defeater for my being rational in accepting theistic belief. What is required, if I am to continue to believe rationally, is a defeater for that defeater. Perhaps I discover a flaw in Democritus' argument, or perhaps I have it on reliable authority that Augustine, say, has discovered a flaw in the argument; then I am once more justified in my original belief.

Of course if this happens, my original belief may still be basic; I do not now accept it *on the basis of* my belief that Democritus' argument is unsuccessful.

*That* fact does not, of course, constitute any evidence at all for the existence of God; but when I believe *A* on the basis of *B* and do so rationally, then *B* is part of my evidence for *A*. In this case, therefore, I would be irrational or at least in some way mistaken if I *did* believe in God on the basis of my belief that Democritus' argument is unsound. It could be the case, therefore, that in certain circumstances my rationally believing *A* requires that I believe *B*, even though rationality does not require and may even preclude my believing *A* on the basis of *B*. If I accept a belief *A* as basic and then encounter a defeater for *A*, rationality may require that if I continue to believe *A*, then I rationally believe there is a defeater for that defeater; but it does not require that I believe *A* on the basis of that belief. It may be that the conditions under which a belief *A* is properly basic for me include my rationally holding some other belief *B*. But it does not follow that if I am *in* those conditions, then *A* is not properly basic for me.

What I have said in this section requires a great deal by way of supplement, qualification, and amplification. I do not have space here for that, but I shall at least suggest some hints for further study.

First, one *prima facie* justification-conferring condition that does not get enough attention is *training,* or *teaching,* or (more broadly) *testimony.* If I ask you your name and you tell me, I have a *prima facie* right to believe what you say. A child is within his epistemic rights in believing what he is taught by his elders. An enormous proportion of beliefs are accepted at least partly by way of testimony: a much higher proportion than one might initially think. You may believe that the Kröller-Müller museum is in Gelderland, The Netherlands. Even if you have been there, you are dependent upon testimony for such information as that *that* museum was indeed the Kröller-Müller and that the area around the museum is indeed part of Gelderland. You are also dependent upon testimony for your knowledge that Gelderland is part of The Netherlands; perhaps you learned this by consulting a map. Indeed, even if you live in a nearby village and are the museum's chief caretaker, you are still dependent upon testimony for these items of information. And testimony, of course, is a *prima facie* justification-conferring circumstance.

Second, what we have been discussing all along is what we might call *weak* justification: a condition satisfied by a person *S* and a belief *p* when *S* is within his epistemic rights in accepting *p*. But there are other interesting and relevant epistemic conditions lurking in the neighborhood. *Being appeared to treely* may confer on me, not merely the *prima facie* right to believe that there is a tree present, but the more impressive epistemic condition of being such that if the belief in question is true, then I *know* it. Call that condition *strong justification.* Being thus appeared to may perhaps also lay obligations on me; perhaps in those conditions I am not merely within my rights in believing that there is a tree present; perhaps I have a *prima facie* obligation to do so.

As I have said, testimony confers a *prima facie* right to believe; but in the typical case the epistemic condition one is in vis-à-vis *p* by virtue of having been *told* that *p* is not as favorable as the condition one enjoys vis-à-vis a proposition — *2 + 1 = 3,* say — that is apparently self-evident. There is a whole range of interesting and relevant epistemic conditions here.[42]

Third, the conditions that confer *prima facie* justification do not inevitably include *belief.* What justifies me in believing that there is a tree present is just the fact that I am appeared to in a certain way; it is not necessary that I know or believe or consider the fact that I am being thus appeared to. What justifies me in believing, on a given occasion, that 2 + 1 = 3 is the fact that it then seems self-evident to me; there is the "clarity and brightness" (Locke) or luminous aura I referred to above. But to be justified it is not necessary that I believe, on that occasion, that my experience is of that character; I need not so much as raise the question. The condition's being satisfied is sufficient for *prima facie* justification; my *knowing or believing* that it is satisfied is not necessary.

On the other hand, what sometimes confers *prima facie* justification upon me in accepting a proposition *p* as basic is a condition that includes my believing some other proposition *q*—where I do *not* believe *p* on the basis of *q*. I learned as a child that there is such a country as China. When I now hear or read something like *leading spokesmen for China today declared the Russian response totally unacceptable,* I am *prima facie* within my rights in believing it; and part of the justifying condition is that I already know or believe that there are such countries as China and Russia. If I did not know or believe that, I would be justified in believing, not the proposition those words do in fact express, but only something weaker—perhaps *there are a pair of things respectively named "China" and "Russia," and leading spokesmen of the first declared the response of the second totally unacceptable.*

Finally, the relation between various justifying conditions and various epistemic conditions can be much more subtle and complex than the above suggests. There may be a pair of conditions C1 and C2, each of which confers *prima facie* weak justification on *p* (for *S*), such that if *S* is in both conditions, then he has *prima facie* strong justification for *p*. On the other hand, these may be a pair of such *prima facie* weak-justification-conferring conditions (for *p*), such that if *S* is in both, then he is *prima facie* obliged *not* to believe *p*. Order may also be important; it may be the C1 and C2 are *prima facie* weak-justification-conferring conditions, such that if *S* is first in C1 and then in both C1 and C2, then *p* is *prima facie* strongly justified for him; but if he is first in C2 and then in both C1 and C2, *p* is only *prima facie weakly* justified for him.

In this connection, consider again the conditions I mentioned above as *prima facie* conferring weak justification on belief in God. Some who believe in God have come to this belief by way of conversion—a deep and relatively sudden restructuring on one's entire noetic structure. Others have been brought up or trained to believe; they originally acquired theistic belief by way of teaching or testimony on the part of their elders and by imitation of their elders. (Like moods and diseases, beliefs can be contagious.) This belief may then be sustained and reinforced by the conditions I mentioned above as weakly justifying belief in God. These conditions, furthermore, may confer a higher epistemic status upon belief in God. One who has been brought up to believe in God has a *prima facie* right to do so; but perhaps one who is brought up to believe and then finds himself in one of the circumstances mentioned above has (*prima facie*) strong justification for believing in God. Perhaps his condition is such that (given that his belief is true and given the absence of contravening conditions) he *knows* that God exists.

### *D. Fideism*

I take up one final question. In *Reflections on Christian Philosophy* Ralph McInerny suggests that what I have been calling Reformed epistemology is *fideism.* Is he right? Is the Reformed epistemologist perforce a fideist? That depends: it depends, obviously enough, on how we propose to use the term "fideism." According to my dictionary fideism is "exclusive or basic reliance upon faith alone, accompanied by a consequent disparagement of reason and utilized especially in the pursuit of philosophical or religious truth." A fideist therefore urges reliance on faith rather than reason, in matters philosophical and religious; and he may go on to disparage and denigrate reason. We may thus distinguish at least two grades of fideism: moderate fideism, according to which we must rely upon faith rather than reason in religious matters, and extreme fideism, which disparages and denigrates reason.

Now let us ask first whether the Reformed epistemologist is obliged to be an extreme fideist. Of course there is more than one way of disparaging reason. One way to do it is to claim that to take a proposition on faith is higher and better than accepting it on the basis of reason. Another way to disparage reason is to follow Kant in holding that reason left to itself inevitably falls into paradox and antimony on ultimate matters. According to Kant pure reason offers us conclusive argument for supposing that the universe had no beginning, but also, unfortunately, conclusive arguments for the denial of that proposition. I do not think any of the alleged arguments are anywhere nearly conclusive, but if Kant were right, then presumably reason would not deserve to be paid attention to, at least on this topic. According to the most common brand of extreme fideism, however, reason and faith *conflict* or *clash* on matters of religious importance; and when they do, faith is to be preferred and reason suppressed. Thus according to Kierkegaard faith teaches "the absurdity that the eternal is the historical." He means to say, I think, that this proposition is among the deliverances of faith but absurd from the point of view of reason; and it should be accepted despite this absurdity. The turn-of-the-century Russian theologian Shestof carried extreme fideism even further; he held that one can attain religious truth only by rejecting the proposition that $2 + 2 = 4$ and accepting instead $2 + 2 = 5$.

Now it is clear, I suppose, that the Reformed epistemologist need not be an extreme fideist. His views on the proper basicality of belief in

God surely do not commit him to thinking that faith and reason conflict. So suppose we ask instead whether the Reformed epistemologist is committed to *moderate* fideism. And again that depends; it depends upon how we propose to use the terms "reason" and "faith." One possibility would be to follow Abraham Kuyper, who proposes to use these terms in such a way that one takes on faith whatever one accepts but does not accept on the basis of argument or inference or demonstration:

> There is thus no objection to the use of the term 'faith' for that function of the soul by which it attains certainty immediately or directly, without the aid of discursive demonstration. This places faith over against demonstration, but *not* over against knowing.[43]

On this use of these terms, anything taken as basic is taken on faith; anything believed on the basis of other beliefs is taken on reason. I take *2 + 1 = 3* as basic; accordingly, I take it on faith. When I am appropriately appeared to, I take as basic such propositions as *I see a tree before me* or *there is a house over there*; on the present construal I take these things on faith. I remember that I had lunch this noon, but do not accept this belief on the basis of other propositions; this too, then, I take on faith. On the other hand, what I take on the basis of reason is what I believe on the basis of argument or inference from other propositions. Thus I take *2 + 1 = 3* on faith, but *21 × 45 = 945* by reason; for I accept the latter on the basis of calculation, which is a form of argument. Further, suppose I accept supralapsarianism or premillenialism or the doctrine of the virgin birth on the grounds that God proposes these doctrines for our belief and God proposes only truths; then on Kuyper's use of these terms I accept these doctrines not by faith but by reason. Indeed, if with Kierkegaard and Shestov I hold that the eternal is the historical and that 2 + 2 = 5 because I believe God proposes *these* things for my belief, then on the present construal I take them not on faith but on the basis of reason.

And here we can see, I think, that Kuyper's use of these terms is not the relevant one for the discussion of fideism. For consider Shestov. Shestov is an extreme fideist because he thinks faith and reason conflict; and when they do, he says, it is reason that must be suppressed. To paraphrase the poem, "When faith and reason clash, let reason go to smash!" But he is not holding that faith teaches something—*2 + 2 = 5,* for example—that conflicts with a belief—*2 + 2 = 4*—that one arrives at by reasoning from other propositions. On the contrary, the poignancy of the clash is just that what faith teaches conflicts with an *immediate* teaching of reason—a proposition that is apparently self-evident. On the Kuyperian use of these terms Shestov would be surprised to learn that he is not a fideist after all. For what he takes faith to conflict with here is not something one accepts by reason—that is, on the basis of other propositions. Indeed, on the Kuyperian account Shestov not only does not qualify as a fideist; he probably qualifies as an antifideist. Shestov probably did not recommend taking *2 + 2 = 5* as basic; he probably held that God proposes this proposition for our belief and that we should therefore accept it. On the other hand, he also believed, no doubt, that *2 + 2 = 4* is apparently self-evident. So given the Kuyperian use, Shestov would be holding that faith and reason conflict here, but it is *2 + 2 = 4* that is the deliverance of faith and *2 + 2 = 5* the deliverance of reason! Since he recommends accepting *2 + 2 = 5,* the deliverance of reason, he thus turns out to be a rationalist or antifideist, at least on this point.

And this shows that Kuyper's use of these terms is not the relevant use. What we take on faith is not simply what we take as basic, and what we accept by reason is not simply what we take on the basis of other propositions. The deliverances of reason include propositions taken as basic, and the deliverances of faith include propositions accepted on the basis of others.

The Reformed epistemologist, therefore, is a fideist only if he holds that some central truths of Christianity are not among the deliverances of reason and must instead be taken on faith. But just what are the deliverances of reason? What do they include? First, clearly enough, self-evident propositions and propositions that follow from them by self-evidently valid arguments are among the deliverances of reason. But we cannot stop there. Consider someone who holds that according to correct scientific reasoning from accurate observation the earth is at least a couple of billion years old; nonetheless, he adds, the fact is it is no more than some 6000 years old, since that is what faith teaches. Such a person is a fideist, even though the proposition *the earth is more than 6000 years old* is neither self-evident nor a consequence of what is self-evident. So the deliverances of reason include more than the self-evident and its consequences. They also include basic perceptual truths (propositions "evident to the senses"), incorrigible propositions, certain memory propositions, certain propositions about other minds, and certain moral or ethical propositions.

But what about the belief that there is such a person as God and that we are responsible to him? Is that among the deliverances of reason or an item of faith? For Calvin it is clearly the former. "There is within the human mind, and indeed by natural instinct, an awareness of divinity. . . . God himself has implanted in all men a certain understanding of his divine majesty. . . . men one and all perceive that there is a God and that he is their Maker." (*Institutes* I, 3, 1) According to Calvin everyone, whether in the faith or not, has a tendency or nisus, in certain situations, to apprehend God's existence and to grasp something of his nature and actions. This natural knowledge can be and is suppressed by sin, but the fact remains that a capacity to apprehend God's existence is as much part of our natural noetic equipment as is the capacity to apprehend perceptual truths, truths about the past, and truths about other minds. Belief in the existence of God is in the same boat as belief in other minds, the past, and perceptual objects; in each case God has so constructed us that in the right circumstances we form the belief in question. But then the belief that there is such a person as God is as much among the deliverances of reason as those other beliefs.

From this vantage point we can see, therefore, that the Reformed epistemologist is not a fideist at all with respect to belief in God. He does not hold that there is any conflict between faith and reason here, and he does not even hold that we cannot attain this fundamental truth by reason; he holds, instead, that it is among the deliverances of reason.

Of course the nontheist may disagree; he may deny that the existence of God is part of the deliverances of reason. A former professor of mine for whom I had and have enormous respect once said that theists and nontheists have different conceptions of reason. At the time I did not know what he meant, but now I think I do. On the Reformed view I have been urging, the deliverances of reason include the existence of God just as much as perceptual truths, self-evident truths, memory truths, and the like. It is not that theist and nontheist agree as to what reason delivers, the theist then going on to accept the existence of God by faith; there is, instead, disagreement in the first place as to what are the deliverances of reason. But then the Reformed epistemologist is no more a fideist with respect to belief in God than is, for example, Thomas Aquinas. Like the latter, he will no doubt hold that there are other truths of Christianity that are not to be found among the deliverances of reason—such truths, for example, as that God was in Christ, reconciling the world to himself. But he is not a fideist by virtue of his views on our knowledge of God.

By way of summary: I have argued that the evidentialist objection to theistic belief is rooted in classical foundationalism; the same can be said for the Thomistic conception of faith and reason. Classical foundationalism is attractive and seductive; in the final analysis, however, it turns out to be both false and self-referentially incoherent. Furthermore, the Reformed objection to natural theology, unformed and inchoate as it is, may best be seen as a rejection of classical foundationalism. As the Reformed thinker sees things, being self-evident, or incorrigible, or evident to the senses is not a necessary condition of proper basicality. He goes on to add that belief in God is properly basic. He is not thereby committed to the idea that just any or nearly any belief is properly basic, even if he lacks a criterion for proper basicality. Nor is he committed to the view that argument is irrelevant to belief in God if such belief is properly basic. Furthermore, belief in God, like other properly basic beliefs, is not groundless or arbitrary; it is grounded in justification-conferring conditions. Finally, the Reformed view that belief in God is properly basic is not felicitously thought of as a version of fideism.

## NOTES

1. W. K. Clifford, "The Ethics of Belief" in *Lectures and Essays* (London: Macmillan, 1879), pp. 345 f.

2. Brand Blanshard, *Reason and Belief* (London: Allen & Unwin, 1974), pp. 400 f.

3. Bertrand Russell, "Why I am not a Christian" in *Why I Am Not a Christian* (New York: Simon & Schuster, 1957) p. 3 ff.

4. Michael Scriven, *Primary Philosophy* (New York: McGraw-Hill, 1966), p. 87 ff.

5. Anthony Flew, *The Presumption of Atheism* (London: Pemberton, 1976), pp. 22 ff.

6. Wesley Salmon, "Religion & Science: A New Look at Hume's Dialogues," *Philosophical Studies* 33 (1978): 176.

7. Richard Braithwaite, *An Empiricist's View of the Nature of Religious Belief* (Cambridge: Cambridge University Press, 1955), p. 32.

8. Gordon Kaufman, *God the Problem* (Cambridge: Harvard University Press, 1972), p. 8.

9. Ibid., p. 85.

10. Ibid., p. 86.

11. A. J. Ayer, *Language, Truth and Logic*, 2nd ed. (London: Gollantz, Ltd., 1946), pp. 114–20.

12. For further discussion of positivism and its dreaded verifiability criterion of meaning, see Alvin Plantinga, *God and Other Minds* (Ithaca, New York: Cornell University Press, 1968), pp. 156–68.

13. This claim has been made by Epicurus, perhaps by David Hume, by some of the French Encyclopedists, by F. H. Bradley, J. McTaggart, and many others. For an influential contemporary statement of the claim, see J. Mackie, "Evil and Omnipotence," *Mind* 64 (1955): 200 ff.

14. C. S. Lewis, *The Problem of Pain* (New York: Macmillan, 1943); and see Plantinga, *God and Other Minds*, 115–55; idem, *The Nature of Necessity* (Oxford: The Clarendon Press, 1974), chapter 9. A more accessible form of the argument can be found in Alvin Plantinga, *God, Freedom and Evil* (1974; reprint ed., Grand Rapids, Michigan: Eerdmans, 1978), pp. 1–50.

15. Alvin Plantinga, "The Probabilistic Argument from Evil," *Philosophical Studies* (1979): 1–53.

16. W. K. Clifford, "The Ethics of Belief," p. 183.

17. Ibid., p. 14.

18. Michael Scriven, *Primary Philosophy,* pp. 102–3.

19. See Plantinga, "The Probabilistic Argument from Evil," pp. 27 ff.

20. See, for example, Plantinga, *The Nature of Necessity,* chapter 10.

21. Blanshard, *Reason and Belief,* p. 401.

22. Scriven, *Primary Philosophy,* p. 103.

23. Roderick Chisholm, *Theory of Knowledge,* 2nd ed. (New York: Prentice-Hall, 1977), p. 14.

24. Alan Donagan, *The Theory of Morality* (Chicago: University of Chicago Press, 1977), p. 134.

25. Aquinas, *Summa Theologiae* (hereafter "ST"), IIa, IIae, I, 5.

26. In fact, these argument forms are self-evidently valid in two senses: (a) it is self-evident that for any instance of the form in question, if the premises are true, then so is the conclusion, and (b) the corresponding conditional of the argument form is itself self-evident.

27. Although the quantification rule presents a bit of a problem in some formulations, in that it does not have the sheer see-through-ability demanded by self-evidence. The fact, incidentally, that propositional and first order logic are not *uniquely* axiomatizable is no obstacle to seeing them as sciences in this Aristotelian sense; nor does the incompleteness of arithmetic show that arithmetic is not a science in this sense.

28. Verum autem est dupliciter considerabile: uno modo, sicut per se notum; alio modo, sicut per aliud notum. Quod autem est per se notum se habet ut principium, et percipitur statim ab intellectu. Et ideo habitus perficiens intellectum ad hujusmodi veri considerationem vocatur *intellectus,* qui est habitus principiorum.

Verum autem quod est per aliud notum, non statim percipitur ab intellectu, sed per inquisitionem rationis, et se habet in ratione termini. (Aquinas, *Summa Theologiae,* Ia, q. 84, a.2; my italics)

29. See Plantinga, *The Nature of Necessity,* chapter 1.

30. Aquinas, *Summa Contra Gentiles* (hereafter "SCG"), I, 13,3.

31. That is, by arguments whose corresponding conditionals are self-evident to us.

32. Aquinas, *De Veritate,* question 14, article 10.

33. Plantinga, "The Probabilistic Argument from Evil," pp. 15 ff.

34. Chisholm, *Theory of Knowledge,* pp. 17 ff.

35. This was suggested by Philip Quinn in his contribution to the APA (Western Division, 1981) symposium on Alvin Plantinga, "Is Belief in God Properly Basic?" *Nous* 15 (March 1981): 41–51.

36. Herman Bavinck, *The Doctrine of God,* tr. William Hendricksen (Grand Rapids: Eerdmans, 1951), pp. 78–79. *The Doctrine of God* is the translation of the second volume of Bavinck's *Gereformeede Dogmatiek,* published 1895–99.

37. John Calvin, *Institutes of the Christian Religion,* tr. Ford Lewis Battles (Philadelphia: Westminster Press, 1960), book 1, chapter 3, pp. 43–44.

38. Karl Barth, *Church Dogmatics,* tr. G. T. Thompson and Harold Knight (Edinburgh: T & T Clark, 1956), volume 1, part 1, pp. 93–95.

39. Roderick Chisholm, *The Problem of the Criterion* (Milwaukee: Marquette University Press, 1973), pp. 14ff.

40. For further comment on the Great Pumpkin objection see Alvin Plantinga, "On Reformed Epistemology," *Reformed Journal*, April 1982.

41. I do not mean to suggest, of course, that if a person believes a true proposition and is justified (in this sense) in believing it, then it follows that he *knows* it; that is a different (and stronger) sense of the term.

42. See Chisholm, *Theory of Knowledge*, pp. 7–15.

43. Abraham Kuyper, *Encyclopedia of Sacred Theology*, tr. J. DeVries (New York: Charles Scribner's Sons, 1898), pp. 128–29.

# The Stranger

George I. Mavrodes

Carol Ten Boom's conscience still troubled her as she settled herself into the airliner seat and looked over the wing toward Chicago's O'Hare terminal.

*I really should have witnessed to her,* she thought to herself. *At least I could have said that I was a Christian . . . or something.*

She was thinking of the girl with the long skirt, braided hair, and gigantic handbag who had offered her a flower in the terminal. A Moonie, she supposed, or maybe Hare Krishna. But she had simply mumbled, "No, thank you," and hurried on, unwilling to be trapped into the persevering conversation which she knew would follow. But now she wondered, as she often did these days, whether she should have gathered her courage to say something about Christ. Had she really denied him, after all, by saying nothing?

These reflections about the past, however, were soon swallowed up by a more current problem. For as the passengers came down the aisle, looking from their ticket envelopes to the seat numbers, one man caught her attention. And no wonder. His dark face was made even darker by his billowing white shirt, and the pleated, folded, white cotton trousers. A fringe of black hair showed beneath his turban, a convoluted knot of fabric, maroon and gray. And as his eyes scanned the numbers on the overhead baggage racks a premonition seized Carol's heart.

Her premonition was true. As she had somehow known he would, the dark man took the seat beside her. He pushed his brief case under the seat in front and awkwardly pulled the belt buckle from beneath him. Maybe he smiled at her. But Carol did not turn to see.

A voice was coming over the intercom now, while the stewardess stood in front, dangling a yellow mask from her hand. Carol heard the voice in snatches: "extinguish all smoking materials and pull the mask toward you, placing it over the nose and. . . ." But though she was only a college senior, Carol had already heard that message many times. She had never seen the masks fall from their overhead compartments, and did not really think she ever would. Nor would she ever use the lower seat cushions as flotation devices. The announcement meant no more to her now than the sound of the engines, or the thrust against her back as the plane gathered speed on the runway.

*He's an Indian, of course,* she thought. *A Hindu. Or maybe a Buddhist.* Or were there any Indian Buddhists? Some religion had died out in India, but she couldn't remember which one. And how did one witness to a Hindu? Or a Buddhist? She had vowed—or was it really a vow?—that she would try to witness to whoever sat beside her. What if he asked her about Karma, or whether she had read the holy books of India? What if he couldn't speak English at all? Maybe that would be lucky, and then she was ashamed of thinking such a thing. And so she opened the book which she had brought along. There was still plenty of time, she thought, hours before they landed in San Francisco. Maybe it would be natural to say something when they were eating. Maybe he would see her bow her head to pray and would ask her about it.

And so she read for a while. But the book was difficult—*The Nature of Necessity*—and she couldn't concentrate enough to make any real headway in it. And then she glanced to her left—involuntarily, or so it seemed—and her eyes met those of her dark neighbor. And for a moment both of them were embarrassed.

"I say, I'm sorry," the man said. "I didn't mean to stare. But one doesn't often see someone reading philosophy in an airliner."

The incongruity between what Carol had expected and the precise British accents which she actually heard left her speechless. She looked down at her book and then at the man again, managing a smile.

"You must be a university student," he said.

"Well, yes," she said. "A college student, I mean. I go to Calvin College. In Michigan."

"Calvin College? I haven't heard of it. Is it named for John Calvin, the reformer?"

"Yes," she said. "It's a Christian college."

"A Christian College!" the Indian said, smiling. "I say, that's splendid! Then you must be a Christian. I'm a Christian, too."

"You are?" Carol could not keep the surprise from her voice.

"Yes," he said. "I was baptized almost six years ago. It was not long before I left for England."

"That's wonderful," Carol said. She would have liked to ask him how he had come to be a Christian, an adult convert as it seemed. But maybe it would seem to be prying. And he said no more about it for the moment.

"You must really like philosophy," he said, nodding at her book.

"Oh, I do." Carol brightened up. She really was enthusiastic about philosophy, and not at all reluctant in discussion. "I'm majoring in it at Calvin, and next year I hope to begin graduate work. I've applied at Yale, the University of Michigan, Cornell, and UCLA."

"I say, that's really good! I'm awfully keen on philosophy myself. I read Greats at Oxford, mostly philosophy. And I. . . . But I haven't introduced myself. I'm Ravi Guptar. Just call me Ravi."

"I'm Carol," she said. "Carol Ten Boom. It's a Dutch name. My grandparents came from the old country. I'm glad to meet you."

"What are you most interested in in philosophy?" he asked her.

"Oh, almost everything, but epistemology especially, and philosophy of religion."

"Really?" he said. "I'm most interested in philosophy of religion, too. I suppose it's because of the way I myself came to believe in Jesus."

"Oh? How was that?"

"It was because of an argument," he went on. "I understand that not many people come that way anymore. And maybe even stranger, it was an argument that I myself constructed."

"Really?"

"I was only twenty at the time, and I hadn't studied much philosophy yet, so it was really crude and rough in spots. But it was on the right track—I'm sure of that. I became convinced that the religion of Jesus Christ is the true way of salvation. So I found some Christians in Madras and was baptized. And I have worshipped God in the Christian way since then."

"That's really strange," Carol said. "I don't think I've ever heard of anyone being converted by an argument. I thought it wasn't even possible. I thought only the Holy Spirit could lead someone to Christ."

"Of course, I don't mean that the Holy Spirit wasn't in it," Ravi replied. "I'm sure that God did lead me by his Spirit. I've often heard Christians say that the Spirit works through sermons, through the Bible, and so on. In my case he worked through an argument."

"But the theistic arguments actually aren't any good, are they?" said Carol. "I mean, they're not sound. Was your argument like the standard arguments in the textbooks?"

"Well, not exactly. It has a part that is rather like Thomas' argument from causality, and a part that is pretty clearly a version of the teleological argument. But overall I haven't seen anything very close to it in the history of philosophy."

"And do you still think that it's sound?"

"Oh, absolutely," he said, "I told you it was pretty crude when I first worked it out. There were some modal mistakes in it, and other mistakes. But it was basically right. And in this past year at Oxford I've reworked the whole thing. I've put it into rigorous form, and now it is a strict demonstration that Christianity is the true religion."

Carol's hesitancy had disappeared by now. They were talking philosophy, and she was confident in that. She wasn't a PhD, but she wasn't a neophyte either, and she had no reluctance to plunge into the discussion.

"A demonstration?" she said. "What do you mean by 'a demonstration'?" And then, hearing the words herself, she blushed and said, "I'm sorry. I didn't mean to sound like a professor."

"Perfectly alright," said Ravi. "It's exactly the right thing to ask. By a demonstration of p I mean a deductively valid argument which has p for its conclusion, and such that each premise is either incorrigible, or self-evident, or evident to the senses."

"And you've got an argument like that for the truth of Christianity? I think some Calvin professors would be surprised to hear that."

"But why?" The young Indian now seemed genuinely surprised himself. "Are there some who are not Christians?"

"Oh, no, they're all Christians. But many of them say that there couldn't be a demonstrative argument or proof for Christianity. Nothing like what you've described. It's a matter of faith."

"Well, I don't know why it shouldn't be faith," Ravi said with a perplexed frown. "But anyway, for better or worse I seem to have this demonstration. We can't do anything about that, can we?"

"I'd be interested to hear it," Carol said. "And maybe we could talk about it?"

"Oh, by all means, by all means! But better to read it than to hear it." Ravi smiled a little apologetically as he reached for his briefcase. "I'm afraid it's a little long. Over 26 pages. Almost 200 numbered propositions. But I've tried to make every premise explicit, and to make every logical move clear and simple."

He pulled out a stapled typescript and handed it to Carol. She saw that the title was "Christianity Demonstrated *More Geometrico.*" And she began to read.

She did not, however, read for long. Not a page, nor half a page, nor even a quarter of a page. For the very first premise—no more than a single line—stopped her. It read, "Jesus of Nazareth rose from the dead."

Carol read the line again. There was no doubt of what it said. And it was clearly marked, "Premise." She looked up, wondering if this were a joke. But Ravi seemed to be smiling in an open and sincere way.

"But Ravi, this premise. . . ." She pointed to it on the page. "It's. . . . I mean, I . . ."

Guptar looked at the page, now a little puzzled again. "Jesus rose from the dead? But that's true, isn't it? That's how I began the journey to Christ."

"But," she said, "of course you can get an argument for Christianity if you can start with premises like that. But it won't be a demonstration. This premise isn't . . . well, I mean it's not . . ."

"I see," said Ravi, smiling easily again. "You think this premise is true, but not suitable for a demonstration. What do you think is wrong with it?"

"Well," she said, "the premises are supposed to be either incorrigible, or self-evident, or evident to the senses. But this one is . . ." And then she stopped.

She stopped because it suddenly occurred to her that maybe Ravi was going to say that the resurrection was evident to the senses, that people had actually seen Jesus alive after his death and burial. Of course, *she* hadn't seen him, but she couldn't deny (since she was a Christian) that someone had seen him. Or, on the other hand, maybe that shouldn't count. But why not? Why should her situation be more definitive than the experience of, say, Mary Magdalene? So maybe that premise did satisfy the requirements after all. Or should the notion of a demonstration be relativized, so that this argument might be a demonstration to some people but not to others?

Those questions rose quickly in Carol's mind, but she had no time to sort them out. So she went ahead with what she had first intended to say. "This first premise isn't incorrigible, or self-evident, or evident to the senses. So the argument can't be a demonstration."

"But it is," said the Indian quietly. "I'm sure of it."

"It's what?" she asked.

"It's self-evident that Jesus rose from the dead."

For a moment Carol simply stared at Ravi, her mouth dropping open. Then she got herself together enough to speak.

"Self-evident? But . . . But how could it be? How could the resurrection possibly be self-evident?"

"Why shouldn't it be?" the man responded. He paused a moment, and then went on. "Look, Carol. You asked me what I meant by a 'demonstration'. Now let me ask you. How do you understand the concept of self-evidence?"

"Well," she said, "the way it was explained in our epistemology class, a proposition is self-evident if just understanding it is enough to make you believe it. You couldn't understand it without believing it."

"Fine!" He smiled at her. "A splendid definition. That's just what I mean about the resurrection."

"It can't be," Carol said. "The self-evident truths are necessary propositions—like 'two plus one equals three' and 'all bachelors are unmarried'. But the resurrection is a historical fact; it's not a necessary truth."

"Of course the resurrection is a historical fact, Carol. And it's not a necessary truth. You're certainly right about that. But why should that prevent it from being self-evident? Why should we suppose that all the self-evident truths are necessary truths?"

"What else could they be?"

"Some of them could be contingent truths. We just have to look and see." Ravi squirmed against his seat belt, trying to turn. "The definition you gave is basically psychological. It defines the notion of self-evidence in terms of the way in which something can be believed, or not believed. Many philosophers have thought that there was an important class of propositions which satisfied that definition. I think they were right about that. But some of these philosophers may also have thought that all self-evident truths were also necessary truths. On that, I think, they are mistaken. At the very least we should ask whether there is some argument which connects the logical notion of necessity with the psychological feature of self-evidence. Do you know such an argument?"

As a matter of fact Carol could not think of any such argument, and so she turned to another problem. "Aren't there a lot of people who understand the claim that Christ rose from the dead but don't believe it?"

"There certainly seem to be," Ravi said. "I don't want to deny it. But here I use a distinction which I was glad to find in St. Thomas—between what is simply self-evident and what is self-evident to someone. It is the latter notion which I am using. The resurrection is self-evident to me, and maybe to some people like me. I'm somebody who has to believe that doctrine as soon as I understand it. And so on. But for those other people it's just not self-evident. They will have to proceed some other way."

Carol now found herself with a variety of questions leading in different directions. One involved a conjecture, and she decided to begin with that one. "Is there anything you believe, Ravi, which you don't take to be self-evident?"

"Oh, sure," he said. "I don't by any means take all my beliefs to be self-evident. The existence of God, for example. I believe it, certainly, but it's not self-evident to me. When I first believed in Jesus' resurrection, I started to read the Bible and other Christian writings. Of course, I found a lot about God in them. But it was almost a year before I believed that there was a God. And then it was because I had worked out the first part of my argument. And it still doesn't seem at all self-evident to me."

"But then why do you think the resurrection is self-evident?"

"Two reasons. One is introspective. When I try to sort out the structure of my own intellectual life from the inside, my belief in the resurrection seems to be self-evident. It has that feel about it. It seems to me that I simply could not fail to believe it if I knew what was there to be believed. I just seem to recognize that disposition as part of my own intellectual machinery, my cognitive 'set'. The other reason is historical. I actually did believe this doctrine as soon as I heard it. The very first time I heard the resurrection mentioned I didn't know what the word 'resurrection' meant. I asked the teacher to explain it. And as soon as he did, I found myself believing the doctrine! I was really surprised, but there was nothing I could do about it. I was stuck with that belief, and I have been ever since."

"But at least you had the testimony of your teacher to go on," Carol said.

"Not at all. The man who explained the resurrection to me was a lapsed Hindu, teaching comparative religion. He's a Westernized naturalist with no sympathy at all for Christianity. I was a firm believer in the resurrection before I ever met a Christian or read a line of Christian literature."

Carol shook her head. "It's incredible. It's so different from anything I've ever heard. I just can't believe it. How could you possibly have mental machinery like that? Where could you have gotten it?"

"But that's an easy question, isn't it, Carol? At least, so it seems to me. I've got no doubt that God gave me that disposition to believe in the resurrection. It was his way of drawing me to Christ. And why not? Surely that's not beyond God's power? If he can give me a disposition to believe my senses, he can also give me a disposition to believe that Jesus rose from the dead."

"But there's a difference, Ravi. Practically all of us believe our senses. But almost nobody—not even Christians—believes in the resurrection the way you do. Surely that difference is important?"

"There certainly is that difference," the Indian replied. "But its importance is more obscure. If you're asking about why there is that difference, I don't have any special theory about it. There are lots of differences among people. Some people have good eyesight, some poor, some are color-blind, some are totally blind. Some people are intelligent, some are dull, some can run a mile in four minutes, some in eight minutes. And so on. Why does God give us different gifts, different abilities? I don't know. But I can thank God for what he gave me, and go ahead to use it as well as I can. And other people can use what he gives to them."

Guptar paused, but Carol said nothing. So he went on. "But maybe you really had a different question. Maybe you think that a disposition which almost everyone has is somehow better than a disposition which only a few people have. But just how is it better? Is the more widespread disposition supposed to be more reliable? But my disposition—even if I'm the only one to have it—is a disposition to believe a particular proposition. And that proposition is. . . . Well, what do you think about it, Carol? What do you say about the resurrection?"

"Well, I think it's true, of course," she said. "Naturally, I'm a Christian. But I don't think it's self-evident."

"No," Ravi said. "But you think it's true. And so you also have to think that my disposition to believe it is reliable. In fact, it's 100 percent reliable. Nothing can be more reliable than that. That can't be the way in which my disposition falls short. Or do you think that in general the dispositions which God gives to a few people are less reliable than those he gives to many people? Maybe you believe that, but I don't. I don't see any reason to believe that God is more likely to deceive one person than two."

At this point Carol decided to try another tack. "Let's go back to the definition of 'self-evidence'. Couldn't someone offer a different definition, maybe entirely in terms of logical necessity, or at least one which made logical necessity a necessary condition for self-evidence?"

"Of course they could," said Ravi. "And on a definition like that, the resurrection will not be self-evident, and my argument will not be a demonstration. But so far that's just a matter of terminology. The real question is whether the new definition is better than the old. Does it pick out a class with some important feature, a class which the other definition ignores?"

"Well, doesn't it?" Carol said. "Necessary truth is an important property, I should think."

"No doubt it is. But is it important here?"

"It sure seems like it. There could be a proposition which you can't help believing, but which is false nevertheless. But adding necessity to the definition of self-evidence will guarantee that what is self-evident is also true."

Ravi smiled. "Of course it will do that. But we cannot make ourselves infallible, or even more learned, by altering a definition. It's harder than that."

"I don't understand what you mean."

"Well, look at it this way. All of the necessary truths are true, so if we build a requirement of necessary truth into the concept of self-evidence, then all self-evident beliefs will be true. But all of the contingent truths are true, too. So if we build contingent truth into self-evidence, then again self-evidence will guarantee truth. Contingent truth will do that job just as well as necessary truth. But in either case we will still be exposed to all the same substantive mistakes as before. We will just have different names for them. Instead of saying that a self-evident belief was false, we will say that a belief thought to be self-evident was not really so. But the substance of the mistake will be the same. The real question is whether something we can't help believing is false. If so, then we are just stuck with that false belief, and there's nothing we can do about it. No reshuffling of our terminology will help us there."

"Well," said Carol, with a doubtful expression on her face, "that sounds right. But somehow I always thought that necessary truths were more solid than contingent truths. But let that go for now. You've got this argument you say is a demonstration. But what good is it if it has to start from something like the resurrection? Isn't that what all this is about?"

"I think that is important—maybe the most important question," Ravi said. "But, at the very least, my argument was good for me. It led me to Christ. And if there is someone with the same dispositions which I have, it may help them in the same way. And if there are people with somewhat different dispositions, but in the same ball park, as you Americans say, then my argument might give them a clue as to how to construct their own arguments."

"But most people aren't like that, are they?"

"No, probably not. And so my argument is not as good as the best imaginable argument. An argument which began with premises which were self-evident to everybody—that would really be something, wouldn't it? I wish I could invent one like that! But I can't, or at least so far I haven't. You've got the best I've been able to do, right there. It's not everything. All I claim is that it's something. It's a rigorous demonstration of the truth of Christianity. It's not a universal conversion machine."

The stewardess was standing beside them in the aisle now, holding two dinner trays. Carol slid the manuscript from the tray table into her lap and picked up the napkin.

"Okay," she said. "Okay. Maybe you're right. Anyway, let's eat. Then I'll read the rest of it."

And to herself she thought, *Maybe it wouldn't have been any stranger, talking to the girl.*

# Christian Experience and Christian Belief

William P. Alston

## I

I take as my starting point the conviction that somehow what goes on in the experience of leading the Christian life provides some ground for Christian belief, makes some contribution to the rationality of Christian belief. We sometimes feel the presence of God; we get glimpses, at least, of God's will for us; we feel the Holy Spirit at work in our lives, guiding us, strengthening us, enabling us to love other people in a new way; we hear God speaking to us in the Bible, in preaching, or in the words and actions of our fellow Christians. Because of all this we are more justified in our Christian beliefs than we would have been otherwise. I am not suggesting that this is the whole ground or that it can do the whole job. I have no aspiration to be a late twentieth-century Schliermacher, spinning the whole web of Christian doctrine out of the personal experience of the contemporary believer. Nevertheless, if I could not find any confirmation of the Christian message in my own experience, I would be less justified in accepting that message than I am in fact. To generalize the point, suppose that no one had ever experienced communion with God, had ever heard God speaking to him or her, had ever felt the strengthening influence of the Holy Spirit in a difficult situation. In that case Christian belief would be a less rational stance than it is in fact.

But though it seems to me plain that somehow this must be so, it is a task of no small magnitude to show how it is so, maintain the position in the face of numerous difficulties, and integrate it with other things that seem equally undeniable. In short, we are faced with a typical philosophical problem.

In the interest of greater focus let me delimit the topic in certain ways.

First I will confine myself to those stretches of Christian experience open to humble lay Christians like myself, who have not undertaken a major contemplative or ascetic discipline, and who have not sacrificed all else to the attainment of an immediate vision of God. This means that I sacrifice the most obvious continuity with the bulk of the philosophical literature on the epistemology of religious experience, which is concentrated, much too narrowly, on mystical experience. It is not surprising that so splashy and easily demarcated a phenomenon as mystical experience should have attracted so much attention, but mystical experience, because of the extreme immediacy and ineffability allegedly involved, poses very special problems not generated by its humbler relatives; and the obsession with mystical experience has led to a serious neglect of the epistemology of the person in the pew.

Second, in order to avoid distracting side issues, I shall not consider experiences that would be termed hallucinatory from a physical standpoint —visions of the saints or of Jesus, literally hearing voices that emanate from no embodied speaker, and the like. I am not setting aside all sensory mediation: I am not excluding, for example, seeing the glory of God in majestic natural scenes or hearing God speak to me in what a friend says or does. It is only sensory *hallucinations* that are being set aside.

Within these limitations I wish to range as ecumenically as possible over the full range of Christian experience—embracing the evangelical sense of having the burden of sin lifted from one after a commitment to Christ, as well as the Catholic sense of the indwelling of Christ in the reception of the bread and wine, ranging over the experience of the Holy Spirit working through one in glossalalia and other "gifts of the spirit," as well as the sense of trust and confidence in God with which a more sober mainliner will begin his or her day.

Third, some stretches of Christian belief are more directly and more obviously open to support by Christian experience than others. If we were to concentrate on the belief that God made all things visible and invisible, that Christ was begotten by His Father before all worlds and is of one substance with the Father, was incarnated by the Holy Ghost of the Virgin Mary, and will come again in glory to judge both the quick and the dead, I might have some considerable difficulty in showing that I can, even partially, confirm any of those items, *individually,* by what happens when I am on my knees in my study. I will start with items of Christian belief that have more obvious connections with our experience as Christians.

1. God will provide for His people.
2. God will forgive the sins of the truly repentant.
3. We have received the Holy Spirit, a source of the New Life. The

fruits of the spirit are love, joy, peace, patience, kindness, goodness, faithfulness, gentleness, self-control.

4. The church is the body of Christ.
5. The Spirit is at work in the church.
6. God speaks to us through the Bible, through the preaching of the gospel, through the lives and actions of those who live in the spirit.
7. God will reveal His will to those who truly seek Him.
8. God will give one the strength to do what He requires of one.

Thus I will be focusing on beliefs as to how God's nature and activities manifest themselves in our lives, rather than bare assertions about the divine in itself. Call these M-beliefs ("M" for "manifestation"). Insofar as I can learn anything from my experience about the existence and nature of God, it is by way of encountering the activity of God in the world. God does not passively sit for His portrait; we cannot just stare at Him, not in this life at any rate. If we come to know God through experience at all, it is through His works, including, pre-eminently, His works in human lives.

So the idea is that beliefs like this tell us what God will do to or for us, how His activity can be expected to impinge on our individual or corporate experience, where His messages for us are to be located, and so on. If we find things turning out in our experience as these principles would lead us to expect, this will lend some confirmation to those principles and hence, indirectly, to the total system in which they are imbedded. Thus the conviction with which we began can be more explicitly spelled out as follows. The Christian beliefs under consideration say that God will manifest Himself in certain ways in our individual or corporate experience. From time to time we find such manifestations in our experience. This provides empirical confirmation for the beliefs in question.

## II

This claim can be attacked, and has been attacked, in a number of ways. I am first going to mention, and reply to, one of the more easily handled objections. Then the rest of the paper will be devoted to a consideration of what I take to be the most serious challenge, the discussion of which will lead us into fundamental epistemological issues.

First, then, it is often contended that one is making a genuine factual claim, one is making a genuine assertion about how things objectively are, only if it is in principle possible to *disconfirm* what one is saying.

Unless one is sticking one's neck out in such a way that the course of experience could decisively show that what one is saying is mistaken, then one is not really claiming that things are one way rather than another objectively.[1] Now it is clear that our examples are not decisively disconfirmable by experience. They are markedly unspecific. They do not say *how* God will provide for His people, *when* or *under what conditions* one can expect a particular fruit of the spirit, just *what* Christ is going to do through His church, and what the *timetable* is. These "somehow-somewhere-somewhen" statements are so formulated that whereas any positive instance will be confirming (since it will be somewhere and so on), there can be no negative instances: whatever happens, you cannot take it as evidence that a fruit of the Spirit will not be received in some other context.

But this is a difficulty for M-beliefs only if the possibility of decisive empirical disconfirmation really is necessary for genuine assertive force. And there are good reasons for denying this. In particular, there seem to be assertions with unimpeachable qualifications that do not pass this test. Consider unrestricted existential generalizations like "There are unicorns (somewhere, at some time)." These too are not susceptible of decisive empirical disconfirmation. No matter how long and how hard we look, without finding any traces of past, present, or future unicorns, it is always possible that there are, have been, or will be some unicorns that have escaped our notice. We may become tired of looking and conclude that the possibility can be safely neglected, as far as our corner of the universe is concerned, but that does not amount to decisive disconfirmation. And despite this, we would all surely agree that if a real honest-to-God unicorn hove into sight, the existential generalization would have been confirmed. Unrestricted existential generalizations like this may have only a limited place in science, but they beautifully illustrate how a statement can be decisively confirmable without being decisively disconfirmable, and how decisive disconfirmability is not necessary for assertive force.

Now for the really serious challenge. "In order that what happens to me be confirmatory of 'God will reveal His will to those who truly seek Him' or 'The Holy Spirit will give me the gift of love if I give it a chance', then I have to be able to recognize (correctly recognize) what happens to me as a case of God revealing His will for me or of the Holy Spirit enabling me to love someone I have difficulty in loving. But whether that is the right way to describe what is going on in the individual case is (almost) as problematic as the existential generalization itself. The tough problem is not the inference from the singular statement to the existential generalization; that is just elementary logic. The tough problem is to determine whether we are justified in conceptualizing our experience in these terms. Does the Christian God really exist, and does He do such things as reveal His will to people, whether to me or to someone else? The only thing I know empirically is that after asking God to reveal His will for me in a certain situation, I had a strong sense that what He wanted me to do was to give priority to work on philosophical theology. All I know by experience is that after responding to the gospel and committing myself to Christ, I became able to feel concern for others in a way I had not done before. Our supposed theological datum has crumbled, under examination, into a purely psychological datum on the one hand and a theological explanation on the other. The theological content comes in only as one possible explanation of these psychological and behavioral phenomena. So before we can use the details of Christian experience to support Christian doctrine we will have to justify explaining such happenings in the Christian way rather than in some other – for example, in the Freudian way – or in terms of some other purely natural psychological mechanisms."

In thinking about how to respond to this challenge we encounter a crucial fork in the road. On the one hand, we could play the game on the terms laid down by the challenger. We could admit that the only thing one knows directly from experience in these cases is that one is having certain experiences: the only real data are subjective. We could then pick up the gauntlet thrown down by our adversary and seek to show that the explanation of these experiences in terms of Christian theology is more adequate than any of its rivals. If we proceeded in this way, we would be admitting that we do not directly experience God in our lives, but we would seek to show that we do have experiences that are best accounted for by supposing that God is "behind" them or "responsible" for them in certain ways.

Instead of embarking on all that I shall explore another tack. I shall resist the bifurcation of Christian experience into psychological datum and theological explanation and defend the original claim that it is God Himself, or, if you like, some activity or aspect of God, that is directly presented or given to our experience in these transactions. That is what I will be doing in the rest of this paper.

But first let us note that in taking this second path we are narrowing our sights even more. We are restricting ourselves to experiences in which the subject takes himself to be directly aware of God, rather than simply being disposed to believe, however firmly, that what is happening in his experience is to be explained by God's activity. Thus if after responding to the Gospel message, I find myself reacting to people in a different kind of way, I may firmly believe that this is due to the action of the Holy Spirit on my soul; but if I do not seem to myself to be directly experiencing the presence of the Holy Spirit, if I am not disposed to answer the question "Just what did you experience?" or "Just what were you aware of?" with something that begins "The Holy Spirit . . . ," then this experience does not fall within our purview; which is not to say that it is lacking in interest or importance. No doubt, this is often a difficult distinction to make, but where it can be made, it will be used in the way indicated.

However I will not be restricting myself to what we might call "focal" experiences of God, those in which the awareness of God is in the forefront of consciousness. I suspect that for many people their assurance of God's existence is at least partly due to a sort of background awareness of the constant presence and creative activity of God, something like our normal background awareness of our own bodies.

## III

How can we defend the claim, in the face of the impressive challenge cited above, that people are sometimes directly aware of God and his workings? Since misery loves company, let us tour some other historically famous difficulties of this sort. First let us visit *l'impasse Phénomène.* Around about the seventeenth century someone had the bright idea of remarking that whereas we had all along been supposing that any normal adult human being could get plenty of empirical data of the form "This log is burning" or "I am seated before the fire in a dressing gown" just by opening her eyes, these supposed data are really hybrids. There is indeed a real datum of the form "I seem to see a log burning" or "A burning-logish sense datum is in my visual field" or "I am being appeared to log-burningly." This datum gets conjoined with an explanation, namely, that it is generated, by a psychophysical process we will pass over in discreet silence, by an actual physical log that is actually burning, to produce the hybrid we uncritically take as a datum. Hence, before we can use our experience as a ground for supposing that there are such things as burning logs, or that a particular log is burning at a particular time, we must find some way of justifying this particular way of explaining the occurrence of sense-data.

It is obvious that this familiar move in the epistemology of sense perception is exactly parallel to the challenge we are considering to the claims of religious experience. If we can figure out what to do in this case, it may help us with our original problem. Perhaps company can do more for misery than just provide more.

First note that the explanation route has not proved fruitful in the sense-perception case. Many thinkers *have* accepted the Cartesian challenge in the terms just specified and have sought to show that our common assumption of an independently existing physical world constitutes the best explanation of the course of our sensory experience. But such attempts have not fared well under criticism. It is dubious that we can specify the purely subjective experiential data to be explained without relying on the "independent physical world" scheme in doing so. And waiving that problem, the arguments for the superiority of the familiar scheme have not been particularly impressive. To go into all this would take a long time, and so I must just register these judgments and pass on.

Of course there is also the phenomenalist gambit of taking beliefs that we get from sense perception to *be* beliefs about actual and possible sense experience, thus relieving us of any gap to be bridged. Again without argument, I shall just take it that this position has been sufficiently discredited, and that we cannot avoid recognizing that the beliefs we form on the basis of sense perception cannot be understood as beliefs about what sensory experiences people would have under certain conditions. I might add that the parallel tack in the religious case—taking beliefs about God to be beliefs about what religious experiences people would have under certain conditions—is equally implausible.

If the epistemic pretensions of sense perception cannot be justified by either of the moves just mentioned, then it seems that here, as in the religious case, our only hope is to reject the bifurcation alleged in the challenge and seek to justify the claim that we do encounter independently existing physical objects in our experience. Put the matter in a somewhat different way. The question concerns the justifiability of a certain *practice* —the practice of forming physical-object beliefs directly on the basis of perception rather than as an explanation of what is perceived or experienced. Another way of characterizing the practice in question is to say that it is a practice of using a certain conceptual scheme (the "independently existing physical object" conceptual scheme) to specify what it is we are experiencing in sense perception. If I may use the term "objectification" for "taking an experience to be an experience of something of a certain sort," then we may say that the practice in question is a certain kind of objectification of sense experience, an objectification in terms of independently existing physical objects. Let us use the term "perceptual practice" (PP) for our familiar way of objectifying sense experience. In parallel fashion I will, for purposes of this paper, use the term "Christian practice" (CP) for the practice of objectifying certain ranges of experience in terms of Christian theology.

We want to consider, with respect to each of these practices, whether we are, or can be, justified in engaging in it. If we are to tackle this question effectively, we must be explicit about the concept of justification involved. So let us say something about that.

## IV

First let us align the concept of the justification of a *practice,* about which we are asking, with the more familiar notion of the justification of a belief. The relationship is very simple. Remember that the practices we are considering are practices of belief formation. Let us call them "epistemic practices."[2] An epistemic practice is a more-or-less regular and fixed procedure of forming beliefs under certain conditions, where the content of the belief is some more-or-less determinate function of the conditions. The practices we are considering belong to a subtype that we might term "experiential epistemic practices," practices in which the conditions are, or include, modes of experience. "Inferential epistemic practices," where the conditions include a certain kind of derivation from other beliefs of the subject, constitute another subtype.

Let us say that whenever a belief is justified, it is so because it is formed in certain circumstances, whether this is a certain kind of experience, the possession of certain reasons, or whatever. Thus a belief is justified because the circumstances of its formation are *of a certain kind* and are related in a certain way to the content of that belief. But then a particular belief is justified if and only if we are justified in engaging in a certain epistemic practice, the practice of forming beliefs with a certain kind of content in circumstances of that kind. The question of the justification of an epistemic practice is, we might say, just a generalization over the question of the justification of particular beliefs.[3] In making a claim as to what justifies a particular belief, we are presupposing that a general epistemic practice is justified. It would seem, therefore, that the concept of the justification of epistemic practices is the more basic one. If we know what practices are justified, we will thereby know what it takes for any belief to be justified, but the converse does not hold. If we could know which beliefs are justified without knowing, in at least some of the cases, what it is that justifies them, we would not have the information we need to determine what practices are justified. Because of the close connection between the justification of beliefs and the justification of practices, I shall in the following discussion freely oscillate between speaking of the justification of beliefs and the justification of practices, though the focus will be on the latter.

The first point about the concept of justification is that it is an evaluative concept, in a broad sense in which this is contrasted with "factual" and includes "normative" (of behavior), as well as "evaluative" in a narrower sense in which it contrasts with "normative." To say that *S* is justified in believing that *p* is to imply that there is something all right, satisfactory, in accord with the way things should be, about the fact that *S* believes that *p*. It is to accord *S*'s believing a positive evaluative status.

Second, there is the point that epistemic justification is a matter of degree. One can be more or less justified in holding a certain belief. This is obvious for justification by evidence, where the degree of justification will be some function of the amount and quality of the evidence; but it holds for experiential justification as well. If I seem to see a car at a distance looming up through the fog, I am less justified in supposing that I see a car than I am if I seem to see a car directly in front of me in broad daylight. Thus we must decide what degree of justification we are asking about. Are we simply asking whether religious experience can justify M-beliefs to some degree or other (to at least a minimal degree)? Or are we asking whether religious experience can justify M-beliefs up to a certain higher level, for example, to a degree sufficient for rational acceptance or to a degree sufficient for knowledge (assuming that other requirements for knowledge have been met)? I take it to be obvious that the first version of the question is to be answered in the affirmative. That question can best be considered by taking a situation in which I have no other basis for either accepting or rejecting the belief, and then by asking whether, in that situation, its seeming to me that God is present to me contributes *something* toward my being justified in believing that God is present to me. In other words, if we contrast one who has that experience and one who does not, stipulating that neither person has any other basis for believing that God is or is not present to him, is it not obvious that the first is, at least, less irrational in holding that belief? If anyone is inclined to resist this judgment, I suspect that it is because he is surreptitiously crediting the person with overriding reasons for supposing the belief to be false.

But I am aiming my sights higher than this. I wish to consider the possibility that one's experience can provide justification sufficient for rational acceptance. From now on I shall use the term "justified" for an epistemic status that is that strong. But in thinking about this question we are forced to introduce a hitherto suppressed complication in the concept of direct experiential justification. Let us think again about the application of this notion to sense experience. A direct realist, in one sense of that term, will hold that I may be justified in believing that there is a tree in front of me just by virtue of the fact that I am currently having a sense experience of a certain sort. But even a direct realist will have to recognize that this will happen only in "favorable circumstances." If I am confronted with a complicated arrangement of mirrors, I may not be justified in believing that there is an oak tree in front of me, even though it looks for all the world as if there is. Again, it may look for all the world as if water is running uphill, but the general improbability of this reduces the justification the corresponding belief receives from that experience, to a magnitude below that required for rational acceptance.

What cases like these show is that even where the justification provided by one's experience is of a magnitude sufficient for rational acceptance, this is only defeasibly so. The justification provided is inherently liable to be overridden, cancelled, or *defeated* by stronger considerations to the contrary. As the examples indicate, such considerations have to do with circumstances in which that perceptual experience was acquired (and/or what the subject knows about those circumstances) and with the likelihood of what is believed in the light of our general knowledge of the world. Thus the justification of beliefs about the physical environment that is provided by sense experience is a defeasible or, as we might say, *prima facie* justification. By virtue of having the experience the subject is in a position such that she will be adequately justified in the belief *unless* there are strong enough reasons to the contrary, unless there are *defeaters* of sufficient strength.

The epistemology of religious experience is even more controversial, but it would seem that where religious experience is taken to provide direct experiential justification for M-beliefs, that justification is taken to be defeasible. The mode of production of the experience is not taken into account here to the extent that it is in sense perception, partly because we do not know as much about how such experiences are produced, and partly because we know even less about which modes of production are most likely to yield veridical experiences. But beliefs about the nature and ways of God are often used to override M-beliefs, particularly beliefs as to what God has spoken to one. If I report that God told me to kill all Wittgensteinians, fellow Christians will, no doubt, dismiss the report on the grounds that God would not give me any such injunction as that. I shall take it that religious experience will, at most, provide *prima facie* justification for M-beliefs.

Getting back to practices, this means that we will have to think of both PP and CP as involving not only a regular procedure of forming beliefs on the basis of experience (where the content of the belief is some function of the character of the experience) but also a procedure of inhibiting, abandoning, or modifying those beliefs in the presence of appropriate defeaters. Thus the practice will involve the capacity to identify relevant defeaters and the disposition to modify belief formation accordingly, as well as a disposition to go from experience to belief in certain ways. It would seem that CP displays less uniformity than PP in this regard. To be sure, there is more diversity in PP than many of us suppose, especially if we look beyond the spatiotemporal boundaries of our culture. Without getting into anything very exotic, there is the point that with the advance of science we learn more about the conditions of accurate observation and hence enrich our stock of possible defeaters. We, but not our distant forebears, override the perceptual inclination to believe that the moon is larger near the horizon than near the zenith or that the moon changes radically in shape and size over the course of the month. But, still, it must be admitted that in our culture there is more diversity in what is taken as a defeater in CP. In some cases but not in others what is taken to be revealed by God in the Bible is given a controlling voice; and among those who proceed in this way there are considerable differences in how this revelation is interpreted. In some cases, but not in others, church tradition can provide defeating considerations. To fix our thoughts, let us think of a form of CP that takes its defeaters from the Bible, the classic creeds, and certain elements of tradition. There will still be differences among subsegments of the community of practitioners so defined, but there will be enough commonality to make it a useful construct.

Next let us make it explicit that the justification about which we are asking is an "epistemic" rather than a "moral" or "prudential" justification. Suppose one should hold that we are justified in engaging in PP or in CP because it makes us feel good. Even if this is so, it would not show that we are *epistemically* justified. But why not? What constitutes epistemic justification? How does it differ from other sorts? We can begin to answer these questions by noting that epistemic justification, as the name implies, has something to do with knowledge, or, more broadly, something to do with the aim at attaining truth and avoiding falsity. At a first approximation I am justified in believing that *p* when, from the point of view of that aim, there is something all right, to be approved, about the fact that I believe that *p*. But when we come to spell this out further, we find that a fundamental distinction must be drawn between two different ways of being in an epistemically commendable position.

On the one hand there is what we may call a "normative" concept of epistemic justification ($J_n$), "normative" because it has to do with how we stand vis-à-vis norms that specify our intellectual duties or obligations, obligations that attach to one *qua* cognitive subject, *qua* truth-seeker. Stated most generally, this is the notion of not having violated one's intellectual obligations. We have to say "not having violated" rather than "having fulfilled" because in all normative spheres, not just the epistemic, *being jus-*

*tified* is a negative status; it consists in one's behavior not being in violation of the norms; otherwise put, it consists in what one has done being *permitted* by the relevant norms, rules, or regulations. It does not mean that what one did was *required* by those norms, that it was one's duty. If my expenses on the trip, for taxis, for example, were justified, that means that they were *allowed* by the regulations; it does not mean that I was obliged to take a taxi. If I am justified, as department chairman, in deciding this matter on my own without consulting the executive committee, that implies that I did not violate any regulations in doing so; it does not imply that I was required to decide it on my own. The regulations may have left me a choice in the matter.

If belief and, more generally, epistemic practices are under direct voluntary control, we may think of intellectual obligations as attaching directly to believing. In that case to say that one is normatively justified in believing that *p* would be to say that one's believing that *p* did not *constitute* a violation of an intellectual obligation. We might think, for example, that one is obliged to refrain from believing *p* where one does not have adequate evidence for *p*. Then if one believes that *p* where one does have adequate evidence, one has not violated that obligation in doing so; and so, to that extent, one is in the clear: one is justified in so believing. And to say that one is normatively justified in an epistemic practice would be to say, more generally, that the adoption of a belief like that in those sorts of circumstances does not *constitute* a violation of any intellectual obligation. But if, as it seems to me, belief formation is not, in general, under voluntary control, obligations cannot attach directly to believing. Even so, I do have voluntary control over moves that can influence a particular belief formation—for example, looking for more evidence or selectively exposing myself to evidence—and moves that can affect my general belief-forming habits or tendencies—for example, training myself to be more critical of testimony. If we think of intellectual obligations as attaching directly to these activities that are designed to influence belief formation, we may then think of *S*'s belief that *p* as normatively justified when the fact that *S* believes that *p* is not due to any violation of intellectual obligations (to engage in or refrain from belief-influencing activities). Thus if my belief that Jim has resigned is one that I would not have if I had been doing what could be reasonably expected of me to train myself to be more critical of gossip, then I am not normatively justified in holding that belief. Again we can generalize this to practices. I am normatively justified in engaging in a certain epistemic practice provided that it is not the case that I would not be engaging in it if I had been conducting myself as I should in my activities that are designed to influence my habits of belief formation.

Now for the second sense of epistemic justification. To say that a person is epistemically justified in this second sense is not to assess her position vis-à-vis obligations or duties to *do* anything: it is not to approve of her *behavior*. It is rather to assess her condition as a desirable or a favorable one from an epistemic point of view, vis-à-vis the aim at the attainment of truth and the avoidance of falsity. It is to say that she is in what we may call an "epistemically strong position." Call this an "evaluative" concept ($J_e$), as contrasted with a "normative" concept of justification. *S* is justified in the evaluative sense in holding a certain belief provided that the relevant circumstances in which that belief is held are such that the belief is at least likely to be true. In other terms, being $J_e$ requires that in the class of actual and possible cases in which beliefs like that are or would be held in circumstances like that, the belief is usually true. Much needs to be done to work out what kinds of circumstances are relevant, how to generalize over beliefs, and so on. Pretending that all that has been done, I would like to suggest that what this boils down to is that the way the belief was formed and/or is sustained is a generally reliable one, one that can generally be relied on to produce true rather than false beliefs.[4] Similarly, if an epistemic practice of belief formation (of forming beliefs of certain types under certain sorts of conditions) is $J_e$, then it is a generally reliable practice, one that will in general produce true rather than false beliefs.

To underline the difference between $J_n$ and $J_e$, let us consider some cases in which a practice is justified in the one sense but not in the other. Consider a naive member of an isolated primitive tribe who, along with his fellows, unhesitatingly accepts the traditions of the tribe. That is, he believes that *p* wherever the traditions of the tribe, as recited by the elders, include the assertion that *p*. He is $J_n$ in doing so, for he has no reason whatsoever to doubt these traditions. Everyone he knows accepts them without question, and they do not conflict with anything else he believes. And yet, let us suppose, this is not a reliable procedure of belief formation; and so he is not $J_e$ in engaging in it. Conversely, a procedure may be in fact reliable, though I have strong reasons for regarding it as unreliable and so would not be $J_n$ in engaging in it; to do so would be to ignore those reasons and so would be a violation of an intellectual obligation. Suppose that I have been presented with overwhelming, though spurious, evidence that for about half the time over the last ten years I have, without realizing it, been in a physiological laboratory where my sensory experience was artifically produced. In this case I have strong reasons for supposing that I cannot tell at a given moment whether or not my perceptual experience is being produced in a normal manner; hence I have strong reasons for regarding my perceptual belief-forming processes as unreliable. Nevertheless they are as reliable as any normal person's.

## V

With this background let us tackle the question of whether one can be justified in PP and in CP, and let us begin with $J_n$. In order to get a handle on this question, we will have to determine what intellectual obligations we have vis-à-vis epistemic practices. Since our basic cognitive aims are to come into possession of as much truth as possible and to avoid false beliefs, it would seem that one's basic intellectual obligation vis-à-vis practices of belief formation would be to do what one can (or at least as much as could reasonably be expected of one) to see to it that these practices are as reliable as possible.[5] But this still leaves us with an option between a stronger and a weaker view of this obligation, corresponding to the famous Clifford-James confrontation over the ethics of belief. To oversimplify, Clifford held that we are obligated to refrain from believing that *p* unless we have adequate reasons for that belief, whereas James held that we are permitted to believe that *p* unless we have adequate reasons for supposing it false. Transposing this to the epistemology of practices, the harsher Cliffordian view is that one is obliged to refrain from engaging in a practice unless one has adequate reasons for supposing it to be reliable. Hence one is justified in engaging in a practice *if and only if* one has such reasons. In the absence of sufficient reasons for considering the practice reliable, one is not justified in it. Practices are guilty until proved innocent. While on the more latitudinarian Jamesian view one is justified in engaging in a practice provided one does not have sufficient reasons for regarding it as unreliable. Practices are innocent until proved guilty.[6] Let us take $J_{ns}$ as an abbreviation for 'justified in the normative sense on the stronger (Cliffordian) requirement', and $J_{nw}$ as an abbreviation for 'justified in the normative sense on the weaker (Jamesian) requirement'.

Now let us consider whether we are justified, in one or another sense, in engaging in PP. And let us begin with $J_{nw}$. Except for those who, like Parmenides and Bradley, have argued that there are ineradicable inconsistencies in the conceptual scheme involved in PP, philosophers have not supposed that we can show that sense perception is an unreliable guide to our immediate surroundings. Sceptics about sense perception have generally confined themselves to arguing that we cannot show that sense perception is reliable: that is, they have argued that PP is not $J_{ns}$. I shall assume without further argument that our perceptual practice is $J_{nw}$.

The question of $J_{ns}$ can profitably be combined with the question of $J_e$. Not that they are the same. As pointed out earlier, a practice may *be* $J_e$ even though I lack adequate reasons for supposing it to be, in which case I will not be $J_{ns}$ in engaging in it. And the converse is possible as well. Nevertheless, if I set out to discover whether a practice is $J_e$, that is, whether it *is* reliable, then I will also be investigating the question of whether one *could* be $J_{ns}$ in engaging in that practice. For the first thing I will look into is whether I, or other people, already *have* adequate reasons for supposing it to be reliable. And if I discover reasons not heretofore possessed by any, or some, people, this will at least show that it is possible for those people to become $J_{ns}$. Finally, if I show that the practice is unreliable, this will at least provide a strong presumption against a claim to have adequate reasons for supposing it reliable. For these reasons, and since it is doubtful that the mass of perceptual practitioners have had adequate reasons for the reliability of the practice, I shall concentrate on considering whether PP is $J_e$.

It would seem that PP is what we might call a "basic practice," one that constitutes our basic access to its subject matter. We can learn about our physical environment only by perceiving it, by receiving reports of the perceptions of others, and by carrying out inferences from what we learn in these first two ways. We cannot know anything a priori about these matters, nor do we have any other sort of experiential access to the physical world. If this is correct, then the attempt to determine the reliability of perceptual practice faces problems very different from those faced by an attempt to determine the reliability of some restricted method or procedure that is imbedded in some wider practice, the rest of which is taken for granted. Suppose I ask whether the process that led up to my present visual perception of a typewriter is of a sort that is generally reliable. Here I am only putting this particular process in question; I am taking for granted the reliability of PP generally, and I am assuming what we suppose ourselves to have learned about the physical world from that practice and from reasoning based on its products. In this case it is certainly possible to obtain evidence to settle the question. Again, if I ask, in the same spirit, about the reliability of the practice of using mercury thermometers for certain kinds of temperature readings, there would again be a very favorable prospect of settling the matter. In all such cases the rest of the total practice in which these procedures are imbedded (or enough of the rest) is assumed to be reliable; hence we can use those other subpractices, and what has been learned from them, to investigate the point in question. But where a total basic practice is under investigation, we have no such resources. Since this practice, and what is based on it, constitutes our sole access to the subject matter, we cannot carry out a direct investigation of its reliability by comparing its deliverances with how the subject matter is, since we have no other way of determining the latter. How, then, can we proceed?

Since this issue has been in the forefront of the European philosophical consciousness for several hundred years, a number of ideas have been broached that could be construed as attempts to provide such a justification, though the question has rarely been put in just these terms. In the interests of getting to my own positive suggestions I shall just issue a few *obiter dicta* concerning a few samples.

1. There are straightforward attempts at justification, typified by Descartes' appeal to the goodness of God, that make use of premises that have not been obtained from PP itself and hence do not suffer from circularity. However, they are all dubitable, at best, either with respect to the premises or with respect to the support those premises give the conclusion.

2. A recent survey of my colleagues revealed a considerable degree of support for "transcendental" arguments of the Kantian or the Strawsonian type, in which it is claimed that the objectification of sense experience by use of the physical-object scheme is necessary for us to have any experience of anything, or for us to have any conception of ourselves, or. . . . I think that all these arguments exhibit various sorts of difficulties in detail. But even if one of them should succeed, it would still, at best, have shown that our customary perceptual practice is even more deeply imbedded in other aspects of our cognitive practices than we had supposed. Or, alternatively, it would show that we are unable to envisage, in any thoroughgoing way, any alternative to this familiar practice. But both of these results would fall short of showing that this practice is a reliable way of finding out how something actually is.

3. Finally, there are various more popular "pragmatic" arguments. "This practice 'works'; it serves as a basis for accurate prediction; it permits general agreement;" and so on. The basic trouble with all this is that it is blatantly circular. We have to use PP to determine that the predictions we make on the basis of perceptual beliefs often turn out to be correct, and to determine that there is a large measure of agreement in perceptual beliefs. We do not discover this by using a crystal ball or being told by an angel.

This survey would indicate that prospects are not good for providing adequate noncircular reasons for regarding PP as reliable. If no such reasons can be provided, we cannot be $J_{ns}$ in that practice. It does not follow, of course, that the practice is not reliable, and hence it does not follow that the practice is not $J_e$; but it does follow that we cannot have adequate reasons for supposing it to be $J_e$. This leaves us with $J_{nw}$. Since, so far as I know, no one has unearthed any sufficient reason for regarding

PP as unreliable, I shall take it that we do lack such reasons, and hence that the practice is $J_{nw}$.

If we take it that being $J_{nw}$ in engaging in PP is enough to make it reasonable for us to do so, and if we generalize this to all epistemic practices, we will arrive at a general perspective on epistemology that has been enunciated by various thinkers in the last two hundred years but, to my mind, never more persuasively than by the eighteenth-century Scottish philosopher Thomas Reid. According to Reid we have several ultimate sources of belief. These include at least "self-consciousness" (in the sense of awareness of one's own current conscious states), sense perception, memory, rational intuition (that is, "seeing" with the mind's eye that certain things are self-evidently so, for example, two quantities equal to the same quantity are equal to each other), and reasoning, which itself is of various sorts. All normal human beings are endowed by God or nature, or both, with a strong tendency to trust these sources, that is, to form firm beliefs on their basis. Moreover, we do this, for the most part, unhesitatingly and uncritically, though we may question one of these sources on a particular occasion if there is special reason to do so. But are we rationally justified in according such trust? What reason do we have for regarding these sources as reliable? When we consider this question generally, as we did above for sense perception, we see that we are unable to give an adequate noncircular justification for any of the sources. Our only reason for supposing that memory is generally reliable is that its past track record is a good one, and we have no way of ascertaining that without relying on our memory. Again, it is obviously impossible to *argue* for the reliability of reasoning without relying on reasoning to do so. And so on.

Thus, if we are to have any chance of acquiring knowledge, we must simply go along with our natural reactions of trust with respect to at least some basic sources of belief, provided we lack sufficient reason for regarding them as unreliable. In the above terms we must be content with being $J_{nw}$. And if some, why not all? Of course we could, if we chose, accept some sources without any positive basis, such as intuition and reasoning, and then require that other candidates be certified by the former, that is, require $J_{ns}$ for these latter. This is, in effect, what Descartes and many other philosophers have done, when, for example, they held sense perception suspect until its reliability could be shown to follow from self-evident premises. But, as Reid points out, this is to be guilty of arbitrary partiality. Why accept intuition and reasoning without any basis, while refusing to do the same for sense perception? Moreover, these attempts have never met with success. In any event nature has not left us any real choice with respect to the sources listed above. In the absence of special reasons for doubt, we do accept the deliverances of sense and memory willy-nilly, whatever our reflective philosophical views. These matters are too important to be left to the vagaries of philosophical reasoning.

## VI

Now back to our initial question about the justifiability of CP. We have seen that $J_{nw}$ is the most we can have for PP and for our other commonly accepted, basic epistemic practices. How does CP stand in this regard? As for $J_{ns}$, I shall just assume without argument that we no more have an adequate noncircular reason for supposing CP to be reliable than we have in the case of PP. Here, too, although the practice may well be reliable, and so be $J_e$, we have no sufficient *reason* for judging this to be the case. And so CP is not $J_{ns}$, and we lack sufficient basis for supposing it to be $J_e$. If, then, CP is $J_{nw}$, it will be in just the same epistemic position as PP and other commonly accepted, basic epistemic practices; and it will be just as rational to take Christian experience to provide *prima facie* justification for M-beliefs as it is to take sense experience to provide *prima facie* justification for perceptual beliefs. To be sure, we cannot say of CP, as I said of the other practices just mentioned, that it is unhesitatingly engaged in by all normal human beings or that religious experience forces theistic belief on all of us willy-nilly. But this is just a matter of counting noses. If one is put off by that difference, one is succumbing to the "big is good" mentality we are supposed to have outgrown, or perhaps to an egalitarian prejudice in epistemology that would have it that what is not shared by all sorts and conditions of men cannot be the real thing. But why suppose that every valid source of knowledge is equally open to all? Think of the considerable number who do engage in CP. And suppose that they, and we, have no adequate reason for supposing this practice to be unreliable. How, then, could it be denied that *they* are as epistemically justified in this practice as all of us are in the more widely dispersed practices we have been considering?

But we get this conclusion only if CP really is $J_{nw}$. Let us consider more carefully whether this is the case. What reasons could we have for regarding CP as unreliable?

First, we can have the most direct and unquestionably relevant reason for regarding an epistemic practice as unreliable if we have ascertained that its outputs are generally incorrect, or even if we have ascertained that they are not generally correct. We have this kind of reason for regarding many "unscientific" methods of weather prediction to be unreliable. But we can have this kind of reason only where we have some other access to the domain about which the practice in question yields beliefs. In the case of predicting weather by examining entrails, we can simply wait and see what the weather is, thereby using a more deeply entrenched practice as a check on the one in question. Now to the extent that CP yields beliefs about matters that we also have some other, perhaps more favored, way of discovering, its unreliability could be shown in the same way. Perhaps something like this is involved when fundamentalist Christians take it on the "inward testimony of the Holy Spirit" that the Bible is the word of God and then suppose that in the Bible God is telling us about the physical history and constitution of the universe. However, one who engages in CP need not get involved in anything like that. I shall restrict this discussion to a kind of CP that only yields beliefs about God, His nature, and His doings, the truth or falsity of which are not assessable on empirical or scientific grounds.

That still leaves the possibility that we might establish conclusions by philosophical reasoning that contradicts all or many of the products of CP. For example, we might demonstrate the nonexistence of God. Or, contrariwise, we might be able to show that God's nature is such that He could not be doing what He is frequently represented in CP as doing. Finally we might be able to show that CP yields a system of belief that is ineradicably internally inconsistent. (I am not speaking of isolated and remediable inconsistencies that continually pop up in every area of thought and experience.) I do not believe that we are able to accomplish any of this, but I will not have time to argue the point. Instead I will pass on to some other putative grounds for unreliability, the relevance of which is harder to assess.

I believe that many people are inclined to take CP to be discredited by certain ways in which it differs from PP, by the lack of certain salient features of PP. These include the following:

1. Within PP there are standard ways of checking the accuracy of any particular perceptual belief. If, by looking at a cup, I form the belief that there is coffee in it, I can check this belief for accuracy by smelling or tasting the contents; I can get other observers to look at it, smell it, or taste it; I can run chemical tests on it and get other people to do so.
2. By engaging in PP we can discover regularities in the behavior of objects putatively observed, and on this basis we can, to a certain extent, effectively predict the course of events.
3. Capacity for PP, and practice of it, is found universally among normal adult human beings.
4. All normal adult human beings, whatever their culture, use basically the same conceptual scheme in objectifying their sense experience.[7]

It is the first of these features that has been most often invoked in this connection by twentieth-century philosophers. C. B. Martin, in a widely discussed essay, "A Religious Way of Knowing," reprinted as a chapter in his book *Religious Belief*,[8] argues that since there is no such "society of checks and tests" involved in religious experience, we are thereby prevented from taking religious experience to be cognition of anything beyond itself. But though 1 has been focused on more than the others, I think we can see that 1 is just a special case of 2. For our standard checking procedures in perceptual practice presuppose that we know a good deal about the ways in which things can be expected to behave in the physical world. Consider the appeal to other observers. Suppose I think I see a fir tree across the street from my house. What would count as intersubjective corroboration? Surely not *any* report of seeing a fir tree. If someone reports seeing a fir tree in Nepal, that will not tend to show that there is a fir tree across from my house. Nor will the failure of someone in Nepal, or across town, to see a fir tree have any tendency to disconfirm my report. Nor would it disconfirm my report if a blind man or one wholly preoccupied with other matters stands just where I was standing and fails to see a fir tree. The point is, of course, that only observers that satisfy certain conditions as to location, condition, state of the environment (enough light), and so on can qualify as either confirming or disconfirming my report. And how do we know what conditions to specify? We do it in the light of presumed regularities in the interaction of physical objects and sentient subjects. Persons in certain circumstances, and only in those circumstances, will count as possible confirmers or disconfirmers of my claim, because, given what we know about the way things go in the psychophysical world, it is only persons in such circumstances that could be expected to see a fir tree if there is one there. Similar points can be made about the other modes of testing. Since 1 holds of a practice only if 2 holds, one can concentrate on the latter.

It is clear that theistic practice does not exhibit these features.

1 and 2. Religious experience does not put us in a position to make predictions about the divine, despite the persistent claims of apocalyptic groups. God, so far as we can tell from our experience, does not operate in accordance with any regularities discernible by us. We are not able to anticipate God's punishment or forgiveness, the granting or withdrawing of His grace. No more are we able to anticipate where, when, or under what conditions He will enter into a human being's experience. Hence we are not in a position to devise checking procedures, to specify what experiences some other subject would have under certain conditions if what the first subject reported of God is correct.

3. CP is not a common possession of mankind in the way PP is.

This divides into two points. (A) Many people do not engage in CP at all. This includes both those who do not take themselves to be experiencing any divine or transcendent reality at all (some of whom are nominal adherents of Christianity and other religions) and those who objectify religious experience with schemes quite different from that of Christian theology. (B) Most of the practitioners are aware of the presence of God only fleetingly and, for the most part, uncertainly. Awareness of God is usually a dim, elusive matter, lacking in detail and vividness and eminently subject to doubt. It is like seeing something in a dense fog or, in a more traditional phrase, through a glass darkly. All this is in sharp contrast to the clarity, detail, persistence, and irresistible convincingness of sense perception.

4. It hardly requires mention that religious experience gets objectified in terms of radically different conceptual schemes in different religious traditions. The same general sort of experience that a Christian takes to be an awareness of the presence of a supreme personal deity might be taken in Hindu circles as an experienced identity of the self with a supreme undifferentiated unity. Where individuals experience God as communicating something to them, these messages will differ in ways that, generally but not invariably, correspond to the locally dominant theology.

One could quibble over whether the contrast is as sharp as is alleged. Questions could be raised about both sides of the putative divide. On the PP side is it really true that all cultures have objectified sense experience in the same way? Many anthropologists have thought not. And what about the idea that all *normal* adult human beings engage in the same perceptual practice? Are we not loading the dice by taking participation in what we regard as standard perceptual practice as our basic criterion for normality? On the CP side is it really the case that this practice reveals no regularities to us, or only that they are very different from regularities in the physical world? What about the point that God is faithful to His promises? Or that the pure in heart will see God? However, I believe that when all legitimate quibbles have been duly registered there will still be very significant differences between the two practices in these respects. So rather than contest the factual allegations, I will concentrate on the *de jure* issue as to what bearing these differences have on epistemic status.

If the lack of these features is to prevent CP from being $J_{nw}$, then that lack will have to constitute an adequate reason for regarding CP as unreliable.[9] And why should we suppose that? I am prepared to agree that 1–4 are desiderata for an epistemic practice. If we were shaping the world to our heart's desire, I dare say that we would arrange for our practices to exhibit these features.[10] Where we have 3, each of us can feel reassured about the practice by noting that everyone else does it. Where we have 2 and 1, we cannot only acquire the handle on prediction and explanation that we get from a knowledge of regularities, but we are able to distinguish effectively between correct and incorrect reports. Where 4 is present, we are saved the agonizing necessity of choosing between radically divergent conceptual schemes and correspondingly radically different beliefs about the subject matter. Things go more smoothly, more satisfyingly, from a cognitive point of view where these features are exhibited. Since PP possesses these virtues and CP does not, the former is, to that extent and in that way, superior from a cognitive point of view.[11] But granting all this, why should we suppose that the lack of these features indicates unreliability? Why suppose that any practice that lacks *these* cognitive virtues will be, or will be likely to be, unreliable, that is, fail to yield generally correct truths about its subject matter? Why suppose that the lack of those virtues carries with it the lack of this further virtue?

I suspect that one who supposes this to be the case is at least implicitly reasoning as follows: "The possession of 1–4 by PP gives us reason for regarding it as reliable. Hence the lack of these features of CP tends to show it to be unreliable." If this is the way the argument goes, it is defective both with respect to its premise and with respect to the relation between premise and conclusion.

First, the fact that PP possesses these features does not give us a reason for taking it to be reliable, for a reason already brought out on page 118 with respect to feature 2. Our only access to these features is through PP itself. How do we know that PP puts us in a position to make accurate predictions? More specifically, how do we know that the predictions it enables us to make are often correct? Well, if the prediction was that it would rain here tomorrow, we wait and *see* whether it is raining here tomorrow. How else would we determine whether the prediction was correct? And how do we know that different cultures agree, by and large, in the way they objectify sense experience? Again there would seem to be no alternative to relying on observations of the speech, behavior, and written records of various cultures. And so for the other features. We simply have no way of determining these or any other features that are not based on the use of PP, that is, that do not involve relying on PP, taking it to be a reliable source of information about the world. Hence if we tried to take these features as a reason for judging PP to be reliable, we would be involved in a vicious circularity. We would be accepting PP as reliable in order to obtain reasons for accepting it as reliable.

Still, I do not believe that this is the end of the matter. We are plagued with circularity here only because of the contingent fact that we have no other access to these facts about PP. Suppose we did; suppose that we had some power of intellectual intuition that enabled us to "clearly and distinctly perceive" that various practices, including PP, exhibit various essential features, including 1–4. In that case we could use at least some of these features as reasons for regarding PP as reliable. I am not sure about 3, but it would seem that 2 (and its appendage, 1) and 4 would constitute reasons of some significant weight. As for 2, why should it be that by reasoning from what we learn about physical objects in PP we are enabled to anticipate accurately the behavior of those objects if it were not the case that PP yields accurate information as a basis for that reasoning? There would seem to be a rather strong *argument to the best explanation* here. The most natural and plausible explanation of our success would be that we are reasoning from generally accurate information. Again, consider 4. Why should it be the case that different cultures objectify sense experience in pretty much the same way unless that objectification is in all these cases under the effective control of the subject matter itself? Why should a lot of independent, subjectively spawned processes of objectification converge in this way? Again we would seem to have a rather strong argument to the best explanation.

Now in spite of this, since we do not in fact have any alternative access to these features, the features do not provide *us* with adequate reasons for judging PP to be reliable. But since, as we have just contended, they would provide us with such reasons if it were not for the circularity, we must allow that there is some strong connection between these features and reliability, such that if we could ascertain the features without reliance on PP, they would provide us with adequate reasons for an imputation of reliability. We might express that connection by saying that these features (with the possible exception of 3) *manifest* or *evince* reliability. They are (reliable) signs of reliability. They betoken its presence. They are ways in which the reliability of a practice shows itself; they constitute a payoff of the reliability of the practice.

We can restate the anti-CP argument in these terms. Instead of alleging that 1–4 constitute an adequate *reason* for taking PP to be reliable, we will just say that 1–4 manifest or betoken reliability. Since CP lacks these manifestations, it will have to be judged unreliable. The denigrator of CP is now no longer in the position of claiming that the possession of 1–4 by PP gives us an adequate reason for regarding it as reliable, but only that their lack by CP gives us an adequate reason for regarding it as unreliable.

Now that the premise has been cleaned up, we can concentrate on the premise-conclusion relationship. Why should we suppose that the lack of *these* manifestations of reliability gives us an adequate reason for a judgment of unreliability? We must be careful to distinguish between a lack of certain possible reasons for a judgment of reliability and a reason for a judgment of unreliability. The lack of 1–4 means that we lack certain reasons for the reliability of CP that we might conceivably have had, reasons that we would have for the reliability of PP were it not for limitations in the ways we can ascertain the presence of these features. But does it follow that this gives us a sufficient reason for judging CP to be unreliable? Let us approach this question by considering generally the conditions under which X's lack of some manifestation, M, of P gives us an adequate reason for supposing that X lacks P.

First, it provides such a reason when M is a necessary condition of P. Here the absence of M provides a conclusive reason for a judgment of not-P. Thus, since having the sum of the angles equal to 180 degrees is a necessary condition of being a Euclidean triangle, the lack of this property by a figure constitutes a conclusive reason for denying that the figure is a Euclidean triangle. Second, it would still provide an adequate, though not an absolutely conclusive, reason provided we had good reason to suppose it very unlikely that X could be P without exhibiting M, that is, provided that M is to be expected given P. Thus, even if turning blue litmus paper red is not, strictly speaking, a necessary condition of being an acid, we have very good reason for thinking it very unlikely for something to be an acid without reacting in this way; and so the absence of this reaction is an adequate reason for denying that something is an acid.

Now let us consider a case in which these conditions do not hold, and hence where the absence of an M, or a group of Ms, does not constitute an adequate reason for denying that X is P. One way in which a person shows herself to be a good philosopher is by publishing numerous philosophical works that are frequently commented on by other philosophers. And where this is the case, we thereby have a good reason to regard the person as a good philosopher. But if X has not published numerous works, or if she has but they have not frequently been commented on by other philosophers, this does not give us a good reason for denying that she is a good philosopher. Such publication is obviously not a necessary condition of being a good philosopher, nor do we have reason to think it very unlikely that one would be a good philosopher without satisfying those conditions. Many of us are acquainted with a number of good philosophers who do not publish frequently. In these cases we lack the specified reason for taking the person to be a good philosopher, but that does not give us an adequate reason for denying that the person is a good philosopher.

Now how about the case in which X is an epistemic practice, M is features 1–4, and P is reliability? First, it seems clear that the conjunction of 1–4 does not constitute a strictly necessary condition of reliability. Surely it is possible that a practice should consistently yield true beliefs even though it does not give us a basis for prediction, and even though it is not shared by all normal human beings. As for the first of these, (2), it might give us correct information about the disposition and activity of objects of a certain kind at particular moments, even though the behavior of those objects is not regular enough to be predictable, or even though the patterns exhibited by the behavior of these objects is too complex for us to grasp. As for the second, (3), why suppose that reliability is tied to universal distribution? This is no more than an egalitarian prejudice that is more at home in politics than in epistemology. Surely it is quite conceivable that a highly reliable procedure for acquiring information should have been acquired only by a small minority of the human race. And so for the rest.

Second, do we have reason to think that it is highly unlikely that an epistemic practice should be reliable without exhibiting 1–4? Is this a *general* feature of reliable practices, or is it rather a distinctive mark of PP and perhaps a few other practices? Several considerations push us in the latter direction. First, what about the practice of pure mathematics? Here we have a highly reliable practice that does not put us in a position to make predictions. "But that is because it does not deal with entities that are in different conditions at different times, and so here the activity of prediction has no place." Precisely. And if we generalize that point, we can say that whether a practice could be expected to yield prediction, if reliable, depends on the kind of subject matter with which it deals. In a moment we shall apply this principle to the discussion of CP. Second, the epistemic practices involved in the development of mathematics and the physical sciences are, as a whole, not engaged in by all normal human beings and so lack feature 3, even though they are highly reliable. To this it may be replied that this does show that 3 is not to be expected for any reliable epistemic practice, but it may still be expectable for an experiential epistemic practice, any practice of forming beliefs directly from experience, beliefs concerning what the experience is taken to be an experience of. For, so the claim will go, scientific practice goes beyond our universally shared PP, not on its observational side, but only with respect to its higher-level conceptual scheme and the kinds of reasoning and explanation that makes possible. This claim will, of course, be hotly contested by such recent philosophers of science as Hanson, Kuhn, and Feyerabend, who argue that a particular scientific practice involves distinctive ways of perceiving, distinctive ways of going from experience to belief, as well as distinctive modes of explanation and hypothesis formation. But even if that is not granted, there are still less controversial cases of reliable experiential practices that are not universally shared. Consider wine tasting or the kind of aural discrimination that an orchestral conductor has. The former has a reliable way of forming beliefs, directly from experience, about the vintages of wines; the latter has a similar capacity for telling which instrument is out of tune when a number are playing simultaneously. Are we to deny the reliability of these procedures on the ground that they are exercised by a tiny minority of the population? Reflection on cases like these shows us that we are really picking out a sort of common denominator of PP when we judge it to be universally shared by all normal adult human beings. If we were to discriminate perceptual practices more finely, we would find many that are reserved for elites.

Finally consider 4, and let us restrict ourselves to experiential practices. Is it to be expected that any reliable mode of objectification of a certain range of experience (involving the use of a certain conceptual scheme) be such that anyone, or almost anyone, who objectifies experience from the same range uses the same conceptual scheme? Or is this a special feature of PP as it exists in the Westernized world of today? I believe that a careful survey of the whole range of human culture over space and time would reveal that the presently dominant mode of objectifying sense experience is the outcome of a long development in the course of which it had many rivals. It is thought by many anthropologists that events which we conceptualize in matter-of-fact, physicalistic terms have been seen in many cultures as involving spirits, magical powers, demonic forces, and so on. No doubt this is a very controversial area, and many critics deny that there are such differences in modes of perception. But at the very least it is not clear that the presently dominant mode of PP has not had prominent alternatives in the past. And if it has, then the present relative uniformity is a feature of a certain stage of development rather than something that is to be expected whenever a reliable experiential practice is found. Hence, at the very least it is not clear that it is very unlikely for a reliable experiential practice to exist alongside alternative modes of objectification of the same range of experience.

I take it that these considerations suffice to dispose of the claim that the lack of 1–4 constitutes an adequate reason for regarding CP as unreliable. We have seen that the possession of 1–4 by PP is best seen as a rather special situation that pertains specifically to certain fundamental aspects of that particular practice in this particular historical-cultural situation rather than as an instance of what is to be expected of *any* reliable epistemic practice. But it may help to put flesh on this skeleton if we consider briefly how CP in particular might be reliable in the absence of 1–4.

The basic point I will be making is this. The reality CP claims to put us in touch with is conceived to be vastly different from the physical environment. Why should not the sorts of procedures required to put us in effective cognitive touch with this reality be equally different? Why suppose that the distinctive features of PP set an appropriate standard for the cognitive approach to God? I shall sketch out a possible state of affairs in which CP is quite trustworthy while lacking 1–4, and then suggest that we have no reason to suppose that this state of affairs does not obtain.

Suppose, then, that (A) God is too different from created beings, too "wholly other," for us to be able to grasp any regularities in His behavior. Suppose further that (B) for the same reason we can only attain the faintest, sketchiest, and most insecure grasp of what God is like. Finally, suppose that (C) God has decreed that a human being will be aware of His presence in any clear and unmistakable fashion only when certain special and difficult conditions are satisfied. If all this is the case, then it is the reverse of surprising that CP should lack 1–4, even if it does involve a genuine experience of God. It would lack 1–2 because of (A). It is quite understandable that it should lack 4 because of (B). If our cognitive powers are not fitted to frame an adequate conception of God, it is not at all surprising that there should be wide variation in attempts to do so. This is what typically happens in science when investigators are grappling with a phenomenon no one really understands. A variety of models, analogues, metaphors, hypotheses, hunches are propounded, and it is impossible to secure universal agreement. 3 is missing because of (C). If very difficult conditions are set, it is not surprising that few are chosen. Now it is compatible with (A)–(C) that (D) religious experience should, in general, constitute a genuine awareness of the divine; that (E) although any particular articulation of such an experience might be mistaken to a greater or lesser extent, indeed even though all such articulations might miss the mark to some extent, still such judgments will, for the most part, contain some measure of truth; and that (F) God's designs contain provision for correction and refinement, for increasing the accuracy of the beliefs derived from religious experience. If something like (A)–(F) is the case, then CP is trustworthy even though it lacks features 1–4. This is a conceivable way in which CP would constitute a road to the truth, while differing from PP in respects 1–4. If (A)–(F) represents the way it is with God and our situation vis-à-vis God, then the absence of 1–4 does not betoken unreliability of CP, nor would their presence betoken reliability of CP. Quite the contrary. If this is the way things are, then if an epistemic practice were to lead us to suppose that we had discovered regular patterns in the divine behavior or that divine activity is equally discernible by all, that would be a reason for regarding the practice as *unreliable*. Therefore, unless we have adequate reason for supposing that (A)–(F) does not obtain, we are not warranted in taking the lack of 1–4 to be an adequate reason for a judgment of untrustworthiness.

Moreover, it is not just that (A)–(C) constitute a bare possibility. In the practice of CP we seem to learn that this is the way things are. As for (A) and (B) it is the common teaching of all the higher religions that God is of a radically different order of being from finite substances and, therefore, that we cannot expect to attain the grasp of His nature and His doings that we have of worldly objects. As for (C) it is a basic theme in Christianity, and in other religions as well, that one finds God within one's experience, to any considerable degree, only as one progresses in the spiritual life. God is not available for *voyeurs.* Awareness of God, and understanding of His nature and His will for us, is not a purely cognitive achievement; it requires the involvement of the whole person; it takes a practical commitment and a practice of the life of the spirit, as well as the exercise of cognitive faculties. "Blessed are the pure in heart, for they shall see God." "If we love one another, God dwells in us." God is always present; we do not have to travel to distant climes or distant planets to see Him and enjoy His presence. But He reveals Himself clearly, unmistakably, and in detail, only to those who have responded to His call, have made a stable commitment to Him, have put Him at the center of their lives, and have opened themselves to His influence.

To be sure, if in the last paragraph I were arguing for the reliability of CP by alleging that (A)–(C) obtain, then that argument would be vitiated with circularity, since we have no reason for supposing that (A)–(C) obtain, apart from assuming the reliability of CP or some analogous religious epistemic practice. But that was not the point. In calling attention to the fact that CP yields (A)–(C) I was merely reinforcing the negative point that we lack adequate reason for supposing that these conditions do not obtain. So far from that being the case, insofar as any epistemic practice claims to tell us anything about the matter, what it tells us is that they do obtain. Thus the basic point is still the negative one. We do not have adequate reason for supposing that (A)–(F) do not obtain, and, therefore, we are not justified in taking the absence of 1–4 to provide an adequate reason for the unreliability of CP.[12]

## VII

Suppose the points I have made so far are granted. More specifically, suppose it to be granted that a fully reflective, knowledgeable person in our society can be $J_{nw}$ in engaging in CP and that she cannot be justified in any other sense in engaging in PP and other commonly accepted, basic epistemic practices. Let us suppose it granted, furthermore, that CP yields a picture of its subject matter that is such as to tend to protect it from imputations of unreliability and so, in this way, is self-supporting. Nevertheless, one might still feel the need for some further recommendation of CP. Granted that we cannot reasonably expect to be able to develop a cogent noncircular argument for the reliability of CP, one still might wonder if there is some way in which CP "proves itself," as PP does with its payoffs of prediction and control of the course of events. Those are the fruits of PP with which it rewards its devotees. Are there analogous fruits of the practice of CP, fruits which provide its devotees with a token of its authenticity that may serve to encourage them to persevere?

Perceptual practice proves itself, insofar as it does, by providing us with a "map" of the physical and social environment that enables us to find our way around in it, to anticipate the course of events, and to adjust our behavior to what we encounter so as to satisfy our needs and achieve our ends. This is the basic function of sense perception in our lives, and it carries out that function with reasonable success, as it itself testifies. To discover the appropriate fruits of the Christian enterprise, we have to ask what its basic purpose or function is. It is clear that it is not primarily a theoretical or speculative function, any more than in the former case, but it is not the same kind of practical function either. It is rather the transformation of the individual into what God intended him to be. This is what, from within the Christian life, its basic goal is revealed to be. It would seem, then, that Christian practice proves itself insofar as it enables the individual to transform himself, or to be transformed, in ways that when they occur will be seen by the individual as supremely fulfilling, as the actualization of his real nature, as what God had planned for him.

At this point it may help us to bring in another epistemological practice hitherto unmentioned, namely, interpersonal perception, our awareness of other persons as persons. There is controversy over whether to regard this as an autonomous practice or simply as a department of perceptual practice, but I shall adopt the former view. That is, I shall suppose that we have a practice of objectifying certain ranges of our experience in terms of the presence, condition, characteristics, and activities of other persons, and that this practice can no more be justified from the outside than any of the others we have been considering. It is, in a way, intermediate between PP and CP. In particular, and this is the point I want to stress at the moment, its internal self-justification is not so purely in terms of predictive efficacy as is PP. To be sure, by perceiving what we do of other persons we are thereby enabled to anticipate their behavior to some extent, and this is of pragmatic value. But persons are notoriously less predictable than things, and the value of this practice for our lives is not restricted to that payoff. To compensate for this relative unpredictability there is the possibility of entering into communication, fellowship, competition, and so on with other persons. And, most basically, that is what this practice enables us to do. We might, analogously, rephrase the above statement about the function of CP by saying that it enables us to enter into communication with God and thereby to become what God has intended us to become.

Please note that I am not suggesting that we can justify particular Christian beliefs by pointing out that one will become a better person if he accepts them or anything of the sort. I am rather suggesting that the feature just imputed to CP is a favorable one, one that enables it to satisfy our basic needs.

But *does* Christian practice prove itself in this way? It follows from points that I have been repeating too often that this cannot be decided except from inside, though outsiders can find out something about this from hearing what insiders say, seeing what they do, and reading what they write. That is the stance I will be taking. And at this point I must make explicit something that has been suppressed, or at least unmentioned, up to this point. It is really inappropriate to compare the situation of the ordinary Christian believer, even the serious, devout, and committed Christian believer, vis-à-vis CP with the situation of the normal adult human being vis-à-vis PP. For we are all masters of the latter practice. We emerged from our apprenticeship in early childhood, long before we reached the stage of philosophical reflection on these matters. But in Christian practice we are, almost all of us, at the stage of early infancy, just beginning to learn to distinguish the other reality from ourselves, just beginning to learn to recognize the major outlines of the landscape, and, one should add, just beginning to learn to respond to them appropriately. Hence we must look outside our own experience to the tiny minority that qualify as masters of the spiritual life, both for some intimation of what mastery of this practice is like and for an answer to the question of whether this enterprise proves itself by its fruits. We cannot hope to arrive at a definitive answer to that question from the outside. Of course there is a remedy for that—to get inside. But that is an arduous and time-consuming task, not one to be attempted in the course of an essay. Meanwhile we must glean such hints as we can from the lives, works, and thoughts of the likes of Mother Teresa of Calcutta as to what it is to be more than babes in the experience of God, and as to what it is to respond to this experience in the ways it indicates.

But I fear that the course of the argument has led me into a region that calls for the expertise of a preacher or a spiritual director rather than that of a philosopher, and so I must take my leave.

## NOTES

1. This position is often associated with Karl Popper. See, for example, his *The Logic of Scientific Discovery* (London: Hutchinson & Co., 1959), chapter 1, section 6. It should be noted, however, that Popper puts this forward only as a necessary condition for an assertion's counting as a part of *empirical science.*

2. You may call them "doxastic" or "cognitive" practices if you prefer.

3. Note that the relationship would be less close if we were concerned, as we are not, with the justification of the *belief* that the practice is justified or that it is reliable. We are not talking about being justified in any such higher-level *belief* about the practice. One might be justified in *engaging* in the practice without even having any such belief.

4. And not just that the practice has a good track record up to now; rather it is a lawlike truth that beliefs formed in accordance with that practice, in those kinds of circumstances, are at least likely to be true.

This formulation can be weakened in various ways without violating the spirit of the conception. If we want to allow that perceptual beliefs about the physical environment are, by and large, justified in this evaluative sense, while admitting that they may all be somewhat off the mark, we can weaken "true" to "closely approximating the truth" and further require the practice to include procedures for progressively correcting and refining these first approximations.

5. Note that although $J_n$ and $J_e$ are nonequivalent extensionally as well as intensionally, the above point indicates a crucial conceptual connection between the two. Roughly speaking, to be $J_n$ is to have done as much as could reasonably be expected of one to see to it that one is $J_e$.

6. In giving these formulations I have been making the simplifying assumption that we have complete (direct or indirect) control over what epistemic practices we engage in. If that is the case, then when on the stronger version I have an obligation to do what I can to avoid engaging in practice P because I lack adequate reason for regarding it as reliable, that will be an obligation to avoid P; and so it will be true that I am justified in engaging in P *iff* I have adequate reason to regard it as reliable. We can generalize the formulations so as to avoid reliance on this assumption by simply putting lack of control as another alternative. Thus the stronger version would become: *S* is justified in engaging in P *iff* either (a) *S* has adequate reason for regarding P as reliable or (b) *S* is unable to prevent himself from engaging in P.

7. In attributing these features to PP we are enriching our conception of that practice by including the storage of perceptual beliefs in memory and various kinds of reasonings from those beliefs, as well as their initial formation. We may enlarge our conception of CP in a similar way and even include PP in CP as well. Then in considering whether CP possesses these features we will be thinking of the distinctive portion of CP by virtue of which it "goes beyond" PP.

8. C. B. Martin, *Religious Belief* (Ithaca, N.Y.: Cornell University Press, 1959).

9. To be sure, even if it does constitute an adequate reason it will not follow that no one can be $J_{nw}$ in engaging in CP. For there may well be persons

who do not know that CP lacks these features. Such a person will not have an adequate reason (at least not this adequate reason) for taking CP to be unreliable. Normative justification of practices, like normative justification of beliefs, is situation relative. What I am justified in believing or doing may not be the same as what you are justified in believing or doing. In thinking that these lacks would inhibit $J_{nw}$ if they were an adequate reason for unreliability, we are thinking of persons who are fully cognizant of the relevant facts.

10. At least those practices that deal with objects that act or change through time. Otherwise 2 would be inapplicable.

11. In fact, if we could have things our own way we would, no doubt, bring it about that PP exhibits these features to a higher degree than it does. Our perception, and reasoning thereon, could conceivably reveal regularities to us much more readily and extensively than it does; and if it did then, by the same considerations we would be even better off. And would we not have been better off if there had not been such divergencies as have existed between ways of objectifying sense experience in different cultures?

12. There is also the following subsidiary point. Since CP yields the conclusion that (A)–(C) hold, if we were to take it that they do not hold, in the absence of overriding reason for supposing them not to hold, we would be begging the question against CP. We would be presupposing that it is unreliable in the course of arriving at a judgment on the matter.

# Can Belief in God Be Rational If It Has No Foundations?

Nicholas Wolterstorff

Central to Christianity, Judaism, and Islam alike is the conviction that we as human beings are called to believe in God—to trust in him, to rely on him, to place our confidence in him. To believe in God is our fundamental human obligation. Central also is the conviction that only by believing in God can the deepest stirrings of the human heart be satisfied. Duty and fulfillment here coalesce.

But is it rational for us to believe in God? Is it rational for us to place our confidence in him? Can a person believe in God without performing a *sacrificium intellectus*? One cannot belong to the intelligentsia of modern Western society without having that question come to mind.

Presumably it is rational for a person to believe *in* God only if it is rational for him to believe various propositions *about* God—in particular, that there is such a being as God. The rationality of trusting someone presupposes the rationality of believing that that person exists. And among the objections to Christian belief, as well as to Judaic and Muslim, characteristic of the modern intelligentsia is the objection that it is no longer rational, if ever it was, to believe that God exists. We must choose between treasuring our rationality and assenting to God's existence. We cannot have it both ways. The rational person will have to make his way in the world without supposing that there exists any God in whom he *could* trust. Kafka's castle is empty. The noises we hear are only echoes of our own voices.

Tacit in this characteristically modern objection to theistic conviction is the assumption that if it is not rational to believe some (affirmative) proposition about God, then one ought not believe it. There are a good many theologians in this century who—if I read them correctly—would contest this assumption. They would agree with the objectors that believing that God exists requires throwing overboard the demands of rationality, but they would nonetheless refuse to go along with the conclusion of the objectors that we ought then to cease believing that God exists. Divine revelation, they say, has entered our existence, coming as an assault to our rationality. Accordingly, we must now choose by what principle we shall live our lives—reason or revelation. The believer has thrown in his lot with revelation, and rationality no longer has any claim on him. It is a matter of utter indifference to him whether his theistic convictions are rational. Rationality is only a siren tempter.

In my judgment this is a profoundly misguided response to the challenge I have cited, expressing an untenable view as the place of rationality in our human existence—at least when rationality is understood as I shall be understanding it in this discussion. In my judgment the charge that it is irrational to believe that God exists must be taken seriously by the theist. This is one of the theses I shall be defending.

But first let me formulate more amply the objection to theistic conviction which I see as characteristic of the modern Western intellectual. The objection can be seen as presupposing a challenge, call it the *evidentialist challenge* to theism. And this challenge can be thought of as consisting of two claims: first, if it is not rational to accept some proposition about God then one ought not accept it; and second, it is not rational to accept propositions about God unless one does so on the basis of others of one's beliefs which provide adequate evidence for them, and with a firmness not exceeding that warranted by the strength of the evidence. Someone who holds that this challenge is correct and, in addition, holds, concerning a given theistic believer, that the believer does not meet the challenge, may then be said to accept the *evidentialist objection* to the theistic convictions of that believer.

It is the evidentialist objection to theistic belief that I wish to consider in this paper, and especially the evidentialist *challenge* that lies behind the objection. My interest is not so much in whether the challenge is being met by some believers or in whether it can be met; my interest is more in whether the challenge itself is tenable.

An explanation is immediately in order. In what follows I shall often speak of someone *believing* that God exists rather than of someone *accepting the proposition* that God exists. I shall mean the same thing. Often "believe" is used in such a way that from the fact that someone believes something it follows that he does not know it. That is not how I shall be using it. When I speak of someone believing something, it is not implied that he does not know it. For—to say it once again—I shall use "believe" as a synonym for "accept." And surely if someone knows so-and-so, he accepts it.

As I have already tacitly suggested, the evidentialist challenge and objection to theistic conviction are not distributed evenly throughout modern society. They are found mainly among the intelligentsia. And as I have already said, they are peculiarly modern. One finds them not at all—or hardly at all—before the latter half of the seventeenth century. A corollary of this latter fact is that evidentialist apologetics, construed as the attempt to meet the challenge by offering arguments for various (affirmative) theistic propositions, thus to legitimize theistic belief, or by showing that the arguments theistic believers already have are sound ones, thus to show that theistic belief is legitimate, are also unique to modernity. Until the modern age, Christian apologetics consisted mainly, not in giving or defending arguments *for* Christianity, but rather in answering objections *to* Christianity. It is when the challenge to Christianity is the evidentialist challenge, and when one attempts to cope with the challenge by meeting it or showing that it has already been met, that the offering of "evidence" becomes relevant to the apologist's traditional endeavor. When Tertullian, in his famous and eloquent *Apology,* undertook to answer the objection (among others) that Christians were responsible for the decline in the economy of the Roman Empire, he did not undertake to offer arguments for the truth of Christianity, let alone for the truth of theism.

## I

John Locke was among the first to formulate articulately the evidentialist challenge to theistic belief. It will help to set the stage for our discussion if we consider what he says. Reason, says Locke,

> as contradistinguished to faith, I take to be the discovery of the certainty or probability of such propositions or truths, which the mind arrives at by deductions made from such ideas which it has got by the use of its natural faculties, viz., by sensation or reflection.
>
> *Faith,* on the other side, is the assent to any proposition, not thus made out by the deductions of reason, but upon the credit of the proposer, as coming from God in some extraordinary way of communicating. This way of discovering truths to men we call *revelation.* (*An Essay concerning Human Understanding,* IV,18,2)

Reason is *reasoning* for Locke, and clearly he thinks of it as one among others of our belief-forming processes.[1] Faith is another belief-forming process. It, by contrast, consists in accepting something "as coming from God."

Does that mean, then, that reasoning plays no rightful role in faith? Not at all, says Locke. It is worth quoting him at some length on this point.

> But since God, in giving us the light of reason, has not thereby tied up his own hands from affording us, when he thinks fit, the light of revelation in any of those matters wherein our natural faculties are able to give a probable determination, revelation, where God has been pleased to give it, must carry it against the probable conjectures of reason; because the mind, not being certain of the truth of what it does not evidently know, but only yielding to the probability that appears in it, is bound to give up its assent to such a testimony, which, it is satisfied, comes from One who cannot err, and will not deceive. But yet it still belongs to reason to judge of the truth of its being a revelation, and of the signification of the words wherein it is delivered. Indeed, if any thing shall be thought revelation which is contrary to the plain principles of reason and the evident knowledge the mind has of its own clear and distinct ideas, there reason must be hearkened to as a matter within its province: since a man can never have so certain a knowledge that a proposition, which contradicts the clear principles and evidence of his own knowledge, was divinely revealed, or that he understands the words rightly wherein it is delivered, as he has that the contrary is true: and so is bound to consider and judge of it as a matter of reason, and not swallow it, without examination, as a matter of faith. (*Essay,* IV,18,8)
>
> Whatever God hath revealed is certainly true: no doubt can be made of it. This is the proper object of faith; but whether it be a divine revelation or not, reason must judge; which can never permit the mind to reject a greater evidence to embrace what is less evident, nor allow it to entertain probability in opposition to knowledge and certainty. (*Essay,* IV,18,10)[2]

It is self-evident, Locke suggests, that whatever God has revealed is true. This is something on which we can base our reasoning, our inferring. It is not something for which we must *first* have evidence. But that a given deliverance from the mouth or hand of a human being is a revelation of God is something for which, if we are to be entitled to believe it, we must have other beliefs which constitute adequate evidence for it. If the *content* of the purported revelation is self-evidently or demonstrably false, then we must reject it as a revelation of God. If, on the contrary, it only has the status of improbability, then we must weigh up that improbability against the probability that it is a revelation from God. (Presumably it *is* such "weighing-up" that Locke has in mind. On this point he is not wholly explicit.)[3]

Why is this so? If we are entitled to accept without argument that what God reveals is true, then why may we not also accept without argument that the New Testament, say, is a revelation from God? Because, says Locke, we would then have no way of showing that "the enthusiasts" are irresponsible in their believings. If we affirm the evidentialist challenge, we can then go up to the enthusiast and say, "Give us the evidence that your purported revelations are in fact from God." If he cannot comply, then we can justly conclude that he is believing irresponsibly.

> But to examine a little soberly this internal light and this feeling on which they build so much: The question here is, How do I know that God is the revealer of this to me; that this impression is made upon my mind by his Holy Spirit, and that therefore I ought to obey it? If I know not this, how great soever the assurance is, that I am possessed with, it is groundless; whatever light I pretend to, it is but *enthusiasm*. Does it not then stand them upon, to examine upon what grounds they presume it to be a revelation from God? (*Essay*, IV,19,10)[4]

Of course, this challenge to the enthusiasts is also a challenge to Christian believers: if they do not believe on the basis of adequate evidence that the Bible is God's revelation, they too must give up their religion. But Locke was confident that in the case of Christianity the challenge could be met. He himself undertook to meet it in his book *The Reasonableness of Christianity, As Delivered in the Scriptures.*

Thus far we have found Locke saying that a condition of someone's being entitled to accept so-and-so as a revelation from God is that he has inferred from other beliefs of his, which constitute adequate evidence for it, *that it is* a revelation from God. In fact Locke contends that the connection between this entitlement and this condition is even tighter. He holds that the firmness with which one accepts this proposition must be proportioned to the strength of the evidence for it.

> We may as well doubt of our own being, as we can whether any revelation from God be true. So that faith is a settled and sure principle of assent and assurance, and leaves no manner of room for doubt or hesitation. Only we must be sure that it is a divine revelation, and that we understand it right: else we shall expose ourselves to all the extravagancy of enthusiasm, and all the error of wrong principles, if we have faith and assurance in what is not divine revelation. And therefore in those cases, our assent can be rationally no higher than the evidence of its being a revelation, and that this is the meaning of the expressions it is delivered in. If the evidence of its being a revelation, or that this is its true sense, be only on probable proofs, our assent can reach no higher than as assurance or diffidence, arising from the more or less apparent probability of the proofs. (*Essay*, IV,16,14)

All that has been said thus far presupposes the acceptability of believing that God exists. What, on Locke's view, is the condition for that? Before a person is entitled to believe that such-and-such is a deliverance from God, he must have inferred from adequate evidence that it *is* that. But what about his prior belief that there *is* a God? Must it too be supported by adequate reasoning if the person is to be entitled to hold it?

Yes indeed, on Locke's view. God, says Locke, "has given us no innate ideas of himself." He "has stamped no original characters on our mind, wherein we may read his being." That God exists is not self-evident to us. Yet,

> having furnished us with those faculties our minds are endowed with, he hath not left himself without witness; since we have sense, perception, and reason, and cannot want a clear proof of him as long as we carry ourselves about us. Nor can we justly complain of our ignorance in this great point, since he has so plentifully provided us with the means to discover and know him, so far as is necessary to the end of our being, and the great concernment of our happiness. But though this be the most obvious truth that reason discovers, and though its evidence be (if I mistake not) equal to mathematical certainty; yet it requires thought and attention, and the mind must apply itself to a regular deduction of it from some part of our intuitive knowledge, or else we shall be as uncertain and ignorant of this as of other propositions which are in themselves capable of clear demonstration. (*Essay,* IV,10,1)

Locke then proceeds to argue that each of us knows intuitively that he himself exists, and that "nothing can no more produce any real being, than it can be equal to two right angles." From these two premises he concludes that there must be an eternal being, and he goes on to argue that that eternal being has the characteristics of God. He seems to be of the view that people do in fact believe that God exists on the basis of this argument, and that what he has done is only formulate the argument and show that it is sound.

## II

I have said that the evidentialist challenge and objection to theistic conviction, along with the attempt to cope with that challenge by practicing evidentialist apologetics, are peculiar to modernity. Some will question this claim by pointing to the practice of natural theology among the medievals. The reply is that natural theology was a different project from evidentialist apologetics—even though the same arguments may occur in both.

We may take Anselm and Aquinas as typical. Anselm's motto was that of Augustine: *credo ut intelligam.* In the opening pages of his *Proslogion* he makes clear what that means for him. His goal in the book was to come to know, or understand, what already he believed. "I have written the following treatise," he says, "in the person of one who strives to lift his mind to the contemplation of God, and seeks to understand what he believes." (Preface) "For I do not seek to understand that I may believe, but I believe in order to understand." (Chapter 1)

Knowing a proposition was in general, for Anselm, a state of mind preferable to taking that proposition on faith. Hence Anselm's goal in constructing the ontological argument, as the remainder of the *Proslogion,* was to bring it about that what already he believed he now would know. In his view an essential component in this process of transmuting belief (faith) into knowledge (understanding) was constructing proofs.

Aquinas was no different on these matters. He explicated the concept of knowledge somewhat more rigorously than did Anselm: a person knows only what is self-evident to him or evident to his senses, or what has been demonstrated from such. Likewise he conceives faith somewhat more rigorously, as accepting propositions on the authority of God the revealer. But the goal of natural theology for Aquinas was exactly the same as for Anselm: to transmute what already one believed into something known. Demonstration was seen as indispensable to this transmutation project.

Taking Anselm and Aquinas as typical, it becomes clear, then, that the medievals were doing something quite different in their project of natural theology from meeting the evidentialist challenge. They were engaged in the transmutation project of altering belief (faith) into knowledge. No one in their milieu was claiming that it was permissible to believe that God existed only if one did so on the basis of adequate evidence, and with a firmness not exceeding the strength of the evidence. (Nonetheless Aquinas did, in chapter 6 of his *Summa Contra Gentiles,* defend the thesis "that to give assent to the truths of faith is not foolishness even though they are above reason.")

## III

A variety of questions can be posed concerning the evidentialist challenge to theistic conviction. (Let us henceforth call this *evidentialism.*) One could ask, for example, what reasons the evidentialist has for holding his position. That is what Alvin Plantinga does in his essay "Reason and Belief in God" in this volume. He there suggests that common to all, or almost all, evidentialists is a certain "model" of rationality, a certain criterion for the application of the concept *rational*—the criterion being that of classical foundationalism. Plantinga then goes on to argue that that criterion is unacceptable. I judge Plantinga to be correct in both these contentions. Almost always when you lift an evidentialist you find a foundationalist. But the careful formulation of classical foundationalism by a number of philosophers in recent years has been accompanied by a growing consensus that it is not a plausible criterion of rational belief.[5]

Another way of considering the tenability of evidentialism would be to formulate and defend a criterion of rational belief alternative to that of classical foundationalism, and then to test the truth of evidentialism by reference to this criterion. That is the approach I shall follow in this essay. If successful, it moves us a stage beyond where Plantinga's discussion leaves us. His discussion puts us in the position of seeing that the most common and powerful argument for evidentialism is classical foundationalism, and of seeing that classical foundationalism is unacceptable. But to deprive the evidentialist of his best defense is not yet to show that his contention is false. It is this next step that I shall undertake to execute.

But before a criterion can be offered for the application of the concept of rational belief, we must be sure that we have clearly in mind the concept itself. And here our situation is surely that our English word "rational" is unusually protean, having a large number of different, albeit connected, senses. We speak of many different sorts of things as rational: rational plans, rational strategies, rational actions, rational persons, rational remarks, rational beliefs. And a large number of different claims are made about these different sorts of entities when we say of them that they are rational. Here it is only rational and nonrational *beliefs* that we will have in view. And the fact that the evidentialist connects the nonrationality of a belief with the obligation not to hold it delimits for us the senses of "rational" relevant to our discussion.

An illuminating way to begin is to consider the following passage from John Locke:

> however faith be opposed to reason, faith is nothing but a firm assent of the mind; which if it be regulated, as is our duty, cannot be afforded to anything but upon good reason, and so cannot be opposite to it. He that believes, without having any reason for believing, may be in love with his own fancies; but neither seeks truth as he ought, nor pays the obedience due to his Maker, who would have him use those discerning faculties he has given him, to keep him out of mistake and error. He that does not this to the best of

> his power, however he sometimes lights on truth, is in the right but by chance; and I know not whether the luckiness of the accident will excuse the irregularity of his proceeding. This at least is certain, that he must be accountable for whatever mistakes he runs into: whereas he that makes use of the light and faculties God has given him, and seeks sincerely to discover truth by those helps and abilities he has, may have this satisfaction in doing his duty as a rational creature, that though he should miss truth, he will not miss the reward of it. For he governs his assent right, and places it as he should, who, in any case or matter whatsoever, believes or disbelieves according as reason directs him. He that does otherwise, transgresses against his own light, and misuses those faculties which were given him to no other end, but to search and follow the clearer evidence and greater probability. (*Essay,* IV,17,24)

What Locke assumes here is that there are duties and responsibilities pertaining to our believings. Just as it is not true that "anything goes" in our actions regarding other human beings, so too it is not true that "anything goes" in our believings.

What must at once be added, however, is that our believings may be subject to duties and responsibilities in a number of different *respects.* (This is a point made by Plantinga in "Reason and Belief in God.") Perhaps there are right and wrong ways of acquiring beliefs. Perhaps there are right and wrong ways of maintaining beliefs. Perhaps some beliefs we ought not to hold because of their injurious effects on our psyches. Perhaps sometimes we hold beliefs with more firmness than we ought (or with less firmness that we are permitted). And if there are obligations pertaining to believings at all, presumably there are some pertaining simply to the having or not having of beliefs.

It is clear that at the center of Locke's attention, and at the core of the evidentialist challenge as he issues it, is this last phenomenon: Some beliefs we ought not to *have.* Some we ought to *have.* Some we are permitted to *have.* Some we are permitted not to *have.* For the sake of convenience we might call these *possession obligations* with respect to our believings (and correlatively, *possession permissions*).

But Locke is also concerned, though less prominently so, with the fact that sometimes we hold beliefs more firmly than we ought—and correspondingly, less firmly than we are permitted. We may call such obligations as these *firmness obligations* with respect to our believings.

Not only does Locke assume that there are duties pertaining to our believings; he also makes a suggestion as to the ground of these obligations—or at least, of the possession obligations. He assumes that we human beings are capable of governing and regulating our assent with the purpose in mind of getting more amply in touch with reality—of increasing our number of true beliefs and of avoiding or eliminating false beliefs. And his thought then is that possession obligations with respect to our believings consist in our obligation to so govern our assent as to get more amply in touch with reality. Fundamentally, then, he thinks of possession obligations along utilitarian lines: they consist in the obligations we have to get more amply in touch with reality, getting more amply in touch with reality being taken, in this context, as a good-in-itself.[6]

It may be remarked, parenthetically, that failure to live up to one's possession and firmness obligations and presumably to all other obligations pertaining to one's believings, when all other things are equal, amounts in Locke's view to disobedience to one's Maker. Living up to them, other things being equal, amounts to obedience. Possession and firmness obligations with respect to our believings are rooted in accountability to our Creator.

Now it would seem that if we have the ability to govern our believings with the goal in mind of getting more amply in touch with reality, then we also have the ability to govern them with other goals in mind. Perhaps we can to some extent govern them with the goal in mind of increasing our peace of mind, or with the goal in mind of staying out of trouble with our government. Correspondingly, perhaps we also have obligations for the governance of our believing with respect to some such goals. Kierkegaard thought, for example, that when it came to religious matters, we ought to hold such beliefs as would most heighten the passion in our lives. To distinguish such obligations from those pertaining to governance with the goal in mind of getting more amply in touch with reality, let us call these latter *reality-possession obligations.*

It is clear that Locke connects the concept of rationality he has in mind with the obligations that pertain to our believings—call such obligations our noetic obligations. The rational belief is the belief which does not violate our noetic obligations. The rational belief is the belief which, by reference to our noetic obligations, is permitted, is justified. But if obligations pertain to our beliefs with respect to different dimensions of those beliefs, the question comes to mind whether Locke is perhaps not working with a somewhat more constricted concept of rationality than this catchall concept. I think it clear that he is. For Locke the rational belief is the belief in accord with the reality-possession and firmness obligations that pertain to one's believings. Rationality consists in not violating *those* duties concerning one's believings. To be rational in one's believings amounts to doing as well in the firmness and reality-possession dimensions of one's believings as can rightly be demanded of one. Just as the morally permissible action is the action in accord with the norms for moral action, so the rational belief is the belief in accord with the firmness and reality-possession norms for believing.[7]

Rationality, thus conceived, is connected with truth. Locke sees clearly, though, that the connection is indirect. Rationality is not to be identified with truth in beliefs, nor is it to be thought that the two coincide. Someone may light on truth by chance; about that Locke says, ironically, "I know not whether the luckiness of the accident will excuse the irregularity of his proceeding." Conversely, someone may seek "sincerely to discover truth by those helps and abilities he has" and "may have this satisfaction in doing his duty as a rational creature," while yet he misses truth. He will not miss his reward, though, says Locke. For he will, so far forth, have done his duty.

Truth, though a merit in beliefs, is not an unfallible mark of praiseworthiness in the person, nor is falsehood such a mark of blameworthiness. By contrast, rationality in beliefs *is* an infallible mark of praiseworthiness in the person; irrationality, of blameworthiness.[8] Rationality, unlike truth, is a derivative merit in beliefs, deriving its meritoriousness from merit in the believer—that merit being present in the believer, however, only if he pursues as he ought the merit of truth. The merit of rationality in our beliefs is grounded in the proper governance of our assent. Noetic rationality is grounded in practical rationality.

## IV

Locke assumes—rightly in my judgment—that we have an obligation to govern our assent with the goal in mind of getting more amply in touch with reality. Likewise he assumes—also rightly, I think—that this goal has the two sides of seeking to increase our stock of true beliefs and of seeking to avoid or eliminate false beliefs. Let us scrutinize these assumptions a bit, beginning with a consideration of that latter assumption. To do so it will be helpful to consider Roderick Chisholm's formulation of our intellectual duties. "Each person," he says, "is subject to two quite different requirements in connection with any proposition he considers: (1) he should try his best to bring it about that if that proposition is true then he believes it; and (2) he should try his best to bring it about that if that proposition is false then he not believe it."[9]

Now suppose one took the second of these two requirements seriously but not the first. That is, suppose one had it as one's sole goal to snare as few falsehoods in one's net of belief as possible. What strategy would then be appropriate? Quite obviously the strategy of undertaking to believe as few as possible of the propositions that cross one's mind.

There is nothing better than this that one could do (though even this might well not achieve the result of eliminating all falsehoods, for many of the things we believe, we do so ineluctably). If one wants above all to avoid catching trash fish, one goes fishing as little as possible. But though a serious pursuit of this strategy would be likely to diminish significantly the number of falsehoods believed, that merit would be purchased at the cost of missing out on a great deal of truth. And surely that is an important deficiency in this strategy of incredulity. The extent to which one had gotten in touch with reality would be severely limited.

Suppose, on the other hand, that one took the first of these two requirements seriously but paid no attention to the second. Suppose one had it as one's sole goal to snare as many truths as possible in one's net of belief. What strategy would then be appropriate? Quite obviously the strategy of undertaking to believe as many as possible of the propositions that come to mind—with this proviso: if one cannot believe both a proposition which comes to mind and its contradictory, then one strives to believe that member of the pair, if either, for which one has better evidence. There seems no better strategy than this strategy of gullibility for achieving the goal. If catching as many edible fish as possible is one's only goal, one nets fish indiscriminately—unless one has to make a choice here and there. But though the serious pursuit of this strategy would increase the number of truths one believes, it is also likely to increase substantially one's stock of false beliefs. And that, surely, is a deficiency. False beliefs mark a failure fully to get in touch with reality.

So both goals are necessary: the goal of increasing one's stock of true beliefs and the goal of avoiding or eliminating false beliefs. Accordingly, more subtle strategies will have to be adopted than either that comprehensive strategy of incredulity or that comprehensive strategy of gullibility.

Of course, once we allow that the pursuit of both these goals is necessary for getting in touch with reality, we must also acknowledge the possibility that in specific cases the two goals will yield conflicting results. Upon doing one's best to ascertain whether a proposition is true or false, one may discover that the evidence pro and con is equally balanced. In such a case one has to weigh up which is the worse outcome—that of missing out on truth or that of falling into error.

Yet another matter, pertaining to our obligation to get more amply in touch with reality, must be raised at this point. With respect to which propositions does one have an obligation to bring it about that one believes them if they are true and disbelieves them if they are false? The answer Chisholm gives is *any proposition one considers*. But that seems hardly correct on a couple of counts. Suppose, upon looking at a bean bag, that the thought crosses my mind that it contains exactly 2019 beans. Suppose I then consider that proposition. Is it really the case, in ordinary circumstances, that I then have an obligation to bring it about that I believe this if and only if it is true? Is not the acquisition of true, and the avoidance of false, belief on this matter so unimportant to my life that I have no such obligation—not even *prima facie*? Of course propositions are not in general inherently trivial or important. There may be tasks which *you* have that make it important for *you* to seek to bring it about that you believe there are 2019 beans in the bag just in case there are. But I have no such tasks.

Neither is it the case that our obligation to attain truth pertains just to the propositions we *consider*. Some of the propositions we have never considered are nonetheless propositions that we ought to believe. It may be that we *ought* to have considered them—and having considered, to believe. Or alternatively, it may be that though we have no obligation to *consider* them, nonetheless we do have an obligation to *believe* them. After all, there are ways of coming to believe propositions which do not require *considering* those propositions. Many of the things we believe, and ought to believe, have never been *considered* by us. Considering is involved in only some modes of belief acquisition.

But concerning which propositions, then, do we have reality-possession obligations? Concerning the ones we each do in fact believe, I would say. But what beyond that? Chisholm is correct in his assumption that the propositions with respect to which we have such obligations are only a limited number and that they vary from person to person. We do not have obligations of rationality concerning reality's entire stock of propositions. And the ones each of us does have are always situated obligations. They are contextual obligations. What determines the variance, however, is not that which each person happens to consider. But if not that, what then?

It is difficult, indeed, to formulate an absolutely general answer to this question. And for our purposes here it is unnecessary to try. But worth observing is that one important factor determining the variance is the person's tasks and obligations in general. Some of my tasks and obligations are such that it becomes essential for their implementation that I seek the truth on certain matters and govern my beliefs accordingly. Of course each person's configuration of tasks and obligations is unique. That, then, is what accounts for a good deal of the variance in the obligations of rationality, and in noetic obligations generally. At the same time, it is true that these configurations do not differ in all respects from person to person, which accounts for a good deal of the commonality in obligations of rationality.

A characteristic error of epistemologists has been to suppose that our noetic obligations are disconnected from our other obligations. The truth is that in good measure the particular shape which the obligation to attain truth and avoid falsehood assumes for each person is determined by his obligations in general. Over and over our general obligations require, for their fulfilment, that we seek to get more amply in touch with some segment of reality. Perhaps there are some matters on which a given person ought to seek to attain true belief and eradicate falsehood whether or not those beliefs will serve some *praxis* of his. But that is not in general true. Our noetic obligations arise from the whole diversity of obligations that we have in our concrete situations. In this way, too, rationality is connected with *praxis*.

One last point. It seems in general not true that each of us has the obligation with respect to certain propositions *to do his best* to bring it about that he believes them if and only if they are true. Doing one's best may be more than can rightly be asked of one—well beyond the call of duty. Indeed, doing one's best with respect to some may interfere with doing one's duty with respect to others. What seems rather to be the case is that each of us has the obligation with respect to certain propositions *to do as well as can rightly be demanded* of us so as to bring it about that we believe them if they are true and disbelieve them if they are false.

Of course, the concept of doing as well as can rightly be demanded of one is, unlike that of doing one's best, a normative concept. This, then, is a second point at which we have found it necessary to introduce normative concepts and considerations where Chisholm had only nonnormative ones—the other being at that point where a determination is made concerning the propositions to which our obligations of rationality pertain.

## V

The applicability of the concept of rationality that we are in the process of elucidating presupposes that we human beings are capable of governing our assent, in particular, capable of governing it with the goal in mind of getting more amply in touch with reality. The very image of governing suggests, however, that there are various belief-forming processes or "mechanisms" present in us. A ruler's governance of his subjects does not consist of calling them into existence. It will be important for our subsequent purposes to look more closely at these two phenomena of human nature, that of belief-forming "mechanisms" and that of the capacity for governing these.

It has to be said that the main representatives of the epistemological tradition give us little help here. Though of course they all take for granted the existence of belief-forming "mechanisms" in human beings, they devote scant attention to this phenomenon as such. A characteristic result of this oversight is that the rules they give for "the direction of the mind" prove limited and myopic in application.

To these generalizations Thomas Reid, the eighteenth-century Scottish philosopher, is the great exception. It was Reid's great genius to perceive that if we want to understand knowledge and rationality, we cannot talk only about the abstract relations holding among propositions, along the way making unreflective assumptions about the "mechanisms" which form our beliefs. We must look head-on at the psychological "mechanisms" involved in belief formation. Articulate epistemology requires articulate psychology.

At the very foundation of Reid's approach is his claim that at any point in our lives we each have a variety of dispositions, inclinations, propensities, to believe things—*belief dispositions* we may call them. What accounts for our beliefs, in the vast majority of cases anyway, is the triggering of one and another such disposition. For example, we are all so constituted that upon having memory experiences in certain situations, we are disposed to have certain beliefs about the past. We are all disposed, upon having certain sensations in certain situations, to have certain beliefs about the external physical world. Upon having certain other sensations in certain situations, we are all disposed to have certain beliefs about other persons. Likewise we are all so constituted as to be disposed in certain circumstances to believe what we apprehend people as telling us—the *credulity* disposition, as Reid rather fetchingly called it.

To the belief dispositions of which Reid took note we may add those rather ignoble belief dispositions of which Marx and Freud made so much: our disposition to believe what gives us a sense of security, our disposition to believe what serves to perpetuate our positions of economic privilege, our disposition to adopt clusters of beliefs which function as ideologies and rationalizations to conceal from our conscious awareness the ignobility of those other dispositions, and so on.

The belief dispositions which I have cited thus far are all dispositions which produce their effects *immediately*. We do not normally infer, from other beliefs of ours which we take as good evidence for it, that a person is before us. Rather, upon having certain sensations in certain situations we just immediately believe this. Likewise our memory experiences produce immediately in us certain convictions about the past. Remembering does not consist in going through a process of inferring a belief about the past from other beliefs.

There is, though, another disposition in us of which these remarks are not true. In addition to the features of our constitution thus far mentioned, we are all so constituted that upon judging some proposition which we already believe as being good evidence for another proposition not yet believed, we are disposed to believe that other proposition as well. To this disposition Reid assigned the name of reason. Let me call it the *reasoning disposition.* What the tradition called *mediate* beliefs can now be singled out as those produced by the reasoning disposition, and what it called *immediate* beliefs, those produced by some one of our other belief dispositions.

Not only does Reid call to our attention the various belief dispositions which we actually do, at a given moment in our lives, possess; he also speaks about the origins of these dispositions. It was his conviction, in the first place, that somewhere in the history of each of us are to be found certain belief dispositions with which we were simply "endowed by our Creator." They belong to our human nature. We come with them. They are innate in us. Their existence in us is not the result of conditioning. It must not be supposed, however, that all such nonconditioned dispositions are present in us at birth. Some, possibly most, emerge as we mature. We have the disposition to acquire them upon reaching one and another level of maturation. He says, for example:

> Perhaps a child in the womb, or for some short period of its existence, is merely a sentient being: the faculties by which it perceives an external world, by which it reflects on its own thoughts and existence, and relation to other things, as well as its reasoning and moral faculties, unfold themselves by degrees; so that it is inspired with the various principles of common sense, as with the passions of love and resentment, when it has occasion for them. (*An Inquiry into the Human Mind*, V,7)

But in addition to our innate, nonconditioned, belief dispositions, we adults all have a number of belief dispositions which we have acquired by way of conditioning. Reid calls attention to a certain range of these as being belief dispositions induced in us by the working of the *inductive principle.* The inductive principle is not itself a belief disposition; it is an innate, nonconditioned disposition for the acquisition of belief dispositions. Reid says, "It is undeniable, and indeed is acknowledged by all, that when we have found two things to have been constantly conjoined in the course of nature, the appearance of one of them is immediately followed by the conception and belief of the other." (*Inquiry,* VI,24) And he adds that it is "a natural, original and unaccountable propensity to believe, that the connections which we have observed in times past, will continue in time to come." (*Inquiry,* II,9) An example that Reid offers, of a belief disposition inculcated in us by this inductive principle of our native constitutions, is this: "When I hear a certain sound, I conclude immediately without reasoning, that a coach passes by. There are no premises from which this conclusion is inferred by any rules of logic. It is the effect of a principle of our nature, common to us with the brutes." (*Inquiry,* IV,1)

Reid's thought concerning the workings of the inductive principle can readily be stated in the language of contemporary psychology. What accounts for some of our beliefs is that a process of classical, or Pavlovian, conditioning has taken place. A regular "schedule" has been established in one's experience between phenomena of type A and phenomena of type B, and now one has the disposition, upon experiencing a phenomenon of type A, to believe that there is also a phenomenon of type B. Hence one has acquired a new belief disposition. It is the disposition to acquire belief dispositions in this manner that Reid calls *the inductive principle.*

Vast numbers of our noninnate belief dispositions are not acquired in this way, however, but rather by way of what we would nowadays call *operant* conditioning, working on our native belief dispositions. In Reid's own thought this comes out most clearly in what he says about the credulity principle. It is a moot point whether the credulity disposition is present in us at birth. But very little maturation is required for it to put in its appearance. "The wise Author of nature," says Reid, "hath planted in the human mind a propensity to rely upon human testimony before we can give a reason for doing so. This, indeed, puts our judgment almost entirely in the power of those who are about us in the first period of life; but this is necessary both to our preservation and to our improvement. If children were so framed as to pay no regard to testimony or authority, they must, in the literal sense, perish for lack of knowledge." (*Essays on the Intellectual Powers of Man,* VI,5)

It was Reid's view that the working of the credulity principle "is unlimited in children" (*Inquiry,* VI,24), in the sense that whatever a child apprehends someone as asserting, he believes. But shortly the principle begins to be "restrained and modified," as Reid puts it. What induces the restraint and modification is the discovery that sometimes the principle produces false beliefs in us. "The principle of credulity is unlimited in children, until they meet with instances of deceit and falsehood." (*Inquiry,* VI,24) Notice: a person's conviction that some of the beliefs produced in him by testimony are false does not *destroy* his disposition to give credence to testimony. Rather, it results in that disposition's becoming restrained and modified. The credulity principle becomes more finely articulated.

We can think of this too in terms of modern conditioning theory.

The original, unqualified credulity principle is altered by way of operant conditioning. One's discovery, or conviction, that certain of one's beliefs thus produced are false, functions as an *aversive* consequence, diminishing to the point of extinguishing the workings of the disposition in such cases. That new, slightly altered disposition is then in turn submitted to the same sort of testing, with the person's convictions, concerning some of the beliefs thus produced, that they are false, again functioning as aversive consequences, and his independent discovery that others are true, functioning as reinforcing consequences, until yet another alteration takes place; and so on and on. Eventually the person is no longer disposed to believe what persons of type P speaking under conditions of type C say on topics of type T, whereas other sorts of testimony he is disposed to believe more strongly than ever (and perhaps more strongly disposed to believe than ever).

I find it surprising that Reid does not emphasize that we are constantly acquiring new belief dispositions by the working of operant conditioning on our other innate belief dispositions as well, not only by its working on our credulity disposition. Reid himself notes about memory that we tend to place more confidence in our memories the more vivid, or distinct, they are. But this is almost certainly a matter of learning. And there is much more that can be said than just this. Other things being equal, one learns to place more confidence in one's memories of yesterday's occurrences than of occurrences in the distant past. One learns to place less confidence in the details of one's memory when one was agitated and upset than when one was observing carefully and calmly. And so on. In short, gradually one learns that one's memory is reliable on certain sorts of matters under certain sorts of conditions, and unreliable on other matters or under other conditions; that modifies the belief dispositions attached to one's memory experiences. The revision can be seen as a selective strengthening and weakening of the original disposition, weakening to the point of disappearance for some cases.

The same sort of thing happens in the case of perception. When, as a child, I rode down a paved road on a hot summer day, I often believed that there was water standing on the road ahead, in the distance, because it definitely looked that way. Now I no longer believe that, even when I am in those same circumstances. For I have learned that it *looks* that way as the consequence of heat waves rising from the pavement without really *being* that way. In general what can be said is this: our native belief dispositions all go through stages of increasing articulation as the result of our experience that some beliefs produced by these dispositions are false, others true.

With this picture in mind of our belief-forming dispositions, let us now look at our capacities for governing the workings of these "mechanisms"—in particular, at our capacities for governing their workings with the goal in mind of more amply getting in touch with reality. As we now move to this second level, we leave Reid behind.

To a great extent it is in our power to *govern* the workings of our belief dispositions—not now to alter them, but to govern their workings. And often it is because it is in our power to govern their workings that we are culpable for our believings and our failings to believe. For one thing, it is often in our power to determine whether a triggering event for some disposition will occur. For example, it was in my power to go over and look at the tire; if I had, the sensations received would have triggered in me the belief that the tire was flat. There are also more subtle and interesting examples than ones like this, however. Often it is in our power to bring it about that we will *notice* something when in situations where that is noticeable. For example, one can set oneself, or fail to set oneself, to notice speed-limit signs when entering villages; and setting oneself to do so makes it highly likely that one will. It is for this reason that police officers are often right in holding us accountable for not knowing what the speed limit in a given village is. So too one can try, or fail to try, to *remember* something; and making an effort to remember often makes it much more likely that one will. For this reason one can often rightly be held accountable for not remembering something—for not having correct beliefs on a certain matter. (Strictly speaking, this last case is a case, not of having it in one's power to determine whether a certain belief disposition will be triggered, but of having it in one's power to determine whether a certain belief is *sustained.* Believing is not an event but an enduring state. A full discussion of the matter would systematically distinguish between factors *initiating* such a state and factors *sustaining* such a state.)

Not only is it often in our power to determine whether a certain triggering event for some belief disposition will occur; likewise it is sometimes in our power, even when an event does occur that characteristically would trigger the disposition, to determine whether or not the disposition will become operative. We can *resolve* or *determine* that a disposition will not become operative, and sometimes at least such a resolution is effective. For example, one can resolve to resist the workings of one's credulity disposition and come to no belief as to what transpired in marital disputes until one has heard out both parties; in the absence of the resolution one would have believed the tale of the first party. Or again: one can resolve to resist the workings of one's memory disposition and no longer to believe that what one seems to remember as having happened when one was in situations of great stress did in fact happen. So, too, one can resolve to resist the workings of one's reasoning disposition and hold no belief about the size of one's checking-account balance until one has gone over the figures at least twice. Obviously, repeatedly resolving to resist the operation of some belief disposition in certain sorts of situations may eventually result in that disposition's being extinguished for those sorts of cases.

The resolve to resist the activation of a belief disposition, even in the presence of an event which, were it not for this resolve, would trigger the disposition, may sometimes take the form of leaving one, not in a state of suspension of belief, but in a state of continuing to believe as one did. Suppose, for example, that a certain belief of Vern's is deeply embedded in the whole structure of his personality, his life-style, his career, and so on. It gives him great comfort. Or he has spent twenty years of work in physics on the premise that this is true. In short, he has deep motivations for hanging on to this belief. Suppose that then someone comes along and presents him with evidence that this belief is false. It would seem that in some such cases it is in Vern's power to accept the evidence and change his mind, but equally in his power to resist changing his mind. That is to say, it is true not merely that in some such cases his mind *is changed* but also that in some such cases it is in his power *to change* his mind, or at least to *let* his mind *be changed.* It is in his power to acknowledge the force of the evidence, give up his resistance to the conclusion, and change his mind; but equally it is in his power to cling stubbornly to what he has always believed and treat the evidence as not conclusive.[10]

And now what about the case so dear to the heart of the classical epistemologist: the case of a person considering some proposition and then deciding to believe it, or to disbelieve it? Perhaps the *considering* is here unimportant. Does it ever happen that we *decide* to believe something? Must a full picture of our belief-forming processes, and of our capacity to govern them, have this sort of case in mind as well?

Perhaps so. Of course it may be that some cases of resolving to resist the working of some belief disposition are also cases of deciding to believe or not to believe so-and-so. Perhaps that is true of the last case considered, the case of Vern. But be that as it may, let us consider a case in which a resolution to resist is not in the picture. Suppose that one is a member of a jury and has agonized long hours over which of two conflicting witnesses to believe on a certain matter. May it be that eventually one *decides to believe* what one of them said and to disbelieve what the other said? One could have made the opposite decision, but as a matter of fact this is what one decides to believe. In some cases of conflicting testimony one just finds oneself persuaded that one witness is speaking truth and the other not. May it be that in other cases one decides? If so, that decision is probably accompanied by a decision to the effect that the *evidence* for the veracity of the one witness is slightly stronger than the evidence for the veracity of the other. This would then be a second point at which a decision to believe occurs in such a case.

So the full picture that emerges is something like this: we each have a variety of belief dispositions, some of which we share with all normal, mature human beings, some of which we do not; some of which we have as part of our native endowment, some of which are the result of one and another form of conditioning, and probably some of which are the result of having resolved to resist the workings of some native or conditioned disposition. In addition, we each have a variety of capacities for governing the workings of these dispositions. To some extent it is in our power to determine whether a certain (sort of) triggering event for a disposition will occur. And to some extent it is in our power to determine whether the disposition will be activated even if an event does occur which characteristically would activate it. Perhaps we also have the capacity in certain (relatively rare) circumstances to *decide* whether to believe something.

It must be clearly noted that rationality, thus conceived, is in good measure person specific and situation specific. When I was young, there were things which it was rational for me to believe which now, when I am older, it is no longer rational for me to believe. And for a person reared in a traditional tribal society who never comes into contact with another society or culture, there will be things rational to believe which for me, a member of the modern Western intelligentsia, would not be rational to believe. Rationality of belief can only be determined in context—historical and social contexts, and, even more narrowly, personal context. It has long been the habit of philosophers to ask in abstract, nonspecific fashion whether it is rational to believe that God exists, whether it is rational to believe that there is an external world, whether it is rational to believe that there are other persons, and so on. Mountains of confusion have resulted. The proper question is always and only whether it is rational for this or that particular person in this or that situation, or for a person of this or that particular type in this or that type of situation, to believe so-and-so. Rationality is always *situated* rationality. (Some thinkers in the modern world seem to have concluded from the fact that a nonsituated theory of rationality is untenable that the concept of rationality itself must be discarded. They have become historicists. We have seen, and will see, no reason whatsoever to draw this conclusion.)

## VI

And now it is easy to see why the theist cannot simply dismiss out of hand the charge that his theistic convictions are nonrational. Nonrationality in one's beliefs is the sure sign that some of one's obligations have been violated. Accordingly, a person cannot meet the charge that one of his beliefs is nonrational by announcing that he has chosen not to live by the canons of rationality, anymore than he can meet the charge that he has acted immorally by announcing that he has chosen not to live by moral obligations. He can meet it only by *contesting* the charge.

There is yet a deeper reason why the theist, at least if he is a Christian, Jew, or Muslim, cannot just dismiss out of hand the demands of rationality. Such a person will always perceive our human obligations as related, in one way or another, to the will of God. God wills that we do what we ought to do. When a theist believes nonrationally, he acts in violation of the will of the very God in whom he believes—unless it be the case that there are extenuating circumstances.

However, it is also easy to see now that the charge lodged against the theist, that he holds his theistic convictions nonrationally, is not a *decisive* charge, in the sense that it does not *follow* from the nonrationality of the belief that he ought to give up believing that. We can see, in short, that one of the two principal components in the evidentialist challenge to theistic conviction is untenable.

The most obvious, and perhaps least important, point to make here is that what grounds the nonrationality of some beliefs is not *what* is believed but *how* it is believed: it is believed with the wrong degree of firmness. Hence, from being told that someone holds some one of his beliefs nonrationally one cannot infer that he ought not to believe that.

But second, the nonrationality of a belief—as, following Locke, we have conceived it—results from the fact that one has not done as well as one ought to have done in governing one's belief-forming "mechanisms" toward the goal of getting more amply in touch with reality. But as we have already seen, one can presumably conduct such governance with other goals in mind; and perhaps with respect to such alternative governance there are also obligations. If so, it may well be that though a given belief represents inadequate governance with respect to the goal of getting more amply in touch with reality and is, accordingly, a nonrational belief, it represents *adequate* governance with respect to some other goal. Further, it may well be that governance with respect to that other goal has priority over governance with respect to getting more amply in touch with reality. We in the West for several centuries now have assumed that nothing could take priority in belief governance over our obligation to expand our hold on truth and to avoid or eliminate falsehood in our beliefs. It is difficult to perceive, though, what defense could be given for this. And if the assumption is in fact false, then here is a second way in which it may come about that a person is permitted to believe something that is not rational for him to believe. Maybe in some cases it is even true that he *ought* to believe it in spite of its nonrationality.

Lastly, there is more to life than governing aright the *what* and the *how* of one's assent—and so too there is more to life's obligations than the obligation to govern aright one's belief-forming "mechanisms." Sometimes these other obligations of life take precedence over those governance obligations, again with the result that one is permitted to believe something that is not rational to believe. Perhaps I did not calculate my bank account figures carefully enough for me to believe rationally that the balance is $53.09. But perhaps I had to choose between spending more time calculating and taking my son to see the Phillies play in the World Series. In this conflict of obligations I may have made the right decision, to calculate quickly and go off to the game. Our obligation to govern our assent aright often takes time to carry out, and sometimes the time taken is wrongly taken from the time needed to carry out some other obligation. For this reason, too, from the fact that someone holds a belief nonrationally it does not in general follow that he ought not to hold it.

When we speak of a person as *justified* in holding some belief, often, perhaps always, what we mean is that the person is *permitted* to hold that belief. So another way of putting the point above is that a person may be justified in holding a belief even though he does not hold it rationally. What is true, of course, is that if a person holds a belief rationally, then *other things being equal,* he is justified in holding it—or to put the same point in other words, then he is *prima facie* justified in holding it. But other things may not be equal, with the result that though he holds it rationally, he is nonetheless not justified in holding it. It will sometimes be convenient in what follows to say of the person who believes some proposition rationally that he is *rationally* justified in holding it—from which it does not follow that he is justified *tout court* in holding it.

Now that we have introduced the word "justified" into our discussion, a few cautions should be sounded. For one thing, *being justified* in one's belief that so-and-so is different from *justifying* one's belief that so-and-so. To be justified in believing that so-and-so is to be in a certain *state.* To justify one's belief that so-and-so is to perform a certain *action.* Most of the beliefs we are justified in holding are such that we never justify them—never even attempt to do so. Probably most are such that we could not do so—depending, of course, on the standards adopted for success in performing the action of justifying.

Second, we speak sometimes of one proposition justifying another, but that too is a different matter. One proposition justifies another when it is good evidence for the other. But justification, on the concept I am using, is not a relation between propositions. It is a relation between a *person* and some one of his *believings*.

Last, an unjustified belief of a person is, not one that he ought to give up, but one that he ought not to have had. Thinkably, now that he has it, he *cannot* give it up. Similarly, the immoral act is not the act that the person ought to undo, nor, always, the act that the person ought to cease doing. It is the act that the person ought not to have done.

## VII

Up to this point we have been trying to get before us, as clearly as possible, that concept of rational belief which is characteristically used in the evidentialist objection to theistic conviction. It is not at all an idiosyncratic concept. Though no doubt there are other concepts attached to our English word "rational," there can be little doubt that this is one of them. It is time now that we move to the second stage of our project—that of trying to formulate a *criterion* for the correct application of this concept.

Given our discussion thus far, we can now put somewhat more precisely the contention of the evidentialist. His claim is that theistic conviction, to be rational, must be arrived at, or at least reinforced, by the process of inference. Each of us has a wide variety of belief dispositions, innate and learned. From this whole array the evidentialist picks out the *inference* mechanism as that which must evoke or reinforce theistic conviction if it is to be rational. Only that will do. And of course he adds that the premises from which the inference proceeds must in fact provide adequate evidence for the conclusion.

This provocative contention raises all sorts of questions as to which sorts of beliefs may serve as premises for the inferences. What sorts of propositions are candidates for evidence? With respect to which sorts of propositions must theistic beliefs be evident? Obviously theistic propositions are themselves not eligible. Which ones are? These questions pose many interesting issues, some of which are explored by Plantinga in his essay in this volume. For our purposes we can set them off to the side. For we wish to test evidentialism by matching it up against a criterion for rational belief.

The criterion I propose will actually be a criterion for a somewhat narrower concept than that of rationality as thus far delineated. Here I shall not at all attempt to specify conditions for permissible *firmness* of conviction. I will attempt only to specify conditions for rationally accepting a proposition at all. We are looking simply for the justifying circumstances for the acceptance of propositions.

A criterion which has recently entered the arena of philosophical discussion, after the collapse of classical foundationalism, is that of *reliabilism.* Reliabilism says, roughly, that a given belief of a person is rationally justified if and only if that belief was produced or is sustained in him by a reliable process or mechanism. Just as some thermometers are reliable and some unreliable, so too some belief-producing and belief-reinforcing mechanisms are reliable and some unreliable. Our rationally *justified* beliefs are those produced or reinforced by the reliable mechanisms. Here is how Alvin Goldman, one of the first proponents of the theory, states its basic contention:

> Granted that principles of justified belief must make reference to causes of belief, what kinds of causes confer justifiedness? We can gain insight into this problem by reviewing some faulty processes of belief-formation, i.e., processes whose belief-outputs would be classed as unjustified. Here are some examples: confused reasoning, wishful thinking, reliance on emotional attachment, mere hunch or guesswork, and hasty generalization. What do these faulty processes have in common? They share the feature of *unreliability:* they tend to produce *error* a large proportion of the time. By contrast, which species of belief-forming (or belief-sustaining) processes are intuitively justification-conferring? They include standard perceptual processes, remembering, good reasoning, and introspection. What these processes seem to have in common is *reliability:* the beliefs they produce are generally true. My positive proposal, then, is this. The justificational status of a belief is a function of the reliability of the process or processes that cause it, where (as a first approximation) reliability consists in the tendency of a process to produce beliefs that are true rather than false.[11]

One thing to be kept in mind in reflecting on this theory is that it is not fully accurate to speak simply of reliable and unreliable mechanisms. The situation is rather that a given mechanism is reliable under certain conditions and for certain ranges of inputs and outputs and is unreliable under other conditions and for other input ranges and output ranges. Another thing to be kept in mind is that a mechanism which has produced mainly truth under certain conditions and for certain ranges of inputs and outputs is not yet, thereby, a *reliable* mechanism with respect to such conditions and ranges. For it may be that though it is unreliable for such conditions and ranges, yet, as luck would have it, when it did in fact operate under those conditions and within those ranges, it produced mainly truth. The mechanism which is genuinely reliable for given circumstances and ranges is the one which *would* produce mainly truth under such circumstances and for such ranges. Reliability is an implicitly counterfactual concept.

Perhaps the main challenge facing the reliabilist in the articulation of his theory is that it is not the least bit evident how we are to pick out the mechanism which produced a certain belief—indeed, it is not the least bit evident that in general there is such a thing as *the* mechanism. What, for example, is the mechanism in the case of the child in the primitive tribe who believes something on the say-so of his elders? Is it that of believing something on the say-so of someone else? Of believing something on the say-so of one's elders? Or believing something on the say-so of *those* elders? If the reliabilist theory is to be applicable, we must be told how, for a given belief, we are to pick out the mechanism that we are to scrutinize for reliability, and how we are to select the sort of conditions, and the input/output ranges, with respect to which that mechanism would have to yield mainly truth for the belief to be rationally justified. I understate the point when I say that this is a *daunting* challenge.

But even without that challenge having been met, I think it can be seen, relying on our ordinary intuitive notion of these matters, that reliabilism, no matter how formulated, will not be a correct criterion of rational belief. In the first place, though it is true that a good many more of the beliefs that we intuitively feel to be rationally justified will turn out justified on this criterion than on the criterion of classic foundationalism, nonetheless, the criterion is still too constrictive. For there are unreliable mechanisms which yield rationally justified beliefs. Suppose, for example, that some belief is produced by an unreliable mechanism, but the agent has no good reason to believe it unreliable—and, more strongly yet, has adequate reason to believe that it was produced by a reliable mechanism. Whatever instructions the reliabilists eventually give us, telling us which mechanisms under which circumstances we are here to check out for reliability, it seems possible that such a situation would arise. And if it does, is not the person in whom that unreliable process produces that belief rationally *justified* in thus believing? Is he not doing as well in the use of his belief-governing capacities, toward the goal of getting more amply in touch with reality, as can rightly be demanded of him? If a scientist develops an instrument for acquiring certain information, and if all the evidence available to him points to the reliability of that instrument, even though it is in fact unreliable, is he not rationally justified in believing the deliverances of that instrument? Was he anywhere remiss in the use of his assent-regulating capacities? What more could rightly have been demanded of him?

Just as there can be rationally justified beliefs produced by unreliable mechanisms, so too there can be rationally unjustified beliefs produced by reliable mechanisms. Suppose that some belief of some person is produced by a reliable mechanism, but all the evidence available to the person points to the conclusion that it is unreliable. Suppose, in fact, that the evidence is so strong that the person would be rationally unjustified in believing the mechanism reliable. It would seem that such a situation could in fact arise; if it did, the person would not be rational in continuing to believe the deliverances of that reliable mechanism. Perhaps the case is just the reverse of that considered in the preceding paragraph: A scientist has developed an instrument for obtaining information on certain matters, but on the evidence available to him, the results are largely in error. In fact, however, they are highly accurate—something which is not discovered until, say, fifty years later. If the scientist, against the evidence for his discovery's unreliability, nonetheless continues to believe its deliverances, surely he is rationally unjustified in his belief.

Last, suppose that some belief is produced and sustained in a person by a reliable process, but in this particular case the person has adequate evidence that the belief is false—not evidence that the process producing it is in general unreliable, just evidence that in this particular case the belief produced is false. Surely in this case too the person would not be rational in believing what was in fact reliably produced. And there can be such cases: I may believe something on the say-so of what I know to be a thoroughly reliable authority; nonetheless, I may acquire evidence that in this particular case what I thereby came to believe was mistaken. If so, I ought to give up my belief. (This would be a case in which one reliable process yields the belief B*p,* and another the belief B*not-p.*) If I fail to do so, I would not be using my belief-governing capacities as well as can rightly be demanded of me.

For these reasons, reliabilism is incapable of filling the void left by the demise of classic foundationalism.[12]

As I now propose to offer my own criterion for rationally justified belief, we must keep clearly in mind the project on which we are engaged. Our project is not to give advice to the person who is wondering whether to believe a certain proposition or whether to keep himself from believing it. Rather we are looking at the person who already has an array of beliefs, so as to give him and others a criterion for picking out those which it is rational for him to hold from those which are not. We are after, not rules for the direction of the mind, but a criterion for separating one's rational beliefs from one's nonrational beliefs.

At the outset a few words should be said about the "ought implies can" principle in its application to beliefs. A rather natural formulation of this principle is that if it is not in a person's power at a given time to cease from believing a certain proposition, then he is rationally justified in believing that proposition. But probably most beliefs are of this sort; I cannot just up and decide to believe that I am not now awake. On the other hand, most of the beliefs a person has at a given time are such that there are some things he *could have done* such that if he had done them, he would not then have the belief. And sometimes these are things he *should have done*. Exactly when they are that is by no means easy to say, however.

The connection between beliefs, volition, and justification is a large dark area, and it would seriously distract me from my main purpose here to enter that area so as to be able to say exactly what the "ought implies can" principle comes to in the area of belief. I think we all feel intuitively that it does come to something. But what exactly that something is, is surely going to prove difficult to say. Let us suppose, though, that some explanation of "could not have" is possible, and let us suppose that some qualifications can be added, so that it turns out true that if a person could not have refrained from believing *p*, then he is rationally justified in believing *p*. Let us then call any belief of a person which, in that sense and with those qualifications, is one he could not have refrained from believing an *ineluctable* belief of his. And let us call the remainder of his beliefs his *eluctable* beliefs. My concern here will be to formulate a criterion for rationally justified *eluctable* beliefs.

One way to get hold of the central contention of the criterion I wish to propose is to note the structure of the objections I have lodged against the reliabilist criterion. The objections were of this sort: If a person has *adequate reason* to cease from some one of his beliefs, then he is rationally unjustified in holding it even if it was produced in him by a reliable process. And if a person *lacks adequate* reason to cease from some one of his beliefs, then he is rationally justified in holding it even if it was produced in him by an unreliable process. The phenomenon of *adequate reason to cease believing* was central in my objections. I suggest that this phenomenon is in fact the central determinant of rationality in beliefs.

Another way to get hold of the theory's central contention is to return to something that Reid said. It will be remembered that Reid thought that there is in all of us a *credulity disposition*—a disposition to believe what we apprehend people as telling us. At first, on Reid's view, this disposition is undifferentiated and unarticulated—as children we believe whatever we apprehend anyone as telling us. But gradually we discover that what certain sorts of people tell us on certain sorts of topics is false. What the rational person then does, says Reid, is resolve to resist the workings of the credulity principle in such cases and no longer accept such testimony. (Eventually this results in the disposition itself being modified.)

Says Reid: "when our faculties ripen, we find reason to check that propensity to yield to testimony and to authority, which was so necessary and so natural in the first period of life. We learn to reason about the regard due to them, and see it to be a childish weakness to lay more stress upon them than reason justifies." (*Essays on the Intellectual Powers,* VI,5)

Thus it is Reid's view that we are *prima facie* justified in accepting the deliverances of the credulity disposition until such time as we have adequate reason in specific cases to believe the deliverances false, or until such time as we have adequate reason to believe the deliverances unreliable for certain types of cases. Our situation is not that to be rationally justified in accepting the deliverances of the credulity disposition we need evidence in favor of its reliability. Rather, we are rationally justified in accepting its deliverances until such time as we have evidence of its *un*reliability for certain types of cases. The deliverances of our credulity disposition are innocent until proved guilty, not guilty until proved innocent.

So, I suggest, it is in general—with one important exception to be mentioned shortly. A person is rationally justified in believing a certain proposition which he does believe unless he has adequate reason to cease from believing it. Our beliefs are rational unless we have reason for refraining; they are not nonrational unless we have reason *for* believing. They are innocent until proved guilty, not guilty until proved innocent. If a person does not have adequate reason to refrain from some belief of his, what could possibly oblige him to give it up? Conversely, if he surrenders some belief of his as soon as he has adequate reason to do so, what more can rightly be demanded of him? Is he not then using the capacities he has for governing his beliefs, with the goal of getting more amply in touch with reality, as well as can rightly be demanded of him?

The exception to which I alluded was this: Suppose that someone has undertaken to alter some native belief disposition, or to cultivate some new belief disposition, for perverse reasons, or for reasons having nothing to do with getting in touch with reality. The extent to which such undertakings, such resolutions, can be successful seems to me severely limited. But no doubt they sometimes have their effect. For example, it may well be that if some person undertakes to disbelieve everything another says, not because of his experience that what the other says is often false, but rather because of his hostility to that person, this will eventually result in his granting the speech of that person less credibility than otherwise he would—*and less than he ought.*

Above I affirmed the innocent-until-proved-guilty principle for beliefs. Here we are dealing with noninnocent belief *dispositions.* And it seems evident that the outcomes of a noninnocent disposition should not be accorded the honor of innocence until their guilt has been proved.

I suggest that, from the standpoint of rationality and its governing goal of getting in touch with reality, the only acceptable reason for undertaking to revise one of one's belief dispositions is that one justifiably believes it to be unreliable. (It is to be remembered here that many of our belief dispositions *get* revised by conditioning; we do not *undertake* to revise them.) If one undertakes to revise it for some other reason, and succeeds, then the disposition, with respect to the points of revision, is no longer innocent with respect to rationality. It has been *culpably revised.* Now if a given belief is produced by a culpably revised disposition, and *solely* by such a disposition, then it is not a belief rationally held. Correspondingly, if a person's *not* believing something in a certain situation is due to the working, or the nonworking, of a culpably revised disposition, then his *not*-believing is not rational.

The innocent-until-proved-guilty principle which I have affirmed for beliefs must be understood as applying just to those not produced by culpably revised dispositions. A person may well find himself in the situation where he does not have adequate reason to surrender a belief produced by a culpably revised disposition. Nonetheless the belief is not held rationally, for the disposition producing it was not innocent on this matter.

What we have so far then is this:

> (I) A person *S* is rational in his eluctable and innocently produced belief B*p* if and only if *S* believes *p*, and it is not the case that *S* has adequate reason to cease from believing *p*.

Rationality in one's beliefs does not await one's believing them on the basis of adequate reasons. Nonetheless, the phenomenon of having reasons does play a central and indispensable role in rationality—a rationality-*removing* role.

But formula (I) is only a first approximation. A number of revisions are necessary before we have a satisfactory criterion. First, though, an explanation is necessary of what I have in mind by "adequate reason." Perhaps it can rightly be said of a person who has the belief that he feels dizzy that he has a *reason* for that belief—namely, *his feeling dizzy.* In that case his reason would be a particular event. Perhaps, too, it can rightly be said of a person who believes that he is seeing a red car, in an ordinary case of perception, that he has a *reason* for this belief—namely, *its seeming to him that he is seeing a red car* (that is, his having a red-car-seeing experience). In this case, too, his reason would be a particular event. In short, sometimes the reason for a belief of ours may be the event which caused the belief (the event which triggered the operative disposition).

But when here I speak of "reason," that is not what I have in mind. I do not mean the disposition-triggering event. What I mean by "reason" is to be explained by reference to the workings of Reid's reasoning disposition. Sometimes what accounts for our believing some proposition *p* is that we believed some other proposition *q* which we judged to be good evidence for *p*. When that occurs, I shall say that the person believes *p* *for a reason*. And the reason is just the already believed proposition *q*.[13] Someone believes *p* for an *adequate* reason, then, if he believes *p* for a reason, if that reason is evidential support for *p*, and if the conjunction of that reason with the other things *S* believes that are relevant to *p* is also evidential support for *p*. And last, a person *has* an adequate reason for believing *p* if there is some proposition *q* which he believes such that *if* he believed *p* for the reason that *q*, he would believe it for an adequate reason.

It is to be noted that whether a person's belief that *q* provides him with an adequate reason for his believing *p* depends, in general, on the other beliefs that person has. Accordingly, it is never strictly speaking true that the reason on the basis of which he believes *p justifies* him in believing *p*; by itself it does not do that. Suppose, for example, that I believe my brother is on campus, and I do not believe I have ever seen or heard of a close look-alike to him. If I now believe that my brother is standing in the courtyard outside my office, and believe this for the reason that I see someone who looks just like him standing out there, I might very well be rationally justified in my belief. The belief that I see someone who looks just like my brother standing out there might be an adequate reason for believing that my brother is in the courtyard. But suppose now that in addition to all those beliefs I also have the belief that my brother is sitting with me in my office engaged in conversation with me. Then my belief that I see someone who looks just like my brother standing out there in the courtyard would not be adequate reason for believing that he is in the courtyard. If I believed the latter proposition for the reason that the former is true, I would not thereby be rationally justified in believing that latter proposition.

Let us return now to that initial approximation, formula (I). I said that a person is rational in holding some belief of his if and only if it is not the case that among his beliefs there is adequate reason for him to cease from that belief. But this will not quite do. For suppose that though *S* does not have adequate reason to not believe *p*, he *ought to have*. The fact that within the totality of his beliefs there is not to be found adequate reason for him to cease from believing *p* is a fact which itself marks a failure to govern his assent as well as can rightly be demanded of him. For example, perhaps his not having adequate reason to cease from believing *p* is due to the fact that his calculations were done very hastily, when he *knows* that they were done hastily, knows that hasty calculation is a most unreliable method of arriving at truth, and had it in his power to be less hasty. As a second approximation to a satisfactory criterion we can say this:

(II) A person *S* is rational in his eluctable and innocently produced belief B*p* if and only if *S* believes *p*, and *S* neither has nor ought to have adequate reason to cease from believing *p*.

This revision of our initial formulation was made in the light of the conviction that sometimes a person ought to have adequate reason to give up some one of his beliefs when in fact he does not. But may it not sometimes be that the converse is true? May it not sometimes be that a person has adequate reason to cease from some one of his beliefs, when in fact he ought not to have? Suppose that the totality of his beliefs does contain adequate reason to cease from believing *p*, but suppose that some of those beliefs he ought not to have. He has them only in violation of his rational responsibilities. If that were altered, the totality of his beliefs would no longer constitute adequate reason to cease from believing *p*. Surely a person in such a situation is in fact justified in believing *p*.

The point is correct, but no emendation is required. For by definition if *S* has *adequate* reason for believing *p*, then within the totality of what he believes there are certain propositions such that if he believed *p* on the basis of those, his doing so would place him in a *prima facie* justifying circumstance with respect to his belief B*p*. But if he is not *prima facie* justified in believing those, then his believing *p* on their basis cannot make him *prima facie* justified in believing *p*. Or so at least I shall assume. I shall assume that a person's believing *p* on the basis of *q* makes him *prima facie* justified in believing *p* only if he is *prima facie* justified in believing *q*. If a person is not justified in holding some one of his beliefs, that defect is passed on to the third and fourth generations of those beliefs that he holds on the basis of that one.[14]

But there are other reasons for revising our formula (II). In making the revisions we shall have to take a fateful step whose full significance will not become evident until later, in section IX.

## VIII

Consider the case in which a person has adequate reason to cease from believing *p* but does not realize that he does. This sort of case comes in two versions. It may be that in failing to realize that he has adequate reason to cease from believing *p*, he has failed to use his belief-governing capacities as well as can rightly be demanded of him. There it is—right before his eyes. But he does not realize it. And his failure to realize it is due to inexcusable absent-mindedness on his part, or haste, or whatever. On the other hand, his failure to realize the nature of his situation may be wholly excusable. The fact that among his beliefs there is adequate reason to cease from believing *p* may be so subtle, or the connections so hard to grasp, that he could not rightly be expected to have noticed it.

It is obvious that these two sorts of cases must be treated differently. The latter leaves his justification in believing *p* unaffected; the former does not. So a third approximation to our desired criterion can be formulated as follows:

(III) A person *S* is rational in some eluctable and innocently produced belief B*p* of his if and only if *S* does believe *p*, and either:
  (i) *S* neither has nor ought to have adequate reason to cease from believing *p*, or
  (ii) *S* does have adequate reason to cease from believing *p* but does not realize that he does, and is rationally justified in that.

One more qualification is required to reach our final formulation. Suppose a person believes *p*, and in addition holds the belief, call it C, that his other beliefs provide adequate reason for him to cease from believing *p*. Suppose also that he is mistaken in that belief C. What does this do to the epistemic status of his belief that *p*?

Note that this type of case comes in three varieties:

(i) The person is mistaken and rationally unjustified in the belief C. The belief C is not rationally permissible for him.
(ii) The person is mistaken but rationally justified in the belief C. It is rationally permissible for him to believe C. But it is not rationally obligatory that he believe it. It is rationally permissible for him not to believe it.
(iii) The person is mistaken in the belief C but would not be rationally justified in ceasing from holding C. It is rationally obligatory that he hold it.

It is obvious that case (i) leaves the status of the belief B*p* unmodified. A person's believing that he has adequate reason to cease from believing *p*, when in so believing he is violating his duties of rationality, does not remove rational justification from his belief that *p*.

It is not so clear what is to be said about case (ii). We are to suppose that a person believes *p* but also happens to hold the belief C that his other beliefs constitute adequate reason to cease from believing *p*. And we are to suppose that he is mistaken, though rational, in that upper-level belief—rationally permitted to hold it, though not obliged to do so. What is permitted of him in this situation?

Ought he to give up his belief that *p*, a belief which he would be fully rational in holding if he did not also have the belief that he has adequate reason to cease from holding it? Does his permissibly, though mistakenly, having that upper-level belief C that his believing *p* is nonrational put him in the situation where he is no longer rational in holding B*p*? Well, why would it do that? Why is it not equally permissible for him to go the other way and surrender that upper-level belief of his? What reason indeed would there be for his being obliged to go one way rather than the other?

Does that mean, then, that he is permitted to go either way? And what about the possibility that he is permitted to continue to believe both?[15] Without decisively resolving the issue, let me assume for our purposes here that it *is* permissible for him to hang on to his belief that *p*—leaving open the issue of whether this is permissible only if he surrenders the upper-level belief that *p* is not held rationally. There will be no great difficulty in revising our criterion as necessary if this assumption proves incorrect.

Case (iii) clearly does alter the epistemic status of believing *p*, however. If the person is not only justified in believing but also rationally obliged to believe that his other beliefs constitute adequate reason to cease from believing *p*, then he has but one choice: to give up his belief that *p*.

Our criterion then becomes this:

(IV) A person *S* is rational in his eluctable and innocently produced belief B*p* if and only if *S* does believe *p*, and either:

(i) *S* neither has nor ought to have adequate reason to cease from believing *p*, and is not rationally obliged to believe that he *does* have adequate reason to cease; or

(ii) *S* does have adequate reason to cease from believing *p* but does not realize that he does, and is rationally justified in that.[16]

My central thesis, now, is this: *S* will have done as well as can rightly be demanded of him in the use of his belief-governing capacities toward the goal of getting more amply in touch with reality if and only if all of his beliefs are innocently produced and none of those is nonrational on this criterion.[17]

Throughout I have been assuming that we are rational and nonrational not only in our believings but also in our *not* believings. The criterion for rationally not believing is wholly parallel to that for rationally believing:

(V) A person $S$ is rational in an eluctable and innocently produced case of not believing $p$ if and only if $S$ does not believe $p$, and either:

(i) $S$ neither has nor ought to have adequate reason to believe $p$, and is not rationally obliged to believe that he *does* have adequate reason to believe $p$; or

(ii) $S$ does have adequate reason to believe $p$ but does not realize that he does, and is rationally justified in that.

## IX

The criterion I have offered for rationality in beliefs openly and unabashedly makes use of normative concepts in its formulation. Indeed, it makes use of the very same normative concept for whose application it is a criterion. Accordingly, to understand the criterion one must already grasp the concept, and to apply the criterion one must already know how to apply the concept. These features of our criterion will give some readers pause in accepting it. They will feel that what is wanted out of a criterion has not been achieved.

When one's goal is to *introduce* a concept to someone, then of course one must avoid using the concept in one's introduction. That has not been my aim here. I have presumed that we already have the concept of being rational, of being rationally justified in one's beliefs. Earlier in my discussion I made some clarifying comments about that concept, pointing out its connection to responsibilities, in that way trying to make as clear as possible which concept I had in mind. My hope was that thereby the reader either would acquire the concept or would acquire a clearer view of a concept which already he had. Here in this section my goal has been to formulate a criterion for the application of this concept that the reader already has in mind. It is true, of course, that in trying to formulate a criterion for the application of a normative or evaluative concept one may set as one's goal to make use of no normative or evaluative concepts. That has not been my goal. My goal has simply been to find a criterion which is correct and illuminating. Whether or not the criterion itself makes use of the concept for whose application it is a criterion is, in principle, irrelevant to that goal. A criterion which does not make use of the concept may prove unilluminating; a criterion which does make use of the concept may prove illuminating.

In that it uses the very concept for which it is a criterion, my criterion is similar to the now customary way of thinking of necessity: It is said that a necessarily true (that is, not-possibly-false) proposition is one which is true in all possible worlds. But no one supposes that this formula can be used to introduce the concept of necessity to someone who lacks it; its circularity makes it useless for that purpose. Furthermore, to apply this formula for the not-possibly-false proposition, one must already be able to apply the concept of possibility. Nonetheless, it is evident from the philosophical literature of the last decade and a half that this way of thinking about necessity and possibility has proved extraordinarily illuminating. I intend my criterion to function in a similar way: namely, to provide us with an illuminating way of thinking about rationality and its conditions.

It may be added that reliabilist and foundationalist criteria, if they are to come anywhere near being satisfactory, must also make use of some normative concept. Consider, for example, the reliabilist criterion: *S* is justified in his belief B*p* if and only if *S* does believe *p*, and B*p* was produced (or is sustained) in *S* by a reliable mechanism. Suppose that though B*p* was not produced in *S* by a reliable mechanism, nonetheless *S* believes that it was and is rationally justified in that belief. Surely then *S* would be rational in believing *p*. Suppose, conversely, that B*p* *was* produced in *S* by a reliable mechanism, but *S* ought to believe it was produced by an unreliable mechanism. Surely *S* is then *not* rational in believing *p*.

Or consider the criterion of the classic foundationalist. Suppose that *S* believes *p* on the basis of certain incorrigible and self-evident beliefs of his. And suppose that though these beliefs do not provide adequate evidence for *p*, nonetheless *S* believes they do and is rationally justified in that. Surely then *S* is rational in believing *p*. Suppose, conversely, that those basic beliefs *do* provide adequate evidence for *p*, but *S* ought to believe they do not. Surely then *S* is not rational in believing *p*.

I conclude that any satisfactory criterion for rational belief will have to be not only a *noetic* criterion, making explicit or tacit reference to the beliefs of the person but also a *normative* noetic criterion, making explicit or tacit use of of some such normative concept as that of justification or obligation. In recognition of these facts the criterion I have offered not only takes the phenomenon of *not having adequate reason to surrender one's belief* as the key phenomenon determining rationality; it adds to this an explicitly noetic-normative component.

## X

Let me comment briefly on a few other features of the criterion. (1) The criterion does not assist us in sorting out adequate from inadequate reasons for refraining from beliefs. If at a certain point one is uncertain as to how to make this discrimination, the criterion will not help to resolve that uncertainty; it will not instruct one to resolve it in a certain way. In that respect the criterion is purely formal. But of course the criterion as a whole is not purely formal. It tells us what relation must obtain between a person and some one of his beliefs for him to be rational in holding that belief. In that way it tells us what to look for when trying to determine whether a certain belief of a certain person is rational. Begin, it says, by scrutinizing that person's beliefs to see whether they contain adequate reason for him to give up the belief in question. This is different from what the reliabilist would say, and different from what the classic foundationalist would say.

It would seem that an adequate reason to surrender a certain belief will always be of one or the other of two sorts: It will be evidence that the proposition believed is false or evidence that the disposition which produced the belief is unreliable (for that sort of triggering event, and that sort of outcome, under such circumstances).[18] If that is so, then the next step to take in fleshing out this criterion is to develop a theory of evidence and a theory of reliable belief-producing dispositions. (Incidentally, if it is true that adequate reasons to cease from a belief often consist of evidence that the disposition accounting for the belief is unreliable, then the reliabilist was on the right track in suggesting that rational justification in beliefs has something to do with reliability of belief-producing mechanisms. What it has to do with it, however, is different from what he thought.)

(2) Given its "innocent-until-proved-guilty" posture, the criterion does not say that only those beliefs which a person holds for reasons are ones which he is rational in holding. Beliefs are induced in us by a variety of dispositions; rationality does not attach only to those produced by our reasoning-disposition. Nonetheless, it may well be the case that many of our beliefs are such that we are not rational in holding them unless we do so for reasons. We must not allow our conviction that this is not true of all beliefs to lead us into supposing that it is true of none.

(3) On the criterion I have offered, a person is rationally justified in all his beliefs until such time as he has acquired certain conceptual equipment and the ability to make use of that equipment. Before that time his system of beliefs may lack a variety of merits, but until, for example, he has grasped (or ought to have grasped) the concept of a reason, he is doing as well in governing his believings as can rightly be demanded of him. Accordingly, there is probably a time in the life of each child when he is rationally justified in all his beliefs. Increase in knowledge makes noetic sin possible.[19]

(4) The criterion offered is clearly not a foundationalist criterion. Fundamental to the foundationalist's vision of the structure of rational belief is the distinction between immediate beliefs and mediate beliefs. As the reader will have surmised, I judge this to be a tenable distinction. And for many purposes it is an important distinction to have in mind. Traditional theories of justified belief and of knowledge, traditional disputes between skeptics and antiskeptics – these often cannot be understood without an understanding of the immediate/mediate distinction. But for a criterion of rational belief the distinction proves otiose. The criterion I have offered is a unified criterion, applying in the same way to mediate and immediate beliefs alike.

Is it then a coherence criterion? Yes, perhaps so. In the central place that it gives to the phenomenon of *no adequate reason to surrender one's belief* it is an example of what John Pollock has called "negative coherence theories." However, in its incorporation of a normative component it goes beyond traditional coherence theories. Perhaps the time has come for us to discard the supposition that the foundationalist/coherentist dichotomy is an illuminating principle of classification.

## XI

Frequently an objection of the following sort is lodged against the criterion I have proposed. Suppose a person takes a fancy to a proposition and just up and believes it. Suppose, further, that he neither has nor ought to have any adequate reason to give up that proposition. Then by our criterion he is rational in his belief. But surely he is not.

The truth is that by our criterion he most assuredly is not rational in his belief. The "mechanism" operative in this imaginary case – one may well doubt whether there really is any such "mechanism" and whether anybody really can believe in this fashion, but let that pass – the "mechanism" operative is that of believing what one takes a fancy to. But certainly any normal adult human being not only ought to know but also *does* know that this is a most unreliable "mechanism" of belief formation. Knowing that, he has a very adequate reason indeed for giving up that belief.

## XII

Our Reidian approach to epistemology downplays the significance of reasoning. Reasoning is but one among many modes of belief formation. And it is not unique in producing rationally held beliefs. Other "mechanisms" of belief formation produce rational beliefs as well.

Yet in spite of this, *reasons* occupy a central role in the criterion I have offered. Is there not some oddity, some discrepancy, in this? Granted that *having reasons* is not the same as *reasoning*. But they are not unrelated. How does downplaying the role of reasoning fit with emphasizing the role of having reasons?

Well, suppose one wants to dislodge some belief that someone has—perhaps the person just took something on someone else's say-so which one believes to be false. How might one proceed? If it is a matter whose truth can be determined by perception, one might do what one can to put the person in the situation where he himself can determine by perception the truth of the matter. Upon being put in that situation, the person might very well believe the testimony of his senses over the testimony of that other person. He may be so made or conditioned that the perceptual disposition (coupled with the disposition to "see" that the deliverance of the perceptual disposition is in conflict with the deliverance of the credulity disposition) operates more powerfully than the credulity disposition. A hierarchy in the strength of these dispositions would operate in such a case.

Depending on the case, another thing one might try to do is give the person a *reason* for supposing that what was said to him is false. *That* may induce him to give up the belief—the situation again being that whatever are the dispositions behind the reasons, they prove to be more powerful than those which produced and/or sustained the belief in question. Now sometimes when we give someone reasons for believing or not believing so-and-so, we induce new beliefs in that person. Perhaps the person comes to believe things on *our* say-so. Or what we say prods him into "seeing" connections among his beliefs which he had not seen before. In this latter case, even though what we say induces the belief, the person does not accept it on our say-so. Of course, giving reasons for believing or not believing something does not always induce new beliefs in the person. Sometimes one just brings forcefully to the person's attention what he believed anyway. (Maybe he did not *believe* that he believed it; sometimes that is what one changes.)

I think we can see now why reasons have a special status. It may be that some available perceptual experience would dislodge what a person believes on testimony. I, on the outside, may know of the availability of that experience and may see to it that the person has that experience. But how could the person himself be obliged to obtain this experience without so much as believing, or being obliged to believe, that the experience is available? By contrast, if there is amongst his *beliefs* adequate *reason* to surrender that belief of his which he accepted on testimony, then we can demand of him that he take note of that—unless the connections are too subtle to expect a person of his intelligence to notice them. Reasons have a special status simply because the contents of our minds have a special accessibility to us and ought accordingly to be taken note of. If amongst those contents there are certain beliefs such that if the person becomes fully aware of them and of their connections to that original belief, that original belief (in the absence of culpable resistances) would be inhibited, then he should let that happen. He cannot be expected to range over the whole world in search of what might inhibit his beliefs. He can be expected to range through his own mind, however.

Let us dig deeper yet in these somewhat speculative reflections. Suppose someone believes *p,* and also has an adequate reason *q* to believe *not-p;* and suppose further that the person sees all the logical and evidential connections involved in this. Add to this that the dispositions involved have not been culpably revised. Then his situation is that one innocent disposition yields the belief that *p,* another yields the belief that *q,* and yet another yields the belief that *p* conflicts with *q.* What reason is there in this situation for him to go one way rather than another? Why not give up the belief that *q* and keep the belief that *p,* rather than vice versa? Or why not give up the belief that *p* and *q* conflict?

Usually we have no choice in the matter. We come with various innate belief dispositions. These gradually become revised, and in good measure they are revised because the deliverance of one disposition conflicts with that of another, and the one yields. Gradually hierarchies of forcefulness develop. We trust vision more than testimony in some circumstances and on some matters; we trust one kind of memory, and one kind of perception, more than another; and so on. And these facts of our nature are the end of the matter. Deeper we cannot go. We cannot *show* that the totality of these dispositions leads us to truth. Of course we can rail against these native dispositions and the hierarchies of forcefulness that gradually emerge. We can undertake to revise these for some reason other than that they have proved unreliable. The Christian, though, will have a reason for not thus railing, for accepting our native and naturally developed noetic dispositions as trustworthy. He believes that we have been made thus by a good Creator. (Of course, in this very process the Christian is trusting the testimony of inference.) It is true that he may well acknowledge that some of our dispositions are signs of our fallenness, not part of our pristine nature, so that they are unreliable. The dispositions of which Marx and Freud made so much are examples. But the Christian will trust that the unreliability of such as these will show up.

To some this will look alarmingly slippery. Should we not *establish* the reliability of a belief disposition before we trust it—provided, of course, that we *can* restrain our trust in it? Well, how, if we are going to trust no belief disposition whatsoever until proved reliable, are we going to prove it reliable? In the very process we shall have to *assume* that some *are* reliable. Alternatively, suppose we acknowledge this fact and, taking for granted the reliability of some, try to establish the reliability of the others by reference to these? But which shall we pick as the touchstones? Surely any choice here, at this fundamental level, will be completely arbitrary.

Perhaps some of the deep motivation of the classical foundationalist comes to light here. Perhaps he thought that he could get around this unavoidable trust in our noetic dispositions as a whole by starting with propositions that we can "see" to be true, and then by reference to these establish the reliability of those dispositions which produce the acceptance of propositions that we do not just "see" to be true. But a fundamental objection arises immediately. Cannot one have the *experience* of "seeing a proposition to be true" when in fact it is false? And cannot one *think* one has this experience when one has some other?

There is in all of us a complex and natural flow of belief formation. In this natural flow we can and do, and sometimes should, deliberately intervene. The rules of rationality are in effect the rules of such intervention. They instruct us, in effect, to bring our other relevant beliefs into consciousness. Once we have done this, our created nature then once again does its trustworthy work of dispelling the original belief or confirming it (or neither)—provided that we do not culpably interfere.

## XIII

And now at last we can return to our beginning. Can belief in God be rational if it has no foundations? Could a person be justified in believing that God exists (or some other affirmative theistic proposition) without the justifying circumstance consisting in the fact that he believes it on the basis of other beliefs of his which he judges to be good evidence for it? Could a person whose belief that God exists is one of his immediate beliefs nonetheless be rationally justified in that belief? Or is it the case that if our theistic convictions are to be rational, they must be formed or reinforced in us exclusively by the "mechanism" of inference?

People come to the conviction that God exists in the most astonishing diversity of ways. Some pick up their theistic convictions from their parents; presumably it is the credulity disposition which is at work in such cases. Some find themselves overcome with a sense of guilt so vast and cosmic that no human being is adequate as its object. Some fall into a mystic trance and find themselves overcome with the conviction that they have met God. Some in suicidal desperation find themselves saying, "Yes,

I do believe," whereupon they have a sense of overwhelming peace. The evidentialist proposes slicing through all this diversity. One's belief that God exists is rational only if it is formed or sustained by good inference—by inferring it from others of one's beliefs which in fact provide adequate evidence for it. In the light of the criterion proposed, what is to be said about this claim?

What our criterion instructs us to consider is whether it is possible that there be a person who believes *immediately* that God exists, and at the same time has no adequate reason to surrender that belief. Or more precisely, whether there is a person who at the same time neither has nor ought to believe that he has any adequate reason to surrender that belief. Might a person's being in the situation of believing immediately that God exists represent no failure on his part to govern his beliefs as well as can rightly be demanded of him with respect to the goal of getting more amply in touch with reality?

I see no reason whatsoever to suppose that by the criterion offered the evidentialist challenge is tenable. I see no reason to suppose that people who hold as one of their immediate beliefs that God exists always have adequate reason to surrender that belief—or ought to believe that they do. I see no reason to suppose that holding the belief that God exists as one of one's immediate beliefs always represents some failure on one's part to govern one's assent as well as one ought.

However, those abstract and highly general theses of evidentialism no longer look very interesting, once we regard them in the light of the criterion offered. One of the burdens of this paper has been that issues of rationality are always situation specific. Once the impact of that sinks in, then no longer is it of much interest to spend time pondering whether evidentialism is false. It seems highly likely that it is. But the interesting and important question has become whether some specific person—I, or you, or whoever—who believes immediately that God exists is rational in that belief. Whether a given person is in fact rational in such belief cannot be answered in general and in the abstract, however. It can only be answered by scrutinizing the belief system of the individual believer, and the ways in which that believer has used his noetic capacities.

Perhaps a theistic believer who is not of any great philosophical sophistication has heard a lecture of Anthony Flew attacking religious belief, and perhaps he finds himself unable to uncover any flaws in the argument. Or perhaps he has heard a powerful lecture by some disciple of Freud arguing that religious belief represents nothing more than a surrogate satisfaction of one's need to feel secure, and perhaps, once again, he can find no flaw in the argument. It would appear that if this believer has puzzled over these arguments for a reasonable length of time, has talked to people who seem to him insightful, and so on, and still sees no flaws in the argument, then he is no longer rationally justified in his belief—provided, of course, he does not have evidence in favor of God's existence which counterbalance these. And it makes no difference now by what "mechanism" his theistic convictions were formed in him! By contrast, the person who has never heard of these arguments, and the person who justifiably believes them not sound, is in a relevantly different situation.

It is important to keep in mind here our main earlier conclusion, however. From the fact that it is not rational for some person to believe that God exists it does not follow that he ought to give up that belief. Rationality is only *prima facie* justification; lack of rationality, only *prima facie* impermissibility. Perhaps, in spite of its irrationality for him, the person ought to continue believing that God exists. Perhaps it is our duty to believe more firmly that God exists than any proposition which conflicts with this, and/or more firmly than we believe that a certain proposition *does* conflict with it. Of course, for a believer who is a member of the modern Western intelligentsia to have his theistic convictions prove nonrational is to be put into a deeply troubling situation. There is a biblical category which applies to such a situation. It is a *trial,* which the believer is called to endure. Sometimes suffering is a trial. May it not also be that sometimes the nonrationality of one's conviction that God exists is a trial, to be endured?

## XIV

And what, lastly, about the enthusiasts who so vexed Locke? Locke was persuaded that the enthusiasts claiming private revelations were irrational and, accordingly, irresponsible. They were acting in disobedience to their Creator. But if we do not demand of everyone in the field of religion good evidence for their convictions, said Locke, then we will simply have to acknowledge that anything goes. The concept of rational belief will simply have to be discarded. So Locke undertook to provide good evidence for his Christian convictions, and he challenged the enthusiasts to act likewise.

The evidentialist challenge which Locke laid down to the enthusiasts is untenable. But that does not mean that one is speechless in the face of crackpots. It does not mean that anything goes. Rather than demanding evidence from the enthusiast, one offers him adequate reasons for the falsehood of his beliefs. Sometimes he may concede the point and give up his convictions. In other cases, no doubt, he will continue merrily believing. But in this respect the approach implied by our criterion is surely no worse than Locke's. Locke's issuance of the evidentialist challenge was not noticeably effective in snuffing out British "enthusiasm"!

## APPENDIX

A reply to my contention in section IX, that an adequate criterion for rational justification in beliefs will itself have to incorporate, tacitly or explicitly, some normative concept, might go along the following lines. This contention may well be true for the *subjective* concept of rational obligation and justification. Surely it is not true for the *objective* concept. But the standard criteria for rational justification which have been proposed —classic foundationalism, reliabilism, and so on—should be seen as criteria for the *objective* concept. Accordingly, what was said in section IX does not touch these criteria. When these are understood as criteria for objective rational justification, there is no need for them to incorporate some normative concept. The objector might go on to charge that I have served the cause of confusion by failing to distinguish, more sharply than I did, my *no-adequate-reason-for-surrendering* proposal concerning objective rational justification from the normative-noetic qualifications attached so as to make it a criterion for subjective rational justification.

I think it will help to unravel the issues here if we turn, for a moment, from the noetic to the moral domain and consider the arguments of those who call for a distinction between objective and subjective obligation within the field of morality. Consider, for example, what Richard B. Brandt says on the matter in his book *Ethical Theory:*

> The definition of "moral obligation" we have outlined makes it possible for a person to make mistakes about his obligation. He may *think* his feeling of obligation is "objectively justified" when in fact it is not. This seems acceptable; we do think that people are sometimes mistaken about their duty or obligation. . . . Yet there is something wrong, as [an example] will make clear.
>
> [S]uppose a physician examined a patient suffering from allergies in 1920, when nothing was known of allergies. The physician advised and performed a series of operations (on the patient's nose and sinuses, for example) at considerable cost to the patient in suffering and money. Was the physician's behavior consistent with his moral obligations? We certainly incline to say it was. According to our total theory, as described above, however, it seems he did *not* do his duty, since, if he had been fully informed (including information about allergies), he would have felt obligated to treat for allergies.[20]

Brandt goes on to try to unravel this case by distinguishing between an *objective* and a *subjective* sense of "duty" and "obligation." The physician did his duty, says Brandt, if "duty" is used in the subjective sense. He did not do his duty if "duty" is used in the objective sense.

But is this correct? Is it true that, in some (standard) sense of the word "ought," the physician did not do what he ought to have done? I suggest that it is not. There is no (standard) sense of the word "ought" according to which Brandt's physician did not do what he ought to have done. I am assuming that the issue at stake here is not to be unraveled by the distinction between *prima facie* obligation and all-things-considered obligation.

If there were such an objective concept of obligation as Brandt proposes, one could believe and assert that *S* ought to do *y*, while yet with full sincerity advising *S* not to do *y*, praising him if he does not do *y* and blaming him if he does, and treating him as culpable if he does do *y*. This would be so if one used "ought" in the objective sense. For culpability is thought to attach to the subjective concept of obligation but not to the objective. I suggest, however, that there is no such concept of obligation. Our concept of obligation is inextricably connected with how we treat people: with the advice we give them, with our dispensing of praise and blame, with our treating of them as culpable. If one does believe that *S* ought to do *y*, then one cannot with sincerity advise him not to do *y*, or praise him for not doing *y*, or treat him as culpable if he does do *y*. The so-called *subjective* concept of obligation is the only concept of obligation there is.

But can we not simply judge whether the physician's action is or is not enjoined by objective moral law? Certainly we can. But to judge it to be enjoined by objective moral law is to assert, or imply, that he ought to do it. And, once again, one cannot believe that he ought to do it and with sincerity enjoin him not to do it. There is no difference between acting in accord with one's obligation and doing as well as can rightly be expected of one.

There is, indeed, a certain truth which those who make the objective/subjective distinction are trying to get at. In the case of Brandt's example that truth is this: A physician dealing with the same medical case that Brandt's physician was dealing with, but who differed from Brandt's physician *in that he was fully knowledgeable* on all relevant moral and medical facts, would be obliged to act differently from the way Brandt's physician was obliged to act. But quite obviously that does not imply that there is some concept of obligation according to which Brandt's physician is obliged to act as that fully knowledgeable physician would be obliged to act.

Of course, when confronted by Brandt's medical case, we can ask what a fully knowledgeable physician dealing with this medical case would be obliged to do. We can also, if we wish, *stipulate* that sometimes we will use the word "obliged" in such a way that Brandt's physician is "obliged" to do whatever a fully knowledgeable physician dealing with this case would be obliged to do. And we may, if we wish, call this the *objective* sense of "obligation." But that does not tell us what Brandt's physician—who after all is not fully knowledgeable—is obliged to do, using the word "obliged" in its normal English sense. The English word "obliged" is not as a matter of fact used to express that concept.

This analysis of the situation has implications for how we understand standard theories of moral obligation (which are not intentionalistic in character). Such theories should not be viewed as telling us what we—who are far from being fully knowledgeable persons—ought in fact to do. If viewed that way, they are radically deficient. Rather, they are best understood as theories which tell us what a person who is fully knowledgeable on the relevant facts ought to do. To get from that information to what we, in our concrete situations, ought to do, we must in the appropriate way take account of our justified error and ignorance.

Consider, for example, a hedonistic utilitarian who holds that the criterion for right action is the greatest pleasure of the greatest number. Such a theorist does not really have in mind that, of the options that confront a person at a given time, the one which would in fact produce the greatest happiness of the greatest number is the one he ought to perform. Rather, he means something like this: An agent who is fully knowledgeable as to the pleasurable consequences of his various options for action, and as to how the moral law applies to actions having such consequences, ought always to choose that option which yields the greatest happiness of the greatest number. For on the utilitarian's view a fully moral agent will always have it as his goal to bring it about that of those options for action which face him on any occasion, he will perform that one which yields the greatest happiness of the greatest number.

You and I, however, are not fully knowledgeable agents. Furthermore, some of our error and ignorance is justified. Accordingly, even if we have adopted the goal that the utilitarian recommends, it may well turn out that sometimes an alternative which would not yield the most pleasure is nonetheless such that we ought to try to perform it (if we did not try to perform it, given our state of error and ignorance, that would indicate a lack of commitment to the goal); and sometimes an alternative which *would* yield the most pleasure is such that we ought not to try to perform it. Our performing it, given our state of error and ignorance, would indicate that we were not fully committed to the goal of doing what will give the greatest happiness.

In short, it may well be that of some less pleasurable actions it is true that we ought to perform them, and of some more pleasurable actions, that we ought *not* to perform them. But if so, it will not be true that we ought always to do what is (in fact) most pleasure-yielding, and to avoid what is (in fact) less pleasure-yielding. Nonetheless we ought to have it as our goal to make this proposition true: Always we perform (what is in fact) the most pleasure-yielding of the options that confront us.

Similar things are to be said about the obligations of rationality. The person who does in fact have adequate reasons for refraining from his beliefs whenever he ought to have them, and who is fully knowledgeable about the presence and absence of such adequate reasons, ought to surrender a given belief as soon as he has adequate reason to do so. For he, along with everyone else, should have it as his goal to cease believing something as soon as he has adequate reason for doing so—other things being equal. For each proposition *p* which he believes, he should seek to make it true that he ceases to believe *p* as soon as he has adequate reason to do so.

But you and I are not such fully knowledgeable epistemic agents. We are often in justifiable error and ignorance on relevant matters. Because of that, there will be propositions we believe for which we have adequate reason to cease believing but which we are nonetheless permitted, even perhaps obliged, to believe; and there will be propositions we believe for which we do *not* have adequate reason to refrain but which we are nonetheless obliged to cease from believing. Almost certainly for each of us there is some proposition *p* which we believe of which it is not true that we are rational in believing it if and only if we lack adequate reason to refrain. Nonetheless each person should strive to bring it about that there is no proposition which he believes for which he has adequate reason to refrain.

What we learn from the analogy to the moral case is not that the criterion for rational belief which I have proposed is merely a criterion for the subjective sense of obligation. We learn something in the opposite direction: namely, that standard moral theories apply, as formulated, only to a person who is in a certain kind of ideal noetic situation. To apply to us in our factual fallen situations, they would have to take into account what we are and are not rationally justified in believing and in ceasing from believing.

## NOTES

1. Sometimes he also includes under reason our faculty for apprehending what is *evident* to us.

2. Cf. *Essay,* IV,19,4: "*Reason* is natural *revelation,* whereby the eternal Father of light, and Fountain of all knowledge communicates to mankind that portion of truth which he has laid within the reach of their natural faculties. *Revelation* is natural *reason* enlarged by a new set of discoveries communicated by God immediately, which reason vouches the truth of, by the testimony and proofs it gives that they come from God. So that he that takes away reason to make way for revelation, puts out the light of both."

3. Compare this passage: "God, when he makes the prophet, does not unmake the man. He leaves all his faculties in their natural state, to enable him to judge of his inspirations, whether they be of divine origin or no. When he illuminates the mind with supernatural light, he does not extinguish that which is natural. If he would have us assent to the truth of any proposition, he either evidences that truth by the usual methods of natural reason, or else makes it known to be a truth which he would have us assent to by his authority, and convinces us that it is from him, by some marks which reason cannot be mistaken in. Reason must be our last judge and guide in everything. I do not mean that we must consult reason, and examine whether a proposition revealed from God can be made out by natural principles, and if it cannot, that then we may reject it. But consult it we must, and by it examine whether it be a revelation from God or no: and if reason finds it to be revealed from God, reason then declares for it as much as for any other truth, and makes it one of her dictates." (*Essay,* IV,19,14)

4. Cf. *Essay,* IV,18,11: "If the boundaries be not set between faith and reason, no enthusiasm or extravagancy in religion can be contradicted.—If the provinces of faith and reason are not kept distinct by these boundaries, there will, in matter of religion, be no room for reason at all; and those extravagant opinions and ceremonies that are to be found in the several religions of the world will not deserve to be blamed; for to this crying up of faith in opposition to reason, we may, I think, in good measure, ascribe those absurdities that divide mankind. For men, having been principled with an opinion that they must not consult reason in the things of religion, however apparently contradictory to common sense and the very principles of all their knowledge, have let loose their fancies and natural superstition; and have been by them led into so strange opinions and extravagant practices in religion, that a considerate man cannot but stand amazed at their follies, and judge them so far from being acceptable to the great and wise God, that he cannot avoid thinking them ridiculous and offensive to a sober, good man. So that, in effect, religion, which should most distinguish us from beasts, and ought most peculiarly to elevate us as rational creatures above brutes, is that wherein men most often appear most irrational, and more senseless than beasts themselves."

5. I have argued for the rejection of classical foundationalism in Nicholas Wolterstorff, *Reason within the Bounds of Religion* (Grand Rapids, MI: Eerdmans, 1976).

6. Though in principle there may be other obligations that we have with respect to our believings, it is only these governance obligations of which Locke takes note. They are the only ones relevant to his purpose—as indeed to mine.

7. It is clear from the above that one can attach the word "rational" to

other facets of our noetic obligations than these. Perhaps here is also the place to remark that the word "rational" need not be directly hooked up to obligations but can be used simply to pick out a merit in beliefs concerning which one may or may not have obligation. This is connected with the comments about the concept of justification in note 12 below.

8. Provided the person has, or ought to have, the necessary conceptual equipment. See note 19 below.

9. Roderick Chisholm, *Theory of Knowledge,* 2nd ed. (Englewood Cliffs, N.J.: Prentice-Hall, 1977), p. 15.

10. There is another analysis of the resistance cases I have cited that ought to be considered. Perhaps the situation is not that the person resists believing, but that he resists acting in appropriate ways on what he does believe. Though I of course acknowledge that there are cases of this sort, it does seem to me that sometimes the resistance is a resistance to the believing. Probably a thorough adjudication between these two analyses would require a perusal of the relevant psychological literature. Such perusal has entered far too little into philosophical epistemology.

11. Alvin Goldman, "What Is Justified Belief?" in George S. Pappas, ed., *Justification and Knowledge* (Dordrecht: D. Reidel, 1979), pp. 9–10.

12. Might it be that the reliabilist, rather than giving a plainly incorrect criterion for rationally justified belief, is formulating a criterion for a different concept of justification than that with which I am dealing? Well, there is evidence that Goldman, for example, *thinks of* the concept of justification differently from how I think of it. He says this: "There may well be propositions which humans have an innate and irrepressible disposition to believe, e.g., 'Some events have causes'. But it seems unlikely that people's inability to refrain from believing such a proposition makes every belief in it justified." ("What Is Justified Belief?" p. 4) Now if a certain belief of a person really is ineluctible, then his holding that belief is no indication that he has failed to use his belief-governing capacities as well as can rightly be demanded of him; for one cannot rightly demand of a person what he cannot do. Accordingly, on the concept of justification with which I have been dealing, such a person is clearly justified in his belief, contrary to what Goldman says. So may it be that the philosophical literature presents us with two different concepts of rationally *justified belief*—not merely various criteria for *one* concept, but two different concepts for which theorists attempt to offer criteria? The one would be a normative concept. A person is (rationally) justified in believing *p* just in case in doing so he conforms to certain obligations that bear on him. And a reasonable assumption is that if he could not have failed to believe *p,* then he is not obliged not to do so. On this concept a person is, roughly speaking, rationally justified in his beliefs just in case he is doing as well in his believings as can rightly be demanded of him. The other concept of justified belief would be a purely evaluative concept. The word "justified" would pick out a certain merit in beliefs, a desirable feature of beliefs; "unjustified" would pick out a demerit in beliefs, a blemish. And a belief would have these merits and defects whether or not it was in any way within the control of the person to have or not have the belief.

The truth, in my judgment, is that there is no such concept of justification as this purely evaluative concept. The situation is not, I think, that Goldman and others are offering a criterion for a different concept of justified belief from that for which I propose to offer a criterion. The situation is rather that Goldman misapprehends the nature of the concept of justified belief. No doubt this misapprehension plays a role in his adopting the criterion he does.

In a person's system of belief we can pick out certain merits which lie between, as it were, all the beliefs being true and all the beliefs being in accord with what can rightly be demanded of that person. Perhaps some of those merits are picked out with our word "rational." And no doubt one of those in-between merits is that of all the beliefs being well-formed or sustained. But the word "justified" does not pick out that merit. The test cases will be those in which the belief is not reliably formed but in which we agree that the person could not rightly be expected to believe otherwise than he does. So look once more at our example of the young person in a primitive tribe. Can it really correctly be said of him that he is *not justified* in believing as he does? I suggest that there is no sense of the English word "justified" such that that can correctly be said of him.

Incidentally, there is a passage in Goldman's essay in which he himself is on the verge of recognizing that the one and only concept of justification is a normative concept. After considering a case which in his judgment calls for a revision in his unqualified reliabilist theory, he says, "So what we can say about Jones is that he *fails* to use a certain (conditionally) reliable process that he could and should have used. . . . So, he failed to do something which, epistemically, he should have done. This diagnosis suggests a fundamental change in our theory. The justificational status of a belief is not only a function of the cognitive processes *actually* employed in producing it; it is also a function of the processes that could and should be employed." (Ibid., p. 29)

13. In the sense of "reason" cited in the preceding paragraph the *event* of a person's believing *q* and believing that it is good evidence for *p* may be his reason for believing *p*.

14. Suppose that someone who believes *p*—perhaps because someone told him that *p* is true—later finds that the evidence for *p* is exactly balanced with that against *p*, that is, with that for *not-p*. What then constitute the obligations and permissions of rationality? Well, the "innocent-until-proved-guilty" principle which we are exploring says that he is permitted to continue believing *p*, for *p* has not been proved guilty. On the other hand, it would seem that he is also permitted to refrain from believing both *p* and *not-p*. What he is *not* permitted to do is to proceed to believe *not-p* on the basis of his awareness that the evidence for *p* and for *not-p* is equally balanced, for he should realize that believing thus is an unreliable "mechanism." (Shortly we shall see more clearly the relevance of this fact.) Of course, if the person had entered this situation believing *not-p* rather than *p*, then the opposite of all these things is true. Then he is permitted either to continue believing *not-p* or to believe neither *p* nor *not-p*, but not to believe *p* on the basis of his awareness that the evidence pro and con *not-p* is equally balanced. This yields what seems initially to be the paradoxical result, that of two people surveying the very same evidence and making the same responsible

judgment as to its weight, one may be permitted to believe *p* but not *not-p*, the other to believe *not-p* but not *p*.

Consider a different but related case. Suppose that a person who believes neither *p* nor *not-p* comes responsibly to the conviction that the evidence for these is equal. What ought he to do? Quite clearly, to refrain from believing either *p* or *not-p*. For to believe either of these on this basis is to believe it on account of what he should realize to be an unreliable "mechanism." Again, suppose that a person who believes *both p* and *not-p* discovers that the evidence for these is equal—and also notices that he believes both, and notices that they cannot both be true. (He may, of course, have been believing both without believing *p and not-p*.) What should, or may, he do? Once again, he is not permitted on the basis of his awareness of his situation to give up one and hang on to the other, for that would be to believe on account of what he should realize to be an unreliable "mechanism." Clearly what he is permitted to do, though, is give up both. But what about the last possibility, that of hanging on to both? Well, the "innocent-until-proved-guilty" principle would in fact seem to say that he is permitted to do this. And though at first this result takes one a bit aback, maybe it is correct. I think, however, that rarely will a person be able to do this—at least for any length of time. And we have already seen that he is not entitled, on the basis of his realization of the situation, to give up either one of them and hang on to the other. He is entitled only to give up both. (Surely such a person would not be rational in believing *p and not-p*. And it is surprising that this would be so, while at the same time it is rational for him to believe both *p* and *not-p*, realizing that they are contradictory.)

15. This last would be most in line with the conclusion drawn in note 14 above.

16. Consider someone who believes that *p* and who earlier held that same belief and held it nonrationally, having adequate reason to cease from holding it. Suppose that in the interim, though he retains the belief B*p*, he forgets those reasons. Suppose also that he is rationally justified in that forgetting; his not believing those reasons later on is rational on his part. And suppose that neither now nor at any time after all those events had transpired was there anything else in his situation relevant to the rationality of this belief than that he once held it in defiance of adequate reasons to give it up and later remembered it but justifiably forgot those reasons. Is he now, at this later point, still nonrational in holding that belief, even though now he neither has nor ought to have adequate reason to cease from that belief? If he *is* still not rational in holding it, then we have to insert a qualification into the above, assuring that the nonrationality of such a belief remains, even though now the person neither has nor ought to have adequate reason to give it up.

17. With this qualification: As mentioned before, the criterion makes no attempt to specify the rationality of the *firmness* with which beliefs are held.

18. Perhaps the rational person tolerates different degrees of unreliability for different sorts of propositions. This is an important issue which I cannot here explore.

19. Of course, the fact that all of some tiny child's beliefs are rationally *justified* does not imply any praiseworthiness on his part. Though lack of justification implies culpability, justification does not imply praiseworthiness. One could, of course, add some qualification to our criterion for rational belief so that it did imply this. Then, on the criterion, though the tiny child would not be unjustified in his beliefs, he would also not be justified.

20. Richard B. Brandt, *Ethical Theory* (Englewood Cliffs, N.J.: Prentice-Hall, 1959), pp. 360–61.

# Turning

George I. Mavrodes

Huyos settled himself on the stone bench and leaned back against the cool wall. He was in a sort of spacious but secluded pocket formed by the convoluted walls which surrounded the main square of his city. Between two walls he could see a slice of the square, and in the background he could hear the sounds of commerce and movement. The sky was blue and the sunshine bright. As other people came in to take their places on the benches and ledges he reflected on his own good fortune. And he had no intimation of the darkness which would fall upon him before an hour had passed.

The church has had many great doctors, he thought to himself, but perhaps not so many as one in every generation. Many Christians had never sat with a master such as Frisius. But in this alcove Frisius taught publicly two mornings a week. By custom and habit those who came regularly had places to sit. But anyone was welcome to come, and there were always people in back who were curious to see the famed preacher. Huyos had come like that at first, but he had come back, and back, until now he was a regular, and had his place. And he counted himself fortunate in the providence of God.

As the great clock finished striking the hour Frisius arrived, striding immediately to his accustomed place. Conversation ceased, as if cut by a knife. Without preliminaries Frisius spoke an invocation, asking for God's blessing there. And then he spoke to the people.

"Today," he said, "we are to begin to speak about the Decrees of God. But first I must say something else. For last week I mis-spoke myself, and I was rebuked for it by the Elder Sumisian."

He smiled a little then, almost shyly, and added, "But gently though, as is the courtesy of one who has lived long in the love of God."

Almost everyone there knew Sumisian by sight, though few knew him well. He was an old man, white of hair and beard, long a Christian. He came sometimes to hear Frisius, but not always. If he came early, the younger men would make room for him to sit; but if he came late, he would stand in back of the crowd. And he never spoke, even on the rare occasions when Frisius invited questions and discussion.

"You remember," Frisius went on, "that I said that our faith in God must be wholehearted and without reservation, a matter of total commitment. And that must be true of every aspect of our faith in God, including, for example, our belief that God is. That, too, must be something which we do from the bottom of our hearts, holding back no measure of assent. And it was there that I mis-spoke.

"What I said was that the degree of our belief should be total and unconditional. Those words were ill-chosen, though my intent was good."

Latecomers were still joining those who stood around the edges, but none of the regular attenders was distracted. For it was not often that Frisius had occasion to correct himself in public, though he did not hesitate to do it when convinced of an error.

"What I had in mind," Frisius went on, "was the doctrine of those who say that the degree of our belief that God exists should be proportional to the weight of the evidence which lies in favor of that belief, or to our assessment of that evidence. Such people study arguments for the existence of God, they collect the evidences for the resurrection of our Lord, they seek to determine the authorship of the biblical books, they trace the derivation of one manuscript from another. And they set that evidence, or their judgments about it, as conditions on the depth of their assent to the reality of God or to other cardinal doctrines of our faith.

"When I said that our belief must be unconditional, I had this doctrine—and this practice—in mind, and I meant to reject it. And in that, I think, I made no error."

"Such people," he continued, "must always be unstable, driven as a wave of the sea. For their faith is at the mercy of opinion about the evidence, and they must always keep before them the possibility that tomorrow's post may bring new evidence and so require some new adjustment in the depth of their commitment."

Normally, Huyos had no trouble in keeping his attention on the lecture. Often at the end of the hour he could recall no incident which transpired, nor what anyone there had worn, but only what Frisius had said. This day also began in that way, but gradually an uneasiness forced itself upon his attention, so that he had to notice it too. And when he did he realized that it had been there, in a sense, before he noticed. It had *grown* in him.

With this realization there came also two others. The first was that the uneasiness had a peculiar quality. It was gentle yet, not intense, but it had about it the flavor of dread. There was in it the apprehension of something not merely frightening but outside of the ordinary range of dangers — one feared to face it, perhaps, but one also did not know where to turn to face it or to flee from it.

The other realization was that the uneasiness was not spontaneous. It grew out of something which he had noticed. But he had noticed in that peculiar way in which one notices and does not notice, so that one does not know what it is that he has noticed. Huyos was sure there was something — he had seen something, heard it, smelled it — but what it was he could not say. But the dread grew out of what he noticed. And it seemed to him that he must still be noticing it, and the unease deepened.

"The books of the philosophers are many," Frisius was saying, "and in the library one may see their journals lying rank upon rank. Every conference hears a new argument spoken, every month sees a new refutation in print. But it is not only the philosophers. The historians, for example, do not readily yield to them in pride of ingenuity, inventiveness, originality. Their opinions also fill shelves. . . ."

And in Huyos it was as if there were two persons. One of them listened to Frisius. But the other scanned inward and outward, searching for the omen upon which the feeling was built.

Could it be something which Frisius was saying, Huyos asked himself. Well, possibly. But it seemed unlikely to him, for Frisius' words seemed plain and true (and Huyos did not yet know that there is also a darkness which has its home in the truth). So he searched in the scene before him, he listened to the background sounds, he tested the air with his nose. But he did not find what he sought.

"That is what I meant to reject," Frisius said. "But what I said was that our believing must be unconditional, not governed by a condition. And that, as Sumisian reminded me, is false. For there is a condition laid upon our believing, a condition to which we are duty-bound to submit. And it is not a new condition, not a special one. It is the one great and fundamental condition which lies upon all human life — indeed, upon all that is created. It is that all things, *all things,* are to be done within the will of God."

And Huyos heard him and continued his search. And the dread deepened, little by little.

"Eating and drinking, marrying and giving in marriage, lying down and rising up, all are to be done within God's good pleasure, and as he appoints them to us. We may not lawfully seize them unbidden, nor refuse them when called. And our believing, too, is subject to the same great requirement. Not every idol is made of stone, and if we were to say that believing has no need of obedience, that cognition is autonomous and lies outside of the sovereignty of God, there we would have made an idol of the mind itself. We would exalt a creature above or beside God.

"What we are to believe, then, and how much we are to believe it—that is for God to command and for us to obey. This is the condition which governs our intellectual life, and the noetic aspect of the faith. And the great doctrines of the Christian faith are those which God wills for us to believe without reservation, without dependence upon evidence, from the bottom of our hearts."

Frisius paused, and looked around. For a moment his eyes met those of Huyos, and passed on. And still Huyos seemed to himself to see, and not to know what he saw.

"I turn now to the subject of the morning," Frisius said. "It is that of the Decrees of God. . . . "

As Frisius went on with his lecture Huyos' feeling subsided until soon only the memory of it was left. And he knew, too, that the omen was gone. There was no further use in looking outward for it. If he was to find it at all, he must find it in his memory. And there he continued to search.

When the teaching session was over, Huyos walked slowly across the square, his head down. The fact for which he sought seemed to lie beneath the surface of his consciousness, like a shifting shape seen dimly under water. He probed for it and probed again, and his feet carried him past the bookstall of his friend, Luxon, which stood at the corner of the Street of the Tinsmiths.

Actually, Huyos' lodging was in the Street of the Tinsmiths, so he had come that way out of habit, without thinking. And as he passed, Luxon called out to him.

"Good morning, Huyos. It is a fine day from the Lord, is it not?"

Luxon had owned the bookstall for years. Newspapers, magazines, popular books, and a section for pornography. But since he had become a Christian, two years before, the pornography had gone. Those shelves, freshly painted, now displayed a selection of Christian books. And the girlie magazines were replaced with a rack of Christian periodicals. Luxon even stocked two or three scholarly theological journals, though of course the sales of these were rather slow.

"Good morning, Luxon," Huyos said, glancing up. And he passed on and turned the corner.

"Huhh," Luxon said to himself. "I wonder what's eating him." And he turned to serve a customer.

As Huyos turned westward into the Street of the Tinsmiths his shadow fell before him on the cobblestones. And as that happened the probe in his mind touched at last what it was seeking and locked on it, as a magnet clamps a bar of steel. His foot came down on the street and stopped as though it too were locked.

"That's it!" he said aloud. "It was his shadow."

The scene at the lecture came back before his mind's eye, as vivid as if he were carried back an hour in time. He saw the crowd, and Frisius standing in the sunlight lecturing, with his shadow slanting away from him. And Huyos saw that as he spoke the shadow grew imperceptibly darker. The change itself, that is, was imperceptible, but soon it could be seen that Frisius' shadow did not match the others. It was deeper, darker. And where his shadow should have merged with that of the wall, it did not disappear. Instead, the one darkness overlay the other, and one could still see the outline of the head and shoulders, a shadow upon a shadow. And as the scene played out in memory so also Huyos felt the dread stirring again.

And, then, as Frisius turned to the Decrees in the remembered lecture, his shadow lightened again as it had been before.

Huyos started up the street slowly, still wrapped in the folds of thought.

"So that was what I noticed," he said to himself. "Of course, he could not see it himself, for as he spoke to us he faced the East, and his shadow fell behind him. But I wonder if any of the others saw it. . . . I wonder if Sumisian was there today."

# Jerusalem and Athens Revisited

George I. Mavrodes

What is the relation between faith and reason? That is an old question, and it has sometimes been put in the form of an ancient metaphor, "What has Jerusalem to do with Athens?" But perhaps we should read that metaphorical question literally for a moment. If we do that, then we realize that Jerusalem and Athens have a host of different relations to each other. Geographical relations, for example, and economic, religious, cultural and military relations to boot. If we read the question metaphorically now, there may again be a variety of relations which belong to its answer. This paper is largely about just two of them, and of how they may react upon one another.

One way of construing the question at hand is to rephrase it as the question "Is theistic belief (or its more specific variant, Christian belief) rational?" I think that two other contributors to this volume construe the question in this way, or at least they address themselves to the latter question. And their answer to it, briefly put, is "Yes, belief in God is indeed rational."

That Yes, however, may easily be misunderstood. And part of this essay is devoted to distinguishing it from another sort of Yes which might also be spoken in response. Some of what is involved here may be made clearer by an analogy. Think of a party of explorers who, as they come across various rivers and lakes, ask the question "Is this water safe for drinking?" And suppose too that in a certain lake the water is heavily contaminated with some noxious bacteria. In that case the true answer to their question is "No, this water is not safe for drinking." Yes, that is the true answer, but perhaps it is not fully informative. For it may also be true that the water could readily be made safe, perhaps by boiling. It would be very useful for the explorers to know that, and so useful for their answer to incorporate somewhere that information.

That lake can be contrasted, however, with a pure mountain stream. That water, wholly uncontaminated, is safe for drinking *just as it stands.*

And no amount of boiling will make it safer. And we can think also of a lagoon, into which some subtle toxin has been introduced, a toxin which cannot be removed. That water is irremediably unsafe.

Now, the lake is in one important way like the lagoon. The water is unsafe as it stands. But in another way the lake is like the stream. That is, knowledgeable people need not despair of drinking it. It would not be surprising if some people, anxious not to lose this latter important information, were to fall into saying (somewhat carelessly) that the lake water *is* safe, perhaps adding now and then, "As long as you remember to boil it."

Now, many secular philosophers, and some religious ones (such as Sören Kierkegaard), have thought that, vis-à-vis rationality, theistic belief is rather like the lagoon. It is irrational, and this irrationality cannot be remedied. Others, including many Christian philosophers, have thought that it was more like the lake. In some circumstances theistic belief is irrational, but it can be made rational. (And usually philosophers who have thought this have also thought that they know how to make it rational.) And still a third group, perhaps smaller than the others, holds that theistic belief is most like the mountain stream. Nothing can be done to make it rational, because it is rational just as it stands.

Now, partisans of both of these latter two groups may say that theistic belief is rational. But that verbal congruence, though it signals a genuine area of agreement, also masks an important divergence. For according to one of these views attempts to make theistic belief rational are unnecessary and useless, while according to the other they are necessary and useful. We shall need to return to this distinction soon.

The analogy of the water, however, does not exhaust the ambivalences with which we shall be involved. For in it I have assumed that the expression "safe to drink" has a single well-understood sense. But the question "Is theistic faith rational?" suffers from the fact that rationality is itself sometimes construed differently by different philosophers. And such people will then be, in effect, trying to answer different questions. I shall try to separate two such questions.

## A PERMISSION TO BELIEVE

### *Rationality vs. Reasons*

If one seeks a Reformed view, one can hardly do better than to begin with Calvin.

> Yet they who strive to build up firm faith in Scripture through disputation are doing things backwards. For my part, although I do

> not excel either in great dexterity or eloquence, if I were struggling against the most crafty sort of despisers of God, who seek to appear shrewd and witty in disparaging Scripture, I am confident it would not be difficult for me to silence their clamorous voices. And if it were a useful labor to refute their cavils, I would with no great trouble shatter the boasts they mutter in their lurking places. But even if anyone clears God's Sacred Word from man's evil speaking, he will not at once imprint upon their hearts that certainty which piety requires. Since for unbelieving men religion seems to stand by opinion alone, they, in order not to believe anything foolishly or lightly, both wish and demand rational proof that Moses and the prophets spoke divinely. But I reply the testimony of the Spirit is more excellent than all reason.[1]

On reading this passage one gets the impression that Calvin was not at all eager to cater to the desires of these partisans of reason, these people who want rational proof and so on. They get rather short shrift here. They have, however, received a more sympathetic response from many other theologians and apologists. For example, a twentieth-century writer, Clark Pinnock, proposes to supply "reason enough," reason enough to commit oneself to Christ in trust and obedience. And he describes his project in this way:

> I am writing, then, for those who do not believe and for those who experience difficulties in their believing. "Wisdom is calling out. Reason is making herself heard" (Proverbs 8:1). As one who struggles with faith in the setting of the secular university, I think I am sensitive to the pervasive influence of secularity in the modern world. I know what it is like to feel that we live in a relative and contingent universe and can do without God and salvation. I do not have to imagine the doubts and uncertainties people feel when the demands of the gospel confront them. But I am also convinced that the Christian world view is adequate intellectually, factually and morally. And I delight in this opportunity to share with others the evidence I have discovered.[2]

It would seem that if Pinnock is successful, then those who desire to have a reason for their belief will be able to find it.

Perhaps even Alvin Plantinga and Nicholas Wolterstorff, Reformed scholars who have essays in this volume, may seem to be more sympathetic to the claims of reason than was Calvin. For they are ready to argue that it is indeed perfectly rational to believe in God. But perhaps this is too hasty, and they may be closer to Calvin than might appear. For Calvin's "crafty" despisers of God may be construed as holding that it would not be rational for them, in their present circumstances, to believe. And they may be challenging Calvin and his successors to *make* it rational, by supplying them with something which they do not now have, presumably a reason for belief. But Plantinga and Wolterstorff, I think, completely reject the project of making theistic faith rational. Like Calvin they have no intention of providing unbelievers with reasons to believe or, for that matter, of providing believers with reasons to continue in their faith. And so they may be, after all, not very far from the position of the *Institutes*.

But what then is the point of their arguments about rationality? As I understand it, their claim is that theistic faith is not to be *made* rational. Rather, it is *already* rational, just as it stands. Unbelievers do not need to be provided with something which they do not now have, in order that their conversion may be rational. They are already in circumstances in which it would be reasonable for them to believe. And believers are not properly subject to the charge of irrationality. For their faith is perfectly rational.[3]

But what of those theists who, though they believe, can give no reason for their belief? They have no argument for the existence of God, they cite no evidence, and so on. Is their belief indeed rational? Plantinga and Wolterstorff reply that it certainly is. Indeed, the main line of their argument is that, perhaps contrary to much common assumption, theistic belief has absolutely no need of reasons and evidence in order to be rational. It is rational to have belief in God as one of your "basic" beliefs—that is, as a belief which is not held on the basis of any other belief. And they hold, for the most part, that the characteristic and preferred way to hold theistic beliefs is in this basic way. The mature and well-instructed believer will have no reasons for his faith. (I say that this is their view "for the most part" because in a curious article Wolterstorff appears to deny it. I come back to that later.)

### *Permissions and Reasons*

In thinking about this claim it is important not to overestimate its strength or its consequences. It is not as strong as it might at first seem. Plantinga and Wolterstorff claim that belief in God is rational. Those who have it at all have it rationally, and those who do not have it would be rational in adopting it. But this does not entail that atheists are irrational in their atheism or that it would be irrational for believers to abandon their faith. And convincing someone that it would be rational for him to believe in God does not amount to giving him a reason for believing in God. And so there would be nothing paradoxical or perverse in someone's agreeing that it would be rational for him to believe in God and yet cheerfully persisting in his atheism. Or, to put all of these points more carefully, that is the way things are, *given the Plantinga-Wolterstorff sense of "rationality."*

The reason for this is that these philosophers construe rationality as equivalent to a moral (or quasi-moral) *permission.* For me to have a belief rationally is for me to be within my rights, my epistemic rights, in holding that belief. If I violate no rule of intellectual morality in holding the belief, then I am justified in holding it, and I hold it rationally. My rational beliefs, then, are those which I am permitted, within the bounds of intellectual morality, to hold.[4]

It is a feature of the logic of permission, however, that a permission is not equivalent to a duty and that a person may have, and often does have, equally good permissions for two or more incompatible courses of action. We recognize this all the time in ordinary (nonepistemic) contexts. I may be perfectly well within my moral and legal rights in walking down the sunny side of the street. It does not follow that I *ought* to walk on the sunny side, that I have any sort of duty to do so. For it may also be within my rights to walk on the shady side. Consequently, the fact that I am permitted to walk on the sunny side cannot itself be a reason for walking there. And there is nothing perverse or paradoxical in a person's agreeing that he has a right to walk on the sunny side but continuing to walk on the shady side. For that, too, may well be within his rights.

In just the same way, if we construe rationality as a sort of epistemic permission, then the fact that a certain belief is, or would be, rational is not a reason for holding it. And there would be nothing queer (or uncommon, for that matter) in rejecting beliefs which one recognizes as rational.

There might, of course, be some other, perhaps stronger, sense of "rational" in which the fact that a belief is, or would be, rational is a strong reason—maybe even a conclusive reason—for adopting it. And, *given that sense,* it would be strange to admit the rationality of the belief but to reject the belief itself. The claim that theistic belief is rational in this stronger sense, however, would require different arguments from those which Plantinga and Wolterstorff marshall. And their actual claims are couched in terms of the weaker sense of rationality.

Their claims, however, though not as strong as might at first appear, are not inconsequential for Christian faith. For while the fact that a belief is rational, in this sense, is not a reason for holding it, the rationality does eliminate a possible reason for *not* holding it. Again, this has its parallel in nonepistemic contexts. If it were illegal to walk on the shady side, that would be a reason, I suppose, for not walking there. If someone, however, could show that it was not in fact illegal—we had simply misunderstood the law, perhaps—then the apparent reason for not walking there would disappear. In the same way, the fact that a certain belief would be irrational is a reason (though perhaps not a conclusive reason) for not holding it. If someone could show that it is not, in fact, irrational, then this apparent reason disappears. Now there might be people who would believe in God were it not for the fact that they think that such a belief would be irrational. And there might be believers who are unsure about their faith, who are perhaps even on the point of abandoning the faith, because they suspect that their belief is irrational. If there are such people, then the Plantinga-Wolterstorff line of argument may help them. For it will eliminate this barrier which stands in the way of their believing.

### *Positive and Negative Apologetics*

Are there really any people like that, people who would believe in God (or who would continue believing) if only they could be convinced that it was rational to do so? This question may be usefully compared with another. Are there people who would believe in God (or who would continue believing) if only they could be convinced that there was some positive reason, some evidence, in favor of that belief? Since (as we have already noted) the fact that a belief is rational is not a reason in favor of it, these are two different questions. And the first is a special case of a more general question, that of whether there are people who would believe were it not for something which they take to be a reason *against* holding that belief. A person who thinks that there are people of this sort may well think it to be useful to engage in what we may call "negative" apologetics. That is, he may think it useful to show that apparent reasons against theistic belief (for example, the problem of evil and such) are not as strong as they appear, that they will not stand up under careful scrutiny, and so on. Negative apologetics consists of refuting and rebutting arguments against the faith. Plantinga and Wolterstorff apparently do believe that such things are useful, and their arguments for the rationality of religious belief appear to be examples of negative apologetics.

A person who believes that there are people who would believe if they had reasons which supported the faith might well think it useful to engage in "positive" apologetics. This would be the attempt to provide such reasons—arguments for the existence of God, for example, or some such thing. The history of Christian thought, of course, provides many examples of positive apologetics.

Some people, however, who take negative apologetics to be useful are not at all enthusiastic about positive apologetics. Since the two questions about the circumstances under which people would believe are different, it is possible to return different answers to them. And it may in fact be characteristic of Reformed theology to make just that distinction. At least, in the curious article to which I referred earlier, Wolterstorff maintains that Reformed theology does characteristically return different answers to these questions. (And he apparently endorses this approach himself.) He says that the Reformed tradition has been "skeptical of the benefit of giving evidence" but also that it has "characteristically gone on the attack against objections to Christianity."[5] And he tries to explain why this is so.

Why are Reformed thinkers skeptical of the value of positive apologetics? Here arises one of the curious features of this article. We might have expected Wolterstorff to say that it is because one needs no evidence for belief in God: it is rational to believe without a reason. But in fact he says almost the opposite. Speaking of a typical case of unbelief, Wolterstorff says, "What the Reformed person would suspect as operative in this and other cases of unbelief is not so much insufficient awareness of the evidence, as it is resistance to the available evidence."[6] And so the Reformed analysis of unbelief, according to Wolterstorff, is that people already have plenty of evidence but they resist it. So it is not useful to give them any more evidence.

It is not easy to see what to make of this way of speaking about evidence, given the other views about the rational status of theistic belief. Maybe it represents a deep ambivalence in Reformed thought, a tendency to oscillate between holding that belief in God is backed by plenty of evidence and holding that it involves no evidence whatever. But anyway, if what Wolterstorff says here is correct, then the general thrust of the traditional "world-based" theistic arguments—arguments such as the cosmological and the teleological—must be correct. For Wolterstorff suggests that it is the "richly complex design of the cosmos and of ourselves" which constitutes the universal evidence for God's existence. And this is just the sort of thing on which such arguments focus. Of course, one or another such argument may be faulty in its formulation, but the general idea of such argumentation must be correct, and not only in the minimal sense that there are sound arguments of this sort for the existence of God. Such arguments would also be correct in that they would formalize the grounds on which believers actually held their faith, and they would express evidence on which unbelievers could actually adopt the faith.

Perhaps, however, Wolterstorff's reference to evidence here is simply an inadvertence, not to be taken very seriously. For he also says that Calvin did not believe that we infer God's existence from the world's design. And there is some reason to think that Wolterstorff may be confusing the concept of evidence with something else. He claims (and also attributes the claim to Calvin) that human beings have a natural tendency or disposition to believe in God and that this disposition is triggered or activated by our observation of the beauty and wonder of the world.[7] And it looks as though he may be taking this fact—the activation of a disposition to believe—as equivalent to evidence for the resulting belief. But that would be a mistake.

In general, the fact that a certain circumstance, event, and so on—call it "C"—activates a disposition to form and hold a certain belief, B, does not at all make C evidence for B. Some men, for example, apparently have a disposition to believe that they are wonderful entertainers, and this disposition is activated by drinking two or three cocktails. That fact, however, does not make the existence of alcohol *evidence* that these people are great entertainers. We need not deny either the disposition or its triggering mechanism in order to maintain that the resulting belief is groundless. In the same way, the mere fact that the design of the world naturally triggers a belief in God does not constitute that design as *evidence* of the existence of God. And people may resist the activation of that disposition without thereby resisting *evidence*.

No doubt there are cases in which something which triggers a disposition to believe is also evidence for the corresponding belief. (In fact, we may have a general disposition to believe in accordance with evidence.) But the triggering relation and the evidential relation are not identical. Maybe the design of the world is, after all, good evidence for the existence of God. But the fact that it naturally triggers the belief does not show that it is. And perhaps Wolterstorff, given his unenthusiastic attitude toward positive apologetics, would not be much interested in trying to show that it is.[8]

### *Reason and Rationalization*

This possible ambivalence about evidence, however, is not the only (or even the most interesting) curious feature in this article. The second—and this one apparently does run deep in Reformed thinking—involves the differing responses to our two earlier questions, the different attitudes toward positive and negative apologetics. The Reformed apologist, we remember, is described as "skeptical of the benefit of giving evidence," but he goes "on the attack against objections to Christianity." Is there a rationale for this difference? Wolterstorff believes that there is, and he tries to derive it from the Reformed analysis of unbelief. But in fact that analysis does not support this divergence of attitude.

Suppose we ask some unbeliever why he does not believe, and he responds (as Bertrand Russell claimed he would reply, even to God himself), "Not enough evidence!" According to the Reformed analysis (as Wolterstorff presents it) this reply is not really informative if it is taken at face value. It does not accurately represent the real source or dynamic of unbelief. It expresses, not the rationale of unbelief, but rather its *rationalization.* It conceals—indeed, its purpose is to conceal—the real source of unbelief. The facts of the case are that (on one interpretation) the unbeliever has plenty of evidence or (on the other interpretation) that he needs no evidence. In either case he is resisting something, either evidence or a natural disposition, and this resistance is driven by a sinful desire not to acknowledge God. The unbeliever says he does not believe because he has no evidence, but we know better. He does not believe because of sin.

Well, what to do? Here, Wolterstorff claims, we can learn something from Freud and Marx, for they uncovered and analyzed some of the other rationalizations which also infect our intellectual lives. And what we can learn here is that

> Given its sources, the way to relieve someone of an ideology or rationalization is not to lay in front of him or her evidence for its falsehood. Usually that won't work. One must get at those hidden dynamics and bring them to light. Critique or therapy, rather than presenting evidence, is what is required.[9]

Well, perhaps so. At least, assuming that the analysis is correct, there is something plausible, even if not compelling, in the prescription. But now think of asking another unbeliever why he does not believe. He says, "Because I have counterevidence. I have objections to theistic belief. It is irrational, and there is the problem of evil, and so on." Not really a surprising response. But the curious thing is that Wolterstorff appears to accept this response at face value. He treats it as if it were really informative, and not merely as a rationalization. It is apparently worthy of being met "head-on" and is not simply to be circumvented by therapeutic procedures. The Reformed apologist goes on the attack against such objections. And so the apologist argues—actually seriously argues—that theistic belief is rational rather than irrational, that the problem of evil can be solved, and so on. Is not that a curious response?

Why does not the Reformed apologist rather say, "All this talk about counterevidence, objections, irrationality, the problem of evil, and so on, is just a smokescreen, a mere rationalization. It is useless to argue about such things. It would be futile to produce theodicies and defenses with reference to evil, or to show that theistic belief is rational after all. These alleged objections are symptoms of a deep-seated resistance against the truth of God. What is needed is therapy, the evangelist's analogue of the psychoanalyst's couch. When the resistance is overcome, the objections will not amount to a hill of beans!"

I do not know why the Reformed thinker does not respond in this way. Whatever reason there is for thinking that "No evidence!" is a rationalization also supports the judgment that "I have objections!" is a rationalization. In fact, it would be a little surprising if a deep-seated and sinful resistance to God did not give rise, in sophisticated people, to rationalizations in the forms of objections, counterarguments, and so on. And if rationalizations call for therapy, why then therapy it should be.

We may nevertheless still feel that there is something useful in refuting objections—in showing that the occurrence of evil is not incompatible with God's existence, for example, or in showing that we violate no intellectual duty in believing in God. And this suspicion, I think, is correct.

This suspicion parallels another, a suspicion about the propriety of positive apologetics. If we think that unbelief is basically a matter of resistance, then there is something plausible, as I said before, in undertaking some therapeutic procedure. But that is not the *only* plausible response. If we think that someone is resisting or ignoring evidence, then we might try to make that evidence still more insistent, more explicit, and so on. That, too, seems to be a plausible response. And that, of course, is what the positive apologist tries to do. He tries to find something which the unbeliever already knows and acknowledges, and to show that this acknowledged fact supports, in one way or another, the belief that God exists. And *both* of these approaches, that of the apologist as well as that of the therapist, strikes us, I think, as plausible.

The apologist, of course, is not bound to be successful. Every valid argument is reversible. Someone who is determined to remain an atheist at all costs can always buy consistency by denying the apologist's premise, even if this means giving up some previously acknowledged conviction. In this way a sound argument may make its hearer more ignorant than he was before. But the possibility of failure is not peculiar to the apologist. Unbelievers can, and often do, resist nonapologetic endeavors to bring them into the faith. Many attempts to dissolve or circumvent the noetic effects of sin by nonevidential means produce no noticeable results. According to a famous Reformed acronym, indeed, the grace of God is irresistible. Perhaps it is, but the methods of his human servants, whether of the apologetic or therapeutic variety, do not seem to share fully in that efficacy.

We are, then, in something like the following position. We can agree with Wolterstorff that it is plausible to undertake "critique and therapy" in the case of someone who pleads insufficient evidence as his reason for unbelief, and that it is also plausible to "go on the attack" against objections to the faith. But also (and apparently against Wolterstorff) we want to hold that it is plausible to meet the charge of insufficient evidence "head-on" by trying to make the available evidence plainer and more explicit. And we can also hold that it is plausible to undertake nonevidential procedures to deal with objections and counterarguments.

### *Belief and Unbelief*

Must a person who thinks in this way therefore reject Wolterstorff's Reformed analysis of unbelief, the analysis which proceeds in terms of sin and resistance? No, or at least not completely. What he needs is the claim that the epistemic situation is complex, especially so in the case of deep-running beliefs which are intimately connected with many aspects of one's life, both cognitively and otherwise. When we direct our attention to certain aspects of that complexity, then the evidentialist approaches seem plausible. But other aspects of the same complex make nonevidentialist procedures seem attractive. Wolterstorff seems to focus upon one sort of aspect when he considers people who complain about lack of evidence, and on the other sort of aspect when objections are raised. But it would be better to recognize the complexity of both sorts of cases.

Perhaps the complexity arises in more than one way. For one thing, unbelievers are not characteristically walking textbooks of logic, any more than are believers. They are not monoliths of single-mindedness and consistency. No, in them there is a mixture of motives and a mixture of principles, not all of them readily harmonizable. In theological terms we might say that in them there is both the image of God and the mark of the beast, and that (at least if they are in any real way "hearers" of the Gospel) both grace and sin abound in their lives. Any realistic appraisal of how they can usefully be approached with the truth of theism, or of Christianity, must take into account the mixed character of their own situation.

There may also be other sources of complexity. Maybe we do not yet have at hand an illuminating model of epistemic realities, either as they are or as they ought to be. Plantinga and Wolterstorff work within the structure of "foundationalist" epistemology. In this scheme every belief is either "basic," and so held without evidence and on the basis of no other beliefs at all, or else it is "derived." If it is derived, then it is held on the basis of those other beliefs from which it is derived and which provide it with whatever support it may have. The relations of derivation and support are strictly one-way, and so derived beliefs must ultimately get their support from basic beliefs. One naturally thinks of the model of a building, in which each brick rests on one or more other bricks until one comes to the foundations, which rest upon no part of the structure at all. But perhaps this scheme is somehow too simple.

Readers of this volume who are theists might usefully try the following experiment on themselves. Pause for a moment and consider your own belief that God exists, just as it stands right now. (Nontheist readers might consider some comparably deep-running component of their own belief systems.) Is that belief, as it functions right now in your own intellectual life, based upon some other beliefs which you hold? And if so, what are those other beliefs, and *how* is the belief in God's existence based on them? (That is, by virtue of what relation do these other beliefs support this one? Do they entail it, for example, or render it probable, or what?) It will not be surprising if many readers are puzzled by this reflection and find themselves at a loss to answer these questions. For some very sophisticated and thoughtful people, who have considered these questions at great length, are apparently in a similar quandary. Plantinga, for example, sometimes argues that the belief that God exists is properly basic, and that it will in fact be basic in the cognitive system of any mature and well-instructed believer. But at other times, or in other moods, he suggests that this belief is not basic but derived, and that the theist's really basic beliefs are something like *God made the world,* or *God helped me when I was in trouble,* or *God speaks to me when I read the Bible,* or something of the sort.[10] Now, these latter beliefs are themselves religious and theistic beliefs. They seem openly to be about God and so on. And so the claim that the belief that God exists is derived from them is not exactly like the claim that it is derived from some more neutral-sounding belief such as *Some things change* or *Arctic terns perform marvelous feats of navigation.* But, then, it is not very much like the claim that *God exists* is basic, either. What are we to make of this ambivalence? Why does not Plantinga come down firmly on one side or the other, opting either for the basicality or the derivative character of *God exists*? At the very least, why does he not tell us what status it holds in his own belief structure, that of a sophisticated believer who has long pondered these questions? One has the impression that he is unable to settle these questions to his own satisfaction.

In a well-settled and stable building every brick has a firm place. Either it sits on top of some other part of the structure, or else it does not. Must we suppose that there is some comparable fact about Plantinga's cognitive structure—that the belief that God exists either is or is not in the foundations, and that is all there is to it? If so, why the ambivalence? Is it that though there is a fact there, Plantinga is not in a good position to discover it? Is it that he cannot get a good clear view of his own cognitive structure? Well, perhaps. It is certainly a possibility. But recognizing this possibility will probably make us more tolerant of a person who claims that in *his* epistemic building some other beliefs are the basic ones and properly so.

Alternatively, we might come to suspect that the ambivalence arises because there is no such fact there to be discovered. That is, we may suspect that the picture of the building with its firmly placed bricks is not a suitable model of our intellectual life, and that somehow—though we may not know just how—the real situation is different or more complicated.

In any case, we can retain the Reformed analysis of unbelief without any compulsion to take up different attitudes toward the propriety or utility of positive and negative apologetics. And if it seems plausible to us, as it does to me, to suppose that negative apologetics may sometimes be appropriate and useful, we may also, without any logical difficulty, suppose the same of positive apologetics.

### *Alternative Projects*

There are, of course, still other projects which we may have in mind when we undertake to examine faith and reason. We may, for example, simply want to set the record straight. That is, we may simply want to register, "for the record," what we take to be the truth in the face of some contrary claims by an unbeliever. In that way we do not let the claims of unbelief go unchallenged, though in recording our challenge we may not concern ourselves greatly with the question of just who may benefit from it.

Setting the record straight, however, may be attempted in more than one way. If some atheist asserts that belief in God is irrational, for example, we might content ourselves with merely contradicting him. We would, that is, simply assert that belief in God *is* rational, and let it go at that. But, on the other hand, we might try to go further, producing some argument in an attempt to *prove* that theistic faith is rational. That would be a different and more ambitious project.

The atheist, too, might have attempted to go further. He might have put forward some argument in support of his charge of irrationality. In that case we would have at least three alternatives by way of setting the record straight. We could simply assert that the faith is rational, or we could produce a positive argument in support of its rationality, or we could undertake to refute the atheist's argument. Between them Plantinga and Wolterstorff engage themselves in versions of all three of these projects in this volume. (But it may be significant that Plantinga does not put forth a positive argument to support his view that theistic belief is, or can be, properly basic.)

But now, what of the atheist who asserts, not that theistic belief is irrational, but rather that it is false? He claims, that is, that there is no God. Might we not want to set the record straight on that point also? If so, then we have again two alternatives which parallel those pertaining to rationality. We may simply assert that there is a God, or we may try to support this claim with some argument. If the atheist puts forward some argument of his own in support of his atheism, then we have three alternatives, again paralleling the earlier triad. We may simply assert that there is a God, we may support that claim with an argument, or we may try to refute the atheist's argument.

Both Plantinga and Wolterstorff assert without hesitation that there is a God. In that way they set the record straight against this sort of atheistic claim. And Plantinga, at least, also engages in the project of refuting arguments which purport to show that there is no God. He has written extensively, for example, in refuting various atheistic arguments from evil. But both Plantinga and Wolterstorff suggest that there is something very suspect, to say the least, about undertaking the third alternative, that of providing a positive argument in favor of theistic belief. There is a "Reformed objection" to this project.

Against a person who argues that belief in God is irrational, then, one can set the record straight in three ways. But if he argues that belief in God is false, we can set it straight in only two ways. We cannot, or should not, produce a positive argument in favor of theistic belief. Or so, at least, it is suggested. And why should that be?

Well, maybe we cannot reply to the atheist in the third way because there simply are not any good arguments for God's existence. Of course, some people try to reply in this way, like Pinnock, but their arguments are failures, defective in some important way. And nobody can do better. According to this view there just is not any good natural theology to be found. If this is true, then we would have an explanation of why positive apologetics cannot be a way of setting the record straight.

Now, in fact Plantinga sometimes appears to believe that there are not any good arguments for God. In *God and Other Minds* he examined several traditional lines of argumentation and concluded that they were defective. And in this volume he asks again whether these arguments, singly or together, constitute proofs of God's existence. His answer is "no doubt they don't."[11] In the same place, however, Plantinga says that these arguments probably do provide evidence for God's existence, even "sufficient" evidence. And the ontological argument, he says, "is just as satisfactory, I think, as any serious argument philosophers have proposed for any important conclusion. . . . The ontological argument provides as good grounds for the existence of God as does any serious philosophical argument for any important philosophical conclusion."[12] But if natural theology can be *that* good, as good as the best arguments anywhere in serious philosophy, good enough to provide sufficient evidence for belief in God, then why should not it too be part of setting the record straight? And why should we not put forward these powerful arguments as *proofs* of God? According to what standard do they fall short of being proofs?

In *God and Other Minds* Plantinga said:

> What the natural theologian sets out to do is to show that some of the central beliefs of theism follow deductively or inductively from propositions that are obviously true and accepted by nearly every sane man (e.g., some things are in motion) together with propositions that are self-evident or necessarily true.[13]

This is put forward as a criterion of success in natural theology. Perhaps Plantinga also takes it, or something very much like it, to be a criterion of success in the project of proving something. And perhaps it is against this standard that the theistic arguments are judged to be failures.

This criterion is a curious mixture of stringency and laxness. It is, on the one hand, highly restrictive of the premises to which a natural theologian may properly appeal. These premises, if they are not necessary truths, must be either self-evident (that is, I suppose, such that no one could possibly understand them without believing them) or else obvious and believed by nearly every sane man. It is easy to see that many attempts at theistic argumentation, regardless of what their virtues may be, fail to meet this requirement. Popular versions of the teleological argument, for example, generally begin with some remarkable feature of the natural world, such as the amazing navigational abilities of the arctic tern. But it is not a necessary truth that arctic terns have these remarkable abilities, nor is the fact that they do a fact which is believed by nearly every sane man. Millions and millions of people, maybe even half the people in the world, have never heard of arctic terns and have no beliefs at all about them. And so those arguments do not satisfy the Plantinga criterion.

In one respect, however, this criterion is strangely lax. For, as it stands, it allows the natural theologian to use as a premise just any *necessary* truth which he pleases. The other clauses in the criterion stress the requirements of obviousness and universal acceptability. But necessary truths, though of course they are true, need not be at all obvious or believed by nearly every sane person. So there might be arguments which satisfy this criterion even though they have very obscure and doubtful premises indeed.

More importantly here, there may be theistic arguments which satisfy this criterion. Indeed, maybe Plantinga himself has developed such arguments. In *The Nature of Necessity* he puts forward a couple of versions of the ontological argument and then says:

> What shall we say of these arguments? Clearly they are valid; and hence they show that if it is even possible that God, so thought of, exists, then it is true and necessarily true that he does. The only question of interest, it seems to me, is whether its main premiss—that indeed unsurpassable greatness is possibly exemplified, that there is an essence entailing unsurpassable greatness—is *true*. I think this premiss is indeed true. Accordingly, I think this version of the Ontological Argument is sound.[14]

Now, if these arguments are indeed sound, then the proposition *God exists* is not only true; it is necessarily true. But every necessary truth follows logically from some other necessary truth. In fact, every necessary truth follows very simply from some other. For consider any proposition, *p*, no matter how obscure. If *p* is a necessary truth, then so also is

(1) *p*, and $3 + 5 = 8$.

And *p* follows from (1) by one of the most elementary operations in logic. So if Plantinga is right about the necessary truth of *God exists,* then the derivation of *God exists* from a conjunction such as (1) would satisfy his criterion for success in natural theology.

It may be said that if *God exists* is in need of a proof, then so also is (1). That may be right, but as it stands, Plantinga's criterion takes no account of such facts. That is why I say it is strangely lax. Perhaps, however, that is merely inadvertent. It would be in the spirit of this criterion to strengthen it by restricting the acceptable necessary truths to those which are obvious and universally believed, just as the contingent premises are restricted. That would make the criterion uniformly stringent. And just this amendment is apparently accepted by Plantinga. He believes that his own version of the ontological argument is sound, and its premises (if they are true at all) are necessarily true. But he says of it:

> It must be conceded, however, that argument A is not a successful piece of natural theology. For the latter typically draws its premises from the stock of propositions accepted by nearly every sane man, or perhaps nearly every rational man.[15]

And he is correct in recognizing that the premises of his argument, even if they are necessarily true, are not universally accepted.

Now when the Plantinga criterion is strengthened in this way, it is very restrictive indeed. "The stock of propositions accepted by nearly every sane man" is, I would suppose, a very small stock, and in all probability not very much of interest follows from it. Plantinga is almost surely right in thinking that no piece of natural theology is successful in terms of this criterion, and that no other piece of serious philosophical argumentation satisfies it either. But so what?

We can, if we wish, define terms such as "proof" and "natural theology" in terms of this highly restrictive criterion. In that case there will be no successful theistic "proof." Or we can reject that definition and propose some other. In that case there may well be a successful "proof" of God. But that difference, so far, would be a merely verbal one. The fact is, however, that every sane man knows a lot of things which are not accepted by nearly every sane man. I know where I live, for example, and whether I had breakfast this morning, and what the weather is like as I write here in Ann Arbor. But the vast majority of "sane men" have no opinion at all about my breakfast or the Ann Arbor weather. And each of them, in turn, no doubt knows something which I do not. And every one of us can endeavor to extend his own knowledge, and that of his acquaintances, by reasoning and arguing on the basis of what *they* know, even if it is not universally accepted. Whether we call such arguments "proofs" is a matter of terminological choice. But it is a question of substance as to whether such a procedure, whatever we may call it, is one which is legitimate and useful as a part of Christian evangelism and nurture. That brings us to the second part of this paper.

## A REASON FOR BELIEVING

### *Rational Ambitions*

A person who wants his beliefs to be rational, in the Plantinga-Wolterstorff sense, has so far put forth a minimal ambition for his beliefs. His desire is analogous to that of a person who wants his actions to be legal. Many people, in fact, have that desire about their own actions, and there is nothing wrong with it. But hardly anyone satisfies himself with such a minimal ambition. Most people also want something else for their actions. They hope that they will be profitable, for example, or pleasant, or useful, or something of the sort. Now, the desire that one's actions be legal is itself a legal desire. But, in most systems of law it is also legal to desire, and to strive for, something more than mere legality in one's actions. It is generally legal, that is, to strive to make your actions useful, pleasant, and so on. In a similar way, a desire for one's beliefs to be rational is itself a rational desire. That is, one does not violate any intellectual duty (nor, I suppose, any other duty) by having such a desire. But this is by no means our only permissible desire about our beliefs. Most people, I would think, want something more than rationality for their beliefs. At least some of these additional ambitions must themselves be intellectually permissible. And so we must remember that the desire for our beliefs to be rational is not the only rational desire about our beliefs.

Now one persistent and common desire which people have for their beliefs is that those beliefs should be true, should correspond somehow with reality, should "tell it like it is," and so on. This truth ambition would seem to be a rational desire. At least it is hard to believe that a person who wants to believe truths so far as possible is thereby violating an intellectual duty. And some people who ponder the relations of faith and reason may in fact be wondering whether there is something called "reason" which can help them achieve this truth ambition with respect to their religious beliefs.

Now, a desire that one's actions be legal is not identical with the desire that they be profitable. Nor are these desires intrinsically incompatible. But there may be some particular action which is profitable, though not legal, or vice versa. In a similar way, it seems quite clear that the truth ambition should not be construed as identical with the rationality desire, for there may be (and no doubt there are) beliefs which are rational in the Plantinga-Wolterstorff sense, but which are not true. It may nevertheless be thought that rationality tends toward truth, in the sense that if we believe in the rational way, then we will have a good chance of approximating the truth ambition, perhaps the best humanly available chance. Is that true?

### *Rationality and Truth*

It is not easy to formulate the question involved here in a satisfactory way. Consider for the moment a bizarre case. Imagine a person who orders his intellectual life in this way. Whenever a possible belief comes to his attention, he formulates it as clearly as possible in a proposition. Then he flips a coin. If it comes up heads, he believes the proposition he has just formulated. If tails, then he believes the negation of that proposition. This person is hardly a model of critical thinking, and no doubt he will often (though by no means always) believe what he has no right to believe. That is, he will often believe irrationally. Nevertheless, it looks as though this procedure will probably yield, over the long haul, about 50 percent true beliefs. Is there some general, and humanly available, procedure which gives good promise of yielding better results than flipping a coin?

Well, is P-W rationality such a procedure? If a person were to believe only what it is rational for him to believe, would he probably do better than merely breaking even in terms of truth and falsehood in the long run? Initially at least it is far from clear that the answer is Yes. P-W rationality is very strongly circumstance dependent. So a young woman who grows up in an isolated and benighted culture in which she is constantly surrounded by bizarre superstitions will be within her intellectual rights, and hence rational, in believing those superstitions herself. It would be too much to suppose, for example, that she has a duty to invent the germ theory of disease, or even that she has a duty to reject the witch doctor's theory which is accepted by all of her elders. But we may well suspect that a woman who thus accepts the beliefs of her tribe, though she is rational in doing so, will do worse then break even with respect to truth. She would do better on that score by flipping a coin.

This observation, however, does not settle the matter. For one thing, we have treated this case somewhat prejudicially. It is rational for this woman to accept the tribal superstitions. OK. But since P-W rationality is only a sort of permission, it may also be rational for her to do something else. Maybe it would also be rational for her to accept the germ theory of disease, or at least to withhold belief from the witch doctor's theory. She would be within her rights, that is, in doing these things, although, of course, it is unlikely that she would ever think of doing them. But if there is more than one rational option, then the choice of one of these options rather than the other cannot be ascribed to rationality itself. And if we want to assess rationality, then we should abstract from those other factors which influence choice. Perhaps we should therefore put our question in the following way. Suppose that this tribal woman also chooses her beliefs by some randomizing procedure, but only from among belief candidates which are rational for her. Will she do better, in terms of truth, than the person who chooses at random among *all* belief candidates, with no concern for rationality? My guess is still that she will not, and that in her case rationality will remain an impediment in the quest for truth.

Someone may object, however, that we should not assess the worth of rationality and its relation to truth solely on the basis of "worst-case" examples. For there are also better circumstances. We can easily imagine a young man, more fortunate than the lady, who grows up in a sort of cognitive utopia, surrounded by elders who are almost entirely paradigms of wisdom and knowledge. We readily imagine that if he limits himself to rational beliefs, even if otherwise he selects them randomly, then he will do better than break even in terms of truth. And maybe that is correct.

Let us say that a person is in "rationality-negative" circumstances if the sort of combination of rationality and randomness described above would probably yield no more than 50 percent true beliefs in the long run. And circumstances are "rationality-positive" if such procedures would do better than break even. The tribe is rationality-negative, and the utopia is rationality-positive. But now, leaving aside these hypothetical tribes and utopias, what is our own circumstance, or that of our friends?

Maybe it is natural to think, initially at least, that of course *we* are in rationality-positive circumstances. We must be much closer to the utopia than to the tribe. But it may be difficult to think of any ground for this confidence which is not just an assumption. After all, it may also be natural for the tribal woman to believe that her circumstances are rationality-positive, and it may well be rational for her to think so. After all, if she accepts the elders' superstitions, then she will also believe that, by and large, the elders are people of wisdom and knowledge. That is, she will describe the tribe much as I have described the utopia. And this may serve to rouse some suspicions in our own minds when we find ourselves describing our own situation in similar ways.

However that may be, we may make a further distinction. If we distinguish circumstances in assessing rationality, we may also distinguish subject matters. Leave aside science and so on for the moment and focus on religion. If an ordinary person in our culture were to choose his religious beliefs randomly from those which would be rational for him, would he do better than to break even? I suspect that he would not.

Well, maybe my own judgments here are unduly pessimistic. Maybe our circumstances, even vis-à-vis religion, are rationality-positive after all. Even so, a person might still have an ambition to do better, in terms of truth, than a simple reliance upon P-W rationality can achieve. That need not be (though it may be) a desire to proceed outside the canons of P-W rationality. For that rationality, I repeat, is only a permission, and it often permits alternatives. So a person may want some procedure to *add* to P-W rationality, a procedure which will improve his chances of truth by guiding him among the alternatives which P-W rationality leaves open.

### *Reasons and Beliefs*

Procedures intended to have that result have often themselves been described or named in terms of "reason" or "rationality." It might be useful to consider briefly here such an alternative conception of rationality. Clark Pinnock, in a book already mentioned, often refers to what is reasonable and rational in matters of belief. He does not, I think, provide an explicit definition of rationality. But I suspect that he does not construe it simply as a sort of permission, as a matter of being within one's epistemic rights. For one thing, Pinnock seems to relate rationality more closely to truth than do Plantinga and Wolterstorff. He says, for example, "I take the question of truth very seriously. I do not believe we need to commit ourselves without reasonable grounds."[16] And he often (as in this quotation) connects the notion of reason and so on with that of grounds and evidence.

Now, we need not dispute at length over a definition of "rationality." The substance of the matter is that Pinnock thinks that there is some humanly available procedure which can be applied to religious matters and which gives people a good chance of arriving at true beliefs. (His own views of how good that chance is are rather modest. He professes only to achieve "reasonable probabilities." But I suppose he means them to be at least above 50 percent.) His preference is to talk about this procedure largely in terms of rationality, reasonableness, reason, and such, and in that he follows a long, if rather vague, tradition. But whatever we call it, what is this procedure and does it in fact give us a good shot at religious truth?

Outlining his "model of rationality," Pinnock identifies two elements. One is an "interaction with the external world" which gives us a knowledge of reality. The second is a procedure of drawing reliable conclusions from this data "by thinking consistently and coherently."[17] (By the "interaction" Pinnock may mean only sense perception. But I think he does not say so flatly, and some of his discussions of religious experience would fit better with a somewhat broader understanding of what the interaction might be.) And the bulk of the book is Pinnock's attempt to apply this procedure to the central claims of Christianity.

Now, Pinnock certainly seems to believe that this two-pronged method —interaction with the world and consistent thinking—gives us a good chance of getting at the truth. I suppose that he would readily hold that it is better than flipping a coin. But in fact he provides no reason for thinking so. He gives us no reason to think that a person who forms beliefs on the basis of sense perception, or of any other apparent interaction with an external reality, will do better in terms of truth than a person who believes in a totally random manner. Nor does he give us any reason to suppose that what he calls consistent and coherent thinking is truth-preserving, or even that it preserves truth more often than not. There is no argument at all in the book in support of such positions, positions which are nevertheless essential to Pinnock's project. He simply scoffs a little at the skeptic who is likely to raise such questions, and lets it go at that. Some people might be inclined to support such positions by reference to the veracity and goodness of God. But Pinnock may not find that suggestion attractive, feeling that it would be inappropriate to argue *from* God in the opening chapter of an argument *to* God.

Pinnock could, however, adapt to his own use a suggestion made by Plantinga and Wolterstorff. These latter philosophers say, we remember, that people have a natural tendency or disposition to believe in God.

Pinnock might well say that people have a natural disposition (implanted in them, no doubt, by God) to form and accept beliefs on the occasion of sense perception, or in response to other experiences, and to recognize and rely upon certain sorts of arguments as truth-preserving. And he can go on to say that he is relying on these natural dispositions himself and is writing for other people who are also willing to rely on them. Such a claim would be plausible, and at least as plausible as the thesis about our disposition to believe in God. There is, after all, even more apparent universality to reliance upon sense perception and logic than to belief in a God or gods. And the difficulty which we have in taking general skepticism at all seriously is testimony to the strength of this disposition in ourselves.

There is no obvious reason, of course, why *both* of these claims should not be true. We may have several natural dispositions which pertain to believing. And if we do, then it would seem plausible to appeal to, and to rely upon, some of these dispositions in confirming the propriety of the others. Which of the natural dispositions would fill the various roles would depend upon which ones were apparently in doubt, and which ones accepted, in any particular case.

I say that Pinnock may well be relying on natural tendencies. But a natural tendency to believe may be *reliable* in the following sense. It is reliable if proceeding in accordance with that tendency yields more than 50 percent true beliefs. (A tendency would be perfectly reliable if it yielded nothing but true beliefs.) As I said earlier, Pinnock does nothing to show that the tendencies on which he relies are in fact reliable. But of course I take them to be reliable myself, and so, I suppose, do most of my readers here. They are, after all, tendencies on which we do in fact constantly rely. If we are right in that, then Pinnock's general procedure, that of appealing to experience and logic, does give us a good shot at the truth. We can expect that this method will, over the long run, probably give us better results than flipping a coin. We can call this procedure "reason" or something of the sort, or we can if we wish give it a quite different name. Its reliability, and the desirability of using it, is not a function of its name.

Perhaps then the question about positive apologetics (natural theology and so on) can be put in this way. Are there any beliefs which are generated by reliable natural tendencies – perhaps the tendencies on which Pinnock seems to rely – which support the belief that God exists? If there are not, then the project of positive apologetics would seem doomed to failure. But if there are, then it may have some chance of success. A person who did not find himself ready to rely on whatever natural tendency he may have to believe in God might feel no hesitation with respect to these other beliefs. And since proceeding in this way would seem to him to promise a good chance of satisfying his truth ambitions, he might go ahead, on the basis of some Pinnock-type argument perhaps, to accept the belief that there is a God.

### *The Strength of Belief*

Here there is a last difficulty which I wish to consider. It arises most clearly in connection with apologetic projects such as that of Pinnock, which openly profess to supply us only with probabilistic arguments, though it also applies, I think, to evidential approaches which are not expressed in probabilistic terms. Suppose that we supply a person with evidence, and he thereby comes to believe that there is a God and so on. So far, so good. Or is it? Will the belief which the person acquires in this way be of any religious significance, or will it simply add one more to this person's stock of opinions?

The question I am here raising is not that of whether propositional beliefs—beliefs that something is the case, such as the belief that there is a God—are *sufficient* to constitute a religion such as Christianity. I, at any rate, have no inclination to suppose that they are. But while not sufficient, some such beliefs might be *necessary* for Christianity. It is hard to see, for example, how someone could be a Christian if he did not believe that any god existed. And so propositional beliefs might be religiously significant even if they are not sufficient to constitute a religion in themselves. Nevertheless, it is often thought that propositional beliefs will be religiously significant only if they are held in a certain way. Most often it is said that such beliefs will function properly in a religion only if they are held very strongly, with full commitment, and so on. But it is also often suggested that beliefs held upon evidence, especially if the evidence is explicitly partial and probabilistic, will be (or ought to be) held only tentatively, weakly, with less than full commitment and so on. And so there is the suspicion that a belief adopted on the basis of evidence will in fact not be a religiously significant belief. Wolterstorff suggests that there is at least some puzzle involved in explaining "the relation between believing with some tentativity that Christianity is the best explanation of various phenomena and adopting the trustful certitude of faith."[18] That is the problem I discuss here. If a person believes on evidence, will he have "that certainty which piety requires"?

It is important to note that we do not avoid this problem (or rather, its analogue) by advocating that religious beliefs should be held as basic beliefs. That a belief is held in the basic way guarantees that it is not held on the basis of other beliefs. It does not at all guarantee that the basic belief is held strongly, or with "trustful certitude," or with an invincible tenacity in the face of contrary evidence, or anything of the sort. And in fact, when I look at those of my own beliefs which seem to be the clearest and most plausible candidates for being basic beliefs, many of them turn out to be things which I do not believe especially strongly and which I can easily imagine giving up if some contrary evidence should appear. So about basic beliefs, too, we must ask, "Will they be held strongly enough to perform the religious function expected of them?" And the fact that they are *basic* beliefs does not supply the answer.

An answer may nevertheless be at hand. It seems to me that there is a good bit of plausibility in saying that there is a natural human tendency to hold religious beliefs rather strongly, if one holds them at all. Or perhaps the fact is that there is a more general tendency to hold one's "life-orienting" beliefs, whether religious or otherwise, strongly. If there are these natural dispositions, then we can expect that religious beliefs which are held in the basic way will generally be held strongly. Or possibly we would rather say that it is the secret operation of the Holy Spirit which generates the required certitude in our religious beliefs. That too is possible. But in either case it would be the content of the belief, and not its basicality, which was relevant to its strength.

Both of these sorts of answers, however, are also available with respect to certainty in beliefs held on the basis of evidence. In those cases, too, either a natural disposition or the power of the Spirit may well generate whatever intensity of conviction is necessary for spiritual and religious significance. Of course, we might ask whether this in fact happens. I personally have no reason to suppose that people who profess to hold their religious beliefs on the basis of evidence characteristically believe in any unusually weak way.

Plantinga and Wolterstorff, however, sometimes seem to suggest that such believers *ought* to have weak beliefs. The strength of their belief ought somehow to match the evidence, and so, at least if they construe the evidence merely probabilistically, the belief ought to fall well short of full conviction. So the position seems to be that while it is legitimate and rational to have full conviction (in theistic belief) on the basis of no evidence at all, it is illegitimate and irrational to have full conviction on the basis of partial, even though substantial, evidence.

This doctrine does not seem to be fully persuasive as it stands. How could it be supported? By an appeal to authority? It is true that many eminent philosophers have said that our beliefs ought to be somehow or other proportional to the evidence. David Hume, for example, said, "A wise man proportions his belief to the evidence."[19] And before him John Locke had said "the grounds of probability . . . are the foundations on which our assent is built [and] so are they also the measure whereby its general degrees are, or ought to be, regulated."[20] And many later philosophers have echoed these sentiments. But I cannot recall that those philosophers have given any argument in support of this alleged intellectual duty or value. Are we bound to accept their judgment in this matter?

In any case it seems clear that Plantinga and Wolterstorff cannot consistently accept the full-blooded doctrine of proportionality as it is espoused by Locke, Hume, and their many followers. For according to that doctrine a proposition which was supported by no evidence at all should be accorded zero degree of belief, or at least a degree of belief lower than that of any proposition which was supported by evidence. But this does not sound at all like that certainty which piety requires. So Plantinga and Wolterstorff must reject this general proportionality doctrine.

Perhaps they favor some modified version of this doctrine, to the effect that beliefs which are held on the basis of evidence should have their strength proportional to the evidence. But if we can reject the full-blooded doctrine of proportionality, why should we not also reject this version? For any person, N, and possible belief, P, there are many belief-related questions we can ask. We can ask whether N believes P, how strongly she believes it, whether it is in her case a basic or a derived belief, whether she is justified in believing it at all, whether she is justified in believing it as strongly as she does, and so on. These are distinct questions. Consider a case in which a woman believes in God because the evidence favors that belief (and let it even be true that she would not have believed if the evidence had gone the other way), and she believes with full commitment even though she takes the evidence to be not fully conclusive. If questions of rationality arise, why should we not reply that it is rational for her to hold this belief because the evidence favors it, and it is rational for her to be fully committed because there is a natural human disposition to hold this sort of belief very strongly if one holds it at all? I know of no reason to think that these replies are not satisfactory, and so I think that we should reject the doctrine of proportionality altogether. If we do that, however, the present difficulty disappears.

## SUMMARY

In this paper I have tried to distinguish two concerns, both of which may be put in terms of a question about rationality. Without using that terminology, however, one of them can be put this way: "Are we within our intellectual rights in believing in God?" And the other one can be put as: "Is there reason to suppose that belief in God is true?" In one sense the first of these questions is the easier to answer, and (in my opinion, at least) some real progress is made on it in other essays in this volume.

The second question is also easy to answer, in a certain sense. It is true that God exists, and true also that God has not left himself without testimony and evidence in the world. If we say such things, we shall speak truths. But saying them, at least in this blunt way, will in many contexts not be useful. And it is the useful way of answering that question which is hard. That requires not merely saying that there is evidence but somehow exhibiting it in such a way that it really does strike someone as *evidence,* so that its evidential and epistemological force becomes actually operative. That is hard, and no apologist is fully successful in it. But the other side of that coin is that it is not impossible, and there are no doubt many who have been partly successful in this project.

## NOTES

1. John Calvin, *Institutes of the Christian Religion,* ed. John T. McNeil, tr. Ford Lewis Battles (Philadelphia: Westminster Press, 1960), p. 79 (bk. 1, ch. 7, sec. 4).

2. Clark Pinnock, *Reason Enough* (Downers Grove, IL: Inter-Varsity Press, 1980), p. 10.

3. More cautiously, they hold that faith *can* be rational, and believers can be in position to believe rationally, without the necessity of anything else being done for them.

4. "To say that it is rational for me to believe something is to say that I am *justified* in believing it. And to say that I am justified in believing it is to say that I am *permitted* to believe it. Further, to say that I am permitted to believe it is to say that believing it is *not in violation of the norms* that pertain to my believings—that my believing it does not represent any failure on my part to have governed my believings as I ought to have done." Nicholas Wolterstorff, "Is Reason Enough?" *The Reformed Journal,* 31: 4 (April 1981): 23.

5. Ibid., p. 22.

6. Ibid.

7. Ibid.

8. It is not clear just how far Wolterstorff endorses the characteristic Reformed rejection of positive apologetics. Maybe he believes only that such apologetic efforts are not useful in the "typical" situation but may be valuable nevertheless in a few cases. Cf. ibid., pp. 20 and 22.

9. Ibid., p. 22.

10. Alvin Plantinga, "Reason and Belief in God," pp. 73–74, 79.

11. Ibid., p. 18.

12. Ibid., pp. 18–19.

13. Alvin Plantinga, *God and Other Minds* (Ithaca, NY: Cornell University Press, 1967), p. 4.

14. Alvin Plantinga, *The Nature of Necessity* (Oxford: The Clarendon Press, 1974), pp. 216–17.

15. Ibid., pp. 219–20.
16. Pinnock, *Reason Enough,* p. 10.
17. Ibid., pp. 16–17.
18. Wolterstorff, "Is Reason Enough?" p. 21.
19. David Hume, *An Enquiry concerning Human Understanding,* sec. 10, pt. 1.
20. John Locke, *An Essay concerning Human Understanding,* bk. IV, ch. 16, 1.

# The Collapse of American Evangelical Academia*

George Marsden

By the midtwentieth century being evangelical and being a scholar were widely viewed as incompatible traits. Indeed, by 1950 the American evangelical scholarly community was in disarray. Scattered evangelical academic institutions boasting a few competent scholars survived, but only in ethnic, regional, and denominational pockets or in the intellectually suspect fundamentalist movement. Few outsiders took these institutions seriously or realized they existed. Some competent Christian scholars could be found in American universities, but evangelical thought would seldom have been counted as a part of American academic life.

Evangelical academia, if noticed at all, seemed from the prevailing liberal humanist perspective the vestiges of a lost civilization. Only seventy-five years earlier almost all of America's leading colleges and universities had borne the deep imprint of their evangelical connections.[1] Academic thought had been largely evangelical thought. In 1950, however, persistent ideas of intellectual progress encouraged the view that traditional religious outlooks were declining irreversibly. Advanced scientific views were supposed to be replacing backward religions, superstitions, and prejudices throughout the world. The actual decline of evangelical academia during the past two generations lent credence to such hypotheses.

The particular issue I wish to address is, What was the intellectual component in this demise of evangelical academia and scholarship? Was the collapse significantly related to the intellectual stance characteristic

*I am indebted to Richard R. Johnson, Mark Noll, the late Dirk W. Jellema, and my colleagues at the Calvin Center for Christian Scholarship for their very helpful comments. I use "evangelical" to include theologically conservative Christians who emphasize the Gospel message of the salvation of sinners through the atoning work of Christ and the authority of Scripture.

of nineteenth-century American evangelicals? Today this question has renewed significance. Since 1950 American evangelicalism has begun to recover intellectually. This recovery has brought renewal of some thought patterns prominent in nineteenth-century evangelicalism. It is important to inquire, therefore, as to the extent these thought patterns were structural weaknesses that contributed to the original collapse. Does their renewal involve building similar weaknesses into evangelical thought today?

The answers will not be simple. The complexity of history precludes most single-cause explanations. American evangelical academia did not collapse simply because of an intellectual error. Comparable secularizing transformations occurred almost everywhere in the Protestant world during the nineteenth century. The positivist claims that modern science provides the only sure ground for certainty combined with the modern historical model of explanation in terms of origins seemed for a time a nearly irresistible intellectual combination. Only strongly institutionalized authority, as in the citadels of Roman Catholicism, was able to withstand such tendencies on a large scale, and then at the cost of sacrificing some academic respectability.

The new ideas gained popularity in Protestant lands such as America not simply by the force of argument but also because they provided explanations that fit many social trends toward secularization.[2] In America, for instance, the long dominance of evangelicals in the colleges was built directly on the ethnic dominance of "Anglo-Saxon" Protestants. Priority of settlement gave this group social and economic dominance and hence control over private (and even much of state) education. By the late nineteenth century, however, ethnic and religious heterogeneity was becoming an overwhelming reality in American culture, so that such dominance had to give way. Americans' professed democratic ideals in fact conflicted with the virtual control of higher education by one religious outlook. The new naturalistic and scientific explanations had the appeal not only of its arguments but of fitting a social need, offering a new and seemingly neutral basis for refashioning education. It also provided a compelling secular account of the dynamics of a civilization that in many areas was losing its religious orientation.

Another of the many social factors contributing to the triumph of the new views was the rise of professionalism. Whereas in 1800 someone like Thomas Jefferson could be an expert in virtually every field of knowledge, by the late decades of the century professional specialization was the key to success. The rise of the universities reflected this cultural trend. The Ph.D. thesis, a demonstration of technical expertise in an area accessible only by specialists, became the prerequisite for entry into academic life.[3] By contrast, nineteenth-century evangelical colleges had been havens for generalists, theologian-philosophers who provided the community with advice in economics, politics, morality, and often in natural science. The new specialists who were taking over by the end of the century could usually outclass the old-time teachers in any of the specialties.[4] Moreover their new concept of being "scientific" meant simultaneously to specialize and to eliminate religiously derived principles from their disciplines. The technical achievements of this new specialization thus reinforced prejudices against evangelicalism, which had been heavily committed to the older generalist approach.

Such factors, formidable as they were, do not seem quite to account for the displacement of the nineteenth-century evangelical outlook turning into such a total rout. One might imagine the revolution in American higher education having taken quite different forms. The rise of pluralism might not have driven out the old establishment so entirely. Excellent Christian colleges (say Oberlin or Wellesley) might have continued as both excellent and Christian even through the dim days for evangelicalism in the first half of the twentieth century. Moreover, evangelical Christian education might have made some adjustment to the university system as Catholic schools did. One of the most puzzling features of American academic life today is that even in these times of evangelical resurgence there is still not a full-fledged evangelical university in America. Why was the severance of evangelicalism from the main currents of American academic life so total?

With only social or cultural explanations the answers to these questions surely would remain incomplete. The specifically intellectual factors are, at least, essential aspects of the picture. Most obviously the academic revolution involved a remarkable change among intellectuals in their view of authority. For evangelicals the Bible stood beside the highest scientific and historical authorities whenever it spoke on such matters. Moreover, it also spoke definitively on many areas that science by itself could not reach. The new combination of scientific positivism and historicism, however, struck particularly hard at the Bible itself, questioning its accuracy at innumerable points and offering alternative naturalistic and seemingly scientific explanations for the rise of human religious beliefs. In simplest terms, the intellectual aspect of the revolution involved the replacement of the old authorities with the new in all but the obscure crannies of American academia.

In reality, of course, this intellectual revolution was much more complex. Battle lines were seldom neatly drawn between secular humanists who reverenced science and history and Bible-believing evangelicals who did not. Rather, a whole spectrum of middle positions attempted to reconcile Christian faith with modern intellectual trends. Some were frank expressions of humanist faith in mankind with a touch of Christian ethics thrown in. Others were modernist theologies, claiming a distinctly Christian heritage but insisting that God continued to reveal himself in the best of modern science and culture. Others were explicitly evangelical positions that attempted to ground Christian faith on truths of the heart or on moral sentiments insusceptible to scientific or historical attack. After 1930 neo-orthodoxy provided Americans an alternative that preserved traditional Christian theology while keeping the core of sacred history in a transcendental realm likewise immune to scientific-historical criticism.

A peculiarity of these middle positions, however, is that they flourished in American academia almost solely in theological institutions. They generated few, if any, alternative nontheological educational institutions or even academic organizations. The reason for this striking absence is not hard to surmise. Every one of these middle positions endorses to some degree the historical and scientific canons of the day. They thus maintained cordial relations with American academia by conceding its virtual autonomy. Their solution to the crisis in authority was to grant the authority of the new science and history, but to emphasize that this authority was limited to certain secular domains. Picking up and vastly accentuating a theme present in the thought of their evangelical predecessors, indeed found in almost all Christian thought, they now rested the entire weight of their apologetic on the point that Christianity went far beyond that which mere scientific reason could reach. They differed from most of their predecessors, however, in suggesting that Christianity had to do only with the aspects of things wholly immune from scientific or historical inquiry. Secular institutions, accordingly, were the proper location for such inquiries.

More traditional evangelicals, however, are the focus of the present inquiry. During the twentieth century they did not concede that Christianity involved exclusively the aspects of things beyond scientific and historical inquiry. The Bible, they insisted, was an historical book in some ordinary ways, even if it was also God's revelation. Many of its claims were in principle susceptible to the same sorts of intellectual analysis as any other claims. Faith and scientific reason were not at odds.

Why was this view, once dominant in America higher education, so preemptively banished from most of American academia? Why did proponents of this view lose virtually all their institutional strongholds? Was there some defect in their defenses of biblically based Christianity and its proper relation to reason, especially scientific reason?

The most incisive analysis of this subject appeared in a 1961 essay by a Princeton philosopher, James Ward Smith, "Religion and Science in American Philosophy."[5] Smith pointed out that among American Protestants there was no crisis of science versus religion associated with the first, or Newtonian, scientific revolution. The American Puritans and their heirs, by and large, embraced the new science with enthusiasm. Their accommodation of Protestantism to science, however, was "superficial." With the notable exception of Jonathan Edwards, says Smith, their accommodation involved simply adding the corpus of modern scientific knowledge to the body of ideas they accepted. They saw these conclusions of modern sciences as additional evidence for the theistic argument from design. Such reconciliation of the new science with Christianity was superficial because they did not closely examine or challenge the speculative basis on which the modern scientific revolution was built. Rather than challenging modern science's first principles, they came to be among the chief defenders of these principles. They were entirely confident that objective scientific inquiry could only confirm Christian truth.

Despite Christians' struggles with Deism and Enlightenment skepticism, this reconciliation of Christianity and modern science by the method of addition generally worked well until the second scientific revolution, that associated with Darwin. Suddenly, rather than the prestige of modern science lending support to Christianity, the supposedly neutral scientific methodology turned its forces directly against Christian thought. Out of nowhere, it must have seemed, came an unprecedented scientific assault. The Christian community, having thoroughly trusted science and the scientific method, had welcomed them, even parading them as their staunchest friends. So, according to Smith's thesis, this superficial accommodation left them with no defenses when the celebrated ally proved to be a heavily armed foe. No mere Trojan horse, we may add, had been imported into the Christian citadel. The very foundations of their defensive walls had been built by Greek philosophers and their modern scientific heirs and hid massive forces potentially hostile to the Christiain religion.

Elaborating such themes briefly, we can see that rather than supporting the old argument from design, nineteenth-century science suddenly produced a series of alternative explanations for the apparent order and purpose in reality. The divisions of the intellectual armies of this revolution usually had two features in common. They claimed for themselves the full prestige of the positive scientific methodology. They also had adopted (as it turns out, quite paradoxically) later-nineteenth-century historical assumptions. That is, they viewed reality, not as essentially stable with fixed truths, but as essentially in process of development. The scientific methodology was applied to explaining that development, with the assumption that such developments could be understood best in terms of natural forces observable by scientific method itself. These assumptions, that life was best viewed as processes and these processes were susceptible to scientific analysis, were behind most of the major intellectual assaults offering alternatives to the Christian explanations of reality. Darwinism offered accounts of the origins of life, of design, and of human intelligence itself. Freudianism added naturalistic explanations for the human sense of meaning, of love and beauty, and of religion itself. Marxism, and similar social explanations, claimed to explain the meaning and apparent direction of history. They offered as well an alternative basis for social ethics. Biblical criticism turned the fire power of such scientific-historical explanation point-blank on the origins of Hebrew religion and the Bible itself. With awesome swiftness the edifice built by the method of addition that had worked so well for Christians in accommodating Christianity to the first scientific revolution had been demolished by the second.

Smith's basic thesis, here considerably elaborated—that the fault in repelling this assault, or even in sensing that it was coming, involved a defect in the American evangelical method of reconciling faith and science —warrants more detailed analysis. Particularly, we can look at how eighteenth- and nineteenth-century American Protestants characteristically viewed the issues concerning faith and reason. We can ask whether their approach was as essentially naive as in retrospect it might seem. And we can consider what we might learn, positively or negatively, from their approach and their experience.

## THE BACKGROUND: THOMAS REID

Until after the Civil War almost all American evangelical theologians built their discussions of faith and reason on principles drawn, at least in part, from the Scottish "Common Sense" school of philosophy. The progenitor of this important school was Thomas Reid (1710–96).[6] Americans also studied Reid's followers, Dugald Stewart, James Beattie, Thomas Brown, and William Hamilton, some of whom (especially Hamilton) modified Reid's views considerably, but in general the Americans' views were readily identifiable as belonging to the Reidian school.[7]

One of the firmest commitments of Reid and his American followers was to the British inductive-empirical school of thought associated with Francis Bacon and Isaac Newton (and more generally with John Locke) concerned above all to establish a firm base for inductive scientific investigation. Reid himself was a great admirer of Bacon, the early seventeenth-century philosopher of science. The influence of "Lord Bacon" on Reid, Dugald Stewart observed approvingly, "may be traced on almost every page."[8] Bacon had taught Newton, said Reid in one of his encomiums, "to despise hypotheses as fictions of human fancy." Newton in turn demonstrated "that the true method of philosophizing is this: from real facts ascertained by observations and experiment, to collect by just induction the laws of nature." Such reasoning from "chaste induction" was a type of "probable" reasoning rather than demonstrative deduction, yet its firmest results were no less certain than those of mathematics. "Probable" evidence, said Reid, often involved many strands, like the twisted filaments of a rope, rather than one argument, yet "many things are certain for which we have only that kind of evidence which philosophers call probable." Evidence from induction, Reid emphasized, "is the only kind of evidence on which all the most important affairs of human life must rest."[9]

By Reid's time, however, the classical foundations on which such inductive scientific inquiry ultimately rested seemed to be crumbling. Classical foundationalism, as it is now sometimes called, was the ideal in the Western philosophical heritage since the time of the ancient Greeks, that a sure structure of knowledge could be built on the absolutely firm foundations of indubitable certitudes. Typically these foundational certitudes included our states of consciousness (such as, I am awake), self-evidently necessary truths (such as 1 + 2 equals 3), and perhaps those things evident to the senses (I am sure I see a tree over there). Such foundationalists typically maintained that these fundamental certitudes did not need to be held on the basis of any other beliefs that one held. They could be taken for granted without demonstration.[10] David Hume, however, an older contemporary of Reid, raised serious questions as to whether such certainty was possible in empirical scientific investigation. By the mideighteenth century John Locke's account of the mental operations involved in empirical knowledge had been widely accepted. External objects, said Locke, stimulate the senses in such a way as to imprint "ideas" of themselves on our minds (which prior to such imprintings were blank). Hume, however, took a skeptical stance toward this account. For instance, he questioned whether we can be certain that these ideas occurring in our minds correspond to anything outside the mind itself. Reason thus seemed to undermine the certainty of the immensely popular scientific empiricism.

Reid's reply to Hume's skepticism revealed his explicit intention to establish a new foundationalism on which inductive science could be based. "All knowledge got by reasoning," he says, "must be built on first principles." He adds that "This is as certain as that every house must have a foundation." Furthermore, some, though not all, of these first principles "yield conclusions that are certain."[11] Reid's account of these first principles arose from his subtle analysis of the psychological mechanisms by which people arrive at those beliefs they take to be self-evident or certain. The conclusion was inescapable, he argued, that our knowledge rests on first principles, or "basic beliefs" (as they are called in this volume), that rest on nothing other than the fact that we find ourselves compelled to hold them. Along with classical foundationalists he said that such foundational principles "seldom admit to direct proof; nor do they need it." These are "the foundation of all reasoning, and of all science."[12]

Reid differed from the classical foundationalists principally in that his close look at those beliefs that people were in practice virtually compelled to hold yielded a considerably expanded set of first principles. Not only did he include states of consciousness, self-evidently necessary truths, and those things evident to our senses, he affirmed also that virtually all normal adults inevitably hold such basic beliefs as the connection between cause and effect, the general regularity in nature, the predictability of some human behavior, the relationship between past and present, the existence of other minds, the continuity of one's self and of others, the reliability of their clear and distinct memories, the trustworthiness of the testimony of others under certain conditions, and the difference between right and wrong. Reid even held that certain beliefs about beauty were compelled in all normal people, and hence universal ("I never heard of any man who thought it a beauty in a human face to want a nose.")[13] People seldom hold any of these beliefs on the basis of reasoning. Rather they are basic beliefs, beliefs not established by arguments, but caused immediately by "common sense," or the belief-producing faculties that underlie all reasoning.[14]

Reid's concern was to reestablish a basis for our certainty about our knowledge of the real world. His philosophy was in this sense a type of "realism," sometimes called "Common-Sense Realism." That there was surely a connection between our certain beliefs and the real world, external to our minds, was itself a dictate of common sense, not susceptible to rational demonstration. Only philosophers or crackpots, he was fond of pointing out, would construct theories that would cast doubt on these common-sense beliefs. Locke's theory of "ideas," for instance, suggested that the immediate (or most direct) objects of our knowledge are our *ideas* about reality. This speculative theory opened the door for the Humean objection that perhaps he had access *only* to our ideas. In fact, Reid insisted, all normal people find themselves compelled to believe that they directly and immediately experience the external world itself. As to the skeptical philosophers who claimed to doubt such things as the existence of the external world, even they ducked when they went through low doorways.

Notably, Reid does not include belief in God among the common-sense first principles. Though as far as I know he does not explain this omission directly, the reasons seem plain enough. For a principle to be a common-sense principle it had to be common to virtually all normal adults in all nations and ages. Of course, we do not believe these first principles *because* we find them to be universal; that would be believing them for a reason. We believe them because we are forced to by the constitution of our natures. Nonetheless, universality is a test for identifying common-sense principles. A negative test is that a person devoid of such beliefs would nearly everywhere be considered a lunatic. Reid says: "All men that have common understanding agree in such principles, and consider a man as lunatic, or destitute of common sense, who denies or calls them into question."[15] Belief in God does not meet this test.

Moreover, in asserting this universality of common-sense principles, Reid is eager to establish the basis for a universal science. Disagreements, he says, often terminate in appeals to common sense. Such disagreements could be avoided if "the decisions of common sense can be brought into a code, in which all reasonable men shall acquiesce." Such a universal code would be a great boon to logic. "And why," Reid adds, "should it be thought impossible that reasonable men should agree in things that are self-evident?"[16] Clearly, a matter so much disputed as belief in God would not qualify as a universally held common-sense foundation stone for such definitive science.

Reid, however, was a moderate Presbyterian, and belief in God played a significant, though often implicit, role in his philosophy. Reid held that the existence of a Supreme Being could be demonstrated by a simple, but irrefutable, process of reasoning. Starting characteristically with a common-sense principle "which we get, neither by reasoning nor by experience," Reid made the major proposition of his argument "That design and intelligence in the cause, may with certainty be inferred from marks or signs of it in the effect." If then we accept as the minor proposition that "there are, in fact, the clearest marks of design and wisdom in the world of nature," then we must conclude that there is a wise and intelligent cause.[17]

This simple argument from design appears to play an incidental role in Reid's philosophy, but the "Creator," the "Almighty," and "the wise Author of our nature" are mentioned constantly in Reid's writings. The Creator has constituted nature and all beings in it with the relationships they have. "The laws of nature," he says with regard to scientific inquiry, "are the rules by which the Supreme Being governs the world."[18] All other beings "must depend upon the nature God has given them; the powers with which he has endowed them, and the situation in which he has placed them."[19] Reid is careful not to argue from the existence of a wise Creator to the reliability of common-sense first principles (which require no argument); nonetheless, when he speaks of beliefs determined by "the constitution of human nature,"[20] he certainly has in mind that these belief-mechanisms and the world that they encounter are constituted by the Creator.[21]

Reid's frequent mention of the Author of our natures reveals an important feature about his thought and that of his nineteenth-century American followers that distinguished their outlooks sharply from later discussions. Almost all philosophies since the later nineteenth century have assumed "the evolution of self-consciousness."[22] An implicit premise usually has been that our mental mechanisms arose simply from natural causes. Such accounts often make what humans call "truth," or at least a good portion of it, a matter of convention. Since our mechanisms for knowing about reality are evolving, "truth" changes with our cognitive development. Furthermore, cultural evolution, a major category of recent thought, often has been interpreted to suggest that "truth" is largely relative to time and place, almost wholly a matter of conditioning and custom.

The naturalistic and evolutionary assumptions on which such attitudes are based were totally foreign to Reid and his nineteenth-century American admirers. They took it for granted that the universe was packed with fixed laws placed there by intelligent design. Reid introduced the fact of evidence of design in the universe as a proposition in his argument for the deity with hardly an explanation. He did note that some ancients had thought "that there are not in the constitution of things such marks of wise contrivance as are sufficient to put the conclusion beyond doubt." Modern science, Reid asserted, in a characteristic eighteenth-century display of the faith in a fixed order that Newtonianism inspired, proved this view obviously fallacious. "The gradual advancement made in the knowledge of nature," Reid observed without elaboration, "has put this opinion quite out of countenance."[23]

## THE BACKGROUND: PALEY AND BUTLER

Christians more directly concerned to defend the faith than was Reid himself took full advantage of the era's widely held belief that natural science had produced irrefutable confirmation of intelligent design in the universe. So the same large group of American apologists who used Reid as the unanswerable reply to general skepticism[24] readily employed William Paley's popular *Natural Theology* (1802) to demonstrate the necessity of theistic belief. Both in nineteenth-century England and America his volume was a widely used text, so that virtually every educated person was acquainted with his arguments.

Paley, like virtually every English-speaking thinker of the era, displayed an implicit trust in empiricism. He claimed that his arguments were built on no special philosophy except some generally accepted "principles of knowledge."[25] He observed also, as Reid and others often said, that an overwhelmingly probable empirical case was virtually as decisive as a logical demonstration. Starting with his famous example of finding a stone and a watch and concluding that the watch must have a designer, Paley built up his probabilistic case by multiplying examples of apparent design in nature, especially in humans themselves. The eye has as much evidence of a designer as the telescope. Moreover, nature reveals a designer with personality, great power, everywhere working on a unified design, present at "the beginning," and (when all was considered) benevolent.[26]

The popularity of Paley reveals an important aspect of the outlook of eighteenth-century Britain and nineteenth-century America. Though the argument from design might be useful to counter adolescent skepticism or the village atheist, for most practical purposes the dictates of natural theology were taken for granted as much by the opponents of Christianity as by its friends. In an age enamored of the order of the Newtonian universe, few doubted that the universe had an intelligent designer. For practical purposes the real debate was between the Deists and the Christians. So Christians and most non-Christians shared a great deal of common ground, especially on first principles. Both agreed that the universe was designed by a Creator who built into it law-structures that humans could discover through scientific procedures. The ghost of David Hume seemed safely enough laid to rest by the likes of Reid and Paley, so that the key question for the apologist was not natural religion, but revealed religion, that is, the Bible.

On this topic the immense popularity of another eighteenth-century figure suggests some of the characteristic assumptions of the nineteenth-century American apologists. Even more than Paley's work, Bishop Joseph Butler's *The Analogy of Religion, Natural and Revealed* (1736) (which in one American edition enjoyed over twenty printings)[27] left its mark on nineteenth-century American thought. Butler too endorsed empirical inductionism as the only safe avenue to the truth.[28] Moreover, as was commonplace, he emphasized that his arguments for Christianity were cumulative and only pointed toward a probability, and did not yield demonstrative proof or absolute knowledge. Nonetheless, he remarked in an often-quoted statement, "Probability is the very guide to life."[29]

Butler's arguments provided some counterparts to those of Reid. Reid established on practical grounds, rather than on argument from evidence, the necessity of trusting in common-sense principles. Butler started at a similar point. Making observations about what we are obliged to believe about nature, he argued for Christianity not by presenting a proof, but by pointing out that virtually the same objections that might be lodged against biblically revealed religion could be made against that which we absolutely rely on as true in nature. Thomas Reid recognized this affinity.

> I know no author who has made a more just and happy use of analogical reasoning than Bishop Butler, in his "Analogy of Religion." In that excellent work, the author does not ground any of the truths of religion upon analogy as their proper evidence. He only makes use of analogy to answer objections against them. When objections are made against the truths of religion, which may be made with equal strength against *what we know to be true* in the course of nature, such objections can have no weight.[30]

## CHRISTIAN AND NON-CHRISTIAN SCIENCE

Reid, Paley, and Butler agreed among themselves and with most of the English-speaking opponents of Christianity on most of their first principles. They were confident that the laws of the human mind were attuned to fixed laws of nature in such a way that careful empirical observation would yield truth. The empiricist tradition dominating much of English thought was gripped by the hopes for dramatic advances in knowledge promised by the scientific method described by Francis Bacon. Newton symbolized the spectacular fulfillments of such promises. For a time this vision of reality was so compelling and the possibility of human advance so promising that few would challenge it. In the early nineteenth century this vision persisted especially in America. "The Baconian philosophy," said Edward Everett in 1823, "has become synonymous with the true philosophy."[31] So great was the reverence in America among scientists, theologians, and most academics for this ideal that a recent historian's phrase, "the beatification of Bacon," seems aptly to describe it.[32]

This blanket endorsement of the Baconian-Newtonian scientific assumptions and method, shared by Christians and non-Christians, had the important implication that, outside of theology, Christians did not consider themselves to belong to any special school of thought. Science, built on firm foundations universally recognized, and proceeding to virtual certainty by careful Bacononian principles of induction, would yield the same results to all inquirers. Christians, who had the advantage of trusting special revelation, had access to some facts that non-Christians refused to acknowledge. Nonetheless, since the Creator had built a definite set of laws into nature and provided laws of the human mind that guided our access to nature's laws, in almost all areas Christians and non-Christians stood on exactly the same footing. Thomas Jefferson, for instance, might be an infidel, but the Declaration of Independence spoke of rights of mankind "endowed by their creator" "self-evident" to all.[33] Such areas were in the domain of science and could be analyzed without recourse to any special Christian teachings.

These assumptions were extremely influential in shaping early American thought and in setting the course of much of American public policy —especially toward education. Their influence is evident, for instance, in virtually all the college texts prior to the Civil War. Francis Wayland, America's most successful college text writer of this era, provides an excellent example for seeing this influence. Wayland, the president of Brown University, was an ordained Baptist minister and a thoroughgoing evangelical. Of his three major texts, *The Elements of Moral Science* (1835), *The Elements of Political Economy* (1837), and *The Elements of Intellectual Philosophy* (1854), the first deals most explicitly with questions of the relations of science to faith. Ethics, he holds, is as much a science as physics: specifically it is "the Science of Moral Law." Wayland was convinced that the laws of morality, essentially "sequences connected by our Creator" of rewards and punishments for various acts, could be discovered "to be just as invariable as an order of sequence in physics." These moral laws may be known by three means: by conscience, by natural religion, and by biblical revelation. These three are thoroughly complementary, differing only in their degrees of certainty and usefulness. Conscience, though certainly providing a universal sense that there is such a thing as right or wrong, does not clearly reveal some important moral laws (as obligations to universal forgiveness) and is often overcome by base passions. Additional moral laws can be discovered by the purely inductive scientific procedures of natural religion—by observing the rewards and punishments God has provided for various acts. Natural religion, however, is an imperfect moral guide also.[34]

Hence a further revelation is required. The moral precepts of revealed religion are "in perfect harmony" with those of natural religion. Revealed religion only goes beyond natural religion. It provides some facts (as about the Atonement or the afterlife) that we could not discover otherwise. The Bible also is "directing us to new lessons, taught us by nature." These clues point us to see how the moral laws observable in nature confirm the precepts taught in Scripture. "So complete is this coincidence, as to afford irrefragable proof that the Bible contains the moral laws of the universe; and, hence, that the Author of the universe—that is, of natural religion—is also the Author of the Scriptures."[35]

Wayland's method in *Moral Science* accordingly is to "derive these moral laws from natural or from revealed religion, or from both, as may be most convenient for our purpose." So, for instance, on Sabbath laws he starts with Scripture and confirms the laws from nature. On laws of property he starts with a mixture of principles from nature and from Scripture. "Everything we behold," he says, "is essentially the property of the Creator," and God reveals how he wants us to use our property. God's will, however, is in perfect accord with scientific analysis, or natural religion. For instance, God reveals that private ownership of property is proper, but this is well demonstrated by economic science which has shown the favorable consequences such an arrangement produces.[36]

A peculiar feature of this way of relating Christianity to the sciences shows up, however, when we look at Wayland's other texts. While the Christian might want to integrate his scientific work with biblical principles, by showing their mutual confirmations, he might just as legitimately deal with the issues as purely scientific ones, with no reference to explicitly Christian considerations. The assumption behind this thinking was that the law structures in creation that science discovers could in no way conflict with scriptural principles. God had created one set of laws. He had endowed us with various means of learning of these laws—including the firm principles of common sense.[37] One could therefore proceed purely on universally accepted principles of science with no fear of conflicting with the Bible.

So in *Elements of Political Economy* Wayland treats his subject as though it were a purely objective science. He acknowledges in his preface that almost every question in political economy could be discussed in moral philosophy. "He [Wayland writes of himself] has not, however, thought it proper in general, to intermingle them, but has argued economical questions on merely economical grounds." For with ethical questions, Wayland maintains, "Political Economy has nothing to do." Rather, questions of economics deal with whether an economical act is "wise," questions that can be settled on inductive grounds.[38]

Wayland's economics is essentially a defense of free enterprise, attempting to explicate the natural system of rewards and punishment (work is rewarded, idleness is punished) that controls economic activity and should not be interfered with. Certainly he thought these were no less God's laws because they could be discovered scientifically. Moreover, Wayland does not refrain from introducing Christianity by the back door. A demonstrable economic fact, he argues, is that the spread of Christianity leads to improvement in education, raising of moral standards, and increases in gross national product. "How much greater benefits does North America confer upon the world," he asks rhetorically, "than it would if it were peopled by its aboriginal inhabitants?"[39]

A number of twentieth-century commentators have suggested that Wayland's approach was basically a species of secularization. Martin Marty, for instance, suggests that a characteristic form of secularization in nineteenth-century America was for Christians to acquiese in a division of labor, separating the "religious realm" from the secular and the scientific.[40] Wayland's wholly scientific approach to *Political Economy* and *Intellectual Philosophy,*[41] for instance, then was inadvertently paving the way for the gradual fading away in the second half of the century of biblical confirmations or the idea of laws of God. Since technical texts in fields such as economics or philosophy did not make these issues explicit, later nineteenth-century thinkers could drop the implicit assumptions entirely with little struggle against Christian alternatives. William Graham Sumner, successor to Wayland as America's leading economist and originally trained for the ministry, remarked that early in his professional career he put his religious ideas in a drawer; years later he opened the drawer and found the beliefs gone.[42] Christian thinkers' encouragement of the independence of science certainly fostered such a quiet, but devastating, revolution in much of academia.

Similar tendencies appear in evangelicals' approaches to the natural sciences. On the one hand evangelical scientists in midnineteenth-century American colleges proclaimed themselves true Baconians, defenders of pure objective inquiry. On the other hand, since all laws were God's laws, inescapable evidence of benevolent design, their science was thoroughly "doxological"—never ceasing to lead us to praise the wisdom of the Creator.[43] They did not lack, then, zeal to relate Christianity to their science. Yet the way they did it was to grant scientific inquiry virtual independence, consistent with Baconian principles of objectivity. The only proviso was that whatever laws were discovered by this autonomous scientific method must be acknowledged as evidence of the wise design of the Creator. As several historians have pointed out, this amounted to a "rickety compromise" between piety and the ideal of absolutely free scientific inquiry.[44]

Natural science was an especially important building block in the edifice of evangelical thought. Far from incidental or peripheral, natural science was supposed to demonstrate design in the universe and hence, as Paley showed, provide important evidence for theism. Moreover, Bishop Butler's analogies suggested striking harmonies between natural and biblical revelation. Evangelicals placed a great deal of weight on the claim that these two sources of knowledge would never conflict. In fact, however, by the midnineteenth century such harmonies were being severely strained. Geology had forced admission that Genesis allowed much greater time periods than previously thought. Numerous other scientific theories in conflict with Scripture were in the air. In fact collapse was imminent.

Evangelical apologists, however, continued to rely on the argument from design with great displays of confidence.[45] Typical is "The Harmony of Revelation and Natural Science," delivered in 1850–51 as part of a series on evidences of Christianity at the University of Virginia (where once the enlightened thought of Jefferson had prevailed). The author, L. W. Green, president of Hampden-Sydney College, insists that "*The theology of natural science,* then, is in perfect harmony with *the theology of the Bible.*" Science "starts with *one instinctive principle, one intuitive conviction,* of the invariable connection between a CAUSE and its appropriate effect." Looking at nature with this intuitive principle, we inexorably are led to a "First Great Cause." At the same time we have an irresistible intuitive conviction of the "*relation between right and wrong,* that there is a moral element in man, and a moral law in the universe, that the *highest power and the highest right are at one, and both are* enthroned, supreme over all worlds." These two intuitions, then, an intuition of sufficient causes and a moral intuition (or, perhaps, a "moral government" intuition), secure human belief in a God of order, design, and benevolence. No amount of scientific evidence, thought Green, could dislodge the conclusions drawn from these intuitively based beliefs. Science could only add evidence of God's astonishing design. Astronomy could discover new worlds, geology might discover new ages, extinct races and species, and incalculable ages for the earth, "yet would the Christian welcome joyfully, and appropriate each successive revelation."[46]

## THE EVIDENCES OF CHRISTIANITY

In the meantime, so long as evangelicals were thoroughly convinced that science must support theism, natural theology was not so much their concern as was the defense of the authority of the Bible.[47] Indeed the Bible was the key issue. For American evangelicals prior to the era of Darwin the chief opponents were Deists and Transcendentalists. Each defended a form of theism known through nature. The real apologetic problem seemed to be, not whether nature pointed toward God, but whether the Bible pointed to the same God. This issue was of supreme importance for Protestants in the age of Enlightenment. America was in unique ways a Bible civilization, the land of *Scriptura sola.*[48] Major issues of the survival of Anglo-Saxon and Christian civilization seemed to rest on the question of the authority of the Bible. In a civilization where in practice the authority of science was seldom challenged, a crucial need seemed to be to demonstrate the congruence of the two authorities.

The evangelical views of the relationships between faith and reason appear most clearly in their arguments used to demonstrate that the Bible was indeed the revelation of the same God known in nature.

Mark Hopkins, famed evangelical teacher ("The ideal college is Mark

Hopkins at one end of a log and a student on the other"), states as typically as anyone the case for Christianity as it stood at midcentury. "Truth is one," Hopkins insists. "If God has made a revelation in one mode, it must coincide with what he has revealed in another." Hopkins presumes, therefore, that we can proceed from what we know with certainty—that which nature reveals—to settle the matter in dispute—the claims of Christianity. Either Christianity harmonized with known truths or it did not. If it did, there was every reason to expect that a scientific inquiry could assemble an overwhelming accumulation of evidences of that harmony. "The Christian religion admits of certain proof," he declares accordingly. All that is required to see this proof is to approach the evidence, not with the prejudices of skeptics, but "in the position of an impartial jury." "This course alone," says Hopkins in Baconian tones, "decides nothing on the grounds of previous hypothesis, but yields itself entirely to the guidance of facts properly authenticated."[49]

Common-Sense philosophy was the starting point of this inquiry. The dictates of common sense provide us with considerable knowledge about nature and human nature. So we should be able to test the congruence of Christian claims with this intuitive and indisputable knowledge. Hopkins agreed with the prevailing opinion that although we were not born with innate ideas, our minds were endowed with innate powers that inevitably led us to certain beliefs.[50] The commonality of these powers and beliefs throughout the race established the "common ground" from which philosophy and the proof of Christianity could proceed.[51] Humans, said Hopkins, were obliged to rely on the authority of their faculties, such as states of consciousness, sense perceptions, memory, testimony, and reasoning, each of which could, under the proper circumstances, yield virtual certainty. Moreover, Hopkins pointed out in typical common-sense fashion an equally firm basis for certainty is "reason" (to be distinguished from reasoning) by which one perceives "directly, intuitively, necessarily, and believes, with a conviction from which he can not free himself, certain fundamental truths, upon which all other truths, and all reasoning, properly so called, or deduction are conditioned."[52] These immediate, noninferential beliefs include much the same list as Reid had proposed, such as the existence of the self, the existence of other personal and rational beings, the existence of the material world, the relationship of cause and effect, the continuity of past and present, mathematical axioms, our sense of choosing, of freedom, and of obligations and responsibilities. "By Reid they were called principles of common-sense, and by Dugald Stewart fundamental laws of belief."[53]

With this common ground to work from, Hopkins could proceed with a major preliminary step in his defense of Christianity: showing that what the Bible reveals is fully consistent with what we already know through nature and natural revelation. "If," he says, "it can be shown that Christianity does not coincide with the well-authenticated teachings of natural religion, it will be conclusive against it." That biblical revelation passes this test establishes a presumption in its favor. On this point Hopkins' arguments are similar to Bishop Butler's in pointing out the many analogies between the two revelations, hence suggesting a single author. Each revelation, for instance, leaves us with incomplete knowledge, not forcing all its truths upon us, and hence leaving us some freedom of judgment and inquiry. The Bible may not be perfectly clear, but then neither is a great deal of what we trust completely in nature.[54]

More positively, Hopkins maintained that he could show that the Christian religion was ideally adapted to the human condition as revealed in nature. "There is a harmony of adaptation," he says, "and also of analogy. The key is adapted to the lock; the fin of the fish is analogous to the wing of the bird. Christianity, as I hope to show, is adapted to man." The human religious nature furnished considerable presumption in this direction. To suppose that the Creator would have created this virtually universal tendency toward religion in mankind and yet not have provided for him a proper object for it "is like supposing that he would create the eye without light." Since every theist (and Hopkins could assume that few in his audience would deny theism) agreed that God was a "moral Governor," they should also admit that such a good Creator probably would reveal himself to his creatures. Moreover, the glaring moral defects of the race made a revelation such as the Bible's seem even more likely. "If a rational being, capable of religion," says Hopkins, "had lost the moral image, and consequently the true knowledge of God and it should be the object of God to restore him, it could be done in no other way than by a direct revelation."[55]

The suitability of Christianity to the known character of humanity is evidenced especially clearly in the correspondences of its moral teachings to human moral needs. Nature revealed a system of morality, of rewards and punishments (as Wayland similarly argued). The Bible taught precisely the same system,[56] but only more precisely, fully, and explicitly. "In fact," says Hopkins,

> moral philosophy, and political economy, and the science of politics, . . . are, so far as they are sound, but experience and the structure of organized nature echoing back the teachings of Christianity. What principle of Christian ethics does moral philosophy now presume to call into question?[57]

Each of these considerations added a strand to the rope that was to form an unbreakable link between what was known from nature and what was claimed in Scripture. To establish Christian truth these Protestants, of course, considered it essential to establish the full authority of the Bible. Such authoritative claims, they held, should be susceptible to analysis. As in almost every other area of life, it should be possible to produce the evidence that would distinguish the genuine revelation from the pretenders. Such evidences might be an accumulation of considerations that, taken as a whole, would be compelling. It would be strange indeed if the true revelation lacked at least enough supporting evidence to establish a strong presumption in its favor.

The arguments for the Bible's authenticity as God's revelation appealed to two areas where human science had access. The moral and religious content of Scripture could, as we have seen, be tested against what was known about morality and religion by simply looking at nature and human nature. In addition, the historical claims of Scripture could be examined like any other historical statements. These two approaches converged in one of the strongest arguments for the Bible's authority. Natural religion and moral philosophy confirmed that the moral teachings of Scripture were unsurpassed. The presence of this exalted moral teaching helped confirm the honesty and integrity of the authors of Scripture in their other claims. "It is incredible and contradictory," says Hopkins, "contrary to all the known laws of mind, to suppose that men whose moral discrimination and susceptibilities were so acute—who could originate a system so pure, so elevated, so utterly opposed to all falsehood—would, without reason or motive that we can see, deliberately attempt to deceive mankind concerning their highest interests."[58]

To this evidence of the integrity of the biblical writers could be added a host of other historical considerations. Prophecies had been fulfilled. The sixty-six books were marvelously unified. Ancient church authorities whose memories reached back to the first centuries affirmed the integrity of the writers and attested their complete trust by being willing to die for their beliefs. The New Testament writers showed similarly total confidence in their claims, and many became martyrs. Their theological claims were confirmed by miracles, to which these authors were eyewitnesses. No contemporary witnesses refuted these miracle claims, even though many thousands of people would have been in a position to do so had fraud been involved.[59] All these evidences confirmed that the biblical writers were witnesses of the highest integrity. We could rely on their testimony, including their claims to be reporting God's revelation, with complete confidence.

Hopkins and the other evangelical writers followed Thomas Reid closely in pointing out that such evidence is "probable" as opposed to demonstrative, "moral" as opposed to mathematical. Lyman Beecher explains this use of "moral": "The difference between demonstration and moral certainty is, that in one case the mind sees the objects of comparison and sees the result, which, of course, is knowledge; but in the other, derives its confidence from the perception of probabilities multiplying till they produce confidence, or moral certainty."[60] Such certainty can become virtually as secure as in the case of mathematical demonstrations. Practically all the important affairs of life, in fact, depend on reliance on such accumulations of probable evidence. Particularly relevant to the case for Christianity is that many important human activities depend entirely on complete reliance on the "probable" evidence of testimony. Courts of law, and all our knowledge of historical figures, depend almost entirely on such testimony.[61] Every normal adult, of course, knows that testimony may deceive. But just as certainly, every society rests matters of life and death on the testimony of witnesses of demonstrated integrity. Reason, of course, often must be used to assemble the evidences of such integrity, but when it does so beyond a reasonable doubt, humans in all ages have accepted such testimony as a ground of certainty.[62] To present the evidences for Christianity, then, is no different than what one might do in other important affairs of life. "The proof of the authenticity of the Holy Scriptures," as Francis Wayland puts it, is "only a particular exemplification of the general laws of evidence."[63]

## FAITH AND REASON

What view of faith and reason emerges from this evidentialist apologetic? On the face of it, it appears that these evidentialists thought that reason must play a very large role in support of faith. "Without reason," says Archibald Alexander of Princeton, "there can be no religion: for in every step which we take, in examining the evidences of revelation, in interpreting its meaning, or in assenting to its doctrines, the exercise of this faculty is indispensable."[64] "Reason is necessarily presupposed in every revelation," echoed his famous student, Charles Hodge.[65] Such statements appear more moderate, however, when we take into account their broad use of "reason." "Reason," as we saw in Hopkins, included reliance in all those common-sense faculties by which people might know things intuitively and directly. So Hodge used the term "reason" to include any capacities for understanding. "The first and indispensable office of reason, therefore," says Hodge, "in matters of faith, is the cognition, or intelligent apprehension of the truths proposed for our reception." "Communication of truth," he explains, "supposes the capacity to receive it."[66]

When the evidentialists, then, spoke of the priority of "reason" in relation to faith, that did not mean at all that a Christian's faith needed to be based on reasoning or arguments. They all agreed emphatically on this point. "It is absurd," says Hodge, "to say that no man believes in God, who has not comprehended some philosophical argument for his existence, it is no less absurd to say that no man can rationally believe in Christ, who has not been instructed in the historical arguments which confirm his mission."[67] Since Christianity was both true and perfectly attuned to human needs, its truth might be recognized immediately. "It is very possible," says Hodge, "that the mind may see a thing to be true, without being able to prove its truth, or to make any satisfactory exhibition of the grounds of its belief."[68] Mark Hopkins explained the case as similar to that of the various disciples believing the evidence when they encountered the resurrected Christ. Some believed just by seeing him. Others had to hear him speak. Others, like Thomas, had to have more proofs and touch the actual marks of the crucifixion wounds.[69]

These observations help clarify the evidentialists' meaning of "evidence." As in the case of "reason," they use a broad meaning that does not necessarily have to do with producing arguments. So when the evangelical apologists make remarks like "man cannot believe, or be obligated to believe, without evidence" (Lyman Beecher)[70] or "faith without evidence is either irrational or impossible" (Charles Hodge),[71] they are not making radical proposals. By "evidence" they seem to mean simply those qualities of something (as an object or the truth of a statement) that can make it evident or apparent to us. Since many things have qualities that make the thing immediately apparent to us, seeing the evidence for something need not involve having any arguments about it.

Charles Hodge clearly explains the role of evidence and of immediate recognition of it in relation to belief in the authenticity of the Bible. The Bible contains sufficient evidence of its authenticity, as truly the Word of God. This evidence is of the sort that, like a truth of mathematics, when one properly apprehends it one simply finds onself compelled to believe it. One finds that the Bible "is so holy, so true, so consonant to right reason and right feeling, that he cannot doubt its truth." These biblical truths are so compelling to those who see them aright because the account of human sinfulness and the provisions for holiness and atonement so exactly suit our condition and needs. "They are truths which have their foundation in our nature and in our relation to God." Whatever other evidences or whatever arguments one may or may not have, when he perceives these truths directly, he does so "on the highest possible evidence; the testimony of God himself with and by the truth to his own heart; making him see and feel that it is truth."[72] Seeing such evidence, then, is not at all dependent on being able to produce an argument or proof.[73]

People, however, may not recognize the evidence for even the plainest truths. This is especially the case with biblical truths. Human sinfulness and moral perversity make them refuse to use their native faculties for recognizing God's truth. So one's moral condition can stand in the way of recognizing even that which is self-evident (especially when the sinfulness that one loves so deeply is that which is being exposed and threatened). "Let a man who hears the forty-seventh proposition of Euclid announced for the first time," explains Mark Hopkins, "trace the steps of the demonstration, and he *must* believe it to be true; but let him know that, as soon as he does perceive the evidence of that proposition so as to believe it on that ground, he shall lose his right eye, and he will never trace the evidence." On the other hand, says Hopkins with regard to biblical truth, "Let 'the mists that steam up before the intellect from a corrupt heart be dispersed,' and truths, before obscure, shine out as the noonday."[74] Seeing such truths might, of course, be aided by arguments. Arguments, however, could not compel belief. What compelled belief is just the seeing of the truth or, put another way, the proper seeing of the evidence.

The acceptance of these truths on God's authority is faith. "Faith," says Charles Hodge, "means belief of things not seen, on the ground of testimony."[75] One trusts what God says and assents to the truths he presents. The Holy Spirit supplies these truths to our hearts, so that the faith is not simply abstract belief, but saving faith.[76] "Faith is founded on testimony," says Hodge. "It is not founded on sense, reason, or feeling, but on the authority of him by whom it is authenticated."[77] Reason accordingly precedes faith, but only in the sense that normal understanding is necessary to apprehend the truth before one believes it. Reason is not the ground of faith, even though it is essential to it. Reason involves faculties necessary for us to see God and what is true; our faith is in God and his truth. Moreover, through faith, or trust in God's authority, we learn truths from the Bible that reason by itself could never teach.

Faith and reason can never conflict. This conviction is central to the entire evangelical outlook. God is the author of all things, so truth discovered in various ways will always harmonize. Faith in the irrational, says Hodge, is impossible. "It is impossible to believe that to be true which the mind sees to be false."[78] Philosophy and theology, he explains, occupy "common ground." "Both assume to teach what is true concerning God, man, the world, and the relation in which God stands to his creatures." Moreover,

> God is the author of our nature and the maker of heaven and earth, therefore nothing which the laws of our nature or the facts of the external world prove to be true, can contradict the teachings of God's

Word. Neither can the Scriptures contradict the truths of philosophy or science.[79]

## THE HIDDEN ASSUMPTIONS

We can return now to the central question of this essay. What, if anything, about this midnineteenth-century American evangelical apologetic made it particularly vulnerable to onslaughts of the scientific revolution associated with Darwinism? Was, as James Ward Smith maintains, this seemingly formidable intellectual edifice in fact built on a foundation of a superficial accommodation to the modern scientific revolution?

The key to the answer to this question seems to have to do with the relation of one's assumptions to what one knows about reality. If careful thinkers find arguments absolutely compelling to themselves, but these arguments soon are widely regarded, even by many sympathetic observers, as specious, chances are that the arguments rested on some questionable hidden assumptions.

The evidentialist apologists were well enough aware of some of their basic assumptions. Charles Hodge, on whom we can concentrate as one of the strongest representatives of the outlook, noted that both the scientist and the theologian must start with "certain assumptions." First, "He assumes the trustworthiness of his sense perceptions." Second, "He must also assume the trustworthiness of his mental operations." Third, "He must also rely on the certainty of those truths which are not learned from experience, but which are given in the constitution of our nature," such as every effect must have a cause and the uniformity of effects from identical causes.[80]

None of these assumptions appears to be especially controversial. Few people would want seriously to challenge the first two, and although some might argue that belief in cause and effect is learned, everyone but a few philosophers and crackpots would agree that indeed we are obliged to assume such beliefs as true. If there is a weakness in this Common-Sense outlook, it does not seem to lie in these acknowledged and widely held assumptions.

Behind these, however, were several other assumptions that were not clearly recognized as such and which appear more controversial. Most striking from a twentieth-century view is the immense confidence they had in the possibility of establishing most of one's knowledge objectively. Starting with the certainties of common sense and following the careful inductive methods of Baconian science, they were confident one could reach sure conclusions, compelling to any unbiased observer, in almost every aspect of human inquiry. Hodge reveals this assumption by constantly speaking of intellectual inquiry as the discovery of "facts." By "facts" he seems to mean states of affairs about reality which are true independently of our knowing them. Once discovered, he insists, "Facts do not admit of denial." "To deny facts," he says in reference to scientific discoveries, "is to deny what God affirms to be true. This the Bible can not do."[81] What seems controversial is, not so much this concept of fact, but rather the wide application it is given. As we have seen, the evangelicals characteristically assumed that the Baconian method would yield indubitable facts in all areas: morality, political thought, economics, and religion. So Hodge describes the Bible as a "store-house of facts." "The Bible is to the theologian what nature is to the man of science."[82] Such facts revealed in God's Word, when properly understood, can be known with certainty as "logical propositions."[83] "They are so set forth, that the meaning of the terms employed, and the sense of the propositions themselves, are understood, and understood in the same way by the renewed and the unrenewed."[84]

The evangelical apologists, of course, recognized bias. Bias, however, was something other people had. "Tell me what a man's philosophy is," said Hodge, "and I will ask him no questions about his theology."[85] They, on the other hand, considered themselves to hold no special philosophy. Their own views were simply open-minded, unbiased, candid, objective, and scientific.

This immense confidence rested on other hidden assumptions. The evangelical apologists' assurance of a high yield of objective certainty in intellectual inquiry rested on their assumptions about nature. Nature, they assumed, was ordered, intelligible, and meaningful. They saw in nature qualities that it would be likely to have only if it were created by a deity much like the God of the Bible—a benevolent Creator and Governor, interested in the welfare of his creatures. The existence of such a benevolent Creator and Governor, then, was in effect a tacit assumption of their outlook. Such a deity, they assumed further, would not systematically deceive his creatures by giving them faulty intellectual mechanisms. Rather, he would ensure that if they used their faculties responsibly, they would gain substantial knowledge about him and about the rest of creation.

The type of confidence they had in common sense also was influenced by this assumption concerning the design of nature. While their convictions about the reliability of common sense may formally have rested (as they did in the case of Reid) on just the fact that people find themselves obliged to trust common-sense faculties and principles, the implications drawn from such observations typically went far beyond what such observations by themselves would sustain. As Hodge (following Reid) remarked in stating his assumptions, common-sense truths were "given in the constitution of our nature." Having been so purposely designed, they could be relied on with perfect security. Moreover, the design of nature was assumed to involve the creation of a single universal human nature. Hence the presumption was that common-sense principles were universal and unalterable. So, as we have seen, Reid thought it possible to establish once for all a universal code of agreed-upon common-sense principles.

Such assumptions greatly abetted the idea that finding truth was essentially an objective process of discovering the "facts." As already observed, most recent twentieth-century ideas of "truth" have assumed an evolution of self-consciousness. With process rather than design as a basic category for thought, "truth" tends to become far more relative to the observer, his time and place. "Facts" commonly are regarded as not fixed, but as some combination of an objective reality and interpretation imposed by the observer.[86]

The weakness in the evidentialists' intellectual system, then, appears to be, not so much in that they started with common-sense assumptions and principles, but in their failure to recognize that a good many other assumptions were in fact functioning in their thought. The role of such assumptions concerning design and a benevolent Designer can be identified more clearly if we take their stated assumptions and add to them premises antithetical to their own, such as "there is no benevolent creator" or even "we do not know whether there is a benevolent creator." With these premises even the reliability of common-sense perceptions looks less secure. The phenomenon that people almost always find themselves trusting common-sense faculties and principles, and even that for the sake of argument they may be obliged to trust them, does not yield a strong presumption that these faculties and principles are especially reliable. Certainly it does not yield any presumption that these are universal throughout the race or unalterable, or that there is one set of assumptions that, in principle, everyone should agree to.

The critical role of the foundational assumptions concerning design in nature and a benevolent Designer became most acutely apparent in the debate over Darwinism. Darwinism was especially threatening to the entire evangelical edifice because it boldly removed the presumed intelligent design of nature and hence the benevolent Designer. Eighteenth- and early nineteenth-century evangelicals, and most of their contemporaries, took the intelligent design of nature to be indisputably a matter of common sense, confirmed by a good bit of reasoning. In fact, however, if one did not first presuppose a benevolent Creator, the intelligence and intentionality of the design was not nearly as evident as supposed. Darwin showed that with a premise such as "we do not know whether there is a benevolent creator" the apparent design and order could be explained at least plausibly on other grounds.

Charles Hodge saw this threat clearly in his famous essay *What Is Darwinism?* (1874), but he could only reassert the common sense of his own position. "The grand and fatal objection" to Darwinism, he said, was that Darwin's principle of natural selection excluded intelligent design. Hodge retorted:

> But in thus denying design in nature, these writers array against themselves the intuitive perceptions and irresistible convictions of all mankind, . . . a barrier which no man has ever been able to surmount.

Hodge bolstered this appeal to irresistible intuition with appeals to Paley and Butler. Paley had produced a "solid irrefragable argument" for a Designer, based on the inescapable evidence of design. "If a man denies that there is design in nature," Hodge argued by analogy, "he can with quite as good reason deny that there is any design in any or in all the works ever executed by man."[87]

The argument was futile as far as the Western intellectual community was concerned. Hodge could claim that the conviction of intelligent design in nature was irresistible and universal, but large parts of the next generations demonstrated that in fact the belief was quite resistible and far from universal. Common-Sense philosophy, claiming to be objective, claiming to rest on no prior assumptions, had no adequate response to such an attack on one of its fundamental principles. The supposed objectivism of the system suffered from a fatal flaw. Common sense could not settle a dispute over what was a matter of common sense.

Even more vulnerable in the evidentialists' defenses of Christianity were the other central pillars in their arguments—the appeals to human religious and moral sentiments. Again, with the tacit assumption of one benevolent Creator these phenomena seemed to point toward a confirmation of Christian claims. So, as we have seen, Mark Hopkins argues, "There is a harmony of adaptation, and also of analogy. The key is adapted to the lock; the fin of the fish is analogous to the wing of the bird. Christianity, as I hope to show, is adapted to man."[88] To first principles of morality, especially, followers of the Scottish philosophy characteristically assigned normative status parallel to the first principles of knowledge. In response to Darwinism, apologists such as Hopkins and Hodge continued to appeal to the supposedly normative principles. Darwinism, they said, could not adequately account for universal religious and moral sentiments.[89] The fact of the matter was, however, that Darwinism *could* account for these phenomena, at least as far as the logic of the case was concerned. Only if one already had a tacit premise that these religious and moral sentiments must have been designed for a purpose did it follow that they were clearly evidence for a Designer. Darwinism, starting with the premise that these phenomena arose naturally, found them to be survival mechanisms—primitive and prescientific ones at that. Such attacks left the evangelical apologetic in a shambles. Great weight had been placed on the analogies of biblical Christianity to what was known about nature. Darwin too saw the contrivances of nature and those of morality and religion as analogous; only in his view they were analogous means of survival with no further point or normative status.

## THE CLAIMS AND LIMITS OF SCIENCE

In *What Is Darwinism*? Charles Hodge perceptively related the immediate issue to the larger questions of science and religion. "Science," said Hodge, was coming to have a new and more limited meaning. Etymologically "science" meant simply "knowledge." It has long had this broad meaning which Hodge himself employed. Recently, however, the meaning was becoming increasingly restricted. "Science" in this restricted sense was limited to "the ordered phenomena which we recognize through the senses." Such a definition gave scientists a disposition "to undervalue any other kind of evidence except that of the senses."[90]

This recent trend to limit the meaning of "science" reflected the philosophical tendencies of the day. Various popular versions of the Kantian distinction between the phenomena and the noumena were being widely circulated and adopted. Two of the most prominent defenders of Darwinism, Herbert Spencer in England and John Fiske in America, made much of this point. The knowledge that we have access to scientifically is limited to the realm of the observable phenomena. We know that underlying these observable phenomena must be some essential qualities or noumena to which we do not have access. All we know about these is that they must exist and that they have effects in the phenomena we observe.[91] So Spencer and Fiske posited a great "Force" or "Power" behind the universe—"the noumenon of all phenomena," as Hodge tagged it.[92] T. H. Huxley, another of the prominent proponents of Darwinism, went further, coining the word "agnostic" to describe his view. "Agnostic" fit exactly the immensely influential intellectual trend growing from these philosophical developments. Positive science, dealing with phenomena, gave us knowledge. Other areas, such as religion or ultimate moral principles, were in the realm of the noumena or the unknowable.[93] So widely have such views of science and religion been adopted in Western culture that we can aptly designate the century after 1869, when Huxley invented the term, as the "age of agnosticism." If the metaphysical aspects of religion were to be discussed at all, they were to be relegated to a realm of "mystery" insusceptible to scientific inquiry.

Hodge recognized clearly enough the beginnings of this trend, but he had little way to counter it. His position was weakened for two related reasons. First, he had as high a view of the powers of pure scientific inquiry as did his most positivistic and secularistic contemporaries. Having had such an exalted view of the possibility of scientific certainty, he and his evangelical counterparts were hardly in a position to discount *prima facie* the extravagant claims of the new science.

The problem, however, went deeper into their basic philosophical stance. Hodge and his evidentialist counterparts claimed to start with a neutral objective epistemology that could be shared by all persons of common sense. Such a view worked well enough so long as there was a general consensus in the culture on certain metaphysical issues. Through the first half of the nineteenth century substantial elements of metaphysical assumptions of the Christian worldview survived. People generally assumed, for instance, that God, other spiritual beings, and normative moral principles were realities that were proper objects of human inquiry and knowledge. When this consensus disappeared, the proponents of a neutral and objective epistemology had little grounds for rebuttal. The question became Were such areas proper areas for scientific inquiry and knowledge? But science itself could not settle a dispute over what was a proper area for scientific inquiry. This was a metaphysical question that had to be decided on some other grounds.

The evangelical apologists had conceded too much. In 1871, for instance, Hodge had boldly stated that the solution to the seeming conflicts of science and religion was simply "to let science take its course, assured that the Scriptures will accommodate themselves to all well-authenticated facts in time to come, as they have in the past."[94] But again the fatal flaw of such objectivism appears. Who was to settle a dispute over what "the facts" were? The new science was excluding whole realms of religion and morality from "the facts." It did not help to respond, as inductivists such as the evidentialists characteristically did, by saying "just look at the evidence." Who was to settle a question of what was "evidence" or of what was possible evidence for what? Hodge complained, in the passage quoted above, that the new science tended "to undervalue any other kind of evidence except that of the senses." But what principle would decide what should be valued as evidence? Common sense might be appealed to. But, as already observed, a neutral common sense cannot settle a dispute over what is neutral common sense.

Here is the point at which James Ward Smith appears to be right in his analysis and critique of the dominant school of American Protestant thought prior to Darwin. With the exception of Jonathan Edwards, evangelicals had developed no effective critique of the first principles on which scientific inquiry rested. They had failed to appropriate Edwards' insight that the prior questions are metaphysical. There is no wholly neutral epistemology that can settle disputes over what areas of human knowledge are neutral and objective. Rather, a Christian epistemology must frankly begin, more or less as does that of Edwards, not only with common sense but also with data derived from revelation. Our understanding of something of the full range of human knowledge is in important ways derived from our belief in a Creator who communicates to his creatures both in nature and Scripture. Commitment to such a view allows us to see in reality the evidences of spiritual things.[95] Lacking such commitment, the modern agnostic sees the same phenomena but does not apprehend their spiritual aspects.

## TWO KINDS OF PEOPLE AND TWO KINDS OF SCIENCE

The question of how these issues might have been worked out in the setting of late nineteenth-century science may be clarified by a comparison. The value of this comparison—with the response of Abraham Kuyper in The Netherlands—is suggested not only by the Dutch-American context in which this essay is written but also by the fact that the evidentialist and the Kuyperian traditions are two of the strongest influences on current American evangelical thought on faith and reason.

Of all the countries in the Western world The Netherlands is the one in which traditional and evangelical Protestantism suffered the least serious decline in numbers and in intellectual influence during the heyday of science and secularism through the first half of the twentieth century. Furthermore, the school of thought of which Abraham Kuyper was the best representative and which substantially influenced the Dutch Protestant community differed markedly from the characteristic stance of American evangelical evidentialists exactly at the point we have been considering. Kuyper himself was not only a theologian but also the founder of a university and the prime minister of The Netherlands from 1901 to 1905, so that his views were well represented in the culture, even though never dominant. Of course, to suggest that the influence of Kuyper's views accounts for the markedly differing degree of impact traditionalist Protestantism had on the culture and the intellectual community of Holland as compared to America would be to oversimplify vastly relations of causes and effects. As emphasized earlier in this paper, many factors help account for the relative intellectual and cultural strength of various religious movements. Nevertheless, just as the evangelical apologists articulated trends in relating Christianity to culture and science prevalent in nineteenth-century America, so Kuyper articulated tendencies in Dutch Reformed thinking that had deep roots. Thus a comparison of the intellectual outlooks, while not meant to reduce the explanation of the differing cultural developments to one of their intellectual components, may provide important clues for seeing how the challenges of the recent scientific age might have been met differently than they were in evangelical America.

Like his American counterparts, Abraham Kuyper believed that in our encounter with reality we are forced to start with the common-sense operations of our minds. The axioms of our thought (such as consciousness of our own self or trust in our senses) are not susceptible to proof, so that "Nothing remains, therefore, but to declare that these axioms are given with our self-consciousness itself; that they inhere in it; that they are inseparable from it; and that of themselves they bring their certainty with them."[96] These common-sense starting points, as the Americans sometimes said also,[97] rested on "faith," as opposed to any demonstration. "By faith," says Kuyper, "you are sure of all those things of which you have a *firm conviction,* but which conviction is *not* the outcome of observation or demonstration." Such faith produces beliefs that are just as certain as any knowledge built on scientific demonstration; indeed, all scientific demonstration rests on such beliefs derived from faith. "All scepticism," Kuyper moreover remarks somewhat extravagantly, "originates from the impression that our certainty depends upon the results of our scientific research."[98]

The point at which Kuyper was departing most radically from the American evidentialists was in insisting that spiritually derived knowledge of God had the same epistemic status and provided the same sort of immediate grounds for certainty as did everyday common-sense experience. Knowledge of God is founded, not upon something prior to itself, but rather on God himself breathing into the minds of humans. This inspiration, the work of the Holy Spirit in communicating from God through Scripture[99] to humans, provides its own certainty. "The sense of this," says Kuyper, "stands entirely in line with every other primordial sense, such as with the sense of our ego, of our existence, of our life, of our calling, of our continuance, of our laws of thought, etc." This sense of "inspiration of God into the mind of the sinner" differs from the general principles of our consciousness in that it is not shared by virtually all people. However, many other valuable inner impulses lack this quality of universality. "Think of the poet, the virtuoso, the hero, and the adventurer. The want of general consent is no proof of want of foundation, and often works the effect, that the conviction becomes the more firmly founded."[100]

With respect to the knowledge of God the crucial element making this immediate knowledge far less than universal is the presence of sin among humans. As much as anything, emphasis on the effects of sin separated Kuyper's thought from the evidentialist, or Common-Sense, theological tradition in America. Whereas in the views of the Common-Sense apologists sin was a factor that could prevent one from taking an objective look at the evidence for the truth of divine things, for Kuyper unacknowledged sinfulness inevitably blinded one from true knowledge of God. Although all people had an innate sense of God, this natural relation was so broken and injured by sin as to be of no use in its present state as a foundation for knowing God truly. Only if one recognized the brokenness of this relationship, that is, only if one recognized one's own sinfulness, could one recognize this sense of God for what it truly was. Such a recognition, however, was not fully possible without God's inspiring communication of special grace.[101]

True knowledge of God, then, could not be founded upon anything other than already having some true knowledge of God specially communicated to one's heart. Hence every effort to prove God to sinners who lack the essential foundation for such knowledge was bound to fail.[102] By contrast, whereas Kuyper thought unrecognized human sinfulness a preventative to true knowledge of God, the American Common-Sense apologists saw it only as an inhibitive. Sin indeed could stand in the way of an objective look at the facts, but the Americans remained confident in the possibility of an objective scientific knowledge available to all intelligent humans. Moreover, they saw no reason why knowledge of God could not be a species of such knowledge.

Kuyper saw the problem as having to do with the concept of objectivity itself. Kuyper and the Common-Sense thinkers agreed that the nature of our consciousness forces us to believe in an organic harmony between subject and object. That is, we must believe that our subjective perceptions of reality can correspond to an actual reality external to ourselves. The Common-Sense thinkers took this correspondence as given, a dictate of common sense, needing no further justification. Kuyper did not quarrel on the immediate and common-sense status of this belief but observed that it was fraught with difficulties unless connected with another primal belief—belief in God as Creator.[103] Whatever necessity we might have to live by the belief in a subject/object correspondence, it could not by itself stand up as a basis for objective science—that is, knowledge for the whole race, not just for individuals. Objective scientific knowledge would have to have the qualities of necessity and universality.[104] In fact, however, scientific thought is riddled with subjectivity. The English, Kuyper observed, were dropping the name "science" for all but the natural sciences, apparently as an admission of the speculative nature of other areas of inquiry. Even in natural science, as soon as they got beyond weighing and measuring, the subjectivity of the theorizing (as Darwinism showed) was becoming conspicuous.

Kuyper explained the reign of subjectivity in terms of the Fall of mankind. In an ideal state of innocence the *subject* of science would be "the universal ego in the universal human consciousness." The *object* would be the cosmos. In such a situation universality of scientific knowledge would be possible, because the relations between subject and subject and subject and object would be so organically constituted as to ensure agreement in knowledge. Sin and the Fall of mankind disrupted this harmonious relationship among subjects and between subjects and objects. So now subjectivism reigns. Each subject is inclined "to push other subjects aside, or to transform the object after itself." Under Satan's influence falsehood is rampant, which is devastating to reliance on personal communication for access to truth. Add to such problems mistakes, self-delusion, delusive imagination, and various ways for distortions in human understandings and relationships to reinforce other distortions and misunderstandings, and the dream of objectivity is obliterated by subjectivism and sin. Such problems are, of course, most devastating in the spiritual science, though they infect all areas of human knowledge where the ego plays an active role in interpretation.[105]

The common-sense starting point in the assumption of a harmonious correspondence between our subjective perceptions and objective reality, however necessary it is for us to rely on it, dies of a thousand such qualifications unless it has some other supposition to support it. And so says Kuyper:

> And however much we may speculate and ponder, no explanation can ever suggest itself to our sense, of the all-sufficient ground for this admirable correspondence and affinity between object and subject, on which the possibility and development of science wholly rests, until at the hand of Holy Scripture we confess that the Author of the cosmos created man in the cosmos as a microcosmos "after his image and likeness."[106]

Though Kuyper is convinced that this is the only good solution to the human epistemic predicament, he presents it not so much as a proof as a confirmation. Human consciousness could be wholly deluded, of course, in supposing a subject-object correspondence, so the argument has a questionable premise. Moreover, no matter how strongly the case is made, many people will refuse to believe that their trust in subject-object correspondence necessitates belief in God. So Kuyper holds the view that God as revealed in Scriptures is known by us, not as a conclusion of an argument, but as a primary truth immediately apprehended as the result of spiritual communication to the human consciousness. People whose hearts and minds are closed to this spiritual communication will not be convinced by arguments. Nonetheless, it remains true that only if the basic truths that we learn immediately by being open to God's Word are added to our basic beliefs will we find adequate explanations to confirm such basic beliefs as our belief in the relationships of subject and object.

Science that includes the Creator of the harmonious correspondences between subject and object among its first principles will differ substantially from science which includes no such principle. There are two kinds of people, says Kuyper, regenerate and unregenerate. Unregenerate do not at all clearly know the Creator. Hence there are two kinds of science. Not that everything that Christians and non-Christians know is different. "There is a very broad realm of investigation in which the difference between the two groups exerts *no* influence." Yet the differences in basic principles mean that the two sciences soon diverge, much as a branch of a fruit tree grafted beside the branch of a wild root. "Near the ground the tree of science is one for all. But no sooner has it reached a certain height, than two branches separate, in the same way as may be seen in a tree which is grafted on the right side, while on the left side there is allowed to grow a shoot from the wild root." Ultimately the goal and direction of these two sciences are at odds with each other, even though in some respects they are alike. Using another metaphor, Kuyper says, "We only affirm that formally both groups perform scientific labor, and that they recognize each other's scientific character, in the same way in which two armies facing each other are mutually able to appreciate military honor and military worth."[107]

Kuyper implemented his theories with the establishment of the Free University of Amsterdam in 1880, an institution in which the theme of the fundamental differences between Christian and non-Christian thought was strongly expressed through most of the twentieth century. Even the presence of this one institution separated the Dutch academic experience from that in the United States, where no major university clearly articulated the conflict between Christian and non-Christian thought as arising at such a primal level. Even in America's surviving Christian colleges such a contrast between Christian and non-Christian thought has until recently not been widely taught. Kuyper's views do seem to offer the kind of critique of the first principles of modern science that James W. Smith said were lacking in American Protestant responses to the Darwinist revolution.

The issue, however, should not be settled so glibly. Kuyper, it seems, had taken into account an assumption in evaluating science that the

Common-Sense apologists had neglected. Nevertheless, his alternative appears to rest Christian faith substantially on the mysterious and inaccessible foundation of the testimony of the Holy Spirit to one's heart. Parallel to the questions that plagued the objectivists (common sense does not well settle a dispute over what is common sense), Kuyper's view seems to have the troubling problem that further appeals to the Holy Spirit will not well settle a dispute over what is truly the voice of the Holy Spirit. Kuyper, in traditional Calvinist fashion, stresses that the Spirit works through Scripture and the body of believers, and these authorities are susceptible to some testing, at least for consistency.[108] Nevertheless, even with these sources of faith practically central, Kuyper emphasizes so much the lack of reasons in coming to faith that the charge of arbitrarily trusting authorities seems a natural one.

Such objections are well articulated by perhaps the greatest proponent of the Common-Sense–evidentialist apologetic, Princeton's Benjamin B. Warfield, in two brief comments on Kuyper's work. Warfield's position, which has had great influence in twentieth-century American evangelicalism, well represents the reasons why Kuyper's views have been unattractive to many American evangelicals.

Warfield professed to find Kuyper's views simply baffling. To him it seemed crucial that the Holy Spirit, though unquestionably primary in granting faith, always worked through means. "The Holy Spirit does not work a blind, an ungrounded faith in the heart." Rather the Holy Spirit granted "just a new ability of the heart to respond to the grounds of faith." So why not expect that there would be sufficient evidence for Christian faith if we only examined it carefully? Faith, said Warfield, is "a form of conviction and is, therefore, necessarily grounded in evidence." To the objection that his stance might seem to make faith dependent on arguments, Warfield retorted simply: "We do not believe in the existence of the sun without evidence because we are not learned in astronomical science." Whether individual believers needed to stop and analyze the evidence was to Warfield of little importance. The important point for Christian apologetics was that the evidence could be analyzed and the faith could be shown to be fully rational.[109]

Lying behind this difference in apologetic strategy was a fundamental disagreement with Kuyper's dictum that there were "two kinds of people" and hence "two kinds of science." Warfield agreed that the regenerate had some advantage over the unregenerate in doing science, but he emphasized that they were doing the same sort of work. Each was working on the same edifice of human scientific knowledge and benefited from the other's accomplishments. Regeneration, he said, made far less difference than Kuyper supposed, since regenerated people remained infected by sin. Moreover, and perhaps more importantly, even if there were sinless men, "Sinful and sinless men are, after all, both men; and being both men, are fundamentally alike and know fundamentally alike." If truth was on the side of the Christians, Warfield reasoned, then in an argument Christianity eventually would triumph. This conclusion rested on an assumption with deep roots in the Common-Sense tradition: "All minds are of the same essential structure; and the less illuminated will not be able permanently to resist or gainsay the determinations of the more illuminated."[110]

The whole argument between these two groups of Reformed Christians rested on differences concerning this question. Did the fact that all human minds were of the same essential structure imply that regenerate and unregenerate know essentially alike? Scripture and other basic Christian assumptions did not clearly settle this issue. Neither did philosophy. In part the difference turned on differing concepts of what is involved in achieving human knowledge. Kuyper, closer to the idealist tradition, while not denying that human minds had similar structures, viewed knowledge in terms of the overall relationships it involved—the organic relationships among Creator, cosmos, and knowing subjects. Doing science, he was convinced, presupposed a whole theory about the fundamental structures of the universe. Knowledge accordingly did not come in isolated packages but was understood by subjects in the context of other beliefs the subject held—beliefs determined either by the subjective urge to remake the universe in one's own image or by proper reverence for God. Warfield, on the other hand, viewed knowledge in an essentially inductionist, or Baconian, fashion. Knowledge was gained by considering evidence and drawing conclusions that that evidence would support. Whether one immediately drew the proper conclusion (as in the nonastronomer's knowledge of the sun) or reached it by carefully weighing evidence and making inferences, the basic idea was the same. Each item of knowledge could exist independently. Knowing depended essentially on looking at the evidence for the individual item. It did not depend substantially on what else one knew or on one's worldview. Once science establishes the evidence and conclusion, the item of knowledge becomes accessible to all rational people, virtually regardless of their other beliefs.

Warfield represented the grand Enlightenment ideal for science, which had deep roots in Western thought dating back to the Greeks. It has been an ideal especially appealing in the United States, a nation founded on principles drawn from Enlightenment thought. Kuyper, coming out of a Dutch "anti-Revolutionary" tradition that sharply criticized these Enlightenment categories, was much more ready to offer a critique of this ideal.

Since Warfield's view continues to have such wide appeal in American evangelicalism, it is worth commenting on this debate. Kuyper seems to have the better of the argument in explicitly relating his philosophy to its Christian assumptions, refusing to accept uncritically the Enlightenment ideal of one science for all humanity, and in providing a basis for building a Christian intellectual outlook that can withstand the claims both of modern science and modern subjectivism. Nevertheless, we should not leave this debate until we have considered why Warfield's views seem to many people so appealing and compelling, and Kuyper's so counterintuitive.

Christianity involves many specific claims about history, morality, and the structure of relationships in the universe. Many of these claims appear to be of the sort that are commonly subjected to analysis when matters are in dispute. In disputed cases the natural thing for humans to do is to examine the evidence for and against the claims in question. Perhaps such an examination will not settle the issue, but at least we should see whether the preponderance of evidence is on one side or the other. To say that such examination of the evidence is irrelevant or of little importance to Christian belief appears to be an evasion. It seems to put Christian claims in a category immune from the tests that we normally use for our beliefs. It suggests to many people that we do not think there is very good evidence to support Christian belief. The evidentialist, on the other hand, is convinced that there ought to be some such evidence. For instance, nineteenth-century apologists made much of the point that if the same God who created the world and humanity also revealed the Bible, there ought to be some evidence of that common authorship. Similarly, if Christianity makes certain historical claims—if it is preeminently a *historical* religion based on God's entering history and becoming to some degree knowable by normal human standards—then there ought to be some evidence favoring the authenticity of those historical claims.

The principal point at which the arguments of the evidentialists failed was, not in supposing that there should be a preponderance of evidence favorable to Christian claims, but rather in supposing that such evidence and arguments constituted conclusive arguments for the truth of Christianity. As we have seen, the general arguments for Christianity do not stand up as logically compelling unless one already grants certain assumptions about reality that virtually presuppose a benevolent Creator. Otherwise alternative explanations can explain the phenomena as logically as can Christianity. Historical arguments are no better, since historical events are typically susceptible to more than one plausible interpretation. Furthermore, sinful people whose minds are adamantly closed to hearing God and his Word will be quick to point out the logical plausibility of the alternatives.

Nevertheless, arguments that are not compelling logically may have great psychological and even intellectual force, particularly for those who are wavering in their resolution to deny the presence of God and his Word. This should be especially true if in fact Christianity accurately describes human conditions and needs and God's saving acts. For instance, if humans indeed have certain moral and religious sensibilities and needs to which the Gospel best responds, then people might well be brought to some intuitive recognition of the suitability of Christianity to their conditions and needs. Compared with secularism, for instance, Christianity may be simply vastly superior in accounting for their actual sense of worth, of right and wrong, or of guilt and of need for redemption and new direction in their lives. This superiority will not appear in that Christianity will be the only hypothesis that can provide a good explanation of these phenomena; rather it may be the one that is the most attractive, given humans' actual needs and sensibilities.[111] How convincing such considerations will be depends of course on the psychological, intellectual, and spiritual condition of the person being addressed. Sin or commitments to other religions will blind many to any such considerations. For others the Holy Spirit may remove such blinders and allow them to see their conditions and needs for what they really are. Such a sight of the true contours of reality may be no more the result of arguments than is the recognition of the beauty of a symphony, but it may be just as much the result of considering the evidence. Once a person has such an insight, the other evidences for Christianity—for instance, that the claims of Scripture are based on testimony of people of apparently high integrity—may add force to the Christian claims, even if not providing arguments to which there is no logical alternative. If people were consistent to their sinful and subjectivistic commitments, they would be, as Kuyper said, unable to be touched by such evidences and arguments. Nonetheless, the Gospel miraculously becomes convincing to sinners who seem to hold the denial of its claims as one of their most basic beliefs. Many are given the insight to see the truth of Christianity even without arguments—or with only a few very informal ones. Others are helped by the spelling out of the evidence. In either case the Holy Spirit helps sinners to see truths that the deepest impulses of their unregenerate natures would have them utterly deny.[112]

Perhaps a similar resolution of the differing approaches to the "two science" questions might be reached. Kuyper appears to say something that is almost essential for the survival of the Christian academic community in a secular setting—that science cannot be regarded as a sovereign domain that sets its own rules to which Christians and everyone else must conform if they are to retain their intellectual respectability. As philosophers of science now are also recognizing, science itself is controlled to substantial degrees by assumptions and commitments.[113] Christians, then, should be free frankly to state their metaphysical starting points and their assumptions and to introduce these into their scientific work in all areas of human inquiry; they should employ underlying control beliefs that differ widely from those of non-Christians.[114]

Nonetheless, despite the impulses to subjectivity, personal knowledge, and special interests that twentieth-century people have become so alerted to, Christians may affirm, as Kuyper and Warfield would have agreed, that "all minds are of the same essential structure." Hence much that common sense affirms is reliable. Among other things, common sense tells us that in fact we can communicate remarkably well even with many people who differ from us quite radically in some perceptions and basic assumptions. So theoretically there is a vast difference between Christian and non-Christian thought—that is, if each were always a logical system consistent with its premises. In reality, however, God has structured our thought so that it is not dominated by such logical categories. Most of what we know goes beyond what is susceptible to logical analysis. Hence radical differences in fundamental assumptions, which might seem to entail wholly incompatible thought systems, turn out to be surmountable in most practical affairs. Warfield is probably right that regeneration does not usually transform people and their thinking as radically as we might like and that our common humanity guarantees us considerable commonality of thought. Hence, the Christian psychologist and the secular behaviorist might find themselves easily able to work together on many psychological projects—to understand each other and to take each other's fundamental assumptions into account. Perhaps the mutual respect and understanding that is in fact possible is, as Kuyper suggested, like that between two contending armies. Nonetheless, through God's grace the relationships between Christians and non-Christians are perhaps more often those of peace than those of open war. Underneath there are warring principles, and these are part of a deeper cosmic contest between the forces of good and evil. Yet the captain in our warfare is the Prince of Peace, so we can rightfully live in peace with our epistemic enemies, even though at some fundamental intellectual levels we may be struggling against them.

* * * * *

In conclusion we can say that the demise of American evangelical academia involved a significant component of intellectual weakness. Specifically, the nineteenth-century evidentialists' overestimation of the prowess of the scientific method seems a serious error. So does the underestimation of the degree to which peoples' thought is of a whole (is made up of a complex and vital relationship among ideas), so that sinfully determined basic first beliefs and commitments can pervade the rest of one's intellectual activity. Nevertheless, despite such overestimations of the possibilities for objectivity, we can learn from the Common-Sense tradition. It emphasizes that many of our beliefs are not derived from other beliefs but arise out of the constitution of our nature. Moreover, regenerate and unregenerate live in the same world and share many of the same experiences. They can communicate with each other. Furthermore, evidences of God's care, power, and provision for salvation abound, and in fact people often see these evidences when presented. The Kuyperian insights qualify these observations by pointing out that such recognition is not founded simply on an appeal to beliefs shared by virtually all people. Rather, sin creates a widespread abnormality. Trust in God which ought to be a spontaneous act providing us with some intuitive first principles of knowledge is lacking in most people. Christians should not be embarrassed to say frankly that this is the issue. If one trusts in God, one will view some evidence differently than a person who basically denies God. If people trust in God, their science and knowledge should have some substantial traits that differ from the science and knowledge of those who basically deny God. Nonetheless, the appeal to trust in God is in a way an appeal to common sense, even though to a suppressed aspect of common sense. The American and the Dutch evangelical-Reformed traditions have offered differing insights on these issues. Evangelical academics in the late twentieth century might benefit by looking at the insights from both these traditions.

## NOTES

1. Mark A. Noll, "Christian Thinking and the Rise of the American University," *Christian Scholar's Review* 9 (1979): 3–16, presents a valuable summary of these developments.

2. For example see Owen Chadwick, *The Secularization of the European Mind in the Nineteenth Century* (Cambridge, England, 1975). By "secularization" I mean here simply the decline of distinctly Christian influences.

3. Burton J. Bledstein, *The Culture of Professionalism: The Middle Class and the Development of Higher Education in America* (New York, 1976). Cf. Noll, "Christian Thinking." A fine account of the impact of professionalism on philosophy is Bruce Kuklick, *The Rise of American Philosophy: Cambridge, Massachusetts, 1860–1930* (New Haven, 1977).

4. Noll, "Christian Thinking."

5. In James Ward Smith and A. Leland Jamison, eds., *The Shaping of American Religion* (Princeton, 1961), pp. 402–42.

6. Some recent and generally favorable philosophical discussions of Reid are found in Stephen F. Barker and Tom L. Beauchamp, eds., *Thomas Reid: Critical Interpretations* (Philadelphia, 1976) and Elizabeth Flower and Murray G.

Murphey, *A History of Philosophy in America* (New York, 1977). See also the work of Nicholas Wolterstorff in this volume.

7. This connection is well documented in many works. For instance, Flower and Murphey, *History of Philosophy in America;* Theodore Dwight Bozeman, *Protestants in an Age of Science: The Baconian Ideal and Antebellum American Religious Thought* (Chapel Hill, 1977); Herbert Hovenkamp, *Science and Religion in America, 1800–1860* (Philadelphia, 1978).

8. Quoted in Bozeman, *Protestants in the Age of Science,* p. 5. For more documentation of Reid's admiration for Bacon see Bozeman, pp. 5–21 passim.

9. Thomas Reid, *Essays on the Intellectual Powers of Man,* ed. Baruch A. Brody (Cambridge, Mass., 1969 [1785]), II: 8, p. 145, and VII: 3, p. 737; Reid discusses "probable reasoning" in VII: 3. "Probable reasoning" includes reasoning on evidence from human testimony, on reputable authority, or based on: the identity of things, some assumptions about human behavior, chances, or induction. The all-importance, even for savages, of inductively determining the "laws of nature" (fire burns, water drowns, etc.) is discussed on p. 736.

10. Descartes provided an alternative version of foundationalism by reducing the basic (or non-demonstrable) beliefs to the minimum—his consciousness that he was thinking—and attempted to derive the rest from that certitude. Reid thought Descartes and his ilk vastly overestimated the importance and the competence of demonstrative reasoning.

11. Reid, *Essays,* VI:4, pp. 596–97.

12. Ibid., I:2, p. 31.

13. Ibid., VI:6, p. 646.

14. Ibid., VI:2, p. 567.

15. Ibid., I:2, pp. 30–31.

16. Ibid., VI:2, pp. 559–60.

17. Ibid., VI:6, pp. 667–69.

18. Ibid., VII:3, p. 735.

19. Ibid., VI:5, p. 616.

20. Ibid., VII:3, p. 736.

21. The mottoes of Reid's first two books are "The inspiration of the Almighty giveth them understanding" and "Who hath put wisdom in the inward parts." S. A. Grave, *The Scottish Philosophy of Common Sense* (Oxford, 1960), p. 159.

22. This is the phrase of a key American transitional figure, Chauncey Wright (1830–75). See Bruce Kuklick, *The Rise of American Philosophy;* and Flower and Murphey, *A History of Philosophy in America,* vol. 2, for discussions of this transformation in America.

23. Reid, *Essays,* VI:6, p. 669.

24. For instance, James Beattie, *An Essay on the Nature and Immutability of Truth in Opposition to Sophistry and Scepticism* (1770), essentially a popularization of the philosophical arguments of Reid, was published in a series entitled *The Evidences of the Christian Religion* (London, 1816).

25. William Paley, *Natural Theology: Selections,* ed. Frederick Ferre (New York, 1963), chapter 6, p. 32.

26. Ibid., passim.

27. Bernard Ramm, *Varieties of Christian Apologetics* (Grand Rapids, 1962), p. 107.

28. Ibid., p. 112. For an affirmation by Butler of the Baconian ideal of reasoning from the "observation of facts" as opposed to "building a world upon hypothesis, like Des Cartes," see Joseph Butler, *The Analogy of Religion, Natural and Revealed to the Constitution and Course of Nature* (London, 1852) [1736]), pp. 75–76.

29. Butler, *Analogy,* Malcom and Barnes edition, quoted in Ramm, *Varieties,* p. 117.

30. Quoted, Butler, *Analogy,* p. 79n.

31. Quoted in Bozeman, *Protestants in the Age of Science,* p. 3.

32. This phrase is from Bozeman, ibid., p. 72. This theme is well documented also in George H. Daniels, *American Science in the Age of Jackson* (New York, 1968); E. Brooks Holifield, *The Gentlemen Theologians: American Theology in Southern Culture, 1795–1860* (Durham, 1978); and Hovenkamp, *Science and Religion in America.*

33. For the considerable influences of Scottish philosophy on Jefferson and the Declaration see Garry Wills, *Inventing America: Jefferson's Declaration of Independence* (New York, 1978). Wills, however, likely overestimates the centrality of these influences in Jefferson's thought.

34. Francis Wayland, *Elements of Moral Science,* ed. Joseph Angus (London, 1860 [1835]), pp. 1, 3, 4, 100, 116–21.

35. Ibid., pp. 219–20.

36. Ibid.

37. Wayland says: "God has created everything double; a world without us, and a correspondent world within us. He has made light without, and the eye within; beauty without, and taste within; moral qualities in actions, and conscience to judge of them; and so in every other case. By means of this correspondence, our communication with the external world exists." Ibid., p. 85.

38. Francis Wayland, *The Elements of Political Economy* (Boston, 1860 [1837]), p. iv.

39. Ibid., p. 132.

40. Martin Marty, *The Modern Schism: Three Paths to the Secular* (New York, 1969), p. 98.

41. Francis Wayland, *The Elements of Intellectual Philosophy* (New York, 1868 [1854]) is essentially a technical account of intellectual mechanisms and faculties in the tradition of Common-Sense philosophy.

42. Paul A. Carter, *The Spiritual Crisis of the Gilded Age* (DeKalb, Ill., 1971), pp. 3–4; Richard Hofstadter, *Social Darwinism in American Life* (New York, 1955 [1944]), pp. 51–66, describes Sumner's career.

43. This tendency is abundantly documented in Bozeman, *Protestants in the Age of Science;* George H. Daniels, *American Science in the Age of Jackson;* E. Brooks Holifield, *The Gentlemen Theologians: American Theology in Southern Culture, 1795–1860.*

44. This is the statement of Bozeman, *Protestants in an Age of Science,*

p. 88, summarizing historian John C. Greene. Hovenkamp, *Science and Religion in America,* makes similar observations.

45. Ibid., passim. For examples of nineteenth-century uses of the argument from design see Charles Hodge, *Systematic Theology* (New York, 1971), 1:215–33, and Robert L. Dabney, *Syllabus and Notes of the Course of Systematic and Polemic Theology* (Richmond, 1927 [1871]), p. 9.

46. L. W. Green, *Lectures on the Evidences of Christianity* (New York, 1854), pp. 463–64. As some of the examples below indicate, evangelical apologists differed somewhat on what they considered intuitive beliefs. Most included, however, a sense of causality and/or moral order.

Green's show of confidence is evident in his remarks on geology: "It furnishes by far the most conclusive of all arguments for the existence of God; explodes the atheistic theory of an infinite series of beings; and thus dispels the last remaining doubt that might otherwise have thrown its shadow over the soul of man." P. 462.

On the centrality of the themes of design, benevolence, and order, cf. Bozeman, *Age of Science,* p. 82.

47. An essay by "a society of clergymen" in *Bibliotheca Sacra* 3 (May 1846), "Natural Theology," lamented that "so noble a department of study should have fallen into unmerited neglect." Pp. 241–42.

48. See Nathan Hatch, "*Scriptura Sola and Novus Ordo Seclorum,*" in *The Bible in America,* ed. Nathan Hatch and Mark Noll (New York, 1982), pp. 59–78.

49. Mark Hopkins, *Evidences of Christianity* (Boston, 1876 [1846]), pp. 97–98 and p. 39.

50. Cf. Dabney, *Theology,* p. 83, and Francis Wayland, "The Philosophy of Analogy," in *American Philosophical Addresses 1700–1900,* ed. Joseph L. Blau (New York, 1946), p. 348, for similar statements.

51. Mark Hopkins, "Grounds of Knowledge and Rules for Belief," *Princeton Review* 57 (January 1881): 1.

52. Hopkins, *Evidences,* pp. 24–27.

53. Hopkins, "Grounds of Knowledge," p. 4; cf. Hopkins, *Evidences,* passim.

Some differences of opinion existed among evangelicals as to the relation of knowledge of God to these intuitive first principles. Charles Hodge held that some sort of general knowledge of God was indeed intuitive and universal. This, he said, the Bible taught. This knowledge was incomplete, so that further instruction was necessary "to give them any adequate knowledge of the nature of God, and of their relations to Him." Hodge, *Systematic Theology,* 1: 199; cf. 191–203. Hodge thought, nonetheless, that it was perfectly legitimate to use the traditional proofs to confirm such intuitive knowledge. Pp. 202–3. The Southern Presbyterian theologian, Charles Dabney, criticized Hodge, saying that Hodge confused intuition with an elementary deduction of common sense (the deduction from an intuitive sense of obligation to an obligator). Dabney, *Theology,* p. 7. Mark Hopkins thought that the natural world was ambiguous in revealing God, and our natural sense of moral obligation might be blinded. So the knowledge of God (from the starry heavens above and moral law within) was not immediate or intuitive, even though it was a simple demonstration.

Dabney and Hopkins appear to be closer to Reid on this point, while Hodge tries to harmonize Common-Sense philosophy with Calvin's view.

54. Hopkins, *Evidences,* pp. 98, 80–91.

55. Ibid., pp. 75 and 48.

56. Hopkins regarded the superiority of Christianity to other religions as needing little argument. Of the chief contender he says: "But I need not spend time in comparing, or rather contrasting, the religion of Mohammed, unsustained by miracles or prophecies, propagated by the sword, encouraging fatalism, and pride, and intolerance, sanctioning polygamy, offering a sensual heaven,—a religion whose force is already spent, which has no sympathy or congruity with the enlarged views and onward movements of these days, and which is fast passing into a hopeless imbecility,—with the pure, and humble and beneficient religion of Christ." Ibid., p. 66.

57. Ibid., pp. 102–3.

58. Ibid., p. 119. Hopkins is not especially concerned with the accuracy of detail of the biblical statements. He says, for instance, that the discrepancies among the Gospels are evidence of their authenticity, since a fraud likely would have tried to make all the details match previous accounts. P. 204.

59. Hopkins, *Evidences,* passim. The impact of Christianity in changing the course of history, especially its demonstrably beneficial moral impact, helped support these claims.

Every evangelical author included a refutation of Hume's arguments on miracles and pointed out that only a prejudice against all miracles would lead one to rule out the authenticity of the biblical accounts. Hopkins, p. 28, says that he will review the well-known arguments refuting Hume because it is still the custom of those who defend Christianity to do so, just as it was "the custom of British ships to fire a gun on passing the port of Copenhagen, long after its power had been prostrated, and its influence had ceased to be felt."

Lyman Beecher, "The Bible a Revelation from God to Man," *Works* (Boston, 1852), 1:219, contrasts the public miracles of the Bible (those of Moses were witnessed by a whole nation that could have revolted against a fraud) to the private miracles of Mahomet and the Catholic Church.

George Fisher of Yale, *Essays on the Supernatural Origins of Christianity* (New York, 1890 [1866]), p. xxvii, expresses complete confidence in authenticating the miracle accounts: "That the narratives of miracles which are given in the Gospels are, in the main, a faithful record of facts which actually occurred, is the result of a sound, unbiassed historical criticism, and must, sooner, or later, be generally acknowledged."

60. Beecher, *Works,* 1:54; Hopkins, *Evidences,* p. 22.

61. Cf. Reid, *Essays;* cf. Wayland, *Intellectual Philosophy,* pp. 317–32.

62. Reid points out the necessity of the mutual aid of reason and testimony in *An Inquiry into the Human Mind* (Chicago, 1970), VI:24, p. 24.

63. Wayland, *Moral Science,* p. 203.

64. Archibald Alexander, *Evidences of the Authenticity, Inspiration, and Canonical Authority of the Holy Scriptures* (Philadelphia, 1848 [1836]), p. 9.

65. Hodge, *Systematic Theology,* 1:49.

66. Ibid.

67. Hodge, "Ground of Faith in the Scriptures," *Essays and Reviews* (New York, 1879), p. 191. First appeared in *Princeton Review* 17 (1845).

68. Ibid., p. 188.

69. Hopkins, *Evidences,* p. 353. Cf. Paley, who responds to the observation that most readers of his *Natural Theology* never doubted the truths he argues for: "Now, I answer that by *investigation* the following points are always gained in favor of doctrines even the most generally acknowledged, supposing them to be true, namely stability and impression. Occasions will arise to try the firmness of our most habitual opinions. And upon these occasions it is a matter of incalculable use to feel our foundation, to find a support in argument for what we have taken upon authority." P. 83. The evidentialists' motives in exhibiting the evidences and arguments in support of Christianity seem to be (1) to aid the doubter and (2) to keep strong the case for Christianity in the ongoing debates in the intellectual world as to which viewpoint is true: evidences of its truth must be available, and these assembled would constitute a stronger case than could be made for any false system.

70. Beecher, *Works,* 1:203.

71. Hodge, *Systematic Theology,* 1:53.

72. Hodge, "Ground of Faith," pp. 189–92.

73. Hodge compares our knowing of this sort of truth to knowing mathematical truths, recognizing beauty or genius and recognizing moral truths. Of the latter he says: "This is not a thing which, in the proper sense of the word, admits of proof. The only possible proof of the correctness of a moral doctrine, is to make us see its truth; its accordance with the law of God, the supreme standard, and with that law as written in our own hearts." Ibid., p. 189.

74. Hopkins, *Evidences,* pp. 20–21.

75. Hodge, *Systematic Theology,* 3:63.

76. Ibid., 3:68–70. Nineteenth-century evangelical writers, of course, differed on their definitions of faith. Hodge, however, is an important representative.

77. Ibid., 3:63.

78. Ibid., 3:83.

79. Ibid., 1:56.

80. Ibid., 1:9.

81. Ibid., 1:57.

82. Ibid., 1:10.

83. Hodge, "The Theology of Intellect and That of the Feelings," II, *Essays and Reviews* (from the *Princeton Review* 22 (1851):609. "Logical" here seems to have no special force, since he has just listed a number of biblical teachings like the Incarnation, that Christ died for our sins, and such. Hodge seems to mean that these beliefs are like the propositions used in logic.

84. Ibid. Hodge adds: "That the one class perceive in the truths thus re-

vealed an excellence, and experience from them a power, of which the other class have no experience, does not alter the case."

85. Quoted in John C. Vander Stelt, *Philosophy and Scripture: A Study in Old Princeton and Westminster Theology* (Marlton, N.J., 1978), p. 147.

86. Cf. my discussion of this point with reference to the historical views of Carl Becker in "J. Gresham Machen, History, and Truth," *Westminster Theological Journal* 42 (fall 1979): 157–75.

87. Hodge, *What Is Darwinism?* (London, 1874), pp. 169, 170, and 173. James R. Moore, *The Post-Darwinian Controversies: A Study of the Protestant Struggle to Come to Terms with Darwin in Great Britain and America, 1870–1900* (Cambridge, 1979), shows that a number of Christian thinkers, notably some conservative Calvinists, viewed Darwinism as compatible with design, pointing out that in principle it raised no new questions regarding the relationship of God's controlling providence and secondary natural means. No longer, however, could they claim with Paley et al. that an intelligent designer was the *only* plausible explanation.

88. Hopkins, *Evidences,* p. 75.

89. Mark Hopkins, *The Scriptural Idea of Man* (New York, 1884), p. 25.

90. Hodge, *What Is Darwinism?* pp. 127 and 129.

91. Spencer, in fact, got this idea directly from the nineteenth-century Scottish philosopher Sir William Hamilton (1788–1856). Hamilton's very influential philosophy combined elements of Reid and Kant. Hamilton held "that our knowledge of mind and of matter is relative and conditioned and that 'of existence absolutely and in itself, we know nothing'." We are, however, compelled to think of something absolute, unknown and unknowable by virtue of a "law of thought." Timothy J. Duggan, "William Hamilton," *The Encyclopedia of Philosophy,* ed. Paul Edwards (New York, 1967), 3:409. Spencer's relation to Hamilton is discussed in Flower and Murphey, *History of Philosophy in America,* 2:528–31. Hodge offered a long critique of this aspect of Hamilton in his *Systematic Theology.*

92. Hodge, *What Is Darwinism?* p. 19.

93. T. A. Goudge, "Thomas Henry Huxley," *Encyclopedia of Philosophy,* 4:101–3. Cf. Ronald W. Hepburn, "Agnosticism," 1:56–59.

94. Hodge, *Systematic Theology,* 1:57.

95. Discussion of Edwards' views has recently been advanced by Norman Fiering, *Jonathan Edwards's Moral Thought and Its British Context* (Chapel Hill, 1981).

96. Abraham Kuyper, *Encyclopedia of Sacred Theology: Its Principles,* trans. J. Hendrik De Vries (New York, 1898 [1894]), p. 136.

97. Hopkins, *The Scriptural Idea of Man,* acknowledges that Sir William Hamilton shows that in a sense knowledge rests on "faith," but Hopkins complains that this is a different use of the word than when "faith" means Christian faith. Pp. 34–39. Benjamin B. Warfield, "On Faith in Its Psychological Aspects" (1911), *Studies in Theology* (New York, 1932), takes a more positive view of Hamilton's position and says it is also Augustine's. In a sense, says Warfield, reason

rests on faith or trust in our understanding, though in another sense "reason underlies all acts of faith." P. 325.

98. Kuyper, *Encyclopedia,* pp. 131 and 95.

99. Ibid., p. 361.

100. Ibid., pp. 356 and 357.

101. Ibid., p. 359.

102. Kuyper sees a more general problem in any effort to get from subject to object without starting with knowledge of God. Cf. quotation below, note 103.

103. "We actually owe all our convictions of the reality of the object exclusively to faith. Without faith you can never go from your *ego* to the *non-ego;* there is no other bridge to be constructed from phenomena to noumena; and scientifically all the results of observation hang in air. The line from Kant to Fichte is the only line along which you may continue." Kuyper, *Encyclopedia,* p. 133.

104. Ibid., p. 90.

105. Ibid., pp. 89, 90, 107, and 107–9.

106. Ibid., p. 83.

107. Ibid., pp. 157, 168, and 156.

108. Ibid., pp. 553–63.

109. Benjamin B. Warfield, *Selected Shorter Writings of Benjamin B. Warfield,* vol. 2, ed. John E. Meeter (Nutley, N.J.: 1973), pp. 98–99, 99, 113, and 105. These comments were first published in 1903.

110. Ibid., pp. 101 and 103.

111. This seems to be the argument of Clark Pinnock's chapter on "pragmatic arguments" in *Reason Enough* (Downers Grove, Ill., 1980).

112. Kuyper likely would agree with most of this. Cf. his similar discussion, *Encyclopedia,* pp. 558–63. He disagreed with the evidentialists over whether the truths of Christianity should be held on the basis of demonstrative arguments based on other premises. So he says of belief in Scripture: "Hence this principium, as such, can be no conclusion from other premises, but is itself the premise, from which all other conclusions are drawn. Aside from this question of demonstrative arguments, however, much of the debate between the two sides revolves around differing terminologies, since much of what evidentialists call belief on the basis of evidence (in their broad sense of that by which something evidences itself) Kuyper would regard as accepted on the basis of faith (i.e. 'becoming firmly convinced of a thing, and of making this conviction the starting-point of conduct, while for this conviction no empirical or demonstrative proof is offered or found.')." Ibid., p. 131.

113. I am indebted to my colleague in the Calvin Center for Christian Scholarship, Robert Manweiler, for his discussions of these points.

114. See Nicholas Wolterstorff, *Reason within the Bounds of Religion* (Grand Rapids, 1976).

# Faith, Reason, and the Resurrection
## *in the Theology of Wolfhart Pannenberg*

D. Holwerda

The task of theology never ends, for theology must respond constantly to the changing motifs that control thought and life in human culture. That task entails the risk that the reformulation of the Gospel may become unduly influenced by motifs that are especially dominant in a given culture. Sometimes motifs may be so dominant and pervasive that critical rejection seems irrational because what is considered rational is determined to a large extent by the basic beliefs held in a particular culture. This essay is a critical survey of this interplay of cultural motifs and Gospel, of reason and faith, as seen in the theology of Wolfhart Pannenberg. The central issue concerns the resurrection of Jesus Christ, because in this century this event has been the test case for theologians wrestling with the relationship of faith and reason.

The resurrection of Jesus Christ and the doctrine of the resurrection of the body lie at the heart of Christian faith and life. The Apostle Paul declared that if there is no resurrection of the dead and if Christ is not raised, then his preaching was in vain and Christians should be pitied. Although initially the early church had to maintain this doctrine against certain gnosticizing tendencies, from the end of the second century until the modern period the church has had no serious conflict concerning this doctrine. No church council was ever called to define its content.

The Enlightenment, however, introduced significant changes in the theological evaluation of this doctrine. Under the impact of certain canons of reason assumed by the historical-critical method, the resurrection lost its central position in the theological interpretation of both the apostolic kerygma and the Christian faith. Since one canon of rationalistic historical criticism was that God does not intervene in the chain of secondary causes, miracles lost their status as historical events. Only those miracles for which a reasonable explanation could be given were granted historical status, such as certain miracles of healing that could be contained within the category of psychosomatic illnesses.[1] Obviously the resurrection fell outside that category and was judged to be merely a psychological miracle, a belief that arose within the minds of the first disciples. As a story the resurrection was considered a myth, that is, a confession that death is swallowed up by immortality, that the real resurrection occurs in the realm of the absolute spirit and not on the plane of history.

This denial of the resurrection as an event in the life of Jesus brought about an unraveling of the fabric of the New Testament. Without an actual resurrection the continuity between the Jesus of history and the Christ of faith disintegrated. Consequently, many argued that it was necessary to choose between the Jesus of history and the Christ of faith, or between Jesus and Paul because Paul was now seen as the second founder of Christianity, an essentially different Christianity whose contours were borrowed from Hellenistic mythologies. The preference, however, was for Jesus, the so-called "Jesus of history," a Jesus no longer interpreted as in the Gospels through the prism of the resurrection. The result of this historical-critical sifting of the text—supposedly sifting the kernel of truth from the husk of traditions in which it was encapsulated, traditions borrowed from a worldview no longer deemed contemporary—was a Jesus who taught ennobling ethical truths. Adolf Harnack, for example, reduced Jesus' teaching about the kingdom of God to the themes of the Fatherhood of God, the brotherhood of man, and the infinite value of the human person.[2]

In such pictures of the "Jesus of history" not only was the resurrection displaced from its central position but the cross as well, except insofar as death was adopted as a metaphor for immortal life. Thus this rationalistic historical-critical investigation produced a drastic revision of the Gospel. Since that time many theologians have been engaged in what could be called pejoratively "a series of salvage operations, attempts to show how one can still believe in Jesus Christ and not violate an ideal of intellectual integrity."[3] For the acceptance of historical criticism seemed to imply that insofar as Christian faith speaks of historical matters, faith must conform to the dictates of reason established apart from faith.

## PANNENBERG'S CONTEXT: DIALECTICAL THEOLOGY

Dialectical theology was in part a reaction to such historical-critical reworking of the data of Scripture. If these data of Scripture must conform to such dictates of reason, the conclusion follows that there is no actual encounter with God in history nor any special revelation of God in history. In spite of their desire to regain a more authentic view of Scripture as revelation, the dialectical theologians did not directly challenge the historical-critical method or its presuppositions. Instead, they attempted to preserve the Scriptures as revelation from God in a manner which could not be touched by historical criticism. Revelation was preserved by fleeing from the arena of history.

The theological stance of Wilhelm Herrmann, a systematic theologian who was the teacher of Rudolf Bultmann and Karl Barth, is a helpful background for understanding the emphases of dialectical theology. During the nineteenth century a modified form of Lessing's "ditch" seemed inevitable to many theologians. Lessing held that accidental truths of history can never become the proof of necessary truths of reason.[4] Since historical truths can never be demonstrated and historical proof is simply what others claimed to have experienced, Lessing believed that only what one experiences himself could be considered reliable proof. The modified form of Lessing's "ditch" which came to govern much theological activity can be stated as follows: "historical judgments of probability can never provide the ground for the certainty of faith."[5] Accepting the fact that the results of historical research are never finally fixed, Herrmann held that faith cannot depend upon historical events. Instead, the immovable fact upon which faith must be based is the inner personal life of Jesus. Through the impression of his person, people are brought into submission to God; and by experiencing the beauty and exalted character of Jesus' personal life, believers receive absolute certainty of the reality of God.[6] Although the picture of this living personality of Jesus is mediated to some extent by the text of Scripture, Herrmann argued that the person of Jesus actually exists behind the text and is ultimately not dependent on it. Consequently, this inner personal life of Jesus cannot be approached by historical criticism. Instead, one encounters it by participating in the sphere of life which it has created, that is, the community of believers. Moreover, once an individual has experienced such communion with God in Christ, the assurance that Jesus lives is based upon the reality of one's own faith.[7]

Thus in Herrmann's view two facts formed the basis for Christian faith: the inner life of Jesus and the conscience of believers by which they know that God communes with them. Out of these must arise the entire content of faith because these constitute the only objective basis that is known. The contrary requirement that faith must accept confessions which affirm certain historical facts, including the resurrection of Jesus, now becomes a demand that people submit to an arbitrary subjectivity. For Hermann consistently insists that the only objective basis for faith lies in "facts which force themselves upon us as undeniable elements in the reality in which we stand."[8] By so grounding the objective certainty of faith in the present experience of communion with God, Herrmann willingly surrendered nature and history to the realm of necessity, and concluded that neither natural science nor historical criticism could pose any threat to the truth and certainty of faith.

While agreeing in many respects with the basic thrust of Hermann's position, Bultmann disagreed with his description of the object of faith. He argued that knowledge of the personality of Jesus is as much historical knowledge as is the knowledge of any other fact in history. Consequently, if faith is dependent upon such a fact, faith would be dependent upon the vagaries of historical research and thus be bereft of certainty. In addition, if the object of faith is historical, then its object would be graspable by reason and faith would no longer be faith.[9] And on the basis of his own radical form-criticism Bultmann held that Scripture itself has no interest in the personality of Jesus, that even the earliest levels of the tradition have been so shaped by the beliefs and needs of the early church that it is impossible to get behind the kerygma to an objective, historical picture of Jesus. Thus faith for Bultmann has no objective historical basis. Instead, Jesus is present only in the kerygma and in the continuing proclamation of the Word. There is no other access to him. Revelation is an encounter with Jesus Christ mediated by the proclaimed Word, and through this encounter the world and its history come to an end. There exists no possibility for demonstrating that such is the case, because it can be known only in the moment of decision. The object of faith transcends the realms of nature and history and is knowable only in the act of faith itself.

Thus, although disagreeing with Hermann concerning what constitutes an historical event, Bultmann's basic view of the relationship between faith and historical event remains remarkably similar. History and nature continue to be viewed as governed by necessity. Hence, for Bultmann the key assumption that controls historical investigation of the text is "the presupposition that history is a unity in the sense of a closed continuum" which "cannot be rent by the interference of supernatural, transcendent powers."[10] The objective world is viewed as a mechanism, a self-contained system of cause and effect existing in objective antithesis to man. The only freedom available to man lies in the moment of decision in which the meaning of the past and the future is decided and thereby unveiled.[11] Bultmann understands history as an address of God calling people to responsible decision over against the past and with a view to the future. But the meaning that is unveiled does not inhere in past events as such; rather, it is an interpretation resulting from a decision in the present. As such it is neither rationally deduced nor inferred, for it is the result of a totally free decision which cannot rationally demonstrate its truth. This free decision is an act of faith.

If for Bultmann faith not only cannot prove itself but must also surrender any claim to an objective basis in historical event because such an objective basis would constitute proof accessible to reason, what happens to the events of salvation proclaimed in Scripture, for example the cross and the resurrection? Obviously, the cross is an objective, historical event, and Bultmann insists on its centrality. However, he argues that as an historical event the cross is simply the fact of the crucifixion of Jesus of Nazareth, a fact that can be adequately explained within the closed continuum of history and can be accepted by unbelievers as well. As such a past fact the cross cannot have for us the significance of being a revelatory or saving event because it is not an event in our lives. Only by becoming a present moment of address in the proclamation of the Word can the cross become revelation and salvation, only when the believer accepts the cross as God's liberating judgment of mankind.[12] Revelation and salvation happen only in the present moment of encounter and decision, but that event of revelation has no verification apart from the decision of faith.

The resurrection is not treated analogously by Bultmann because he believes that it is not an historical event. His reasons are twofold: 1. If the resurrection were an actual historical event, it would constitute a miracle. Since history is assumed to be a closed continuum, such miracles do not happen. Furthermore, to require anyone today to believe in the resurrection of a corpse would demand a sacrifice of the intellect and change faith from its character of free decision into an arbitrary commitment. 2. If the resurrection were an historical event, it would be accessible to the historian. As such it would be an event knowable by all, and hence the object of faith could be verified. Faith would no longer be a free decision.

Consequently, Bultmann interprets the resurrection as a myth expressing the saving significance of the cross. The resurrection proclaims the cross as victory. Belief in the resurrection is a risk because the Word which proclaims the cross and resurrection confronts people with the "question whether they are willing to understand themselves as persons who are crucified and risen with Christ."[13] Because the resurrection is merged with the cross, death with its negation of objective, historical existence now becomes the symbol of life. Of course, such life is not visible or objectively historical, for if it were—since the objectively historical is a realm governed by necessity—it would be death. The objectively historical is at most a veil behind which, or above or beyond which, faith sees but reason can neither perceive nor apprehend.[14] The life of freedom, authentic existence or salvation, transcends the existence contained within the necessities of nature and history. Such belief cannot be verified, for it has no objective basis in nature or history, but it is known in the existential moment of encounter and decision. Faith does not live by sight. It remains a risk.

The general impact of Kant's philosophy upon such representatives of modern theology is obvious, but more particularly Herrmann and Bultmann have been influenced by Marburg Neo-Kantianism.[15] In the light of the advances of science, especially mathematical physics, this Neo-Kantianism refined the Kantian view of the "object." According to Kant the intellect integrates various sensations by means of the categories of thought, and thus any phenomenon becomes a definite object only in and through the act of thought. The Neo-Kantians removed the necessity of sensation by arguing that thought does not need to have its origin outside itself. Instead, the object of thought must be understood by reference to the act of thought itself. Thought constructs, posits, or projects objects, and it does so according to the principle of law. Hence the evidence for the objective validity of any cognitive judgment is not sensory data but the successful integration of the cognitive judgment into a lawful, unified structure of thought. The Marburg Neo-Kantians are rationalists, not empiricists: "to know is to objectify in accordance with the principle of law."[16]

This Neo-Kantian epistemology explains the structure of Bultmann's theology, in particular his attitude toward nature and history. For underlying this epistemology is the assumption of a double human subject. On the one hand, the human subject is the bearer of reason and the creator of the world of objective forms that he knows. As such the human subject is universal, one with all mankind as a participant in the transcendent Spirit or Logos. For this subject of objectifying reason only that counts as reality which is given in the mode of universality and necessity, and reason manifests itself in forms that endure: ideas, institutions, and works of art. On the other hand, the human subject is a unique individual, the subject of his own being and experience, unlike any other person in history. This unique individual is manifest only in the immediacy of the moment and thus finds fulfillment only in the transcendence of nature and history in the distinct sphere of religion. Consequently, because history as knowledge is a series of objectifications developed according to the law which governs that arena, Bultmann accepts as self-evident the belief that history (or any other science) has nothing to do with religion. Religion may not be described as historical because it is the free expression of the individual self and is not the realm of objectification according to the principle of law. Thus Bultmann's basically Lutheran contrast of law and grace, kingdom of the world and kingdom of God, was radicalized by this Neo-Kantian epistemology. The apparent advantage of adopting the Kantian bifurcation of reality and the Neo-Kantian bifurcation of the human subject was that theology could escape the intellectual hegemony of the natural and social sciences without impugning their validity.[17] The result was that theology became an independent "science" freed from the obligation of relating faith and reason and of challenging either the methods or the results of the sciences. However, this so-called advantage had as its unquestioned assumption that the resurrection of Jesus Christ could be nothing more than a postulate of the Christian faith, a declaration of meaning or value for the individual self but not a declaration of historical fact.

A similar separation of faith and reason is evident in the work of Karl Barth. Although strongly critical of Bultmann and holding positions which could have been developed into an attack upon the assumptions governing the historical-critical method, Barth never developed such an attack. His changing view of the resurrection and his defense of theology as a science illustrate this failure.

Initially Barth's view of the resurrection was virtually identical to that held by Bultmann. In his early book on Romans, Barth affirmed that "in the Resurrection the new world of the Holy Spirit touches the old world of the flesh, but touches it as a tangent touches a circle, that is without touching it."[18] Commenting on this early position, Barth said he then understood the resurrection only as "the eternal transcending meaning of all moments in time."[19] The resurrection was not an event in space and time and could be known only in the moment of encounter with God's revelation in Christ. At that time Bultmann believed that he and Barth stood on common ground.

Later Barth recognized in this early position the error of failing to sense the teleology of history, a movement toward a real end, and changed his position to an affirmation of the resurrection as "an historical and therefore temporal event."[20] But even though the resurrection of Jesus happened "in the human sphere and human time as an actual event within the world with an objective content,"[21] it remained for Barth an event not accessible to the historian. While it is not accessible to the historian, it is nonetheless historical because

> It is sheer superstition to suppose that only things which are open to 'historical' verification can have happened in time. There may have been events which happened far more really in time than the kind of things Bultmann's scientific historian can prove. There are good grounds for supposing that the history of the resurrection of Jesus is a pre-eminent instance of such an event.[22]

Barth's position assumes that there are in history at least a limited number of events, such as the resurrection, which can be known only by revelation and not by historical research. Faith in effect sets limits to what can be known by historical investigation, but apart from guarding this limited number of events wrought directly by God, faith attempts no explicit critique of either the presuppositions or the results of historical-critical investigation. Similarly, in the general area of historical criticism Barth developed no critique of its methodology. He suggested that "the critical historian needs to be more critical," but he did not say what that entailed.[23] In theory Barth granted rationalistic historical criticism full sway over Scripture insofar as it is a human word, but in practice Barth seemed to ignore its results.[24] Since revelation is a miracle and is only indirectly related to the text of Scripture, Barth simply claimed that historical criticism can neither grasp nor deny it. Revelation happens in spite of historical criticism and from beyond any arena lying within its grasp. Consequently, while affirming revelation from God received by faith, Barth nowhere develops an integral relationship between faith and reason, revelation and history.[25] They seem to touch each other only as a tangent touches a circle. The Christian faith according to Barth is not a worldview (Weltanschauung), and, therefore, an integral relationship of faith and reason need not and cannot be developed.[26]

Barth's discussion of theology as a science reveals a similar position. According to Barth theology is a science only in the sense that "it follows a definite, self-consistent path of knowledge," a path determined by its object that is God's revelation of himself in Jesus Christ.[27] For this reason theology cannot submit itself to any general concept of science in order to justify itself as a science. Because certain assumptions about an ordered cosmos have determined both the classical and the modern view of science, Barth asserts categorically that theology cannot submit to these assumptions without surrendering the very theme of theology. Nevertheless, he insists on calling theology a science.[28] One reason for so doing, among others, is to demonstrate that there is a science in opposition to the "heathen" concept of science that does not have Aristotle as its ancestor.[29] Implicit in this reason lies the possibility of a radical critique of science, but Barth never develops such a critique. Instead, he makes his case for theology as a science on practical grounds and never challenges the essentially Kantian duality of the noumenal and phenomenal realms. In effect, Barth tolerates the "heathen" concept of science as adequate for its own object. The Barthian challenge occurs only when that concept of science seeks to dictate what theology must be if it is to be a science. Since theology has its own distinct object and assumes a unique faculty (faith) for the knowledge of its object, theology cannot submit to such dictation. Faith must assert its own suprahistorical territorial claims against reason, but faith cannot challenge, influence, or direct reason where reason attempts to grasp its appropriate object in nature or history. Thus, theology is protected as an independent science by assuming that neither theology nor faith can provide a better insight into the structure of historical reality than that provided by the natural sciences.

The theology of Wolfhart Pannenberg is a vigorous protest against these assumptions of dialectical theology. In place of a theology which so minimizes the significance of history for faith that faith becomes a leap in the dark grounded upon nothing other than itself, Pannenberg has begun a theological program whose primary slogan is "revelation as history," a slogan which affirms that faith is based upon historical knowledge whose evidence is available for all to see. Because Pannenberg wishes to overthrow an established mode of theological thinking, the theses he puts forth for discussion are rather bold and admittedly "sometimes one-sided."[30] Thus, it is important to remember the context which shapes the debate. Basically, Pannenberg refuses to accept the prevailing assumption that in order to protect the reality of revelation, it is necessary to declare either that revelation resides only in the meaning of an event, a meaning beyond the grasp of the historical-critical method because the meaning of an event is determined not by detached, scientific investigation but by personal decision, or that revelation occurs in events so unique that they are not part of that history which the historian can investigate. Pannenberg rejects this flight from objective history to the safe harbor of prehistory or suprahistory known only by faith, a flight caused by the pressures of historical criticism. He believes that such flight must be rejected because it turns Christian faith into a subjective, and hence arbitrary, decision and is in any case contrary to the biblical understanding of revelation.

## PANNENBERG'S ULTIMATE FEAR: THE CHARGE OF SUBJECTIVISM

Pannenberg's most basic critique of the dialectical theology of Barth and Bultmann is that it is a form of subjectivism and hence of irrationalism. Consequently, he is himself extremely wary, if not fearful, lest he say anything that would warrant the same criticism of his theological position. The reason for this critique and wariness lies in an important cultural motif that shaped dialectical theology. Dialectical theology was a response not only to the rise of historical criticism but also to the atheistic critique of speech about God. Already in 1799 Fichte had criticized as incompatible with the infinity of God the idea that God as the highest being could be personal. He argued that by applying the term "personal" to God, one was asserting that the finitude of man was constitutive of divine reality.

If God were personal, then limits had been placed on his infinity. Later Feuerbach argued that God is the product of the imagination of man. Although mankind had experiences of infinity, Feuerbach claimed that such experiences were not experiences of God but were actually experiences of the infinity of human essence. Thus, according to Feuerbach, God is but a human projection of mankind's infinite essence.

Karl Barth accepted Feuerbach's critique but added the proviso that it applied only to human religion, not to the revelatory Christian faith. According to Barth all talk of God outside the Christian proclamation was idolatry which issues in man's self-deification, but such talk has nothing to do with the reality of God. Christian proclamation alone can truly speak of God, for in it God is known through God alone. No point of contact for such speech exists in human nature, for knowledge of God requires no basis in human nature—it is created directly by the revelatory action of God. Thus Barth argued that Feuerbach's view that God-talk was simply an illusionary anthropomorphism did not apply to God-talk contained in Christian proclamation because the gospel declares that the God-man relationship is irreversibly a relationship from above to below, from God to man.[31]

Can Feuerbach be defeated so easily? Pannenberg does not think so. Because of Feuerbach theology can no longer simply speak the word "God" without explanation, and if theology follows Barth's theology from above, Pannenberg argues that it will fall into a "self-inflicted isolation of a higher glossolalia."[32] In addition, Pannenberg believes that theology cannot surrender all non-Christian religions to the Feuerbachian critique without endangering itself, for "if the idea of a personal God is everywhere else judged to be a mythological self-interpretation of man, one would hardly be able to prevent this view from having repercussions on Christian theology and its language about God."[33]

Nietzsche's atheism is also an important root of the Western European cultural situation in the twentieth century. Already in Feuerbach there lurked the view of man as an absolutely self-empowered being which Nietzsche affirmed in his central thesis of the will to power. Pannenberg considers Nietzsche's point of view to be simply the logical outcome of the modern, post-Cartesian metaphysics of subjectivity in which truth is related to the self-certainty of the subject. In Nietzsche, subjectivity is expressed in the form of the will, so that even truth itself is but a value judgment of the subjective will. Within such a framework God appears only as the highest value and, as such, a value posited by the human will. In fact, all religious statements are but subjective judgments of the valuating will.

Does Barth's affirmation of revelation from above, of knowing God only through God, effectively counter Nietzsche's claim? Again Pannenberg does not think so. For him Barth's claim is a retreat into supernaturalism, and he argues that such supernaturalistic talk of God depends ultimately on the subjective decision of faith. Since it is the decision of faith that motivates a leap into supernatural truth, such a view plays into Nietzsche's hands. Thus Pannenberg asserts that "wherever faith as decision is constitutive of the truth of its contents, one has not yet departed from the basis of Nietzsche's position, his metaphysics of the will."[34] It is from this perspective that Pannenberg levels the charge of subjectivism against both Barth and Bultmann.

How then does Pannenberg believe it possible to speak of God in a rationally acceptable way, that is, in a manner that effectively escapes the critique of God-talk characteristic of secular atheism? Pannenberg's answer is complex and not yet fully developed, but it includes the following elements. A retreat to traditional theism is ruled impossible. Instead, theology must reformulate the concept of God in relation both to the philosophical question of being and to the subjectivity of modern man, including his sovereignty over nature and his self-transcendence. One can then speak of God only if God is the reality which "supports man in the openness of his freedom."[35] In addition, in view of the contemporary atheism of empty transcendence characteristic of Karl Jaspers and Ernst Bloch, theology must seriously reexamine the biblical idea of the hiddenness of God, a hiddenness even in his revelation.[36] Theology must then proceed to demonstrate that this "empty transcendence" is in fact a personal God, a demonstration which Pannenberg believes can be accomplished by means of the history of religions. Thus, Pannenberg wishes to develop his argument on various levels. However, since he believes it necessary to conduct the argument with atheism on its own grounds, that is, on the basis of the understanding of man's nature, the heart of his answer is the development of a theological anthropology. Without developing all aspects of Pannenberg's position, including his own modified Hegelian perspective, we shall briefly summarize Pannenberg's perspective on the question of God.

The question posed by Pannenberg is this: How can theology escape the dilemma created by the atheistic criticism of theistic conceptions? For, on the one hand, to claim with certain theologians a special status for Christian speech about God is to be vulnerable to the atheistic critique of subjectivism. On the other hand, to follow other theologians in accepting atheistic criticism by interpreting "God-talk" as designating existential relations in the interpersonal realm means the demise of theology and the victory of atheism. The dilemma can be resolved, according to Pannenberg, "only if the claim of Christian proclamation to derive from an experience of God does not remain a mere assertion but is capable of verification."[37] Such verification does not require a neutral court of appeal existing prior to and outside of the biblical revelation of God, for that would not be compatible with the majesty of divine revelation. Instead, it is the revelation of God itself which discloses the truth about man and the world by means of which the truth of revelation is proved. If such is the case, however, how does Pannenberg escape his own charge of subjectivism since his position seems so similar to Barth's? Pannenberg argues, in distinction from Barth, that once the existence of man and the world has been illumined by biblical revelation, thereafter these realities can be *perceived* as being the way they have been characterized by revelation. In other words, since revelation has occurred, it has become part of human experience and human history. Thereafter, quite apart from any appeal to the Bible as authoritative, theology can appeal to the actual existence of man and the world as witnesses for the reality of the biblical God. Since the revelation that illumines the actual existence of mankind and the world is historical, it can be perceived by mankind.

What does Pannenberg mean by referring to the existence of man and his world? A perspective found in the early writings of Barth is used by Pannenberg to develop his own point of view. Barth spoke of the relationship between God and man as the correspondence or even the coincidence of the human question and the divine answer. The divine is, however, materially prior to the human question and in fact elicits the question, for "without the call of the Lord, who in utmost hiddenness is the answer to this question, there would be no laws, no religions, and thus neither would there be that question that manifests itself in them about the most hidden meaning of life."[38] Pannenberg regrets that Barth abandoned this formulation of question and answer out of fear that it did not adequately exclude the possibility of man being able to attain knowledge of God on his own. Barth thought that in the description of man as question lay the possibility of a partial answer concerning God which could be extrapolated from the shape of the question itself. Then revelation would become the captive of human thought. On the contrary, Pannenberg argues that in surrendering this formulation for such reasons Barth "gave up the possibility of claiming human existence as a witness for the truth of revelation."[39]

Pannenberg believes that this formula which speaks of the questionableness of human existence is a suitable and comprehensive expression of contemporary knowledge about man, because many today, including the atheists Camus, Sartre, and the Marxist Ernst Bloch, make use of this basic anthropological insight. They agree that the basic structure of human existence is that of a question seeking an answer for life as a process of inquiry that continually drives a person into the open. This openness of human behavior presupposes a supporting ground that is different from the entire realm of existing things. Mankind seeks a ground which can support itself and all reality. Everyone seeks a power which can support one beyond the limits of present experience, a power which supports one in the openness of one's human freedom. Since many theoreticians agree with the anthropological perspective, including certain contemporary atheists, and since he believes it is basically in harmony with biblical perspectives, Pannenberg argues that this anthropology opens a way to speak rationally about God in contemporary culture.

Of course, this perspective does not by itself demonstrate that this power which mankind seeks is personal and hence God. However, Pannenberg believes that the personal nature of this power can rationally be verified on the basis of the history of religions. The question which man is and the questions which he frames occur only in association with the reality inquired about. To the degree that human existence is motivated by questions about human destiny and fulfillment, to that degree mankind is already borne by the reality toward which such inquiry is directed. Mankind's ongoing experience with this reality becomes the test for the validity of various projected answers, and, consequently, the answers are refined and the questions reformulated because of such experience. This experience of reality is essentially religious in nature, and even philosophical reflection concerning the nature of this fundamental reality only discovers answers derived from human religious experience. The various religions themselves are answers to this basic question of human existence which stem from particular happenings or events in which this basic reality is experienced. Although non-Christian religions are "based on unclear provisional forms of the true answer to mankind that has happened in Jesus Christ"[40] because they distort the happenings on which they are based by understanding the power which upholds all reality as belonging to the realm of finitude, Pannenberg argues that most religions share the conviction that this power that sustains all reality is personal. Thus, even though the answer to the question of human existence is not universally experienced as personal, Pannenberg concludes that the evidence from the history of religions is such that the question about human existence can be understood as a question about God. In fact, interpreting it as a question about God brings out its real meaning. In addition, Pannenberg believes that the "modern metaphysics of man's subjectivity is conceivable only on the presupposition of God."[41]

Finally, to counter the charge that talk of God as a personal being entails a contradiction of finite vs. infinite, Pannenberg argues that the concept of man as a person is itself an article of faith which originates in man's experience with this underlying reality. In his view the terms "person" or "personality" are categories originating in the phenomenology of religion. For example, in the Old Testament the personality of man is derived from participation in the inviolable majesty of God (image of God), and in ancient Greece the stress on the person as an intellectual individual seems to be derived from the religious motif of man as a being that participates in the divine world-reason by virtue of his intellectual essence. Thus the history of religions confirms the formula that the answer (which is divine) determines the question (which is humanity). God's person refers then not to finite limitation but to the "non-manipulatedness of this power which at the same time, however, makes a concrete claim upon man in that happening which is constitutive of religious experience."[42] Talk of God as person expresses God's holiness.

Such a view of God is widespread in the history of religions. Of course, the characteristics of these personal deities vary considerably. Yet, Pannenberg believes that by means of the history of religions one can demonstrate that the God of Israel is set off from all other deities particularly with regard to his freedom of action and his exclusive claim on those in covenant with him. He believes further that these features provide the only adequate basis for the historical nature of man which is valued so highly in the modern world. Reality is experienced as the history of ever-new events moving toward a future which has not yet appeared. Only the God of the Old and New Testaments can be the power that upholds such a reality. For the biblical view of the coming of the kingdom or of the future of God is that God himself will be the answer to "the questionableness of every phenomenon in the world of nature and of mankind that still remains open in the flow of history."[43] In so speaking of God Pannenberg believes that he does justice not only to the atheistic critique of theism while avoiding the charge of subjectivism but also to the actual essence of human nature, to the reality of the history of religions, and to the exclusive claims of the Gospel.

Without critically analyzing Pannenberg's view on the rationality of God-talk, one wonders whether Pannenberg has achieved anything more than an affirmation that on the basis of faith one can argue that Christian claims about God are reasonable or make sense. However, his substantial claim that evidence from the history of religions rationally verifies the personal nature of God, and that this verification is established by reason apart from faith, has not been demonstrated. Instead it seems to this interpreter that the evidence from the history of religions has been selected and interpreted by a prior faith commitment concerning God as personal. In addition, an important question remains: Does not the acceptance of the radical questionableness of man, understood as humanity's openness to ongoing inquiry which continuously proceeds beyond every present situation and every conception of God, endanger the exclusive claims of the Gospel? Pannenberg's answer is simply a confession which accepts the claims of the Gospel. The Gospel is not endangered by these assumptions because man "cannot get beyond the biblical God himself because this God in his almighty freedom is not among the beings existing in the world, but is the Lord of the future, toward whose coming the world is moving."[44] Does such an absolute affirmation rest on reason or on faith? Can Pannenberg finally escape his own charge of subjectivism? He thinks he can with his understanding of revelation as history.

## PANNENBERG AND THE ENLIGHTENMENT

Before Pannenberg's theology of history is developed, it is important to understand his rejection of a central principle on which the Reformation was based. For the Reformers Scripture alone was the final authority for faith and knowledge, but Pannenberg believes that this *sola scriptura* principle of the Reformation is no longer a viable option for theology.

Basically Pannenberg gives two reasons for his rejection of the *sola scriptura* principle. The Reformers could still believe that the historical content of Scripture and its literal sense coincided. However, due to the rise of historical criticism such belief is no longer possible. The scriptural presentation of the history of Israel or Jesus can no longer without qualification be considered to be identical with the actual course of events. Pannenberg accepts Von Rad's thesis that the tradition recorded in Scripture reveals an ongoing appropriation of the past in terms of present experience, an ongoing "contemporanization and actualization" of the redemptive facts of the past.[45] Thus there is a distance between the text of Scripture and the events to which the text witnesses, and, consequently, it is necessary to go behind the text to discover the events of revelation.[46] Because of this theological view of Scripture created by historical criticism, Pannenberg believes that one cannot overcome the dichotomy between faith and the events in which it is grounded by a simple appeal to Scripture. Instead, he believes it is necessary to show that the meaning of the redemptive events attested by Scripture is actually rooted in the events themselves. Such demonstration can be accomplished, according to Pannenberg, only by the exercise of historical reason itself.

The second reason for his rejection of *sola scriptura* lies in the historical distance which is perceived to exist between "every possible theology today and the primitive Christian period."[47] Not only is there distance between the text of Scripture and the events to which it witnesses, but there is also a great gulf between the language and conceptual framework of the scriptural witness and that which is necessary for understanding and communication today. While the Reformers could identify their own teaching with the content of the biblical writings, today—because of the awareness of the deep gulf between the intellectual milieu of Scripture and that of our own time—there can be no simple, naive identification with either Scripture, the Reformers, or the confessions. Contemporary theology must move in a different direction, for it "comes closest to material agreement with the biblical witness when it seriously takes up the questions of its own time in order to express in relation to them what the biblical writers expressed in the language and conceptual framework of their time."[48]

Because of these perceived historical distances between biblical text and event, and between biblical text and modern milieu, Pannenberg judges that an appeal to *sola scriptura* has become an appeal to an authoritarian principle. Such an authoritarian claim, he argues, is no longer considered acceptable where the Enlightenment has become effective, for there "all authoritarian claims are on principle subject to the suspicion that they clothe human thoughts and institutions with the splendor of divine majesty."[49] Hence, if theology assumes that it can simply appeal to the authority of Scripture as a guarantee of the truth of its contents, theology is in effect demanding a sacrifice of the intellect by compelling human reason simply to submit to its truth.[50] Pannenberg totally accepts the Enlightenment demand for the freedom of human reason from all established or external authorities, whether political or religious, because he believes not only that such freedom is demanded by the Christian faith but also that "man's recent coming of age must itself be recognized as the fruit of the Christian spirit."[51]

Contrary to the opinion of many others, Pannenberg believes that it is possible to grant this emancipation from authoritarian structures without losing the real content of the Christian tradition. He believes it possible to distinguish the authoritarian features of the Christian faith from its real essence not only within the ecclesiastical tradition but even within Scripture itself. These authoritarian features are ascribed simply to the times in which the tradition was passed on. For in the biblical world, as well as in the ancient and medieval, authoritarian structures were not only not objectionable because they were so common, but Pannenberg argues that they were also necessary for maintaining "the identity and purity of the Christian tradition."[52] By authoritarian structures Pannenberg has in mind such things as a hierarchial order or the apostolic succession of bishops, obedience to dogmatic formulas, Scripture as a divine word that must be obeyed, and appeal to prophetic inspiration within Scripture.[53] Today, however, due to the rise of historical criticism such authoritarian claims for tradition are no longer credible. Theology should not regret this development because the message of the kingdom of God establishes mankind's freedom from all "unconditional human authority," and, therefore, "in the whole of man's political and intellectual existence, there are no privileged areas exempt from critical reflection."[54] Thus Pannenberg moves inexorably to the conclusion that theology has no choice but to become a critical, rational enterprise free from authoritarian structures. Theology must invite others to make free, rational judgments about the truth and to commitment based upon such judgments.

Pannenberg's belief that a rational theology is both necessary and possible produces a strong defense of theology as a science. In contrast to Karl Barth's refusal to subsume theology under the general concept of science which functions in other areas, Pannenberg accepts that general concept without reservation and accuses Barth of making theology rely on "a subjective act of the will or an irrational venture of faith."[55] For if, as Barth claims, theology is only a critical examination of the language and practice of faith to determine whether it conforms to the revelation of God, a revelation to which faith must obediently submit, then Pannenberg charges that subjectivism reigns in theology. Barth's positive theory of revelation becomes "the furthest extreme of subjectivism made into a theological position" because "Barth's apparently so lofty objectivity about God and God's word turns out to rest on no more than the irrational subjectivity of a venture of faith with no justification outside itself."[56] Consequently, Pannenberg fully accepts the criteria governing what Barth terms "heathen" science because these criteria simply make explicit the requirements of logic. Thus theology, as is the case with any science, must admit that if its statements are uncheckable, they are meaningless.

How does Pannenberg propose to check or verify theological statements in order to defend his claim that theology is a science judged by the same criteria applied to the other sciences? The claim of the logical positivists that a statement is meaningful only if one can determine under what conditions it is true is accepted by Pannenberg, but not the highly restricted kinds of verification permitted by the logical positivists. Instead, Pannenberg proposes to test theological statements by examining the consequences that can be derived from them. His thesis is that "statements about divine reality and actions are testable by reference to their implications for the understanding of finite reality insofar as God is maintained to be the all-determining reality."[57] In other words, to the degree that theological statements open up a deeper understanding of reality or show that nothing can fully be understood in its particular reality without reference to God, to that degree there is corroboration or confirmation of theological assertions. Theological statements are hypotheses that must be tested, and the test is not faith but a rational understanding of reality itself. In Pannenberg's eyes a confessional theology cannot defend itself against the charge that it only rationalizes prejudices.[58] Therefore, if theology is to escape the charge of subjectivism or irrationality, it must become fully rational.

In order to understand what Pannenberg means by a rational theology and how he attempts to "prove" its assertions, it is necessary to understand several basic concepts: first, his concept of "revelation as history" together with his replies to serious questions about this concept arising from both historical criticism and theology; second, his view of reason as it functions in historical criticism; third, his understanding of the relationship between faith and rational insight. Only by grasping Pannenberg's understanding of these basic concepts can one understand his presentation of the resurrection of Jesus as the ultimate basis for his rational theology.

## REVELATION, FAITH, AND HISTORICAL CRITICISM

Pannenberg's theological program is in reality a theology of history. The basic thesis shaping his program is summarized in the following statement:

> History is the most comprehensive horizon of Christian theology. All theological questions and answers are meaningful only within the framework of the history which God has with humanity and through humanity with his whole creation—the history moving toward a future still hidden from the world but already revealed in Jesus Christ.[59]

With this thesis Pannenberg challenges the widely held assumption that revelation is something additional, a supplement added to or hovering above the historical course of events. Instead, for Pannenberg revelation comes not only in history but *as* history itself. Consequently, revelation is there for all to see without the need for acquiring any capacity or perfection in addition to reason which all already possess. The "normal equipment for knowing" is all that one needs to apprehend revelation because it is appropriated simply as "a natural consequence of the facts."[60] In this way Pannenberg wishes to remove Christian faith from what he considers the arena of the irrational and subjective and to place it within rational discourse.

However, if theological knowledge is essentially historical in nature, then the theologian is limited—as is every other person—to pursuing such knowledge through historical investigation, for there is no other avenue by which to gain certainty about past events. The common dichotomy between ordinary history or salvation history as lying beyond the arena of historical research must be rejected. Pannenberg argues that theology cannot tolerate the idea of two different kinds of history occurring on different planes, and the historical method cannot allow that there is a more fruitful way to certainty about past events without acknowledging that that way is the right historical method.[61] Thus whatever limits pertain to historical investigation pertain also to theological knowing. If an event, because of its unique or unusual character, is opaque for the historian, it is no less opaque for the theologian, because no human being can claim any special avenue for knowing the past that is not equally available to any other person. Whatever claims are made for knowledge concerning the past must be confirmed by detailed historical observation.[62]

In order to maintain his position that historical research is the only mode of access to a past event, Pannenberg must consider several problems arising from both historical criticism and theology. For example, since historical-critical judgments assume as criteria present human experience, historical criticism seems to be controlled necessarily by an anthropocentric vision, and it has seemed inevitable to many that historical research must apriori exclude any notion of God or transcendence. How can the historian as historian make any pronouncement at all concerning acts of God? Although Pannenberg recognizes that there has been a fundamental antithesis between the worldview of the historical method and the biblical view of God and history, he argues that such need not be the case and that this antithesis actually hampers the progress of historical research.

While admitting that there is a necessary anthropocentric element in the methodology of historical criticism, Pannenberg argues that the anthropocentric worldview which has characterized modern historical research is unnecessary. Ernst Troeltsch, whose work has influenced the course of historical criticism, held that the historical method rests both on the principle of analogy, which assumes the fundamental homogeneity of all events, and on the principle of the universal correlation of all events. For Pannenberg the problem of the anthropocentric character of historical research does not lie in the principle of correlation. Theology too must assume that biblical events do not exist in isolation from other events but must be understood in correlation with the history of the Near Eastern world, of Judaism and Hellenism. Redemptive history is not a history of another kind or of another realm distinct from the rest of history. Although this principle of correlation has been associated with a rather rigid view of causal relations in historical criticism which has produced an immanentist view of the development of history, Pannenberg maintains that this view of causal relationships is unacceptable not only on theological grounds but also on historical grounds because it "conflicts with the contingency of individual events."[63] Adopting a more general concept of cause, one that is less positivistic and deterministic but which still sees connections between historical phenomena and recognizes that "historical formations are not 'from the first once-and-for-all-time' finished entities,"[64] Pannenberg asserts that theology has no real problems with the principle of historical correlation, but only with the principle of analogy in historical investigations.

The principle of analogy claims that the historical investigator can understand the past only in terms of that which he knows from present experience. Troeltsch has given a classic expression to this principle in the following quotation:

> Analogy with what happens before our eyes and what is given within ourselves is the key to criticism. Illusions, displacements, myth formation, fraud, and party spirit, as we see them before our own eyes, are the means whereby we can recognize similar things in what tradition hands down. Agreement with normal, ordinary, repeatedly attested modes of occurrence and conditions as we know them is the mark of probability for the occurrences that the critic can either acknowledge really to have happened or leave on one side. The observation of analogies between past occurrences of the same sort makes it possible to ascribe probability to them and to interpret the one that is unknown from what is known of the other.[65]

Pannenberg agrees that such an anthropocentric structure by which one proceeds from one's current state of knowledge to disclosures concerning the past is inescapable. What is objectionable in Troeltsch's formulation of the principle, and in much current historical investigation, is the assumption that all events are comprehended within a uniform, fundamental homogeneity of all reality. Consequently, it is claimed that the historian can know only that which is essentially homogeneous with that which he already knows, and that which is truly nonhomogeneous is necessarily declared to be historically unreal. Flowing from such a view is the attempt to discover laws which govern the historical process, laws analogous to those in the natural sciences, but this naturalizing of the historical process happens at the expense of the individuality and particularity of historical events. Pannenberg labels these assumptions a "biased world view"[66] and argues, to the contrary, that analogy should be used to discover the individual and the particular in an historical event rather than merely the typical. The principle of analogy cannot be the basis for disputing the facticity of events which burst analogies with usual events, for it must always be limited by "the particularity that is present in every case in the phenomena being compared."[67] Such a view of analogy would be more in harmony with a theological view of God's activity in history because the emphasis would fall on the individual, the particular and the contingent character of an event. God is not locked into a preexisting historical order. That which is new and never before present can occur, but our knowledge of the new depends upon our use of analogy while recognizing its limitations. In fact, analogy makes it possible to state precisely the unique particularities of an event when compared with analogous parallels. For example, the use of analogy can sharpen our awareness of the uniqueness of the religion of Israel by showing that while there are similarities, Israel's religion is not identical with surrounding religions. Thus, although the principle of analogy with its anthropocentric focus continues to occupy a central position in historical investigation, analogy need not produce or assume an anthropocentric worldview.

However, even if it is possible to amend satisfactorily the principles governing historical criticism, can faith grant that its object is accessible to such historical investigation? A dominant tradition in modern theology has declared that faith cannot surrender its object to historical investigation. One reason given for this position is that since the results of historical research can be expressed only as probabilities, such results can never be an adequate basis for the certainty of faith. Hence the object of faith has been removed from the realm of history to a realm inaccessible to historical criticism by theologians who hold that the object of faith is restricted to the living personality of Jesus, or to the kerygma known only by faith. Pannenberg believes that this attempt to gain greater certainty than is possible in history results inevitably in a flight from history. When that occurs, faith cannot defend itself against the charge that it is based upon itself and hence is based on an illusion.

A somewhat more conservative theological tradition holds with Pannenberg that the historical is the *conditio sine qua non* of faith but maintains that the revelatory character of these historical events cannot be known by historical reasoning. Against this position Pannenberg continues to maintain that if "the revelatory and redemptive significance of the fate of Jesus of Nazareth can be seen only by faith and is in principle closed to the rational investigation of this event, then it is impossible to see how the historicity of the pure facts should be able to protect faith against the reproach that it rests upon illusion and caprice."[68] In Pannenberg's view the revelatory significance must be contained within the event itself; otherwise the unity of revelation and history is destroyed, and faith becomes merely a subjective projection. But if the revelatory meaning belongs to the event itself, Pannenberg argues that "then it will be impossible *in principle* to reject out of hand the idea that the historical investigation of this event, even in its particularity, could and must discover its revelatory character."[69] Even though historical research cannot produce absolute certainty about past events and thus even the events of redemption must be continuously open to historical critical review, Pannenberg does not consider this state of affairs an especially troublesome matter. He simply affirms that the certainty that is achievable is sufficient, even though it is not absolute.[70] Since Pannenberg believes that faith is primarily trust which focuses on the promissory character of an event, he can be satisfied with less than absolute certainty concerning past facts. His absolute certainty concerns the future rather than the *precise* historical shape of the past.

If, however, the revelatory significance is enclosed in the events, how can Pannenberg account for the fact that many historians do not perceive this significance in the events attested in Scripture? Pannenberg claims a similarity between his view of meaning inherent in historical event and Luther's teaching concerning the outer clarity of Scripture. Luther taught that the essential content of Scripture was completely clear, unambiguous and open for all the world to see. Nothing additional was necessary to make the meaning clear, and all objections to its content were judged by common sense (reason) itself to be without force. However, Luther did hold that the Devil had blinded men so that they no longer see the facts that are there to be seen unless they are illuminated by the Holy Spirit. If Luther made such a claim, how can Pannenberg sustain the claim that his own idea that the revelatory significance of events is accessible to reason is in fact similar to Luther's?

To support his thesis, Pannenberg argues that for Luther the illumination of the Spirit, even though always necessary in actuality, is only accidentally required. Truths of Scripture are *in and of themselves* convincing and accessible to reason, but due to the accident that Satan has blinded mankind, the work of the Spirit is necessary. Thus Pannenberg holds that for Luther the Holy Spirit "does not *supplement* reason, but rather *frees* it for its natural function."[71] Consequently, the Spirit is never a supplement to an exegetical or historical argument. With such an interpretation of Luther's position, Pannenberg believes that his own point of view stands on a firm footing within a venerable theological tradition. Faith does not make up for defective knowledge. Knowledge of past redemptive events and their promissory character is accessible to reason, and all that is necessary for knowing is the "normal equipment for knowing." Christian truth is not a gnostic knowledge of secrets reserved for an "in group," but instead Christian truth is wrapped up in events that are open to the general reasonableness of all persons. Through the appropriation of these events by reason one is led to faith, for faith is actually trust in the promissory character of these events which is directed toward a future fulfillment. With such emphases Pannenberg desires to overcome every dichotomy between revelation and history, or faith and reason, which would have as its result the subjectivization of faith.

However, the problem inherent in Pannenberg's position is whether he accounts adequately for the necessary work of the Spirit in the human perception of the revelatory meaning of events. Although he desires to avoid what he calls a gnostic point of view, which apriori limits a secret knowledge to a favored few, the question remains whether Pannenberg himself ascribes to faith an implicit priority over reason even in the acquiring of historical knowledge. It may be possible to argue, as Pannenberg does, that faith does not bring with it private knowledge received apart from the facts which can then be superimposed upon knowledge derived from a public knowing of facts in order to complete it. But it is far more difficult to argue that knowledge is achievable apart from specific faith presuppositions or without the illumination of faith. Or to put the matter in other terms, when Luther teaches in effect that common sense or reason knows the truth of Scripture, he is using "reason" normatively. That is, any use of reason which arrives at conclusions contrary to the truth of Scripture is by definition neither common sense nor a genuine exercise of reason. However, since the illumination of the Spirit is necessary to know the truth of Scripture, one should argue that in Luther's case—at least for knowledge of redemptive events—revelation and faith have priority over reason and in fact control its proper use. Pannenberg rejects such a formulation because of his rejection of every authoritarian principle and its corollary of faith as subjectivism. He prefers to argue that as trust (*fiducia*) requires knowledge (*notitia*) as its basis, although it goes beyond knowledge, so faith requires reason as its basis, although it goes beyond reason. Nevertheless, the question still remains whether Pannenberg does not, like Luther, assume the realities of revelation and faith in his description of reason and its functioning.

Pannenberg's basic thesis that historical research is the only mode of access to a past event, including those proclaimed as revelatory events by Scripture, raises a variety of questions. In addition to those mentioned above, there is a basic question which arises from the historical method itself: On what basis can the historian as historian speak about God? Can he demonstrate by means of historical research that God has revealed himself in Jesus of Nazareth? Pannenberg believes that he can. Although recognizing that a few decades ago such a suggestion would have been laughed out of court, he claims that today it seems not so scandalous except to those who still hold to positivistic theories of science.

How can the case be argued within an appropriate understanding of historical methodology? Although the historian usually works with such a small segment of history that it is hardly possible to raise the question of God, Pannenberg argues that it can be done if the historian has "history as a whole in view, corresponding to the universality of God, whose revelation is the object of inquiry."[72] The question whether God has revealed himself in a given event can be meaningfully addressed only when there is an assumption concerning a "universal-historical horizon." Pannenberg believes that the historian can avoid such an assumption only with great difficulty because every historian approaches the material of history not just with assumptions about human nature but also with "models of courses of events" or ideas about "over-arching continuities." No event can be understood from within itself but must be seen in its continuities with all other events and finally with universal history. Pannenberg finds support in R. Wittman's assertion that "without world history there is no meaning in history," and in the position of R. Collingwood who holds that "research into the particulars of history always presupposes an outline of the whole of history in relation to which the material that has been handed down by tradition is to be interrogated."[73] However, one's idea of the unity of history must not cancel out the contingency of events. Thus if both unity and contingency are to be maintained, a transcendent ground for the unity of history is required. So Pannenberg draws his conclusion that "the God who by the transcendence of his freedom is the origin of contingency in the world, is also the ground of the unity which comprises the contingencies as history."[74] The unity of events is grounded in the faithfulness of God and not in some development which endures from the past into the future. Hence unity and continuity are visible only in retrospect as the faithfulness of God links what is contingently new to that which has been. In Pannenberg's view history is constructed from the future backward, that is, the new event becomes the key to the meaning and unity of the past. Thus it is really the biblical God who alone makes it possible to conceive the unity of history in such a way that the contingently historical is maintained.

Has Pannenberg imposed a faith a priori on historical research? He argues that he has not both because the position can be argued in terms of the historical material itself and because it must be remembered that "it was Israel's history of God and the fate of Jesus which first disclosed to man the understanding of the world as history."[75] Of course, this highly theological understanding of history cannot meet the demands of positivists who contend that continuities must be derived from observations of particulars. But claiming Collingwood on his side, Pannenberg asserts that it has been proven that such a positivistic demand is inappropriate to the historical object as such.[76] His own theological view of history, moreover, can be verified "through subsequent testing by observation of the particulars. Its ability to take into account all known historical details would be the positive criterion of its truth; the proof that without its specific assertions the accessible information would not be at all or would only be incompletely explicable, can be used as a negative criterion."[77] Just as the ancient church had to lay claim to Greek philosophy for its witness to the universal deity of the Father of Jesus, so today, Pannenberg believes, theologians must do the same in the arena of historical research. The biblical witness to God as the Creator demands such consideration.

## A DEFINITION OF REASON

Besides arguing that theology is a rational science because revelation is fully historical and can be perceived by historical investigation, Pannenberg must also define his use of "reason." Although acknowledging that the perfect unity of faith and reason is promised only for the eschaton (1 Cor. 13:12ff.), Pannenberg believes that one should accept neither the ancient and medieval view which assumed a necessary tension between "free, rational insight and obligation to an authoritative norm" nor the modern understanding in which this tension has developed into sharp opposition.[78] The Augustinian position argued that since the truths of faith concern historical facts, faith is always dependent for its knowledge either upon the testimony of eyewitnesses or upon a tradition considered credible and authoritative. Hence the truths of faith must always be believed and cannot be made fully transparent to reason, and Christian doctrine can never be transformed without remainder into rational insights. Science deals with universals that can be known by reason, but since the realm of history is the arena of particulars, there can be no science of history in the strict sense. Consequently, access to knowledge of history is always dependent upon faith, even though Christian faith is, of course, more than the mere acceptance of an historical tradition. However, since the dawn of the Enlightenment with its rejection of belief based on authority as irrational and the use of historical criticism with its rational method of settling appeals to history, Pannenberg argues that an appeal to an authoritative tradition looks like coercion and is in any case in vain. Nevertheless, not just any definition of reason will do. In fact, Pannenberg states that reason as commonly understood cannot have the last word in theology "without violating the exaltedness of the reality of God and his revelation above all human conceptualization."[79] Thus, in order to make a case for a rational theology, Pannenberg distinguishes three typical forms of reason: a priori reason, receiving reason, and historical reason.[80] The first two are judged unacceptable and the last acceptable for reasons which look very much like reasons of faith. At least it is the case that historical reason can only fully understand itself on the basis of what faith knows about the future.

The dominant view of reason in the West from Aristotle to Kant has been the view that reason is controlled by a priori principles, or principles known intuitively by the intellect. Knowledge is the result of applying these principles to data derived from sense experience, and reason is not open to that which is incongruous with these principles. Where such a view of reason reigned, theologians took the position that the contents of Christian faith were supernatural, not derived from these a priori principles and hence beyond natural reason. To escape the problems inherent in this view, it would be possible to suggest, as Luther did, that these natural principles be replaced by the supernatural truths of faith and in this way achieve a unity of faith and reason. Pannenberg does not follow this suggestion. Not only does he consider the traditional view of an a priori reason incompatible with Christian faith, he also holds that the substitution of the truths of faith for a priori principles is incompatible with the freedom of the Enlightenment. The imposition of truths of faith as supernatural principles would be viewed as bondage and not as the fulfillment of reason.

A second view of reason rejects the creative character of a priori reason in favor of an emphasis upon reason as a passive reception of or a being illumined by that which is. Reason observes, and the movement is from that which is to the one who observes it.[81] This view was modeled after Platonic insight and was thought to be amenable also to the reception of supernatural revelation. Pannenberg rejects this view because it depends upon a Greek understanding of truth or reality as that which always is. Reason comprehends only that which is contemporaneously present. However, according to Pannenberg the biblical view is oriented toward the future because truth is a reality which is regarded as history, as that which will show itself in the future. Consequently, the truth of God does not disclose itself to contemplation by reason that is directed only toward that which is present. Instead the truth of God can be grasped only when met by trust in God's faithfulness.[82] Pannenberg believes that this biblical view, while preserving that which is correct in the Greek view —namely, that true being is enduring, stable, and speech about it is reliable—overcomes the Greek dualism between true being and changing sense appearance. It does so by understanding true being not as timeless but as historical and as proving its reliability through history whose future is open.[83] Truth is not timelessly unchangeable but is rather a process that runs its course and maintains itself through change. Consequently, the unity of truth is known only from the standpoint of the end. Pannenberg summarizes his view in this thesis: "Since the emergence of historical consciousness, the unity of all reality is conceivable only as a history. The unity of truth is still possible only as a historical process, and can be known only from the end of this process."[84] Consequently, a view of reason which denies this historical character of truth is inadequate. From this line of critique it is apparent that Pannenberg uses faith as a criterion for the rationality of reason, although he would also maintain that this is the best view of the nature of reality and truth and hence of reason, a view that can be held by those who do not share the presuppositions of Christian faith.

This view of reason which is not antithetical to faith is designated by Pannenberg as "historical reason." By this he has in mind the historical character of reason, the awareness that there is no permanently fixed structure of reason but rather that reason is a process of reflection which moves forward continually from one stage to another.[85] Because thought recognizes the difference between itself and its object, there is a continual process of reflection by means of which imagination brings forth new syntheses. This process is always open, never achieving the synthesis that can be considered absolute and final.

Wilhelm Dilthey is one who developed this historical character of reason. Since every individual experience has its meaning only in connection with life as a whole, since the whole can be seen only in retrospect and since history is never finished, Dilthey held that all assertions of meaning can be only provisional and relative. While agreeing with the basic structure of Dilthey's position, Pannenberg disagrees with the conclusion. He agrees that an individual event or being can be given its definitive meaning only from a fore-conception of a final future of the whole of reality, a future that is still unfinished. But in contrast to Dilthey, Pannenberg draws the opposite conclusion: "every assertion of meaning rests upon a fore-conception of the final future, in the light of which the true meaning of every individual event first becomes expressible in a valid way."[86] Thus human assertion of meaning can be both provisional and valid. This position is a consequence of Pannenberg's view that truth, reality or being, is itself historical and maintains itself through change. Hence truth can be known provisionally and yet validly.

This view of reason is crucial for Pannenberg's theology because reason, like faith, requires the horizon of eschatology. If meaning is dependent upon or derived from an eschatologically constituted whole and if reason ascribes meaning to the present and past on the basis of a fore-conception of this future, then the absolute presupposition for the functioning of reason is this "anticipation of a final future constituting the wholeness of reality."[87] Faith is similar to reason in that it is explicitly directed toward that eschatological future which reason anticipates and from which it derives. In this view the language of faith does not and cannot stand in contradiction to reason. The difference is that reason is properly concerned primarily with present things and consequently runs the risk of forgetting its own presupposition by understanding itself on the basis of the present. Thus faith must remind reason of its own absolute presupposition and in so doing assists reason to become fully transparent to itself in its own reflection. In this way "faith can confirm itself as the criterion for the rationality of reason just by its orientation towards a final eschatological future."[88]

Thus Pannenberg argues that the structure and functioning of reason does not exclude faith. However, can reason know the future or does it depend here upon faith? Or is the fore-conception which reason requires merely a formal postulate without content? If it is, then Dilthey's conclusion concerning the relativity of knowledge would follow inevitably. In order for Pannenberg's position to stand, the fore-conception which reason requires for knowing must have content. In the case of Christian faith, knowledge derives from the preappearance of the eschatological future in the resurrection of Jesus. Since in Pannenberg's view this is the same future from which reason derives, it follows that he must hold that reason can know this preappearance in the history of the resurrection of Jesus. And that is precisely the heart of Pannenberg's rational theology. He holds, not that reason depends upon faith, but that faith depends upon reason.

## FAITH, REASON, AND THE HOLY SPIRIT

Before finally examining Pannenberg's presentation of the resurrection as a meaningful event accessible to reason, we should pursue further his understanding of the relationship between faith and rational insight.

Everything Pannenberg writes is geared to overcoming the irrational bias which dominates much of modern theology. Faith for Pannenberg is not a risk, no ungrounded leap in the dark. If faith has no basis in history, it becomes mere credulity, superstition, or a tediously developed work of faith. In opposition to such irrational tendencies, Pannenberg has posited his astonishing thesis that revelation not only comes *in* history but *as* history and that this historical revelation is universal, open to anyone who has eyes to see and requiring no special equipment for knowing. Critics have responded by charging that Pannenberg either negates the necessity of faith or holds that faith is but an inference from that which reason has established. If reason as such can know the revelatory events, is there any room left for a necessary work of the Holy Spirit? In his desire to oppose irrationalism, has Pannenberg so capitulated to the demands of reason that the requirement to believe the kerygma seems to have evaporated?

Pannenberg's essay "Insight and Faith" is an attempt to answer his critics. Paul Althaus, in particular, charged that Pannenberg's limitation of faith to trust is not the Reformation usage. The Reformation usage embraced three elements: knowledge, assent, and trust. While granting the correctness of this historical note, Pannenberg replies that the adoption of this broader definition in no way alleviates the real issue, namely, the relationship of trust to assent and knowledge. Is faith grounded in knowledge or is it grounded in itself? Althaus holds the view that while historical facts are the essential basis for faith, it is necessary to distinguish knowledge of the facts as such from knowledge of their revelatory, or saving, significance. The former can be grasped by reason (historical criticism), but the latter knowledge is disclosed only in the believing acceptance of the message. Pannenberg finds such a view unacceptable because it looks like the decision of faith becomes the ground of certainty. Faith then grounds itself, and that for Pannenberg leads back to an irrational view of faith.[89] Then the Christian no longer knows whether his faith is in fact based on supportable knowledge or is only a subjective reassurance.

Contrary to such a position, Pannenberg argues that "knowledge of the ground of faith must, as such, logically precede faith."[90] The logic of faith must be distinguished from the psychology of faith. Psychologically both trust and knowledge can be taken up in the same act, and, in fact, trust can exist in the expectation that knowledge will be disclosed. This often occurs where there is an atmosphere of confidence in the reliability of the message. However, that atmosphere has been gradually lost because of theology's flight from facts about history to the realm of meaning and the historicity of the individual. Consequently, theology today must reestablish the credibility of the Christian message, even though not every Christian need undertake this task of proving the trustworthiness of the knowledge that is presupposed. Theology must deal with the logic of faith, and logically knowledge is the presupposed basis or ground of trust.

If the logic of faith requires the priority of knowledge and if one maintains that all knowledge is natural knowledge in order to avoid justifying the truth of the Christian message by a decision of faith, is there any room left for the necessary work of the Holy Spirit? Pannenberg affirms the common Christian confession that belief in the Christian message is effected by the Holy Spirit, but he argues that the Holy Spirit is not the criterion for the truth of the message. The work of the Holy Spirit cannot be substituted for argumentation, because the criterion of truth is the content of the message. Whether a message is true can be ascertained only by referring to the inherent meaning of the reported event. This knowledge of events, while less than genuine faith, constitutes the necessary presupposition for it. Knowledge of events is, for Pannenberg, more than knowledge of some bare facts, for when events are understood in their context, the original meaning is recognizable in the events themselves. Events bring their original meaning with them from the context in which they have occurred. But if events and meaning are open to rational inquiry, does it follow that by the power of one's own intellect one can arrive at knowledge of God? Pannenberg wishes to avoid this conclusion by arguing that it is the events or the message that reports events that bring a person to such knowledge of God. The events or the Gospel reporting them have the transforming power of truth emanating from them. The Holy Spirit works within the Gospel and does not join itself to the Gospel as something additional to it. Through the appropriation of these events true faith is sparked. True faith has to do with the future, with allowing oneself to be grasped by these events and the promise they contain.[91]

If all knowledge is natural knowledge and reason certifies the reliability of the message, how does Pannenberg account for the fact that not all persons agree that the message is reliable and consequently not all believe? His answer is that "an illumination is necessary in order for that which is true in itself to appear evident in this character to a man."[92] The reason that not all persons are convinced by that which is true in itself is that the truth is opposed by prejudgments that are themselves irrationally rooted. Such prejudgments cannot be swept away by rational argument alone. In order for this to occur, illumination is necessary so that that which is clear in itself and demonstrable as true can dawn upon the individual person. In other words, Pannenberg believes that people "must first be brought to reason in order that they may also really perceive the event that reveals the truth of God's deity."[93]

Is Pannenberg's view of illumination the same as Calvin's teaching concerning the internal witness of the Spirit? Not if the internal witness of the Spirit means that "the content of faith is present only for the pious subjectivity—so that its truth cannot be presented in a way that can claim universal binding force."[94] For Pannenberg the Spirit is the power of the word itself, and more basically the Spirit belongs intrinsically to the event of redemption itself, namely, the ministry and destiny of Jesus and especially the resurrection. The resurrection life is a Spirit-reality, and for this reason one can claim that faith is effected by the Spirit, that is, "by the eschatological reality of new life that has appeared in Christ, of which the Christian message speaks."[95] The Spirit is not added to the events or the message but is itself their reality and meaning. Thus Pannenberg consistently shifts the focus away from subjectivity or individualistic piety to the events themselves with their inherent meaning. For him this is a shift away from restricting faith to an intellectual ghetto toward affirming the universally binding force of the truth-content of that faith. Although faith goes beyond reason as trust goes beyond knowledge, nevertheless, "knowledge of the revelatory event establishes the believing trust in which it issues."[96] Thus people must be brought to reason so that faith can transcend what is known about particular events by trustfully embracing the promise which it contains, a promise whose verification or confirmation awaits a future which is quite different from anything imagined.

## THE RESURRECTION: THE CRITICAL TEST OF PANNENBERG'S RATIONAL THEOLOGY

If faith depends upon reason, how can reason know the preappearance of the eschatological future in the resurrection of Jesus? Or to ask the same question in another way, how can reason discover God in Jesus? Pannenberg's method for answering these questions is based on his thesis that the original meaning of an event is recognizable in the event itself because events bring their meaning with them from the context in which they have occurred. The claims of Jesus did not arise in a vacuum. Jesus himself claimed the God of Israel as his authority, and thus the historical context for understanding Jesus includes the Old Testament and Jewish tradition. By discovering the meaning of Jesus' activity and destiny from the original historical context, Pannenberg argues that one thereby establishes the rational basis for judging all subsequent interpretations of the meaning of Jesus.

Pannenberg sketches Jesus' context as follows. The heart of Jesus' message was the God of the Old Testament and the nearness of his approaching reign. How was this God known and understood in the Jewish traditions? The basic biblical assumption is that God is usually hidden. He is not everywhere and always equally accessible, but he can be known only when he chooses to reveal himself. Initially God reveals himself by theophany, but as God's history with Israel continues, theophanies decrease, and it becomes evident that God's revelation of himself is indirect rather than direct. God's self-revelation occurs through historical acts. Events announced by prophets actually take place. Miracles and victories in war become the means by which the God of Israel reveals himself as Israel's God. At first attention is focused on single events, but gradually the entire history of Israel from the promise made to the patriarchs to the occupation of the promised land is seen as God's self-revelation, as evidence for Yahweh's divinity. Since what once had been promised had now been accomplished, this history proved to Israel the divinity of Yahweh.

However, after the exile the past fulfillment of promises could no longer establish the truth of Yahweh's divinity. It could now be seen that the conquest of the land was but a provisional fulfillment of Yahweh's promise, a fulfillment that was less than what was promised. In fact, if there were no subsequent fulfillment, Yahweh's self-revelation could be called into question. Thus it was under the prophetic announcements of doom that a significant change occurred. Israel no longer looked back to the revelation of Yahweh as a past event completed in the conquest but looked forward to the future. The definitive self-revelation of God was an event still to be expected. Gradually the horizons of the prophetic message expanded until Israel expected the final demonstration of Yahweh's divinity to occur not just within the horizons of Israel's history but within the history of the nations. In particular, apocalypticism placed this hope in the distant future, a hope which for the first time embraced the whole history of Israel and the world as a "continuing totality of divine activity realizing a plan which had been decided at the beginning of creation."[97] Only the end of history would finally and definitively reveal the God of Israel. Ultimate knowledge of God has to await the end for "only when all occurrence is ended can the divinity of God be known on the basis of the connection of history."[98] Since the final unity of history will be known only at the end, historical events can be seen in their significance only in the light of this end.

However, if definitive and final knowledge awaits the end, could the apocalyptic writers themselves have had any present certainty that Yahweh is God? Should not doubt be the prescribed attitude until everything has occurred? Granting that the apocalyptic visionaries undoubtedly derived their own certainty from their anticipatory visions, Pannenberg argues that the more sober biblical position affirms that only the actual occurrence of what has been predicted demonstrates its truth.[99] Herein lies the significance of Jesus, for in him the end has occurred in advance.

How can one know rationally that Jesus is the proleptic revelation of the end, and hence of the divinity of the God of Israel? The method requires that one determine the original meaning of Jesus' activity and destiny from its nearest horizon, and that was a horizon shaped by apocalypticism. Although Jesus was not an apocalyptic seer proclaiming visionary descriptions of the end time, his proclamation of the coming reign of God as near at hand was an apocalyptically colored prophecy. According to Jesus the eschatological future of God's reign was no longer reserved for the distant future but was already a power determining the present. In fact, the ministry of Jesus itself was already the dawning of this reign of God. Because Jesus' message brought about this nearness of God, he had to claim for himself the authority of God and that the salvation of mankind depended upon their response to his message. In this respect Jesus differs from the prophetic and apocalyptic tradition because he is aware that he brings something new. His message is not only information about a coming reality but is itself its proleptic appearance. In distinction from the prophetic tradition, Jesus' own person stands in the center, and response to him is a response to the prophetic and apocalyptic tradition, but Jesus cannot be restricted to the limits of that horizon. Instead, it is precisely against the limits of that tradition that Jesus' uniqueness can be seen. What prophets and apocalyptists only knew in advance had now become reality in the person and ministry of Jesus. The end had occurred in Jesus, at least as a proleptic reality.

Although Jesus' message of the near reign of God presupposed an awareness of the expectations developed by the prophetic and apocalyptic tradition, neither his message nor his miracles constituted definitive or unambiguous proof that the reign of God had dawned. As the prophetic word had to be confirmed by future fulfillment, so Jesus' announcement of the final, universal reign of God had to be confirmed by fulfillment. If such fulfillment failed to occur, the basis of his message would be retroactively destroyed.[100] Hence, the acceptance of Jesus' claim during his earthly ministry was actually in anticipation of this final, future confirmation by God himself through the occurrence of the end in history.[101]

According to the testimony of the disciples that confirmation occurred in the resurrection of Jesus from the dead. In the apocalyptic tradition the resurrection of the dead was the end of all history. Of course, that tradition expected the resurrection of all the righteous dead, and to that extent the resurrection of One—separate from the resurrection of all—was not expected. Still, within the horizons of that tradition, if Jesus was raised, his resurrection had to be understood as the occurrence of the end of history in the destiny of this one man. Because the resurrection of Jesus happened, the prophetic and apocalyptic expectation was proven to be, not just empty fantasy, but the truth itself.[102] Nevertheless, because it was the resurrection only of one, Jesus' resurrection could be only an anticipation of the end ahead of time. Apart from the resurrection Jesus' ministry conceivably could have been surpassed by subsequent acts of God, but God's act in the resurrection of Jesus is no longer surpassable by an inner-worldly event.[103] It is the arrival of the end ahead of time. Consequently, Jesus' announcement of the near end was confirmed in that it happened in himself, and the problem implicit in an apocalyptic hope that looks only to the distant future was overcome, for "by the resurrection of Jesus, God himself and his salvation are near to the world for all time to come—no matter how long the world endures. . . . Ultimate reality is already present in the midst of time."[104]

Pannenberg offers a six-point summary of the immediate, inherent significance of Jesus' resurrection.[105] In other words, Pannenberg argues that if one were a contemporary of Jesus sharing the apocalyptic expectation of the resurrection, the actual occurrence of the resurrection itself would—without any further interpretation—communicate the following:

(1) If Jesus has been raised, the end of the world has begun.

(2) If Jesus has been raised, this for a Jew can only mean that God himself has confirmed the pre-Easter activity of Jesus.

(3) Through his resurrection from the dead Jesus moved so close to the Son of Man that the insight became obvious: the Son of Man is none other than the man Jesus who will come again.

(4) If Jesus, having been raised from the dead, is ascended to God and if thereby the end of the world has begun, then God is ultimately revealed in Jesus.[106]

(5) The transition to the Gentile mission is motivated by the eschatological resurrection of Jesus as resurrection of the crucified One. Since the Old Testament and Judaism expected the final revelation of God to occur before the eyes of all people, the beginning of the end in Jesus' resurrection signified the inclusion of the Gentiles into eschatological salvation.

(6) The content of the words of the risen Jesus are to be understood as the explication of the significance inherent in the resurrection itself. Word and event have the same content, that is, the words add nothing new to the significance of the event but only explicate its inherent significance. For example, Paul's Gospel is an exegesis of the appearance of the resurrected Jesus that he experienced and was not audibly communicated to him in completed form.[107]

Pannenberg does not claim that every event is as unambiguous as the resurrection of Jesus. The crucifixion certainly was not, nor are many events in our own lives. Nevertheless, some occurrences contain "such irresistible evidence that there can be no doubt about their meaning for us,"[108] and the resurrection of Jesus is a prime example of such an occurrence. Thus, according to Pannenberg, if one grants that apocalypticism is the appropriate historical horizon for understanding the significance of Jesus and accepts as fact that he rose from the dead, the significance of that event is beyond question. In addition, the resurrection can now be directly the basis of faith without appealing to an authoritative, supplemental revelation. The meaning of the resurrection, which is the self-revelation of God, is carried by the event itself.

If the end of history is the event by which God will definitively disclose his deity, and if that end has appeared proleptically in Jesus, one can discover God in Jesus only through knowledge of his resurrection. But the question whether Jesus was raised from the dead is an historical question which can be answered only by historical arguments. In order to circumvent this necessity, it would be necessary to have present experiences of the resurrected Jesus. Thus Pannenberg holds that the question whether he was raised or not can be answered only by historical inquiry, and apart from such knowledge of the resurrection of Jesus Christian faith cannot protect itself against the charge of illusion.

How can historical argument prove the fact of the resurrection of Jesus? Pannenberg's handling of Jesus' resurrection as an historical problem contains little that is surprising or novel. He repeats the familiar claim that without the assumption of the resurrection it is very difficult to explain the emergence of the Christian community in an historically convincing manner.[109] Its rise would remain forever an enigma. He also adopts the increasingly common viewpoint that objections to the resurrection based on its unusual or unique character are not really historical arguments at all. In fact, such objections are rooted in the belief that only that which presently occurs could have occurred in the past, a belief rooted in an erroneous view of both natural and historical science.

Pannenberg believes that there are two separate resurrection traditions: one focused on the appearances of the resurrected Lord and the other on the empty tomb. These two traditions were originally separate, and only later were they combined. For example, Mark records only the empty tomb, and Paul only the resurrection appearances, whereas both are found in the Gospel of John. Pannenberg judges that Paul's record of the appearances is historically superior because the reports in the Gospels contain so much that is legendary that it is difficult to find a historical kernel in them. This legendary character is seen especially in the tendency to underline the corporeality of the appearances. Therefore, Pannenberg concentrates on the Pauline account of the resurrection appearances to construct his historical argument.

Paul's intention in enumerating the appearances of the resurrected Jesus is "to give proof by means of witnesses for the facticity of Jesus' resurrection."[110] This intention is especially clear in the note regarding the five hundred brethren, most of whom were still alive and could be queried about the matter. The fact that Paul's report is not a disinterested one may not be used to disqualify its serving as historical proof. The vital interest of Paul, or of any historian, could serve to disqualify only if one can demonstrate that such interest prejudices the results of the inquiry, but Pannenberg claims that one can hardly question Paul's intent to give a convincing historical proof by the standards of his time.

How does one know that the Pauline tradition is not a later, freely invented, legendary development? Pannenberg argues for its historical character in the following manner. Paul himself was in Jerusalem within six to eight years after the resurrection. Although he wrote 1 Corinthians in 56 A.D., it is important to note that the formulas used by Paul are derived from an older, originally Aramaic, confession. Paul does not coin these phrases on his own but quotes from an already established tradition. Hence there is hardly sufficient time for legendary development, and Paul's tradition must be treated as historical in nature. In addition, the appearances of the resurrected Jesus were experienced as concrete occurrences from without and not simply as subjective experiences. These appearances can be described as visions in the sense that others present may not have perceived them, for example, Paul's companions on the road to Damascus. Nevertheless, the category of visionary seeing only expresses something about the subjective mode of experience and may not be used to question the reality of the event experienced in this form.[111]

The heart of Pannenberg's historical argument is the rejection of alternate explanations as impossible or less plausible than the explanation which accepts the resurrection as fact. For example, the familiar argument that the appearances of Jesus were merely a product of the enthusiastic imagination of the disciples is rejected by Pannenberg as psychologically untenable. No one trained in Judaism would have responded in such a manner to the death of Jesus, even if they believed him to be the Messiah. In addition, the belief about the eschatological resurrection of Jesus—separated by an interval from the universal resurrection—was a totally new belief. It cannot be explained as a development from previously held beliefs, that is, not apart from the fact of Jesus' resurrection itself. Moreover, the number and temporal distribution of the appearances militates against any explanation based on the theory of mass hysteria.

Objections to the acceptance of Jesus' resurrection have also been raised in terms of historical science. What sorts of possibilities can the historian consider in reconstructing the historical correlation of events? Many historians operate with a view of reality which assumes that resurrections cannot happen, a view which Pannenberg argues is untenable in terms of the presuppositions of modern physics. Science knows only part of the laws of nature, and, in any case, an individual event is never completely determined by natural laws. Conformity to law is only one aspect of what happens. Thus Pannenberg concludes that "natural science expresses the general validity of the laws of nature but must at the same time declare its own inability to make definitive judgments about the possibility or impossibility of an individual event, regardless of how certainly it is able, at least in principle, to measure the probability of an event's occurrence."[112] The judgment about whether or not an event has happened is in the final analysis an historical judgment which cannot be prejudged by natural science. Since the historical tradition has no other viable explanation for the rise of the Christian community, it should accept the resurrection of Jesus as an historical event even if historians and all others know nothing more particular about it than can be derived from the Jewish apocalyptic tradition. In other words, even though the language used to designate the event is essentially metaphorical language, the resurrection of Jesus should not be denied historical status.[113]

Pannenberg admits that from the viewpoint of historical science there remains a real difficulty in speaking of the resurrection of Jesus.[114] The original confession of the resurrection of Jesus is a conclusion which works backward from the appearances to the belief that Jesus did not remain dead, and from this belief, in connection with the empty tomb, to the affirmation of the resurrection. Pannenberg believes there is an inner necessity in this process: if Jesus lives, then he either lives again or is transformed to another "life." But such a conclusion confronts the historian with a real difficulty. An historical event must occur in time and space and thus be distinguishable by its specific time and place from other events. The resurrection of Jesus meets the criterion of occurring at a specific time, but whether it can be satisfactorily located in a specific place remains somewhat problematic. Certainly it occurred in connection with an empty tomb in Jerusalem.

However, the problem is that other events in space must have a continuation in succeeding events which also occur in space and in a continuing relationship with what has preceded. Such is not the case with Jesus himself. There are no such immediately subsequent events in space or even in time. The resurrection is an event in time and space, but the appearances do not require that the appearing reality was itself in space and time. Thus the continuing consequences of the resurrection with reference to Jesus himself escape our view. Jesus has been resurrected to a new life, but he has disappeared from our world. Precisely what occurred historically remains vague. Jesus lives, but what that life is in an historical sense is unknown. Since the historian knows no other such event, he cannot further describe it. According to Pannenberg the historian must affirm the event while recognizing that the rest escapes his judgment. Thus history both declares the resurrection and at the same time "protects the Mystery of the Resurrection of Jesus."[115] However, even though the historian cannot fully describe what the event of the resurrection of Jesus actually is because it transcends what is historically visible, the historian must still name the event. For this there is no category more historically appropriate than the category of resurrection derived from Jewish apocalyptic.

The theological claim that because the resurrection of Jesus is the beginning of a new age it cannot be perceived with the eyes of the old aeon is rejected by Pannenberg. Even though a metaphor must be used to describe the event because the resurrection of Jesus is the beginning of the new creation, the reality of the resurrection has been made known to a certain number of persons living in the reality of the old aeon. Consequently, if one affirms the resurrection of Jesus as an event, it must be affirmed as an historical event. Pannenberg also rejects the assertion of some theologians that faith gives an immediate, prescientific relationship to the past which contains within itself an unconditional certainty about these past events. Although Pannenberg grants that there may be such intuition, he argues that intuition requires confirmation through historical observation in order to know whether a particular intuition is tied to fact or illusion. Thus Pannenberg consistently affirms the principle that the only method of achieving a degree of certainty concerning past events is historical research.

The second line of tradition concerning the resurrection of Jesus is the tradition of the empty tomb. Pannenberg believes that these two traditions of resurrection appearances and empty tomb developed independently of each other. Hence if both are judged to be historically probable, there is dual confirmation of the resurrection tradition. The essence of Pannenberg's argument for the historicity of the empty tomb is as follows: Paul's silence concerning the empty tomb cannot be used against that tradition because Paul is concerned with the relationship between the Christ event and the destiny of believers. The empty tomb "belongs to the singularity of Jesus' fate," which in no way affects the parallel of Christ and the believer central to Paul's proclamation of the Gospel.[116] Thus even if Paul knew the tradition, which Pannenberg considers probably doubtful, it was of little interest in the light of his purposes.[117] However, in Jerusalem the situation was different. There the resurrection could not have been proclaimed unless the empty tomb was an established fact. Critically important is the fact that the early Jewish polemic, which rejected the resurrection of Jesus, shared the conviction that the grave was empty. While granting that the traditions about the discovery of the empty grave are legendary in their textual form, Pannenberg believes that this in no way affects the historical character of the basic tradition. For even apart from the textual traditions in the Gospels, general historical considerations alone indicate that the proclamation of Jesus' resurrection in Jerusalem is hardly conceivable except on the assumption that the grave was in fact empty.

Theories claiming that no one knew where Jesus was buried are considered by Pannenberg as borrowed from the realm of fantasy. There is nothing in the tradition about a search for the grave, nor is there any mention of the matter in Jewish polemic, where it would have had a useful function, if indeed it were the case. But both the Christian tradition and early Jewish polemic assume the fact of the empty tomb.

The relationship between these traditions of the empty tomb and the appearances of the resurrected Jesus is considered extraordinarily difficult by Pannenberg. He follows the scholarly opinion that locates the basic appearances in Galilee. These appearances are primary, and the discovery of the empty tomb is thought to have occurred only after the disciples returned from Galilee. The intertwining of appearances and empty tomb are considered a later, legendary development. In this perspective the two traditions develop independently, and neither occasions the other. Thus Pannenberg concludes that the reality of Jesus' resurrection must be considered "historically very probable, and that always means in historical inquiry that it is to be presupposed until contrary evidence appears."[118]

Throughout his entire argument Pannenberg makes no appeal to an authoritative tradition. His argument is strictly historical and consequently does not go beyond assertions of historical probability. Thus, while arguing that the subjective-vision hypothesis falters for psychological reasons and becomes still more questionable because the empty tomb is historically very probable, Pannenberg admits that the situation would be very different if the discovery of the empty tomb was the occasion for the disciples' journey to Galilee. That theory has been defended, but Pannenberg judges that the assumption that the disciples concluded from the empty tomb that they should return home to Galilee to find Jesus rests upon insufficient psychological motivation. Nonetheless, if such a theory were possible, Pannenberg grants that the case for interpreting the appearances of Jesus as spontaneous visionary experiences would be strengthened. Then the only difficulty remaining would be the broad temporal distribution of the appearances. Thus Pannenberg's case rests upon historical argumentation that reconstructs the tradition in such a way that the reports of the empty tomb prior to resurrection appearances in Matthew, Luke, and John must be judged either as legendary or as containing motives of a dogmatic or editorial sort that are clearly not historical.

Although Pannenberg attempts to build a rational historical argument for the facticity of the resurrection of Jesus, the question arises whether his own faith intuition concerning the resurrection does not predispose him to give greater weight to certain arguments than to others. Psychological motivation is difficult to assess. Perhaps if one did not believe that Jesus was raised, even an argument resting on the assessment that the necessary psychological motivation moving the disciples from empty tomb to Galilee was rather weak might be considered better than an argument which requires one to believe that the resurrection appearances designate a reality existing outside the disciples' own subjectivity. The question can also be raised whether Pannenberg holds, contrary to his own historical assessment which knows nothing about what the resurrected reality of Jesus really is, a view or belief about what that resurrected reality can be. For Pannenberg seems to know that any stress upon the corporeality of that reality is necessarily legendary. Historical argument requires the assessing of various pieces of evidence and weighing a variety of arguments about their correlation. In such arguments about the resurrection of Jesus it seems that a faith commitment to its reality has influenced the structure of the historical argument. Thus the question remains: Has Pannenberg demonstrated by his historical arguments for the resurrection that faith depends upon reason, or has faith in fact subtly or even basically affected the rational weighing of the historical evidence?

## A CRITICAL EVALUATION

Pannenberg is to be commended for grasping the theological pendulum and pushing it in the opposite direction. In a world which has come to doubt that the Gospel makes any claims concerning truth, in which certain theologians even have thought it necessary to surrender virtually all claims to the historical truth of the Gospel in order to preserve the authority of the kerygma, a theology trying to demonstrate the contrary is absolutely essential. For Pannenberg has perceived correctly that the surrender of such historical claims evaporates the Christian Gospel into myth which may have meaning for one's individual subjectivity but which asserts no claims concerning the universal truth of the Gospel. If Pannenberg wanted to demonstrate only for Christians that their faith is reasonable, not irrational, rooted in events in history, and, therefore, not merely a subjective or arbitrary choice, we would not object. In fact, we would agree that the Christian community would be the better for such efforts, and perhaps even the cultural atmosphere in which the Gospel is proclaimed would be improved by such efforts. Though that is part of Pannenberg's stated intention, his theological program assumes a more universal demonstration of the rationality of the Gospel.[119] For Pannenberg's central thesis is that reason precedes faith and provides the foundation on which faith rests. His thesis is, not the traditional "I believe in order that I may know," but the more modern "I know and so I believe." This basic thesis raises some very serious questions.

Since the resurrection of Jesus as historical event is the foundation of Pannenberg's rational theology, we must ask whether he succeeds in constructing a rationally convincing argument for the truth of the resurrection. Has he successfully demonstrated that the resurrection of Jesus was an event in space and time? Basically, that question is impossible to answer in the abstract, for whether a demonstration is convincing or not depends upon perspectives held by those listening to the demonstration. If one believes, as Pannenberg does, that God is active in history and is the most important historical agent, that history is an open process and God is not locked into a prefixed order, and that history is an indirect revelation of God, then the historical argument for the historicity of the resurrection of Jesus gains in plausibility. In fact, one who accepts such assumptions has the right to claim that such beliefs illumine reality and that without such beliefs important aspects of reality are inadequately or erroneously understood. But such assumptions or beliefs seem to grant faith a priority over reason and suggest that reason functions only within the context of faith. Pannenberg, however, resists that position.

What then does Pannenberg succeed in demonstrating about the resurrection and to whom? It would appear that for those holding beliefs or assumptions that differ from Pannenberg's, not much at all. For example, since Pannenberg agrees that the historian must give reasons for what he asserts and not merely rely on authority, he presents a variety of reasons for holding that the resurrection is an historical event. The chief reason is the list of witnesses presented by Paul. While the evidence in this case may be sufficient to argue that Paul is quoting from a primitive tradition and that he intends this listing of witnesses to function as historical proof, the evidence does not logically compel the conclusion that the tradition is true. Establishing a tradition as primitive demands only the conclusion that the earliest community believed it to be true![120] In addition, certain historians argue that since one expects to find miracles, myths, and legends in certain kinds of religious literature, such as the Bible, such phenomena can be interpreted with equal rational validity as interpretations of the significance ascribed to Jesus by the earliest community. Even if one agrees with Pannenberg that there was insufficient time and lack of an adequate psychological context for creating a resurrection myth, can one argue that thereby one has established the resurrection as an historical event in a logically compelling fashion? Is it not rather the case that believing acceptance of the tradition shapes the marshalling of the evidence and thus the conclusion drawn from the evidence?

The argument based upon the empty tomb is a further case in point. Matthew informs us that the Jews said the body had been stolen. Thus one can argue that both Jews and Christians believed that the tomb was empty and that, therefore, certain hypotheses which assume that the tomb was not empty have little historical validity, such as hypotheses about a lost tomb or about primitive taboos which would have prevented anyone from entering the tomb. Nevertheless, the fact of an empty tomb is not limited to a single rational historical explanation. Pannenberg's arguments for the resurrection are adequate for demonstrating rationally that the rejection of the resurrection as historical fact has no greater historical plausibility than the acceptance of the resurrection. In fact, Pannenberg has every right to claim that his arguments have greater historical plausibility, but being convinced that such is the case depends upon a believing acceptance of the event itself.

A basic problem in Pannenberg's theology is the transition from the probabilities of historical reason to the certainty of faith. By agreeing that historical reason produces only judgments of probability while affirming that faith requires absolute trust, Pannenberg creates a dilemma in his theological system. If historical reason produces only judgments of probability, how can Pannenberg avoid the position of those who say that because the story of the empty tomb does not possess a high degree of probability, it can never be the cornerstone of faith? Even if Pannenberg's argument is valid that statements of historical or natural probabilities cannot determine whether a particular event happened or not, the problem remains how one moves from probability to certainty, from reason to faith.

Pannenberg rejects the position that faith gives certainty regarding historical fact. He defines faith only as trust, as an action by which one trusts a promise or surrenders oneself to another. Faith is thus confidence in God who will raise those who are joined to him. But faith is not itself an avenue of knowledge or even some greater confidence that the propositions established by historical reason are true.[121] Thus Pannenberg argues consistently that while faith requires total trust, the necessary historical knowledge on which it rests remains afflicted by a relative degree of uncertainty.[122] In fact, historical reasoning requires *in principle* that one allow the possibility that the eschatological meaning of the history of Jesus could become doubtful to such a degree that the foundation for the certainty of faith would be removed. Pannenberg agrees *in principle* that this is so, but he sees no occasion for apprehension concerning such future developments. Certainly, Pannenberg can plausibly maintain that what must be affirmed theoretically as a possibility need not be envisioned as a threatening actuality, but he has not thereby removed the problem of the certainty of faith.

Can faith achieve certainty greater than reason can provide? The suggestion by Pannenberg that historical certainty and the certainty of faith occur on different levels resolves nothing and, in fact, reinforces the dilemma.[123] The further suggestion that the certainty of faith is rooted in the peculiar nature of this particular historical event—namely, that it is the eschatological event which reveals the meaning of the whole of history—also does not escape the dilemma. Of course, if it were possible to know the resurrection as the eschatological historical event with total certainty, then the historical event could support complete and total trust. But according to Pannenberg it is the task of historical reason to establish that the history of Jesus is this eschatological event, and reason cannot achieve absolute certainty. Thus it appears that Pannenberg has but two choices: either grant that faith *knows* more than reason can provide (and at times Pannenberg seems to suggest that this is so, even though that position contradicts his basic understanding of the relation of faith and reason) or admit that the certainty of faith is dependent upon subjective decision. For if the full meaning of the resurrection, namely, that it is the eschatological event in which God is fully revealing himself in Jesus Christ, requires a step beyond historical knowledge, a leap which reason cannot fully warrant but faith demands, then Pannenberg himself is open to the charge of subjectivism that his entire theological proposal seeks to avoid. It may be a leap of faith which has greater historical warrant than in the case of Kierkegaard or Bultmann, and that may be an advantage, but it remains a leap toward certainty which the evidence established by historical reason cannot sustain.

At times one is tempted to tone down Pannenberg's admittedly "bold and one-sided" statements and give a more moderate interpretation of his theological program. For Pannenberg admits that psychologically one can believe in Jesus without first having established by reason the truth of the matter and that, in fact, many persons have neither the time nor the competence to establish by reason the truth of the matter. Although psychologically this may be the case, he argues that logically knowledge preceeds faith and leads into it. Thus Pannenberg maintains that the logical presupposition of faith is that its truth can be demonstrated. A moderate reading of this position would be that once faith exists, the believer can develop the logic of faith and give reasons for its existence. There are even some statements in Pannenberg that could support such an interpretation. For example, there is the curious statement which affirms that truth as futural "can only be grasped by faith, which trusts in him who will in the future prove himself truly reliable."[124] Here faith is assigned an essential role in acquiring knowledge. And in response to two critics Pannenberg admits that "the movement of faith is already operative in the very perception of historical fact."[125] Such an admission comes perilously close to the position on which this critical evaluation is based. This position agrees that the Christian scholar must engage in rational argument with alternative positions, must challenge various views of reason and critically revise historical methodology.[126] It agrees that Christianity makes truth-claims about reality which may not be surrendered. But, in contrast to Pannenberg's basic thesis, this position holds that the believer has arrived at such a rational understanding of the truth by means of revelation which has compelled assent or produced insight, and hence by means of a revelation which has been grasped by faith. While agreeing that faith does not produce meaning, it maintains that apart from faith such meaning is not perceived. Thus, even if the rational case constructed for the Christian view of reality may be accepted by others as compelling, if it is so accepted, it is because a moment of illumination has occurred which is really an acceptance by faith of the truth of the Gospel. From this point of view illumination is itself the moment of faith which allows one to see and to articulate the truth. Pannenberg, however, restricts illumination to the plane of reason and consistently refuses to grant faith any priority over reason or in any way to speak of faith as the foundation of reason.

Of course, Pannenberg recognizes that when the truth is presented, not all acknowledge it. But he ascribes this to the existence of subjective and irrational factors which cannot be removed by rational argument. Hence illumination or insight is necessary, but such insight is created not by faith but by the truth itself and occurs for Pannenberg on the plane of reason. This understanding of illumination shifts the question of understanding God's revelation from one of sin and guilt to one of intellectual understanding. However, according to Scripture it is not just irrational factors of various kinds which must be overcome for illumination to occur, but it is rather mankind's basic resistance to God himself. Consequently, revelation must be understood first of all in a soteriological framework which graciously meets and overcomes human resistance to the presence of God. Only where such resistance has been overcome can reason be liberated to see the whole of reality as it is in fact. Naturally, the failure to see reality as it is creates or results in intellectual misunderstandings, but the root of such misunderstanding lies in mankind's fundamental resistance to God and his revelation. Thus we would maintain that reason finds itself within the reality of salvation, but reason is not itself the entrance to salvation.[127]

Although it may be tempting to advocate a more moderate interpretation suggesting that Pannenberg wishes only to give a theological interpretation of reason which demonstrates that reason is not inimical to faith because it requires faith's presuppositions for its own proper functioning, Pannenberg's own discussion does not allow it. For he maintains consistently not only that the history of Jesus is logically prior to faith but also that knowledge of that history produced by autonomous historical reason is logically prior to faith and leads into faith. Thus the dilemma mentioned above still exists: if faith requires certainty, Pannenberg must either assume an epistemology contrary to his dominant thesis that faith is not an avenue of knowledge but is dependent upon reason for its foundation, or acknowledge that he has not fully escaped the charge of subjectivism as he himself defines it. The only way out of this dilemma is to challenge the epistemology assumed by the autonomy of reason. Does reason, in fact, establish autonomously its own criteria for validating claims to truth, or is there a prior element of commitment, trust, or belief within which reason functions and on the basis of which it develops criteria for validating claims to truth? The essays in this book assume the latter viewpoint. For example, W. Alston argues the following thesis: "There are a number of irreducibly different sources of beliefs, each of which can be effectively evaluated, if at all, only from within, only by basing the evaluation (at least in part) on beliefs gained from that source. There is no Archimedean point from which we can make impartial judgments on these epistemic claims. There is no strictly noncircular justification of a basic epistemic source."[128] The advantage of this alternative epistemology is that it avoids the dilemma of Pannenberg's scheme while retaining the intention of his program, namely, the insistence upon the truth-claims of Christianity, the necessity of defending these truth-claims by rational means against counterarguments, and the validity of insisting that the truth-claims of revelation illumine reality.

What then about the charge of subjectivity? Need one accept as fact that if faith is essential for knowing the revelation of God, such knowledge is but the creation of human subjectivity? Pannenberg continues to characterize faith as a subjective decision, but by limiting faith to trust or commitment he seeks to escape the charge. However, even if faith is necessary in order to know, need one conclude that such knowledge is but a value judgment or a projection of human subjectivity? If faith is elicited by God's revelation in history and does not exist apart from it, why should this be considered any more subjective than any human act by which knowledge is acquired? If, as Pannenberg himself argues, insight is compelled by acts of God or by reports concerning such acts, and the power which convinces resides in the truth itself, and, therefore, such insight which is necessary but not universal is not open to the charge of subjectivity, why cannot one make a similar case for faith as necessary for knowledge without opening the door to the charge of subjectivity? The fact that Christian faith is not held universally does not justify the charge that it is only a subjective decision, essentially irrational in nature. Undoubtedly, the proposition that $2 + 2 = 4$ is held universally and considered a proposition held rationally. The power which compels this universal acceptance resides in the proposition itself. While the truth of the Christian faith is not held so universally, it does not follow that faith is essentially irrational. For can it not be that certain orders of reality are less accessible than others, that especially where the self-revelation of God is concerned the human sinful condition plays a more dominant role in the suppression of truth? If such is the case, the fact that there is universally less agreement concerning this revelation of God need not suggest that where revelation has created assent, such assent is irrational or merely subjective.

There remains one premise requiring critical assessment. Because of his commitment to the autonomy of reason, reason which cannot be bound by an external authority, Pannenberg reduces revelation to event and understands verbal contexts and/or pronouncements as explications of the inherent significance of revelatory events. For example, the writings of the Apostle Paul are described as an exegesis of the resurrection event and are not considered revelation audibly received by Paul. An intriguing question is whether this understanding does justice to the verbal dimension even within Pannenberg's own framework. His basic thesis that events take their meaning with them from the context in which they occur must be paired with the fact that especially in regard to the resurrection that context is verbal in nature. It is found in the prophetic and apocalyptic writings which existed prior to the event of the resurrection and which constitute for Pannenberg the context within which the resurrection must be understood. In fact, his thesis is that if the essence of this apocalyptic vision is not believed, the resurrection cannot be understood. Therefore, in agreement with Paul's argument in 1 Corinthians 15, Pannenberg declares that "the expectation of resurrection must already be supposed as truth" if the resurrection of Jesus is to be understood.[129]

Thus Pannenberg consistently assumes that belief in resurrection precedes an understanding of the resurrection of Jesus. Does this not imply that revelation in the form of promise, revelation as verbal declaration, demands an acceptance by virtue of itself? Does it not imply that the context for understanding the event is first a promise made by a faithful God and revealed through a prophet? Although the experience of the fulfillment of previous promises may be "adequate" evidence for the faithfulness of God to those who believe, the promise itself requires acceptance or belief prior to and apart from the adequate verification which occurs in the event which fulfills the promise. Not only does faith accept before the confirmation of the promise in events, but prior to the eschaton faith always believes more about the meaning of the central redemptive events than has yet become visible. Thus, even though events are central to the biblical understanding of revelation, verbal revelation, or the promise which forms the context for the understanding of events, is required for an adequate understanding not only of what has not yet happened but also of what has happened. Human reason cannot decipher the meaning of revelatory events by inference from the events themselves but instead requires a promissory or revelatory verbal context which has been accepted by faith as the true context for the understanding of events. If this is correct, there is no reason for accepting the Enlightenment bias against believing an authority or believing on the basis of reliable witnesses. Pannenberg should not, and in fact cannot, surrender the Christian confession of Scripture as the canon for faith.

Pannenberg assumes that the only alternatives are faith grounded upon itself (subjectivism) or faith grounded upon historical events rationally known. There is, however, another possibility. Faith can be understood as correlated with revelation. Such correlation does not require a *sacrificium intellectus,* but it does require a total surrender of the person to God and to his revelation. This revelation accepted by faith becomes, then, the arena within which and on the basis of which reason functions. The slogan *credo ut intellegam* is not a declaration of irrationality but is rather the true understanding of reason.

Pannenberg's theological program is a significant challenge to important cultural biases against the Christian faith. That it does not fully succeed is caused by Pannenberg's own acceptance of a significant cultural bias, namely, the autonomy of reason. Reason is not autonomous, nor does it establish autonomously its own criteria for rationality in matters of either faith or science. Beliefs of various kinds are inevitably involved in establishing the definition of rationality. Such is the thesis of the various essays in this book.

## NOTES

1. Cf. A. Harnack, *What Is Christianity*? (Harper & Row, 1957), pp. 27–28.
2. Ibid., pp. 63–70.
3. V. A. Harvey, *The Historian and the Believer* (Macmillan, 1966), p. 104.
4. G. E. Lessing, *Theological Writings,* tr. H. Chadwick (Stanford University Press, 1957), p. 53.
5. This formulation is by H. Ott, quoted by G. Spiegler, *The Eternal Covenant* (Harper & Row, 1967), p. 5.
6. Cf. W. Herrmann, "How We See God in Jesus," in *Contemporary Religious Thinkers,* ed. J. Macquarrie (Harper & Row, 1968), chapter 9.
7. Cf. R. R. Niebuhr, *Resurrection and Historical Reason* (Scribner, 1957), pp. 6–9.
8. Hermann, "How We See God," p. 73.

9. R. Bultmann, "Bultmann Replies to His Critics," in *Kerygma and Myth,* ed. H. Bartsch, tr. R. Fuller (London: S.P.C.K., 1957), pp. 210–11.

10. R. Bultmann, "Is Exegesis without Presuppositions Possible?" in *Existence and Faith,* ed. S. Ogden (Hodder & Stoughton, 1961), p. 345.

11. Cf. R. Bultmann, *History and Eschatology* (Harper & Row, 1957), p. 120.

12. *Kerygma and Myth,* pp. 39 ff.

13. Ibid., p. 42.

14. Bultmann quotes Erich Frank with approval: "to the Christians the advent of Christ was not an event in that temporal process which we mean by history today. It was an event in the history of salvation, in the realm of eternity, an eschatological moment in which rather this profane history of the world came to an end. And in an analogous way, history comes to its end in the religious experience of any Christian 'who is in Christ'." Bultmann, *History and Eschatology,* p. 153.

15. The Marburg Neo-Kantians are the philosophers Hermann Cohen (1876–1912) and Paul Natorp (1885–1922). Influenced by these philosophies, the theologian Wilhelm Herrmann (1879–1922) became identified with this school of thought.

16. R. A. Johnson, *The Origins of Demythologizing: Philosophy and Historiography in the Theology of Rudolf Bultmann* (Leiden: Brill, 1974), p. 50. For an assessment of the contribution of Neo-Kantianism to Bultmann's theology on which this discussion is dependent, see especially chapter 2.

17. Cf. R. R. Niebuhr, *Resurrection and Historical Reason,* p. 76.

18. K. Barth, *Epistle to the Romans* (Oxford University Press, 1963), p. 30.

19. K. Barth, *Church Dogmatics* (T. & T. Clark, 1936–77), II/1, p. 635 (hereafter referred to as CD).

20. CD, III/2, p. 624.

21. CD, IV/1, p. 333.

22. CD, III/2, p. 446.

23. Barth, *Epistle to the Romans,* p. 8.

24. While claiming it was not necessary to choose between the historical-critical method and the venerable doctrine of inspiration, Barth said if he were forced to choose, he would choose the latter. Many of his critics believed he had chosen for inspiration against the results of historical criticism. Cf. preface to Barth, *Epistle to the Romans.*

25. Pannenberg charges that Barth has escaped the modern problems of history and historical relativism but has not answered the questions posed by Ernst Troeltsch. Thus in Pannenberg's eyes "Troeltsch could have been written last year or the year before. When I read Barth, it is as if I were reading a church father of the fifth century." Cf. W. Pannenberg, "A Theological Conversation with Wolfhart Pannenberg," *Dialog* 11 (1972):294.

26. K. Barth, *Dogmatics in Outline* (Harper & Row, 1959), pp. 59–60.

27. CD, I/1, p. 7.

28. Cf. CD, I/1, pp. 7–8; W. Pannenberg, *Theology and the Philosophy of Science* (Westminster Press, 1976), pp. 270–71.

29. CD, I/1, pp. 10–11.

30. Pannenberg, "A Theological Conversation," p. 286.

31. Cf. K. Barth, *Protestant Thought: From Rousseau to Ritschl* (Simon & Schuster, 1969), pp. 358ff.

32. W. Pannenberg, "Types of Atheism and Their Theological Significance," in *Basic Questions in Theology* (Fortress Press, 1971), 2:189.

33. W. Pannenberg, "The Question of God," in *Basic Questions in Theology,* 2:205.

34. Pannenberg, "Types of Atheism," p. 195.

35. Pannenberg, "Question of God," p. 223.

36. Cf. Pannenberg, "Types of Atheism," p. 199.

37. Pannenberg, "Question of God," p. 207.

38. Ibid., p. 208.

39. Ibid., p. 209. In his later writings, according to Pannenberg, Barth did return to a better position by stressing the relation of all creatures to God's revelation in Christ, and thus affirming that even non-Christian religions are related to the real God and are not simply the ideological self-interpretations of man.

40. Ibid., p. 226.

41. Pannenberg, "Types of Atheism," p. 191.

42. Pannenberg, "Question of God," p. 229.

43. Ibid., p. 232. Cf. also W. Pannenberg, *Theology and the Kingdom of God* (Westminster Press, 1969), pp. 55–58. For a critical discussion of Pannenberg's view of God, reality, and history, cf. B. J. Walsh, *Futurity and Creation: Explorations in the Eschatological Theology of Wolfhart Pannenberg* (Published thesis, Institute for Christian Studies, Toronto, Ontario, 1979).

44. Ibid., p. 233. Such confessional answers at key junctures in Pannenberg's theology are puzzling. They seem to give faith an ultimate priority over reason contrary to Pannenberg's basic position.

45. Cf. W. Pannenberg, "Kerygma and History," in *Basic Questions in Theology,* 1:88–95.

46. A corollary for Pannenberg is his acceptance of the demise of Scripture as a canon assuming material agreement among all its authors. Pannenberg believes that the contemporary emphasis upon the individual tendencies of the authors has effectively destroyed the traditional view of Scripture as canon.

47. W. Pannenberg, "The Crisis of the Scriptural Principle," in *Basic Questions in Theology,* 1:6.

48. Ibid., p. 9.

49. W. Pannenberg, "Response to the Discussion," *Theology as History,* ed. Robinson and Cobb (Harper & Row, 1967), p. 226.

50. Cf. W. Pannenberg, "Faith and Reason," in *Basic Questions in Theology,* 2:51.

51. Pannenberg, "Response," p. 228.

52. Pannenberg, *Theology and the Kingdom of God,* p. 95.

53. Ibid., p. 93. Cf. also Pannenberg, "Response," p. 230.

54. Pannenberg, *Theology and the Kingdom of God,* p. 94.

55. Pannenberg, *Theology and the Philosophy of Science,* p. 273.

56. Ibid., p. 273. The same point is made in the following sentence: "If proof through rational enquiry is ruled out in advance, but for some reason or

other we still want to hold the Christian tradition, nothing remains but the wholly uninsured venture of faith." Ibid., p. 273.

57. W. Pannenberg, "The Nature of a Theological Statement," *Zygon* 7, 1 (March 1972): 11.

58. Ibid., pp. 17–19.

59. W. Pannenberg, "Redemptive Event and History," in *Basic Questions in Theology,* 1:15.

60. W. Pannenberg, "Dogmatic Theses on the Doctrine of Revelation," *Revelation as History,* ed. W. Pannenberg (Macmillan, 1968), pp. 135ff.

61. Pannenberg, "Redemptive Event and History," p. 38.

62. Ibid., pp. 50ff.

63. Ibid., p. 42.

64. Ibid., p. 42.

65. Ibid., pp. 43–44.

66. Ibid., p. 45.

67. Ibid., p. 47.

68. Ibid., p. 60.

69. Ibid., p. 61.

70. Pannenberg summarizes his view of the matter with a quotation from Otto Kim: "a historical conclusion can be regarded as certain when. . . despite the fact that it is not removed from all possibility of attack, it is nevertheless in agreement with all known facts."

71. Ibid., p. 64, n. 129.

72. Ibid., p. 67.

73. Ibid., pp. 69–70.

74. Ibid., pp. 74–75.

75. Ibid., p. 78.

76. Collingwood holds that research does not begin by gathering the greatest possible number of details in random fashion in order to take the second step of exhibiting laws governing them; rather, "a conjecture about the relationships, the historical circumstances, guides one's interest from the beginning." Ibid., pp. 70–71, 78.

77. Ibid., p. 78.

78. Pannenberg, "Faith and Reason," p. 48. Pannenberg believes that the church and its theologians, from the late medieval period onward, have contributed to this sharp opposition between faith and reason in the modern world. By restricting themselves to Scripture and by failing to relate the themes of revelation to other sciences, theologians became advocates of two distinct realms, "a realm of supernatural knowledge and a contrasting realm of so-called natural knowledge." Cf. Pannenberg, "The Crisis of the Scriptural Principle," pp. 1–2, 13. A commendable part of Pannenberg's program is his attempt to regain the concept of the unity of the truth and the significance of revelation for illuminating all areas of knowledge.

79. Pannenberg, "Faith and Reason," p. 46.

80. Ibid.; for Pannenberg's discussion of these forms of reason, cf. pp. 55–64.

81. Cf. W. Pannenberg, "What Is Truth?" in *Basic Questions in Theology,* 2:12. As representatives of "receiving reason" Herder, Kamlah, and Jacobi are mentioned.

82. Although Pannenberg's critique of "receiving reason" is created by his understanding of the biblical view of truth or reality, the role given to faith seems not in harmony with his fundamental view of the relation of reason to faith.

83. Pannenberg, "What Is Truth?" pp. 6–9.

84. Ibid., p. 27.

85. This understanding of reason is traced by Pannenberg from Fichte to Hegel, Dilthey, and Heidegger. Cf. Pannenberg, "Faith and Reason," pp. 59–62.

86. Ibid., p. 62.

87. Ibid., p. 63.

88. Ibid., p. 64.

89. Pannenberg judges this to be but another form of an essentially Neo-Kantian dichotomy of facts and value.

90. W. Pannenberg, "Insight and Faith," in *Basic Questions in Theology,* 2:32, n. 7.

91. Ibid., pp. 34–40. Cf. also Pannenberg, "Dogmatic Theses," pp. 135–39.

92. Pannenberg, *"Insight and Faith,"* p. 40.

93. Ibid., p. 40.

94. Ibid., p. 43.

95. Ibid., p. 42.

96. Ibid., p. 45.

97. W. Pannenberg, "The Revelation of God in Jesus of Nazareth," in *Theology as History,* ed. J. Robinson and J. Cobb (Harper & Row, 1967), p. 122.

98. Ibid.

99. W. Pannenberg, *Faith and Reality* (Westminster Press, 1977), p. 57.

100. Pannenberg, "The Revelation of God," p. 113.

101. W. Pannenberg, *Jesus-God and Man* (Westminster Press, 1968), p. 65.

102. Pannenberg, *Faith and Reality,* p. 58.

103. W. Pannenberg, "On Historical and Theological Hermeneutic," in *Basic Questions in Theology,* 1:179.

104. Pannenberg, "The Revelation of God," p. 117.

105. The six points are taken from Pannenberg, *Jesus-God and Man,* pp. 67–73.

106. Pannenberg argues that when these apocalyptic ideas are translated into Hellenistic terminology and conceptuality, the result is an epiphany tradition which prepares the way for the subsequent doctrine of incarnation. Ibid., p. 69.

107. In support of this claim Pannenberg points to the development in Paul's thought from 1 Thessalonians to Philippians. Ibid., p. 73. This view contributes to Pannenberg's thesis concerning the priority of event over word revelation.

108. Ibid., p. 73.

109. Pannenberg, *Faith and Reality,* p. 72.

110. Pannenberg, *Jesus-God and Man,* p. 89.

111. Ibid., p. 95.

112. Ibid., p. 98.

113. By calling "resurrection" a metaphor Pannenberg is not denying its reality as an event. It is a metaphor because it compares rising from death to rising from sleep. The latter we have experienced, but the former we have not. Thus we know the resurrection only indirectly, and the concept must be termed a metaphor. Cf. *Jesus-God and Man,* pp. 74–76, and "The Revelation of God," pp. 127–28.

114. Cf. W. Pannenberg, "Dogmatische Erwägerungen zur Auferstehung Jesu," *Kerygma and Dogma* 14 (1968):105–18.

115. Ibid., p. 113.

116. Pannenberg, *Jesus-God and Man,* p. 100.

117. Since Pannenberg traces Paul's knowledge of the resurrection tradition to the Jerusalem community, why he considers it probably doubtful that Paul even knew the tradition of the empty tomb is not clear.

118. Pannenberg, *Jesus-God and Man,* p. 105.

119. In a letter of clarification Pannenberg writes, "the question is whether the Christians themselves can be validly convinced of the universal validity of this message—and can also convince, to be sure not 'the modern world,' but indeed individual thinking persons." Quoted by J. Robinson, "Revelation as Word and as History," *Theology as History,* p. 89.

120. Cf. Harvey, *The Historian and the Believer*, p. 110.

121. W. Pannenberg, "Response to the Discussion," *Theology as History,* p. 268, n. 80.

122. Ibid., p. 273.

123. Ibid.

124. Pannenberg, "Faith and Reason," p. 59.

125. Response to Harder and Stevenson in "A Theological Conversation with Wolfhart Pannenberg," *Dialog* (1972):289.

126. Cf. F. Klooster, "Historical Methodology and the Resurrection in Pannenberg's Theology," *Calvin Theological Journal* 11 (April 1976):5–33.

127. Cf. J. W. V. Van Huyssteen, *Teologie Van Die Rede* (Kampen: Kok, 1970), p. 232. Van Huyssteen also suggests that since Pannenberg argues that the personhood of man is ultimately derived from communion with God, he should also do the same for human rationality, that is, it derives its reality and recognizes its limits in relation to God.

128. By beliefs Alston refers both to scientific and religious beliefs. From an unpublished paper, "Experience of God." For the same thesis see "Christian Experience and Christian Belief," pp. 14ff.

129. Pannenberg, *Jesus-God and Man,* p. 81. The same apocalyptic horizon is binding today, for "if this horizon is eliminated, the basis of faith is lost." Ibid., p. 83. In order to show how it can be binding, Pannenberg argues that the expectation of a resurrection from the dead can be established in the modern world as an appropriate and meaningful expression of human destiny.